FINANCIAL MARKET INFRASTRUCTURE AND ECONOMIC INTEGRATION

This book is the first comprehensive study of the interplay between the cutting-edge regulation of financial infrastructure and international economic integration. It tackles a series of important questions: How does the regulation of central counterparties interact with international economic law? Is the WTO able to deal with the regulatory diversity of each country's financial rulebook? Do FTAs foster deeper integration of financial infrastructure services? Can competition law effectively tackle monopolisation and anticompetitive conduct in financial infrastructure?

The book discusses how the liberalisation of financial market infrastructure is achieved within the most prominent international economic integration settings: the WTO, Economic Integration Agreements, and EU competition law. It explores whether a more harmonious relationship between financial regulation and economic integration is feasible, and how it can be achieved. The book demonstrates the existence of both structural barriers to trade and trade-facilitating tools that can impede and foster the further integration of financial market infrastructure. Measuring the depth of liberalisation of financial market infrastructure services in more than 120 FTAs, as well as surveying recent case law of the WTO, the Court of Justice of the European Union, and the practice of the European Commission, the book shows how the economic integration of financial market infrastructure occurs.

An essential read for those seeking to understand how the cutting-edge regulation of financial market infrastructure and transnational systems of economic integration interact with one another.

Studies in International Trade and Investment Law: Volume 30

Studies in International Trade and Investment Law

Series Editors
Gabrielle Marceau
Krista Nadakavukaren Schefer
Federico Ortino
Gregory Shaffer

This series offers a forum for publication of original and scholarly analyses of emerging and significant issues in international trade and investment law – broadly understood to include the whole of the law of the WTO, the public international law of foreign investment, the law of the EU common commercial policy and other regional trade regimes, and any legal or regulatory topic that interacts with global trade and foreign investment. The aim of the series is to produce works which will be readily accessible to trade and investment law scholars and practitioners alike.

Recent titles in this series:

The China-Australia Free Trade Agreement: A 21st-Century Model
Edited by Colin Picker, Heng Wang and Weihuan Zhou

Regional Economic Integration and Dispute Settlement in East Asia: The Evolving Legal Framework
Anna G Tevini

The EU, World Trade Law and the Right to Food: Rethinking Free Trade Agreements with Developing Countries
Giovanni Gruni

Patent Games in the Global South: Pharmaceutical Patent Law Making in Brazil, India and Nigeria
Amaka Vanni

The Nationality of Corporate Investors under International Investment Law
Anil Yilmaz Vastardis

The Regulation of Product Standards in World Trade Law
Ming Du

Investors' International Law
Edited by Jean Ho and Mavluda Sattorova

Rethinking, Repackaging, and Rescuing World Trade Law in the Post-Pandemic Era
Edited by Amrita Bahri, Weihan Zhou and Daria Boklan

Flexible Regional Economic Integration in Africa: Lessons and Implications for the Multilateral Trading System
Timothy Masiko

International Investment Law: An Analysis of the Major Decisions
Edited by Hélène Ruiz Fabri and Edoardo Stoppioni

State Capitalism and International Investment Law
Edited by Panagiotis Delimatsis, Georgios Dimitropoulos and Anastasios Gourgourinis

The European Union and International Investment Law: The Two Dimensions of an Uneasy Relationship
Francesco Montanaro

Financial Market Infrastructure and Economic Integration

A WTO, FTAs, and Competition Law Analysis

George A Papaconstantinou

•HART•

OXFORD • LONDON • NEW YORK • NEW DELHI • SYDNEY

HART PUBLISHING

Bloomsbury Publishing Plc

Kemp House, Chawley Park, Cumnor Hill, Oxford, OX2 9PH, UK

1385 Broadway, New York, NY 10018, USA

29 Earlsfort Terrace, Dublin 2, Ireland

HART PUBLISHING, the Hart/Stag logo, BLOOMSBURY and the Diana logo are trademarks of Bloomsbury Publishing Plc

First published in Great Britain 2024

A catalogue record for this book is available from the British Library.

A catalogue record for this book is available from the Library of Congress.

Library of Congress Control Number: 2023947944

ISBN: HB: 978-1-50996-675-2
ePDF: 978-1-50996-677-6
ePub: 978-1-50996-676-9

Typeset by Compuscript Ltd, Shannon

To my family,
Στην οικογένειά μου.

Foreword

THE RESEARCH QUESTION that the author addresses in this study is as much a contemporary issue as it is an issue for the future: multilateral liberalisation commitments can be affected by regulatory diversity. In fact, they can be legally affected.

As the author shows, domestic antitrust laws influence the quality and quantity of liberalisation commitments. But antitrust laws are not universal. They are unilaterally designed and enforced. The GATS framework is rudimentary indeed. Was it an oversight or a negotiation too far for the WTO framers?

This study sheds a lot of light on this and many other questions. By comparing the workings of EU law with the multilateral (WTO) framework, and the halfway house that a few FTAs represent, the author provides the reader with all the necessary tools to understand the issues surrounding the liberalisation of financial services.

But the study does more than that. It provides an analytical framework to inquire into the limits of multilateral liberalisation. This is a framework of analysis that can be applied in other sectors as well. And the subject-matter chosen, financial services, is ideal to bring to the discussion the key parameters: gains from trade, public order, and the optimal extent of commitments to preserve a healthy balance between the former and the latter.

Petros C Mavroidis
Columbia Law School

Acknowledgements

THIS BOOK IS the result of years of contemplation and research, carried out at some of the most stimulating academic places on earth: Florence, New York and Geneva. However, I have no doubt that I could not have done it without the unwavering support and intellectual encouragement of the extraordinary people who have accompanied me and others who I met along the way. Florence and the formative years of academic research at the European University Institute (EUI) opened my curiosity and passion for economic law and international trade in its multiple dimensions. EUI provided me with the stimulating academic environment to conceptualise and develop this book but, interestingly, this project also evolved in a number of other places, including Geneva, New York City and Brussels.

This project would not have come into fruition without the generous support and guidance of my mentor Petros C Mavroidis at the EUI and Columbia. I would like to thank him for his generosity, patience, tireless support and insightful observations that have fueled this project, not to forget his humour and friendship. He is a source of inspiration to me and I owe him immense thanks for what I know about international trade.

I would like to warmly thank Stefan Grundmann for his support and guidance from the very first inception of the book's ideas, exchanged at Villa Schifanoia, Sala Europa for my EUI PhD panel interview. Since then, he has been providing his insightful input and never stopped encouraging me to pursue innovative ways to approach the regulation of financial markets.

At the World Trade Organization, I had the opportunity and honour to work with Juan A Marchetti whose generosity in sharing his insights and experience on trade in financial services contributed to broadening my knowledge and understanding of trade in financial services. I also convey a special thanks to Hamid Mamdouh, Antonia Carcaniga, Jocelyn Magdeleine, Martin Roy and Tomasz Koziel for rewarding discussions.

During my academic stay at Columbia Law School, this project benefitted hugely from exposure to empirical research in legal scholarship. I had the chance to discuss this project and acquire useful input from professors and scholars. Notably, I would like to acknowledge the importance of discussions with Professor Katharina Pistor, Anu Bradford, John Coffee, Merritt Fox and George A Bernmann. In New York City, I also had the chance to meet and engage in intriguing academic discourse with Thomas Streinz, Julian Arato, Joseph Weiler and Rob Howse.

In Brussels, the book took its final form and shape. I would like to thank my colleagues at the European Commission, in particular Bart de Meester, Mislav Mataija, Lothar Ehring, Michael Fridrich, Krzysztof Pawlowski and Colin Brown, all of whom provided valuable feedback. The stimulating discussions on regulatory aspects of trade and competition enabled me to explore the deeper connection between these very different but very interconnected disciplines. At White & Case LLP, where I worked as an associate attorney, my understanding of the practice of EU and international competition law significantly increased.

This book also greatly benefitted from comments and discussions with distinguished academics in the field, notably Bernard Hoekman, Christos Gortsos, Geert Van Calster, Jan Wouters, Veerle Colaert, Panagiotis Delimatsis, Giortio Monti, Hans Micklitz, Ulrich Petersmann, Ioannis Galariotis, Adam Jakubik and Carlo Cantore.

Moreover, I would like to express my gratitude to the series editors and the editorial team of Hart Publishing for the support and excellent collaboration.

Heraclitus wrote 'Πάντα ῥεῖ' (everything flows); however, some things remain unchanged and one of them is my affection for my family. My parents', Athina and Antony, and my sister's, Chrysa-Aggeliki, unconditional love and support have helped me across all the steps of carrying out this project. My parents have conveyed the joy of pursuing knowledge and I am deeply indebted to them for this. Additionally, my grandparents Ioannis and Aggeliki have always encouraged me to forge my own path and I will always be grateful to them.

This book might never have come to fruition had it not been for my grandfather George A Papaconstantinou – legal scholar and Stanford alumnus – whom I never had the chance to meet. His academic accomplishments have inspired me since my earliest days.

This book is dedicated to my family and specifically, to my daughter, Athena – Emilia, and my wife, Viorica. Their love, patience, companionship and support have helped me navigate all the challenges of this project. I am eternally grateful to them.

Finally, the views and opinions expressed in this book are wholly my own and do not in any way engage or bind the institution I work for.

Brussels, 8 November 2023

Contents

Abbreviations and Acronyms

ATS	Automated Trading System
BIS	Bank for International Settlements
BOE	Bank of England
CCCS	Competition & Consumer Commission Singapore
CCP	Central Counterparty
CDS	Credit Default Swap
CETA	Comprehensive Economic and Trade Agreement
CFTC	Commodity Futures Trading Commission
CMS	Collateral Management Services
CRTD	Consolidated Real-Time Datafeeds
CSD	Central Securities Depository
DB	Deutsche Börse
DOJ	Department of Justice
DTCC	Depository Trust & Clearing Corporation
ECB	European Central Bank
EEA	European Economic Area
EGB	European Government Bonds
EIA	Economic Integration Agreement
EMIR	European Market Infrastructure Regulation
ESCB	European System of Central Banks
ESMA	European Securities and Markets Authority
ETD	Exchange Traded Derivatives
EU	European Union
EURIBOR	Euro Interbank Offered Rates
FCA	Financial Conduct Authority

FRAND	Fair, Reasonable, and Non-Discriminatory
FSB	Financial Stability Board
FTA	Free Trade Agreement
GATS	General Agreement on Trade in Services
GATT	General Agreement on Tariffs and Trade
ICN	International Competition Network
IMF	International Monetary Fund
IOSCO	International Organization of Securities Commissions
IRD	Interest Rate Derivative
ISD	Investment Services Directive
LFT	Less Favourable Treatment
LIBOR	London Interbank Offered Rate
LSE	London Stock Exchange
MA	Market Access
MAD	Market Abuse Directive
MAR	Market Abuse Regulation
MFN	Most Favourable Treatment
MIFID	Markets in Financial Instruments Directive
MIFIR	Markets in Financial Instruments Regulation
MoU	Memorandum of Understanding
NCA	National Competition Authority
NSA	National Supervisory Authority
NT	National Treatment
NYSE	New York Stock Exchange
OTC	Over-the-Counter
PCO	Prudential Carve-Out
PTA	Preferential Trade Agreement
REFIT	Regulatory Fitness and Performance Program
Repos	Repurchase agreements

RTA	Regional Trade Agreement
SIFI	Significantly Important Financial Institution
SME	Small and Medium Enterprise
TBT	Trade Barriers to Trade
TEU	Treaty of the European Union
TFEU	Treaty on the Functioning of the European Union
T2S	Target 2 Securities
UK	United Kingdom
US	United States
WTO	World Trade Organization

List of Figures

List of Tables

List of Cited Case Law

Panel and Appellate Body Reports

EU Courts Jurisprudence and Commission Decisions

US Supreme Court Case Law

List of Discussed Legal Frameworks

1

Introduction

IN THE AFTERMATH of the 2008 financial crisis, the role of financial market infrastructure has emerged at the forefront of important commercial, regulatory, legislative, and political debates. The institutions that are part of financial market infrastructure are: (i) stock exchanges and regulated securities markets – such as Euronext, New York Stock Exchange, NASDAQ, and Hong Kong Stock Exchange; (ii) central counterparties (CCPs, also referred to as clearinghouses)[1] – such as Eurex Clearing, LCH.Clearnet, ICE Clear Europe, and Japan Securities Clearing Corporation; and (iii) central securities depositories – such as Clearing Banking AG, the Depository Trust & Clearing Corporation, the Canadian Depository for Securities, and Switzerland's SIX Securities Services. These institutions are seminal for the operation of financial markets globally as they ensure their efficiency, safety, soundness and they contribute to furthering economic development.

The scope of this monograph, principally, focuses on the new systemic role financial infrastructure (and specifically central counterparties) has acquired. Accordingly, this book evaluates the interplay between the regulation financial market infrastructure in different international economic integration settings. In the wake of the financial crisis, CCPs have been tasked with mitigating the perils attached to the trading of over the counter (OTC) derivatives in the global financial system. OTC derivatives have been largely responsible for the effects of the recent financial crisis, as they contributed to the buildup of systemic risk in financial markets prior to 2007 and spread volatility during the crisis. Notably, those financial instruments played a crucial role in proliferating the risks of the US subprime mortgage market to financial markets across the globe.[2] This, coupled with financial markets' interconnectedness, insufficient

[1] In this book the terms clearinghouses and central counterparties (or CCPs) are used interchangeably.

[2] For literature on this subject, see, for example, J Bullard et al, 'Systemic Risk and the Financial Crisis: A Primer' (2009) 91 *Federal Reserve Bank of St Louis Review* 403; T Somanathan and V Nageswaran, 'The Role of Derivatives in the Global Financial Crisis of 2008' in T Somanathan and V Nageswaran, *The Economics of Derivatives* (Cambridge, Cambridge University Press, 2015) 107; M Scholes, 'Foreword' in TF Cooley et al (eds), *Regulating Wall Street: The Dodd-Frank Act and the New Architecture of Global Finance* (Hoboken, John Wiley & Sons, 2010); S Grima, 'The Current Financial Crisis and Derivative Misuse' (2012) 1 *Online Journal of Social Sciences Research* 265.

supervision and inadequate regulation, resulted in an amplification of the crisis's detrimental effects.[3]

This book discusses the interface between the regulation of financial infrastructure (and specifically clearinghouses as one of the most prominent post-crisis financial market infrastructure institutions), on the one hand, and international economic integration law from a World Trade Organization (WTO) and competition law perspective, on the other, within the context of the post-crisis regulatory environment. This study aims to identify both the existing obstacles and opportunities in the liberalisation of financial market infrastructure and to construct a normative framework according to which further integration would be promoted without jeopardising the stability and soundness of financial systems.

Academic literature developed in the wake of the crisis on both sides of the Atlantic has focused its attention on the economic importance that central counterparties have gained in financial markets and has scrutinised the legislative frameworks regulating their operation.[4] However, scholarship has neglected the role and prominence of financial market infrastructure in general, and clearinghouses in particular, in legal systems of global economic integration. Surprisingly, so far scholars have not paid attention to the elements of international economic law setting out specific disciplines for financial market infrastructure and the extent to which these rules are compatible with, and work along the same lines as, financial regulatory systems.

This book seeks to remedy this lacuna by precisely filling this gap in the literature. The following paragraphs spell out how this study aims to evaluate the relationship between the regulation of financial market infrastructure and economic integration as well as the concrete case studies deployed in this endeavour. Importantly, the concrete obstacles and driving forces of the liberalisation of financial market infrastructure are identified as the direct consequence of this monograph's analytical framework.

[3] In respect of the complementary grounds that supported the exacerbation of the effects of the crisis, see, inter alia, J Crotty and G Epstein, 'Proposals for Effectively Regulating the US Financial System to Avoid yet Another Meltdown' (2008) No 2008-15 Working Paper, University of Massachusetts; S Claessens et al, *Financial Crises: Causes, Consequences, and Policy Responses* (Washington DC, International Monetary Fund, 2014).

[4] See, for example, JL Allen, 'Derivatives Clearinghouses and Systemic Risk: A Bankruptcy and Dodd-Frank Analysis' (2012) 64 *Stanford Law Review* 1079; MJ Roe, 'Clearinghouse Overconfidence' (2013) 101 *California Law Review* 1641; Y Yadav, 'Clearinghouses and Regulation by Proxy' (2014) 43 *The Georgia Journal of International and Comparative Law* 161; SJ Lubben, 'Failure of the Clearinghouse: Dodd-Frank's Fatal Flaw' (2015) 10 *The Virginia Law & Business Review* 127; H Peirce, 'Derivatives Clearinghouses: Clearing the Way to Failure' (2015) 64 *The Cleveland State Law Review* 589; M Lamandini, *Recovery and Resolution of CCPs: Obsessing over Regulatory Symmetry?* (Centre for European Policy Studies, 2018); O Jackson, 'Could EU Go down the Equivalence Route for London CCPs?' (International Financial Law Review, 14 February 2018); P Schammo, 'Caught in a Cross-Fire? The US CFTC and the European Commission's Proposals on Third-Country CCPs' (2018) 39 *Company Lawyer* 277; FV Cerezetti et al, 'Market Liquidity, Closeout Procedures and Initial Margin for CCPs' (2019) 25 *The European Journal of Finance* 599.

This work investigates, on a first level, the interplay between the regulation of financial infrastructure, on the one hand, and the toolkit of international economic integration, on the other. On a second level, this monograph explores the extent to which a more harmonious relationship between those two legal systems is feasible and, if so, by what means it can be achieved. The liberalisation of financial market infrastructure is the common denominator in the analysis of both disciplines. Consequently, the book's analytical framework underscores all the parameters germane to promoting or discouraging such liberalisation.

On the one hand, financial regulation sets forth the rules on how financial institutions carry out their business both at the national and international level, among other things. There are occasions, as in the case of cross-border traded OTC derivatives, where financial regulation in the name of the stability of financial systems extends an extraterritorial reach – meaning, most commonly, that it not only regulates domestic institutions but also scrutinises the business of institutions authorised abroad. The principal considerations of financial regulation are the preservation of financial stability – through, for example, the avoidance of negative externalities and market failures – as well as economic development. Accordingly, financial regulation is tasked with safeguarding a sensitive balance between achieving or contributing to economic growth (by, for example, stimulating capital markets and increasing liquidity) and preventing the realisation of financial turbulence scenarios (by, for instance, monitoring systemically important financial institutions).

On the other hand, international legal systems of economic integration, and most importantly, the law of the WTO, seek – after the General Agreement on Tariffs and Trade (GATT) era – to further integrate the economies of different states with the objective of attaining higher growth and higher levels of economic development for the parties to such international treaties. In this endeavour, the laws of economic integration aim at liberalising the markets for the international trade in goods, services, and intellectual property. Notably, the WTO legal frameworks on economic integration are comprehensive and they include specific sets of rules for the supply of financial services, including the services pertinent to the provision of financial market infrastructure. Importantly, the General Agreement on Trade in Services (GATS) puts forward a thorough framework for trade in financial services that WTO Members' domestic financial regulatory systems have to observe. Following this, legal systems of transnational economic integration at the WTO have their own mechanics for the supply of financial services that directly interact with domestic financial regulation.

Investigating the relationship between the legal disciplines of financial regulation (as a form of domestic law) and economic integration (as part of the international legal order) is crucial to grasp that these two ostensibly separate legal orders are in a constant interplay. The relationship between the two systems determines the level of liberalisation of financial markets and, therefore, it is crucial to understand that the more interconnected they are, the higher the likelihood of further integration. This book discusses the interaction between the two disciplines in the context of three case studies, namely in the context of: (i) WTO law; (ii) the law of economic integration agreements; and (iii) competition law.

The findings of this study indicate that there is much scope for further integrating financial market infrastructure and underscore the obstacles and opportunities of such integration. Moreover, the findings of this book concretely identify the obstacles to the liberalisation of financial market infrastructure for each case study, which may not be justified under the pretext of financial stability. In addition, the examination of the interplay between financial regulation and international economic integration in the context of plurilateral trading system reveals the existence of shortcomings, in the form of silos, possibly generated by the absence of proper institutional channels for the better coordination of the two systems. Importantly, this study's findings indicate what elements are of the essence in liberalising financial market infrastructure (such as, the existence and application of competition law). Exploring this interface is a delicate exercise that requires careful consideration of all the elements relevant to both systems in order to draw firm and legally sound conclusions.

As to the relevant economic aspects, financial market infrastructure institutions tend to provide their services in networks and, as such, network effects characterise their industry. The intrinsic characteristics of network industries, in comparison to other types of markets, are: (i) consumption externalities; (ii) switching costs and lock-in effects; (iii) significant economies of scale and production; and (iv) complementarity, comparability and standards.[5] In addition, another market element closely related to the provision of financial infrastructure services is the existence of large sunk costs. These types of costs are expenses that a company needs to incur to enter a market but cannot recover it if it exits the market. The importance of sunk costs lies with the fact that they can stop a market from being contestable.[6] This book bears in mind these elements to the extent that they serve its analytical framework.

To approach the subject matter of this monograph in a rigorous fashion and to capture all the nuances associated with the interface between the regulation of financial market infrastructure, on the one hand, and legal systems of international economic integration, on the other, we examine three case studies that serve this objective. This study's inquiry is assessed through the lenses of:

- WTO law, to evaluate the tension between the two systems at the multilateral trading system;
- economic integration agreements (EIAs) that liberalise trade in financial market infrastructure services, to assess how the development of plurilateral

[5] See O Shy, *The Economics of Network Industries* (Cambridge, Cambridge University Press, 2001).

[6] For a thorough analysis of contestable markets, see WJ Baumol et al, *Contestable Markets and the Theory of Industry Structure* (New York, Harcourt Brace Jovanovich, 1982).

trade agreements accommodates the relationship between financial regulation and economic integration; and

- the economic law of the European Union (EU), exemplified by the use of harmonised regulatory frameworks and competition law, as the most representative model of deep economic integration among different states.

These three case studies have been selected due to their prominence in the liberalisation of financial market infrastructure and their overall importance as economic integration legal systems. Additionally, these case studies are essential to underscore that the transnational supply of financial infrastructure services and, accordingly, the legal system that surrounds such services, hinges on the terms and conditions of the economic integration model that the transacting parties are subject to. The next paragraphs explain the specific methodological steps undertaken in each of the selected case studies.

In assessing the tension of the regulation of financial market infrastructure at the multilateral trading system, we shed light on the liberalising instruments employed by WTO law to promote international trade in financial services and, subsequently, we examine the consistency of a financial regulatory framework enabling market access of foreign clearinghouses with WTO law. This case study is selected because of the importance of CCPs to the post-crisis overhaul of financial markets, the failure of existing literature to evaluate clearinghouses' role in international economic law, and the truly international nature of clearing derivatives. To that end, once the relevant WTO law applying to trade in financial services has been explained, we, first, examine the existing regulatory framework for 'third-country' clearinghouses put forward by the EU. This is a necessary first step to understand the terms and conditions the EU regulation employs for the transnational trade in clearing services. As a second step, we venture into examining the conformity of the European regime with the GATS relevant obligations and commitments. For the purposes of this inquiry, the consistency of the EU regulatory framework is tested under the GATS most favourable treatment (MFN) provision, the prudential carve-out housed in the Annex of the GATS, and the GATS provisions on domestic regulation and mutual recognition. Finally, we draw conclusions on how further liberalisation of financial market infrastructure can be attained at the WTO.

Due to the great importance of regionalism in the integration of global markets over the last decades,[7] the second case study sheds light on how the liberalisation of financial market infrastructure services, and in particular

[7] Especially since negotiations at the WTO level have been stagnating, the role of the plurilateral trading system has become more prominent. For relevant literature see, inter alia, M Nakatomi, 'Plurilateral Agreements: A Viable Alternative to the World Trade Organization?' [2013] Asian Development Bank Institute Working Papers No 439; BM Hoekman and PC Mavroidis, 'Embracing Diversity: Plurilateral Agreements and the Trading System' (2015) 14 *World Trade Review* 101; BM Hoekman and PC Mavroidis, 'WTO "à La Carte" or "Menu Du Jour"? Assessing the Case for More Plurilateral Agreements' (2015) 26 *European Journal of International Law* 319.

securities' clearing and settlement services, is attained at the plurilateral trading system. In doing so, this study comprehensively maps out how the commitments for clearing and settlement services entered in EIAs compare and contrast with the liberalisation of those services at the multilateral trading system. An empirical analysis is employed in Chapter 4 to capture the intricacies embedded in economic integration agreements and to measure the liberalisation of financial market infrastructure in EIAs in comparison to the WTO benchmark. This methodological approach serves the monograph's broader objective of assessing the interplay between financial regulation and economic integration – in the context of the plurilateral trading system. In brief, as financial market infrastructure services are provided through mode 1 (cross-border supply), mode 2 (consumption abroad), and mode 3 (establishment), the commitments undertaken for market access and national treatment are the key factors for gauging liberalisation. The analysis of this case study relies on the findings based on measuring the liberalisation of clearing and settlement service in EIAs. In this analytical framework, relevant aspects of the role of national financial regulations are factored in. As a result, the relevant political economy pertinent to the liberalisation of financial market infrastructure is highlighted and the driving factors behind the liberalisation of these services are identified.

In the third case study, we explore how the liberalisation of financial market infrastructure is achieved at the EU level because it is one of the deepest economic integration systems we have witnessed globally. The EU integration model is vested with some unique elements that represent its 'comparative advantages' in the liberalisation of markets, the most prominent of which is none other that the application of competition law. Consequently, we discuss the importance of competition and antitrust law for the liberalisation of financial market infrastructure services. In addition, the EU model is the only example where the objectives of financial regulation are closely aligned with its economic integration tools, all aiming at further integrating financial market infrastructure.

Overall, the above-stated methodological steps are necessary to extrapolate where the barriers to the liberalisation of financial market infrastructure lie. This book's analysis aims to promulgate concrete policy recommendations as to what elements could contribute to realising further liberalisation of the relevant markets by striking a closer and more-harmonious relationship between the two disciplines – namely, between financial regulation and economic integration – while ensuring that the integrity of financial systems is not put in jeopardy.

This volume develops as follows: Part I focuses on financial regulation and WTO law. Specifically, Chapter 2 sheds light on the tools WTO law employs to liberalise trade in financial market infrastructure services and Chapter 3 investigates the consistency of the EU financial regulation for foreign clearinghouses with WTO law to highlight the interface between the two disciplines. Importantly, WTO law has delegated sufficient legislative leeway to financial regulators, but, at the same time, it stipulates specific obligations and commitments that WTO Members shall respect. The analysis is developed taking account of this background and aims to underscore possible ways forward for the liberalisation of financial services at the multilateral trading system.

In Part II, the liberalisation of financial market infrastructure services (in specific, securities' clearing and settlement) in the plurilateral trading system is assessed. By identifying, in an empirical fashion, the liberalising patterns of financial infrastructure services in economic integration agreements, we aim in Chapter 4 to pin down the degree to which the systems of financial regulation and international trade law work together. In addition, we aim to identify possible limitations and find common ground for better communication channels which could lead to further integration in the future.

Part III explores the relationship between financial regulation and competition law. Specifically, Chapter 5 discusses how the liberalisation of financial market infrastructure has been facilitated in the EU, through the application and enforcement of competition law and by incorporating competition-incentivising provisions in financial regulatory frameworks. This economic integration model offers deeper integration than the other two and this study aims at underlining how the EU's 'comparative advantages' contribute to further integrating the markets for financial market infrastructure.

Finally, Chapter 6 concludes the work. Having concretely identified obstacles and opportunities in the way of financial market infrastructure's international liberalisation, this chapter suggests possible paths and policy recommendations that can be followed should states decide to further integrate their financial infrastructures.

Part I

Financial Regulation and WTO Law

2

The Liberalisation of Trade in Financial Market Infrastructure Services under WTO Rules

I. INTRODUCTION

AT THE OUTSET, the WTO Agreements cover a wide array of subject matters. The relevant substantive rules in connection with international trade are included in the Agreements in Annex 1 to the Marrakesh Agreement Establishing the WTO.[1] This Annex is further divided into three separate annexes concerning trade in goods (Annex 1A), trade in services (Annex 1B) and trade-related aspects of intellectual property rights (Annex 1C). This book's lens investigates the international liberalisation of financial services. Thus, Annex 1B is the analytical framework we discuss in our assessment of how financial infrastructure services are integrated in the multilateral trading system. Annex 1B consists of the General Agreement on Trade in Services (GATS)[2] and its specific annexes. The GATS was negotiated during the Uruguay Round (1986–1994) and entered into force in 1995. It was the first set of rules for opening financial (and other) services markets that was included in the multilateral trading system.[3] Since then, the GATS has been playing a prominent role in the international framework for the liberalisation and regulation of financial services.

The GATS was the first multilateral and legally enforceable agreement to cover trade in services. The dynamics that led to its 'genesis' came as the consequence of political compromise and vast flexibility is provided to WTO

[1] Agreement Establishing the World Trade Organization, done in Marrakesh on 15 April 1994, UNTS No 31874, published in WTO, *The Legal Texts: The Results of the Uruguay Round of Multilateral Trade Negotiations* (Cambridge, Cambridge University Press, 2000) 4.

[2] ibid 284.

[3] Financial services was one of the sectors for which negotiations and WTO Members' specific commitments were extended and finally agreed in December 1997. The schedules of commitments agreed upon in December 1997 were embodied in the GATS by the Fifth Protocol to the GATS which entered into force in 1999. For more information see SJ Key, 'Financial Services in the Uruguay Round and the WTO' [1997] Group of Thirty Occasional Papers 54.

Members.[4] Progressive liberalisation constitutes the Agreement's compass.[5] In terms of scope, the GATS is applicable to 'measures by Members affecting trade in services'.[6] The Panel in *EC – Bananas III* has stated that the GATS has a wide scope to 'ensure that the disciplines of the GATS would cover any measure bearing upon conditions of competition in supply of a service, regardless of whether the measure directly governs or indirectly affects the supply of the service'.[7] Additionally, the Panel in *EC – Bananas III* defined the scope of application of the GATS in the following terms:

> [N]o measures are excluded a priori from the scope of the GATS as defined by its provisions. The scope of the GATS encompasses any measure of a Member to the extent it affects the supply of a service regardless of whether such measure directly governs the supply of a service or whether it regulates other matters but nevertheless affects trade in services.[8]

Further the Panel in *Argentina – Financial Services* stated that 'as a preliminary matter ... the question of the applicability of the GATS to the measures at issue before evaluating their consistency with the substantive obligations invoked by Panama'.[9] It follows from this that scope is an issue that needs to be examined by WTO judiciary before any discussion into substance is undertaken.

In addition, a distinction between the measures 'as such' and 'as applied' exists.[10] Therefore, it can be maintained that not only the content of WTO Members' financial rulebooks may be under the GATS scrutiny, but also their

[4] See JA Marchetti and PC Mavroidis, 'The Genesis of the GATS (General Agreement on Trade in Services)' (2011) 22 *European Journal of International Law* 689; *cf* R Adlung and A Mattoo, 'The GATS' in A Mattoo et al (eds), *A Handbook of International Trade in Services* (Oxford, Oxford University Press, 2007) 48.

[5] Third recital of the GATS Preamble. See also Panel Report, United States – Measures Affecting the Cross-Border Supply of Gambling and Betting Services (10 November 2004), WT/DS285/R (*US – Gambling*), para 6.313.

[6] GATS, Art I:1; *cf* Appellate Body Report, European Communities – Regime for the Importation, Sale and Distribution of Bananas (9 September 1997), WT/DS27/AB/R (*EC – Bananas III*), para 220; Panel Report, Mexico – Measures Affecting Telecommunications Services (2 April 2004), WT/DS204/R (*Mexico – Telecoms*), para 7.41; Panel Report, European Union and its Member States – Certain Measures Relating to the Energy Sector (10 August 2018), WT/DS476/R (*EU – Energy Package*), paras 7.408–7.410; Panel Report, Argentina – Measures Relating to Trade in Goods and Services (30 September 2015), WT/DS453/R (*Argentina – Financial Services*), paras 7.80, 7.84.

[7] Appellate Body Report, *EC – Bananas III*, para 7.281; Appellate Body Report, Canada – Certain Measures Affecting the Automotive Industry (31 May 2000), WT/DS139/AB/R (*Canada – Autos*), paras 164–66.

[8] Panel Report, *EC – Bananas III*, para 7.285.

[9] Panel Report, *Argentina – Financial Services*, para 7.80.

[10] For relevant jurisprudence, see for example Appellate Body Report, United States – Continued Existence and Application of Zeroing Methodology (4 February 2009) WT/DS350/AB/R (*United States – Continued Zeroing*), paras 181, 79 ('both specific determinations made by a Member's executive agencies and regulations issued by its executive branch can constitute acts attributable to that Member ...'), 87, 259–60; Appellate Body Report, European Communities – Selected Customs Matters, (13 November 2006) WT/DS315/AB/R (*EC – Selected Customs Matters*), para 165; Appellate Body Report, Dominican Republic – Measures Affecting the Importation and Internal Sale of Cigarettes (25 April 2005) WT/DS302/AB/R (*Dominican Republic – Import and Sale of Cigarettes*), para 107 ('... we observe that the Appellate Body has consistently affirmed the right of WTO

application.[11] The definition of a 'measure' is very broad in the GATS, encompassing any type of action in any form taken by Members.[12] The scope of the GATS covers both the treatment extended to services and service suppliers of foreign Members.[13] In the same vein, a 'measure' by a Member 'affecting trade in services' includes measures regarding the purchase, payment, or use of a service, and the access to and use of, in connection with the supply of a service among others.[14]

Moreover, the GATS Annex on Financial Services[15] (hereinafter referred to as the Annex) provides further clarity on defining 'financial services'[16] and 'financial service supplier'.[17] Importantly, the Annex includes in its indicative list, the services inextricably linked to financial market infrastructure, namely:

> trading for own account or for account of customers, whether on an exchange, in an over-the-counter market or otherwise, the following: (A) money market instruments (…); (B) foreign exchange; (C) derivative products (…); (D) exchange rate and interest rate instruments (…); (E) transferable securities; (F) other negotiable instruments and financial assets (…)'[18]

It also includes 'settlement and clearing services for financial assets, including securities, derivative products, and other negotiable instruments'.[19] The panel in *China – Electronic Payment Services* clarified the nature of latter sector:

> [S]ubsector (xiv) encompasses the clearing and settlement of financial instruments sharing essentially the same characteristics as securities, derivative products, and

Members to challenge legislation laying down norms of rules "as such", as well as their right to bring claims against the application of such measures in specific instances …').

[11] For analysis on the application of the GATS in 'as such' and 'as applied measures' see S Bhuiyan, 'Mandatory and Discretionary Legislation: The Continued Relevance of the Distinction under the WTO' (2002) 5 *Journal of International Economic Law* 571. For an overview see also A Yanovich and T Voon, 'What Is the Measure at Issue?' in A Mitchell (ed), *Challenges and Prospects for the WTO* (Cameron May Ltd, 2005). For the potential application of the GATS in the decisions of competition authorities, see B De Meester, 'Testing European Prudential Conditions for Banking Mergers in the Light of Most Favoured Nation in the GATS' (2008) 11 *Journal of International Economic Law* 609; CD Ehlermann and L Ehring, 'WTO Dispute Settlement and Competition Law: Views from the Perspective of the Appellate Body's Experience' (2002) 26 *Fordham International Law Journal* 1505.

[12] GATS, Art XXVIII(a) provides for the definition of a 'measure' that includes laws, regulations, rules, and decisions among others.

[13] Appellate Body Report, *EC – Bananas III*, para 227. See also Panel Report, *Argentina – Financial Services*, paras 7.97–7.98.

[14] GATS, Art XXVIII(c). It shall be borne in mind that the list is indicative according to the Appellate Body Report, *EC– Bananas III*, para 220.

[15] Pursuant to GATS, Art XXIX, Annexes are binding for WTO Members.

[16] GATS, Annex on Financial Services, para 5(a) reads as follows: 'A financial service is any service of a financial nature offered by a financial service supplier of a Member. Financial services include all insurance and insurance-related services, and all banking and other financial services (excluding insurance).'

[17] ibid para 5(b) sets out the following definition: 'A financial service supplier means any natural or juridical person of a Member wishing to supply or supplying financial services but the term "financial service supplier" does not include a public entity.'

[18] ibid para 5(a)(x).

[19] ibid para 5(a)(xiv).

other negotiable instruments. More particularly, (xiv) covers the clearing and settlement of financial instruments which have investment attributes, grant ownership rights and yield financial returns.[20]

In addition, the Understanding on Commitments in Financial Services (hereinafter referred to as the Understanding) is a unique legal instrument in the WTO – although not an integral part of the GATS – which provides a sort of voluntary formula approach to scheduling commitments under certain provisions of the GATS in connection with financial services. Notably, the rules and disciplines set out in the Understanding are not binding on every WTO Member but only on those that opt to abide by it.[21] WTO Members inscribing commitments in accordance with the Understanding have usually inserted a headnote to that effect in the section on financial services of their Schedules of Specific Commitments.[22] Since schedules are an integral part of the GATS, those obligations have become binding on the Members concerned. Members adopting the Understanding may, of course, schedule conditions and/or qualifications to the obligations mandated by the Understanding.[23]

Further, the GATS identifies four ways in which financial market infrastructure services can be supplied by foreign financial institutions in the territory of a WTO Member; these are the four 'modes of supply' set out in the GATS. Under the first two modes of supply, foreign financial institutions, such as trading venues or central counterparties, do not have any physical presence within the territory of the host WTO Member. First, the foreign trading venue can provide services cross-border into the territory of another WTO Member without any physical presence in this territory and without the consumer moving (mode 1).[24] Second, a foreign financial institution can also do this by offering its financial infrastructure services to a consumer who travels from his/her home territory to the territory of the financial institution to receive the service (mode 2).[25] Contrary to those two modes of supply, the other two modes

[20] Panel Report, China – Measures Affecting Electronic Payment Services (16 July 2012), WT/DS413/R (*China – Electronic Payment Services*), para 7.163.

[21] The adoption of this approach was, however, subject to the following conditions as specified in the Understanding: (i) it does not conflict with the provisions of the Agreement; (ii) it does not prejudice the right of any Member to schedule its specific commitments in accordance with the approach under Part III of the GATS; (iii) resulting specific commitments shall apply on a most-favoured-nation basis; and (iv) no presumption has been created as to the degree of liberalisation to which a Member is committing itself under the GATS.

[22] Those headnotes usually read as follows: 'Commitments in this subsector are undertaken in accordance with the Understanding on Commitments in Financial Services'. Some Members have added the following (or a variation thereof): 'These commitments are subject to the limitations on market access and national treatment in the "all sectors" section of this schedule and to those relating to the subsectors listed below.'

[23] See the second indent of the introduction to the Understanding.

[24] GATS, Art I(2)(a).

[25] ibid Art I(2)(b).

involve physical presence of the foreign financial service provider in the host WTO Member. Third, the financial institution can supply services by means of a 'commercial presence' in the host WTO Member (mode 3).[26] Such commercial presence includes 'any type of business or professional establishment', in the form of legal person, branch or representative office.[27] Fourth, the foreign financial institution can provide services by sending a natural person to the host WTO Member (mode 4).[28]

An explanation of the GATS basic mechanics applying to international trade in financial services paves the way to this study's forthcoming analysis. The following analysis provides a high-level account of how the liberalisation of financial services is effectuated in the multilateral trading system under the WTO and sheds light on the GATS-specific tools enabling such liberalisation by investigating the relevant provisions (together with the relevant WTO jurisprudence) which facilitate international trade flows in financial market infrastructure services sectors.

II. THE LIBERALISATION OF FINANCIAL SERVICES UNDER WTO LAW

Liberalisation on trade in services is typically confined by non-tariff barriers that take the form of regulations.[29] This is especially the case for financial services, which is one of the most heavily regulated industries. Nevertheless, the WTO Members' regulatory autonomy is prescribed in the fourth recital of the GATS,[30] and can serve as a valuable means of interpretation. It is assumed that governmental protectionism[31] can be entrenched in Members' regulations and subsequently can be deemed, on a case-by-case basis, unlawful under WTO law. One of the GATS' main objectives, as set out in its Preamble, is 'to establish a multilateral framework of principles and rules for trade in services with a view to the expansion of such trade'.[32] Thus, the promotion of trade in financial services is a designated purpose.

[26] ibid Art I(2)(c).

[27] ibid Art XXVIII(d).

[28] ibid Art I(2)(d).

[29] For a categorisation of barriers to trade in services, see B Hoekman and CA Primo Braga, 'Protection and Trade in Services: A Survey' (1997) 8 *Open Economies Review* 285; RM Stern, 'Quantifying Barriers to Trade in Services', *Development, Trade, and the WTO: A Handbook. Washington, DC: The World Bank* (Washington DC, World Bank Publications, 2002).

[30] The fourth considerandum of the GATS Preamble reads as follows: 'Recognizing the right of Members to regulate, and to introduce new regulations, on the supply of services within their territories in order to meet national policy objectives and, given asymmetries existing with respect to the degree of development of services regulations in different countries, the particular need of developing countries to exercise this right.'

[31] J Bhagwati, 'The Pure Theory of International Trade: A Survey' (1964) 74 *The Economic Journal* 1, 18.

[32] See the second considerandum of the GATS Preamble.

Moreover, the GATS and the WTO system as a whole are conducive to the liberalisation of financial services. The following aspects are prominent in achieving such liberalisation. First, the WTO is a multilateral forum which aims to reduce or eliminate barriers to trade, promote contestable markets and facilitate economic growth and development. The WTO and other international financial bodies (such as the International Monetary Fund (IMF) and the Basel Committee on Banking Supervision) seek to liberalise trade in financial services and reinforce domestic financial systems. The objectives of liberalising trade in financial services and strengthening domestic financial systems (eg by making them more resilient via prudential regulation and supervision) are complementary and mutually reinforcing.[33] Thus, opening financial sectors to international competition and enabling international trade can result in more competitive and efficient markets for financial services.[34]

Second, the GATS sets up a mechanism for WTO Members to assume legally binding commitments in financial services sectors, which are subject to enforcement proceedings under the WTO dispute settlement mechanism. WTO Members' GATS commitments are binding and cannot be withdrawn without compensation of trading partners.[35] Disputes on financial services commitments under the GATS have been the subject of the WTO dispute settlement mechanism in the past and the corresponding WTO jurisprudence put forward the guiding principles according to which WTO Members can design their financial rulebooks to ensure conformity with the rules of the multilateral trading system.[36] It should be noted however that the relief found by a challenging WTO Member can only be prospective.[37]

Third, the GATS is built upon the most favoured nation (MFN) principle, which excludes discrimination between different countries. In accordance with the MFN principle housed in the GATS, a WTO Member shall accord to services and service suppliers of any other Member treatment 'no less

[33] Sydney J Key highlights the relationship between financial sector liberalisation and regulation in this respect and draws a distinction between regulations that amount to anticompetitive trade barriers and regulations that serve legitimate purposes (eg integrity and stability of financial systems). See SJ Key, *The Doha Round and Financial Services Negotiations* (Washington DC, American Enterprise Institute, 2003).

[34] Financial services trade can improve capital markets' efficiency, enhance the quality, availability and pricing of financial services and stimulate innovation in the industry. See, for example, M Kono et al, 'Opening Markets in Financial Services and the Role of the GATS' (WTO, 1997) WTO Special Studies No 1; W Dobson and P Jacquet, *Financial Services Liberalization in the WTO* (Washington DC, Peterson Institute for International Economics, 1998).

[35] GATS, Art XXI.

[36] See analysis below for further information on WTO disputes in connection with financial services.

[37] Dispute Settlement Understanding, Art 19(1) indicates that a panel or the Appellate Body (which is currently non-operational) can only recommend a losing WTO Member to 'bring the measure into conformity' with the applicable WTO Agreement.

favourable' than the treatment it extends to 'like' services and service suppliers of the most favoured foreign nation.[38] The MFN principle has traditionally been at the epicentre of international trade rules and aims to proliferate the benefits of free trade to all the parties to the multilateral trading system. We offer an in-depth review of the GATS provision in the context of trade in financial services in the next section.

III. THE GATS PRINCIPLES CONTRIBUTING TO THE LIBERALISATION OF FINANCIAL SERVICES

Since the GATS has played an important role in opening financial services markets across the globe and has promoted the constant growth of international trade in financial services since 1995, leading to world exports of more than US$ 611 billion in 2022,[39] it is all the more important to explore the GATS-specific toolkit which enables the liberalisation of trade in financial market infrastructure services. In particular, the remainder of this chapter provides an overview of the main obligations and commitments set out in the GATS framework governing trade in financial services which facilitate international commerce of financial infrastructure services (such as trading of derivatives products or clearing and settlement for financial assets). By way of example, the following sub-sections will address questions like:

- How and under what conditions does, in practice, the GATS MFN treatment preclude discrimination between financial infrastructure providers from different WTO Members?
- In what way do national treatment and market access commitments assumed by WTO Members ensure that foreign CCPs are not extended less favourable treatment vis-à-vis domestic CCPs and do not face quantitative restrictions upon market entry?
- To what extent does the GATS put forward specific disciplines on WTO Members' domestic regulation in connection with financial infrastructure services?

[38] GATS, Art II, para 1. The GATS permits certain departures from the MFN obligation in cases of economic integration agreements, one-time exemptions to be taken upon the entry into force of a WTO Member's Schedule of Commitments and does not apply to recognition agreements. For a more detailed discussion on the MFN principle, see below.

[39] This is evidenced by the increase in the world exports of financial services which grew from US$ 71.6 billion in 1995 to US$ 366.2 billion in 2007 and US$ 611.2 billion in 2022, accounting for 16% of the US$ 3.82 trillion digitally delivered services exports. See WTO, Financial Services, Background Note by the Secretariat, 3 February 2010 (S/C/W/312 S/FIN/W/73), and WTO, 'Global Trade Outlook and Statistics' (WTO, 5 April 2023) www.wto.org/english/res_e/booksp_e/trade_outlook23_e.pdf accessed 25 July 2023.

- How can investment banks from two different WTO Members provide cross-border derivatives trading services based on recognition agreements under the GATS?
- When and under what requirements can the GATS prudential carve-out for domestic regulation of financial infrastructure be in breach of a WTO Member's market access or national treatment commitments or its MFN obligation?
- Does the GATS pose any restraints on the subsidisation of WTO Members' financial infrastructure providers?

The analysis below responds to those questions and perhaps, more importantly, offers the tools to readers to reply to questions of a similar nature in connection with the supply of trade in financial services: (i) by explaining the mechanics of the GATS legal framework applicable to financial services; (ii) by putting the relevant jurisprudence (ie WTO Panel and Appellate Body reports) into context; and (iii) by providing concrete examples from relevant practice on how the liberalisation of financial market infrastructure services occurs.

This section proceeds as follows: First, in sub-section A, I provide an overview of the architecture of the GATS most-favoured-nation obligation and explain its importance for the supply of financial infrastructure services; in sub-section B, I focus on how national treatment and market access commitments undertaken by WTO Members contribute to the liberalisation of financial infrastructure services by reducing (or removing) barriers that discriminate against foreign services and/or service suppliers with respect to market entry and operation in a host country and by prohibiting quantitative restrictions; in sub-section C, I discuss the condition under which the GATS discipline on domestic regulation can ensure the openness, transparency and procedural fairness of WTO Members' rulebooks on financial infrastructure; in sub-section D, I focus on how mutual recognition agreements under the GATS foster the liberalisation of financial market infrastructure services among the WTO Members subject to those arrangements; in sub-section E, I discuss the role of the GATS prudential carve-out for financial services and explain that by its very purpose (ie to ensure the financial stability, integrity and resilience of domestic systems) it contributes to the liberalisation of financial market infrastructure services; finally, in sub-section F, I touch on the subsidies discipline under the GATS and discuss any possible implications on WTO Members' financing of financial infrastructure service providers.

A. Most Favoured Nation

As mentioned above, non-discrimination constitutes the cornerstone of the world trading system and MFN is the most representative obligation in the GATS. GATS Article II:1 provides that: 'With respect to any measure covered by this

Agreement, each Member shall accord immediately and unconditionally to services and service suppliers of any other Member treatment no less favourable than that it accords to like services and service suppliers of any other country'. This GATS provision stipulates that services and service providers of any WTO Member shall not receive less favourable treatment than like services and service providers of any other WTO Member. The Annex to the GATS on Article II sets out the conditions according to which WTO Members are exempted from the obligation in Article II:1.[40] In respect of exemptions from Article II of the GATS in connection with financial services, the Fifth Protocol to the GATS provides that the Schedules of Commitments and List of Exemptions from Article II concerning financial services annexed to this Protocol replace the financial services sections of the Schedules and List of Exemptions of that Member.[41]

To fall within the scope of MFN, two criteria must be satisfied: first, financial services or service suppliers (such as trading venues or clearinghouses) from Member X shall be considered 'like' services or service suppliers from Member Y in accordance with GATS, Article II; second, if such services are considered 'like', a WTO Member must not accord 'less favourable treatment' (LFT) to Member X in comparison to Member Y. The following analysis takes account of the concepts of 'likeness' and LFT within the GATS in light of the recent WTO dispute settlement reports which focus on financial services.

i. 'Likeness' under the GATS Article II

The determination of discriminatory behaviour in WTO law depends on the concept of likeness. Like services or service suppliers from different Members cannot be accorded differential treatment. However, if they are not considered like, they can be treated differently. Extensive WTO jurisprudence on likeness exists in trade of goods,[42] but the focus of this book lies with services. The panel

[40] See WTO (n 1) 308. WTO Members were allowed, upon their accession to the WTO, to enter certain exceptions to the MFN obligation in their list of MFN exemptions.

[41] See the Fifth Protocol to the General Agreement on Trade in Services (S/L/45, 3 December 1997), which was adopted by the Committee on Trade in Financial Services on 14 November 1997 (S/L/44, 3 December 1997). By way of background, the negotiations on financial services were extended until the end of 1997 when a final agreement among WTO Members was reached. For background discussions, see Key (n 3).

[42] Appellate Body, European Communities – Measures Affecting Asbestos and Products Containing Asbestos (12 March 2001) WT/DS135/AB/R (*EC – Asbestos*), para 102, refers to the requirements promulgated by the GATT working party report on Border Tax Adjustments. These criteria relate to: (i) the properties, nature, and quality of the products; (ii) the end-uses of the products; (iii) consumers' tastes and habits or consumers' perceptions and behaviour in respect of the products; and (iv) the tariff classification of the products. *cf* Appellate Body Report, *Argentina – Financial Services*, para 6.30. With regard to those criteria, the Appellate Body observed that '[a]s in the context of trade in goods, however, we equally consider that the criteria for analysing 'likeness' of services and service suppliers are simply analytical tools to assist in the task of examining the relevant evidence, and that they are neither a treaty-mandated nor a closed list of criteria that will determine the legal characterization of services and service suppliers as "like".' See Appellate Body Report, *Argentina – Financial Services*, paras 6.31–6.32.

in *Canada – Autos* held that 'to the extent that the service suppliers concerned supply the same services, they should be considered like'.[43] This statement is drafted broadly, and seems to disregard the complex nature of services and the role of regulation, which adds further complexity to this assessment. Additionally, it could restrict the right of WTO Members to regulate the supply of services on the basis of national policy preferences. The GATS likeness determination differentiates from the standards set out by WTO jurisprudence for goods. Allowances must be made for Members' regulatory framework divergences that can complicate the conditions of 'likeness'. Recently, WTO case law has broadened our understanding of how trade norms can filter WTO Members' prudential frameworks. It has also provided guidance on how 'likeness' can be established between service providers from different jurisdictions.

The Appellate Body *in Argentina – Financial Services* held in respect of 'likeness' of the GATS Article II:1 that 'the determination of "likeness" of services and service suppliers must focus on the competitive relationship of the services and service suppliers at issue'.[44] Additionally, the Appellate Body noted:

> Thus, we consider that the concept of 'likeness' of services and service suppliers under Articles II:1 and XVII:1 of the GATS is concerned with the competitive relationship of services and service suppliers. This is consonant with the Appellate Body's understanding of 'likeness' in the ambit of trade in goods. In *EC – Asbestos*, the Appellate Body held that the word 'like' in Article III:4 of the GATT 1994 is to be interpreted as applying to products that are in a competitive relationship, and that therefore a determination of 'likeness' under Article III:4 is, fundamentally, a determination about the nature and extent of a competitive relationship between and among products. As the Appellate Body noted, '[i]f there is – or could be – no competitive relationship between products, a Member cannot intervene, through internal taxation or regulation, to protect domestic production'.[45]
>
> Further, in the context of trade in goods, the Appellate Body noted that there is a spectrum of degrees of 'competitiveness' or 'substitutability' of products in the marketplace. The assessment of such a competitive relationship requires a market-based analysis. The Appellate Body also stated that not all products that are in some competitive relationship are 'like products', and that it is difficult, if not impossible, in the abstract, to indicate precisely where on this spectrum the word 'like' falls. In our view, the same is true with respect to 'like services and service suppliers', and, thus, the likeness of services and service suppliers can only be determined on a case-by-case basis, taking into account the specific circumstances of the particular case.[46]

[43] Appellate Body Report, *Canada – Autos*, para 10.248; *cf* Panel Report, *EC – Bananas III*, para 7.322.

[44] Appellate Body Report, *Argentina – Financial Services*, para 6.24; *cf* Appellate Body Report, European Communities – Measures Prohibiting the Importation and Marketing of Seal Products (22 May 2014) WT/DS401/AB/R (*EC – Seals Products*), para 5.82, Appellate Body Report, *EC – Asbestos*, para 99.

[45] Appellate Body Report, *EC – Asbestos*, para 117.

[46] Appellate Body Report, *Argentina – Financial Services*, paras 6.25–6.26.

Notably, the competition concept is adopted from the GATS Article XVII, and can prove to be a useful guide in the process of assessing whether services or service suppliers are like. Although the *China – Electronic Payment Services* panel queried the determination of likeness for both services and service suppliers,[47] the Appellate Body understands these terms *in tandem*, and suggests they should not be examined in isolation.[48] Specifically, the Appellate Body in *Argentina – Financial Services* noted that:

> the reference to 'services and service suppliers' indicates that considerations relating to both the service and the service supplier are relevant for determining 'likeness' under Articles II:1 and XVII:1 of the GATS. The assessment of likeness of services should not be undertaken in isolation from considerations relating to the service suppliers, and, conversely, the assessment of likeness of service suppliers should not be undertaken in isolation from considerations relating to the likeness of the services they provide. We see the phrase 'like services and service suppliers' as an integrated element for the likeness analysis under Articles II:1 and XVII:1, respectively. Accordingly, separate findings with respect to the 'likeness' of services, on the one hand, and the 'likeness' of service suppliers, on the other hand, are not required. Because the 'likeness' analysis serves to assess the competitive relationship of the 'services and service suppliers' at issue, the particular features of that competitive relationship, in the circumstances of any specific case, will determine the relative weight to be accorded in the analysis of 'likeness' to considerations relating to the service and the service supplier, respectively. In any event, in a holistic analysis of 'likeness', considerations relating to both the service and the service supplier will be relevant, albeit to varying degrees, depending on the circumstances of each case.[49]

Moreover, regarding the difference between trade in goods and trade in services (especially concerning the modes of supply in the latter), the Appellate Body noted that:

> the different modes of supply as defined in Article I:2 exist only in trade in services under the GATS, and not in trade in goods under the GATT 1994, and, accordingly, the analysis of 'likeness' of services and service suppliers may require additional considerations of whether or how this analysis is affected by the mode(s) of service supply.[50]

Furthermore, the presumption approach refers to the case where the complainant can establish 'likeliness' by merely illustrating that the measure in question distinguishes between services and service suppliers based exclusively on origin. This 'presumption' has been accepted by numerous panels for trade in goods,[51]

[47] Panel Report, *China – Electronic Payment Services*, paras 7.698–7.709.
[48] Appellate Body Report, *Argentina – Financial Services*, para 6.29.
[49] ibid.
[50] ibid para 6.33.
[51] Panel Report, Colombia – Indicative Prices and Restrictions on Ports of Entry (27 April 2009) WT/DS366/R (*Colombia – Ports of Entry*), paras 7.355–7.356; Panel Report, United States – Certain Measures Affecting Imports of Poultry from China (29 September 2010) WT/DS392/R (*US – Poultry (China)*), paras 7.424–7.432.

and recently endorsed by the Appellate Body in the context of services.[52] Nevertheless, the perimeter of the 'likeness' presumption is narrower for trade in services; this is due to inherent complexities of services sectors, distinctions between services and service suppliers, varying modes of supply,[53] and domestic regulations, which define the realm of operation of service suppliers alongside with consumers' preferences, that all need to be borne in mind.[54] Interestingly, in *Argentina – Financial Services* the panel concluded that 'it is not the origin per se which determines ... but the regulatory framework inextricably linked to such origin'.[55] The Appellate Body reversed the panel's finding because its analysis erred in fulfilling the presumption of 'likeness' criteria.[56]

The Appellate Body in *Argentina – Financial Services* held that, with respect to the applicability of the presumption approach in the context of trade in services:

> While these complexities do not, as a matter of principle, render the presumption approach inapplicable in the context of trade in services, the scope of this presumption is more limited than in trade in goods. Whether and to what extent such complexities have an impact on the determination of whether a distinction is based exclusively on origin in a particular case will depend on the nature, configuration, and operation of the measure at issue and the particular claims raised.[57]

Moreover, the Appellate Body stated that:

> in keeping with the general rule that the burden of proof rests upon the party that asserts the affirmative of a particular claim, the complainant bears the burden of making a prima facie case that a measure draws a distinction between services and service suppliers based exclusively on origin.[58]

According to the Appellate Body:

> if a panel finds that the complainant has failed to make a prima facie case that a measure provides for differential treatment based exclusively on origin, then the panel must engage in an analysis of 'likeness' of services and service suppliers on the basis of the relevant criteria adapted to trade in services, as addressed above, before it may proceed to the analysis of less favourable treatment.[59]

These benchmarks for determining 'likeness' between service providers furnish clear filters for evaluating whether financial market infrastructure providers

[52] Appellate Body Report, *Argentina – Financial Services*, paras 6.38, 6.52, 6.61.
[53] Panel Report, *China – Electronic Payment Services*, para 7.704.
[54] Appellate Body Report, *Argentina – Financial Services*, paras 6.38–6.41.
[55] Panel Report, *Argentina – Financial Services*, para 7.166.
[56] Appellate Body Report, *Argentina– Financial Services*, para 6.61.
[57] Appellate Body Report, *Argentina – Financial Services*, para 6.40. See also para 6.52 of the Appellate Body Report.
[58] Appellate Body Report, *Argentina – Financial Services*, para 6.42.
[59] ibid, para 6.43.

(such as trading venues or central counterparties) from third countries are like or not. However, case-by-case analysis is required to establish whether the conditions are met. It should be mentioned that the burden of proof always lies with the party that asserts an affirmative claim.[60] The role of regulatory frameworks has been stressed by WTO judiciary in the determination of 'likeness' for services and service-suppliers – especially in the context of financial services. The analysis below sheds light on the second condition of the MFN in the GATS.

ii. LFT under GATS Article II

LFT is embedded in both GATS Articles II:1 and XVII; the WTO judiciary holds that both provisions employ the same standard.[61] The Appellate Body in *Argentina – Financial Services* offered its appraisal on the nature of 'treatment no less favourable' housed in those two articles of the GATS. As regards Article II:1 of the GATS, the Appellate Body noted:

> 6.105 Turning to Article II:1 of the GATS, we note that this provision does not further define the term 'treatment no less favourable'. Furthermore, we recall that Article XVII:1 contains a national treatment obligation, whereas Article II:1 contains a most-favoured-nation obligation. Nonetheless, the operative parts of these provisions are similarly worded, in that a Member is required to accord 'treatment no less favourable' to 'services and service suppliers of any other Member'. Both provisions serve the function of prohibiting discrimination against foreign services and service suppliers vis-à-vis like services and service suppliers. Although the immediate context of this term in Articles II:1 and XVII:1 is not expressed in identical words, and Article II does not contain the elaboration of the 'less favourable treatment' standard found in Articles XVII:2 and 3, the Appellate Body has found that both provisions share the essential nature of anti-discrimination provisions, and cover both de jure and de facto discrimination.[290] Thus, the elaboration on the meaning of the term 'treatment no less favourable' contained in Article XVII, and in particular in Article XVII:3, should also be pertinent context to the meaning of the same term in Article II:1.
>
> 6.106 We note that, in *EC – Bananas III*, the Appellate Body upheld the panel's finding that the EC licensing procedures in that dispute conferred less favourable treatment under both Article II and Article XVII of the GATS. In so doing, the Appellate Body based its findings under both provisions on the same notion of 'less favourable treatment'. Specifically, the Appellate Body agreed with the panel that various aspects of the EC licensing procedures at issue created less favourable conditions of competition for service suppliers of the complainants' origin.[291] The Appellate Body's findings indicate that, on substance, the concept of 'treatment no less favourable' under both the most-favoured-nation and national treatment provisions of the GATS is focused

[60] Appellate Body Report, United States – Measures Affecting Imports of Woven Wool Shirts and Blouses from India (25 April 1997) WT/DS33/AB/R (*US – Wool Shirts and Blouses*), paras 14, 335.
[61] Appellate Body Report, *Argentina – Financial Services*, paras 6.105, 6.106; *cf* Appellate Body Report, *EC – Bananas III*, para 233.

> on a measure's modification of the conditions of competition. This legal standard does not contemplate a separate and additional inquiry into the regulatory objective of, or the regulatory concerns underlying, the contested measure. Indeed, in prior disputes, the fact that a measure modified the conditions of competition to the detriment of services or service suppliers of any other Member was, in itself, sufficient for a finding of less favourable treatment under Articles II:1 and XVII of the GATS.[62]
>
> [290] Appellate Body Report, *EC – Bananas III*, para 233.
> [291] Appellate Body Report, *EC – Bananas III*, paras 240–248 [remainder of footnote not reproduced]

The Appellate Body in *Argentina – Financial Services* crystallised the notion of LFT. It underlined that both de jure and de facto discrimination are covered by the scope of Article II and it made clear that Article II is informed in determining the notion of 'less favourable treatment' by the more elaborate language included in Article XVII of the GATS. Most importantly, for both provisions the crucial element that qualifies whether certain measures extend LFT is based on the modification of the conditions of competition to the benefit of services or service suppliers of a WTO Member in comparison to like services or service suppliers of another Member – as stipulated in Article XVII:3.[63]

Jurisprudence developed for goods agreements does not always chime with the mechanics of the GATS due to their structural differences.[64] Nevertheless, the GATS legal requirement for establishing LFT has been recently delineated by the Appellate Body for trade in financial services, as said. A measure fails to confer 'treatment no less favourable' if it modifies the conditions of competition to the detriment of services or service suppliers of any other Member in comparison to like services or service suppliers of, respectively, any other country or the Member imposing the contested measure.[65] Thus, the driving force of LFT is the relation between the measure in question and whether this measure alters the conditions of competition between like service suppliers.[66]

Regulatory frameworks admittedly affect trade in services. Indeed, it all depends on the standard of review for LFT to determine whether differential

[62] Appellate Body Report, *Argentina – Financial Services*, paras 6.105–6.106. See also Panel Report, *EU – Energy Package*, para 7.489.

[63] Art XVII reads: 'Formally identical or formally different treatment shall be considered to be less favourable if it modifies the conditions of competition in favour of services or service suppliers of the Member compared to the like services or services suppliers of any other Member.' For GATS, Art XVII (National Treatment), see the analysis below.

[64] The LFT standard in the GATT is identical to the one in the GATS; see Appellate Body Report, *EC – Seals Products*, para 5.90. The Technical Barriers to Trade Agreement does not employ the same LFT legal standard because it requires an additional step not justifiable in the GATS geometry, namely the 'legitimate regulatory distinction'; Appellate Body Report, United States – Measures Affecting the Production and Sale of Clove Cigarettes (4 April 2012), WT/DS406/AB/R (*US – Clove Cigarettes*), para 182.

[65] Appellate Body Report, *Argentina – Financial Services*, para 6.151.

[66] See Appellate Body Report, *EC – Bananas III*, paras 244, 246; Panel Report, *China – Electronic Payment Services*, paras 7.712, 7.714.

treatment is extended or not. Evaluating whether a measure leads to modifying the conditions of competition at the expense of like service suppliers 'must begin with scrutiny of the measure, including consideration of the design, structure, and expected operation of the measure at issue'.[67] However, this type of regulatory assessment will not go beyond the content of the GATS and change its internal balances. The panel in *Argentina – Financial Services* attempted an alternative to the text of the GATS treaty interpretation of the LFT, which resembles the approach devised by the Agreement on Technical Barriers to Trade (also known as the TBT Agreement). The panel's analysis went beyond just taking account of the regulatory aspects relating to services that may affect the conditions of competition, and attempted to justify LFT on 'certain regulatory distinctions'.[68] This stance disregards the broader GATS taxonomy, which favours Members pursuing their national policies and at the same time provides the prudential exception that financial regulations can be justified under.[69] Conversely, the TBT Agreement has this regulatory distinction in the determination of LFT, but does not furnish exceptions as the GATS does. Ultimately, the Appellate Body did not endorse the panel's interpretation.[70] It stated that to the degree that evidence pertaining to the regulatory aspects has a bearing on the conditions of competition, it might be taken into consideration, subject to the specific characteristics of the case.[71]

Moreover, the Appellate Body in *Argentina – Financial Services* observed that this interpretation of the LFT standard was also aligned with the structure of the GATS, according to which 'Members can utilise certain flexibilities available to them uniquely under the GATS, when undertaking their GATS commitments, and their obligations are qualified by exceptions or other derogations contained in the GATS and its Annexes.'[72] The Appellate Body further noted:

> Through these flexibilities and exceptions, the GATS seeks to strike a balance between a Member's obligations assumed under the Agreement and that Member's right to pursue national policy objectives. A Member's right to pursue national policy objectives is recognised in the preamble of the GATS, including the third and fourth recitals. The term 'national policy objectives' in the preamble, which is general and undefined, may cover a wide array of objectives, and Members retain various means to pursue these objectives. To begin with, measures pursuing national policy objectives may be taken outside the sectors or supply modes covered by GATS Schedules. Furthermore, a Member may pursue a wide range of policy objectives while acting

[67] Appellate Body Report, Thailand – Customs and Fiscal Measures on Cigarettes from the Philippines (17 June 2011), WT/DS371/AB/R (*Thailand – Cigarettes (Philippines)*), para 134.

[68] Panel Report, *Argentina – Financial Services*, paras 7.212, 7.232.

[69] The GATS prudential exception is discussed below. For a comprehensive and thoughtful analysis, see CM Cantore, *The Prudential Carve-out for Financial Services: Rationale and Practice in the GATS and Preferential Trade Agreements* (Cambridge, Cambridge University Press, 2018).

[70] Appellate Body Report, *Argentina – Financial Services*, paras 6.151–6.153.

[71] ibid, para 6.127.

[72] ibid, para 6.112.

> consistently with its obligations or commitments assumed under the GATS. Indeed, a Member's commitments under the GATS could in some cases serve to further its national policy objectives. Where measures are found to be inconsistent with a Member's obligations or commitments under the GATS, the GATS provides for various mechanisms, such as Article XIV, which take account of policy objectives underlying such measures. This balance, too, reinforces the established legal standard for 'treatment no less favourable' under the non-discrimination provisions of the GATS, that is, whether a measure modifies the conditions of competition to the detriment of like services or service suppliers of any other Member. Where a measure is inconsistent with the non-discrimination provisions, regulatory aspects or concerns that could potentially justify such a measure are more appropriately addressed in the context of the relevant exceptions. Addressing them in the context of the non-discrimination provisions would upset the existing balance under the GATS.[73]

The GATS Article II:1 LFT status quo provides clarity as to how like services or service suppliers are to be treated. If national regulatory frameworks impact on the conditions of competition between like services or service suppliers, then differential treatment at odds with the MFN principle is extended. The LFT test does not consider regulatory intent and/or objectives but rather gravitates around the real effects as the result of the modification of the conditions of competition for foreign 'like' services or service suppliers. In light of the above, it is clear that to ensure MFN treatment in the area of financial services, financial regulators need to craft their prudential and supervisory frameworks taking into consideration that 'like' services and service suppliers from third countries have to be accorded equal treatment. As discussed above, the MFN treatment is a general obligation, which is only subject to WTO Members' exemptions from GATS Article II enshrined in their Schedules of Commitments. The following sub-section on market access (GATS, Article XVI) and national treatment (GATS, Article XVII) focuses on how those disciplines result in the liberalisation of financial services sectors and explores their legal mechanics.

B. Market Access and National Treatment

The GATS articles on market access and national treatment are included in Part III of the GATS, titled 'Specific Commitments'. As a result, both market access and national treatment within the GATS are not unconditional general obligations but rather they are effectuated on the stipulation that WTO Members inscribe specific comments on the basis of one or more modes of supply.[74] It should be noted that any of the entries under the GATS Article XVI (market access) or XVII (national treatment) may vary between full commitment without limitation ('none') and full discretion to apply any measure falling within

[73] ibid, paras 6.114–6.115.

[74] For a detailed discussion on the methodologies for listing commitments, see B Hoekman and P Sauvé, 'Liberalizing Trade in Services' [1994] WTO Discussion Paper No. 243.

the ambit of the relevant article ('unbound').[75] Following this, WTO Members have undertaken Schedules of Specific Commitments which are attached to the GATS and form an integral part of the treaty.[76] Those commitments determine the degree to which specific GATS obligations on market access or national treatment apply in certain services sectors or subsectors (such as the financial sector). The WTO judiciary noted that because a WTO Member's obligations concerning a particular service depend on the specific commitments that it has undertaken regarding the sector or subsector within which that service falls, a specific service cannot fall within the different sectors or subsectors; meaning that the sectors and subsectors in a WTO Member's Schedule must be mutually exclusive.[77] In addition, as mentioned above, certain WTO Members have decided to enter their commitments on the basis of the Understanding on Commitments in Financial Services. It is worth noting that several WTO Members (including the US and the EU) have modelled their commitments in financial services sectors in line with Understanding.[78]

The WTO adjudicatory bodies clarified that:

> A [WTO] Member may limit the extent to which it grants market access or national treatment for the services listed in its Schedule, by inscribing the 'conditions or qualification' (which we refer to more simply as 'limitations') mentioned in Article XVII either under 'limitations on market access' or under 'limitations on national treatment'. A Member's obligations on market access and/or national treatment are determined with reference to any such limitations inscribed in its schedule.[79]

Thus, to define the degree of a WTO Member's national treatment commitments in connection with the services at issue, one needs to examine the WTO Member's Schedule of Commitments to assess whether, with respect to the relevant mode of supply, there are any limitations inscribed beside the relevant service, in the market access or national treatment column, or in market access or national treatment column of the horizontal section of the WTO Member's Schedule. In the absence of any limitation on national treatment, the term 'None' would be used; conversely, where the WTO Member undertakes no national treatment commitment with respect to a service, the word 'unbound' is inscribed.[80]

[75] See, for example, Appellate Body Report, *US – Gambling*, para 215.

[76] GATS, Art XX:3 reads: 'Schedules of specific commitments shall be annexed to this Agreement and shall form an integral part thereof.' For an interpretation of this provision by the WTO judiciary, see Appellate Body Report, *US – Gambling*, paras 159–160. See also Panel Report, *US – Gambling*, para 6.45.

[77] Appellate Body Report, *US – Gambling*, para 180.

[78] For a more detailed discussion of the scope of the Understanding in connection with market access and national treatment, see below.

[79] Panel Report, *EU – Energy Package*, para 7.235. See also Panel Report, *China – Publications and Audiovisual Products*, para 7.944.

[80] For a broad overview of the GATS, see WTO Secretariat, 'The General Agreement on Trade in Services – An Introduction' (WTO) www.wto.org/english/tratop_e/serv_e/gsintr_e.pdf accessed 25 July 2023.

In light of the above, it is evident that the GATS is a flexible agreement that involves only gradual liberalisation of (financial) services at the pace and national prerogatives of WTO Members which enter market access and national treatment specific commitment on a voluntary basis. Having explained the principal mechanics concerning WTO Members' specific commitments inscribed in their GATS Schedules, the forthcoming analysis elaborates on the market access and national treatment obligations set out in the GATS and, specifically, the extent to which they contribute to the liberalisation of financial infrastructure services while ensuring that WTO Members maintain discretion in designing their financial regulation.

i. Market Access

The market access provision in the GATS removes various quantitative restrictive measures on the entry and operation of foreign services and service suppliers in the market of a host country and contributes significantly to the liberalisation efforts in financial services sectors since the entry into force of the GATS.[81] In particular, market access plays an important role in opening markets for foreign services and service suppliers through WTO Members' undertaken commitments, thus leading to 'international contestability of markets'.[82] 'Market access' as a term appears very broad and seemingly covers all types of trade barriers to entry and operation.[83] However, GATS, Article XVI on market access has a very specific scope, focusing on removing primarily *quantitative* limitations on the overall provision of services in WTO Members' markets – so long as those Members decide to list those sectors, subsectors, or activities in their Schedule of Commitments.[84] The GATS does not define market access but instead offers a list of restrictive measures (mostly of a quantitative nature) which are typically used by host countries to refuse entry to services and service providers

[81] For empirical research shedding light on the degree of liberalisation of trade in financial services defined by commitment enshrined in the GATS, such as the ones on market access, see JA Marchetti, 'Financial Services Liberalization in the WTO and PTAs' in JA Marchetti and M Roy (eds), *Opening Markets for Trade in Services, Countries and Sectors in Bilateral and WTO Negotiations* (Cambridge, Cambridge University Press, 2009); JR Barth et al, 'World Trade Organization Commitments vs Reported Practices on Foreign Bank Entry and Regulation: A Cross-Country Analysis' in AN Berger et al (eds), *The Oxford Handbook of Banking* (Oxford, Oxford University Press, 2012).

[82] For a study focusing on the liberalisation of trade in financial services as the result of the GATS and the negotiating agenda in the Doha Round, see Key (n 33).

[83] Market access is defined as 'the ability of a company or country to sell goods and services across borders'. For the definition and a short analysis, see Investopedia, 'What Is Market Access in International Trade?' (Investopedia, 30 September 2021) www.investopedia.com/terms/m/market-access.asp#:~:text=Market%20access%20refers%20to%20the,is%20the%20most%20common%20contex accessed 25 July 2023.

[84] See discussion above.

from third countries. In the following paragraphs, we provide an overview of this GATS provision's scope and mechanics in light of the recent WTO dispute settlement reports in the area of trade in services, which offer clarifications on the interpretation of the market access provision set out in the GATS.

At the outset, GATS, Article XVI on market access reads:

> 1. With respect to market access through the modes of supply identified in Article I, each Member shall accord services and service suppliers of any other Member treatment no less favourable than that provided for under the terms, limitations and conditions agreed and specified in its Schedule.[8]
> 2. In sectors where market-access commitments are undertaken, the measures which a Member shall not maintain or adopt either on the basis of a regional subdivision or on the basis of its entire territory, unless otherwise specified in its Schedule, are defined as:
>
> (a) limitations on the number of service suppliers whether in the form of numerical quotas, monopolies, exclusive service suppliers or the requirements of an economic needs test;
> (b) limitations on the total value of service transactions or assets in the form of numerical quotas or the requirement of an economic needs test;
> (c) limitations on the total number of service operations or on the total quantity of service output expressed in terms of designated numerical units in the form of quotas or the requirement of an economic needs test;[9]
> (d) limitations on the total number of natural persons that may be employed in a particular service sector or that a service supplier may employ and who are necessary for, and directly related to, the supply of a specific service in the form of numerical quotas or the requirement of an economic needs test;
> (e) measures which restrict or require specific types of legal entity or joint venture through which a service supplier may supply a service; and
> (f) limitations on the participation of foreign capital in terms of maximum percentage limit on foreign share-holding or the total value of individual or aggregate foreign investment.
>
> [8] If a Member undertakes a market-access commitment in relation to the supply of a service through the mode of supply referred to in subparagraph 2(a) of Article I and if the cross-border movement of capital is an essential part of the service itself, that Member is thereby committed to allow such movement of capital. If a Member undertakes a market-access commitment in relation to the supply of a service through the mode of supply referred to in subparagraph 2(c) of Article I, it is thereby committed to allow related transfers of capital into its territory.
>
> [9] Subparagraph 2(c) does not cover measures of a Member which limit inputs for the supply of services.

The six limitations on market access set out in Article XVI(2) of the GATS are summarised and concrete examples in the context of financial market infrastructure are given to explain how these restrictive measures, of primarily quantitative nature, may apply in practice. First, limitations on the number of services suppliers (eg monopolies or exclusive rights for the supply of financial infrastructure services or measures limiting the number of central counterparty licences that will be granted in a WTO Member). Second, limitations on the total value of service transactions or assets (such as measures limiting the value of financial instruments' clearing transactions to a specific percentage of total mandatory clearing transactions in the WTO Member concerned). Third, limitations on the total number of service operations or on the total quantity of service output (eg limitations on the number of over the counter (OTC) derivatives trading operations by foreign trading venues). Fourth, limitations on the total number of natural persons that may be employed in a particular service sector or that a service supplier may employ (eg limitations on the number of foreign employees in a WTO Member's central securities depositories). Fifth, measures which restrict or require specific types of legal entity or joint venture through which a service supplier may provide a service (such as measures requiring specific types of juridical person to supply financial infrastructure services or prohibitions to establish direct branches). Sixth, restrictions on the participation of foreign capital in terms of maximum percentage limit on foreign shareholding or the total value of individual or aggregate foreign investment (eg measures prohibiting foreign investors from owning more than a specific percentage of the shares of central counterparties in the WTO Member undertaking the commitment).

The examples above show that the GATS market access provision is designed to address government intervention in the services industry that quantitatively restricts entry or establishment of foreign services or service suppliers to a country's domestic market for committed services sectors.[85] This type of trade barrier is not uncommon in Members' financial services industries, which are heavily regulated – in part to tackle some of the market failures endemic to the industry.[86] For example, if a WTO Member has fully bound 'settlement and clearing services' for all modes of supply in its Schedule, a restrictive measure like the ones described above would be in violation of the GATS. For completeness, it should be noted that if such a restrictive measure were to be adopted to maintain the financial soundness and integrity of the system, a potential breach of GATS, Article XVI could be justified under the GATS prudential carve-out, if its requirements were met.[87]

As to the precise function of the market access provision in the GATS, the Appellate Body stated that:

> Article XVI of the GATS sets out specific obligations for Members that apply insofar as a Member has undertaken 'specific market access commitments' in its Schedule. The first paragraph of Article XVI obliges Members to accord services and service suppliers of other Members 'no less favourable treatment than that provided for

[85] That is, services sectors expressly inscribed in a WTO Member's schedule in the Art XVI market access column.

[86] For a thorough analysis of the underlying rationale behind financial regulation, especially in the context of the recent financial crisis, see Cantore (n 69) 5–63; *cf* C Goodhart et al, *Financial Regulation: Why, How and Where Now?* (Abingdon, Routledge, 1998).

[87] For a discussion on the prudential carve-out, see below.

under the terms, limitations and conditions agreed and specified in its Schedule.' The second paragraph of Article XVI defines, in six sub-paragraphs, measures that a Member, having undertaken a specific commitment, is not to adopt or maintain, 'unless otherwise specified in its Schedule'. The first four sub-paragraphs concern quantitative limitations on market access; the fifth sub-paragraph covers measures that restrict or require specific types of legal entity or joint venture through which a service supplier may supply a service; and the sixth sub-paragraph identifies limitations on the participation of foreign capital.[88]

Following this, it is clear that the degree of market access 'openness' is intrinsically incumbent on WTO Members' commitments inscribed in their GATS Schedules. Moreover, despite the absence of a definition for market access in the GATS, the Appellate Body effectively fleshed out the scope of application of this provision by explaining the nature of the restrictive measures under Article XVI.

With respect to the introductory heading of Article XVII:2 as context for the interpretation of one of the six subparagraphs included in that provision, the Appellate Body noted that

> the chapeau to Article XVI:2, refers to the purpose of the sub-paragraphs that follow, namely, to define the measures which a Member shall not maintain or adopt for sectors where market access commitments are made. The chapeau thus contemplates circumstances in which a Member's Schedule includes a commitment to allow market access, and points out that the function of the sub-paragraphs in Article XVI:2 is to define certain limitations that are prohibited unless specifically entered in the Member's Schedule.[89]

In respect of the restrictive measures covered by the market access provision in the GATS and specifically whether the limitations listed in Article XVI(2) are a *numerus clausus* or not – which has been disputed by WTO Members and scholars alike[90] – the WTO judiciary confirmed that:

> [t]he ordinary meaning of the words, the context of Article XVI, as well as the object and purpose of the GATS confirm that the restrictions on market access that are covered by Article XVI are only those listed in paragraph 2 of this Article.[91]

[88] Appellate Body Report, *US – Gambling*, para 214.

[89] ibid, para 233.

[90] For academic discussion and diverging views on the subject in the aftermath of the *US – Gambling* Appellate Body report, see P Delimatsis, 'Don't Gamble with GATS – The Interaction between Articles VI, XVI, XVII and XVIII GATS in the Light of the US – Gambling Case' (2006) 40 *Journal of World Trade* 1059; F Ortino, 'Treaty Interpretation and the WTO Appellate Body Report in US–Gambling: A Critique' (2006) 9 *Journal of International Economic Law* 117; PC Mavroidis, 'Highway XVI Re-Visited: The Road from Non-Discrimination to Market Access in GATS' (2007) 6 *World Trade Review* 1.

[91] Panel Report, *US – Gambling*, para 6.318. See also Appellate Body Report, *US – Gambling*, paras 6.298–6.299.

It also confirmed that '[t]he six types of measures form a closed or exhaustive list, as indicated by the wording of the chapeau to paragraph 2 ("the measures ... are defined as")'.[92]

This was also confirmed by the Panel in *China – Electronic Payment Services*, which observed that the market access obligation of the GATS 'applies to six carefully defined categories of measures of a mainly qualitative nature'.[93] Along similar lines, the Panel in *Argentina – Financial Services* observed that:

> the list of measures in the six subparagraphs of Article XVI:2 is not only exhaustive but also fulfils the function of establishing clearly, exactly and precisely the types of limitation on market access that are prohibited and hence may not be maintained or adopted in those sectors where a Member had adopted specific commitments, unless it has specifically mentioned this possibility in its Schedule.[94]

While more restrictive in terms of liberalisation prospects, the author endorses the interpretation according to which GATS, Article XVI(2) includes an exhaustive list of measures, as this appears to reflect better the text of the agreement as prepared by the drafters of the WTO Treaty and it offers more legal certainty by not giving rise to ambiguity as to the exact content of the provision. In any event, WTO adjudicating bodies have construed the provision in a pragmatic manner that – while it does not expand the number of the restrictive measures defined in the GATS Article XVI:2 – captures conduct the nature of which is quantitative, irrespective of whether this quantitative nature is expressed in numbers or not.[95]

In addition to the GATS, the Understanding on Commitments in Financial Services offers a sort of a formula approach to scheduling commitments under Article XVI of the GATS concerning financial services. Given the importance of this instrument in setting the norm for WTO Members' commitments in financial services, the following paragraphs explore the most prominent features housed in the Understanding concerning 'market access'. First, the Understanding complements Article VIII of the GATS (monopolies) by providing that WTO Members having adhered to the Understanding shall include in their Schedules any existing monopoly rights in financial services sectors and shall endeavour to eliminate them or reduce their scope.[96] The Understanding provides further GATS-plus treatment by fleshing out an obligation on government procurement,

[92] Panel Report, *China – Publications and Audiovisual Products*, para 7.1353.

[93] Panel Report, *China – Electronic Payment Services*, para 7.652.

[94] Panel Report, *Argentina – Financial Services*, para 7.418. See also Panel Report, *EU – Energy Package*, para.7.648.

[95] For a more detailed discussion, see Delimatsis, 'Don't Gamble with GATS – The Interaction between Articles VI, XVI, XVII and XVIII GATS in the Light of the US – Gambling Case' (n 90) 1067–68.

[96] See para B.1 of the Understanding. Notably, this obligation also extends to activities carried out by a public entity for the account of WTO Members' governments, which, if provided on non-market conditions, would normally be considered '*services supplied in the exercise of governmental authority*' and, therefore, fall outside the coverage of the GATS. See subpara 1(b)(iii) of the Annex on Financial Services.

according to which WTO Members must ensure that when procuring financial services, public entities in their jurisdictions accord foreign services providers established in their territories MFN and national treatment.[97] In addition, the Understanding provides that WTO Members shall offer financial service providers of any other Member the right of establishment ('commercial presence') for all financial services sectors.[98] Moreover, according the Understanding '[a] Member shall permit financial service suppliers of any other Member established in its territory to offer in its territory any new financial service'.[99] Finally, the Understanding puts forward a 'best endeavour' obligation 'to remove or to limit any significant adverse effects on financial service suppliers of any other Member' in connection with a category of measures.[100] It goes without saying that the obligations in the Understanding are covered by the GATS prudential carve-out (discussed below).

In light of the above, it is evident that the Understanding goes beyond the degree of liberalisation of financial services sectors set out in the GATS for the WTO Members that adhere to it. Since several WTO Members have opted to adopt the 'market access' standards found in the Understanding, its effect on opening financial markets to foreign services and service suppliers (in cases where, for example, a country procures the services of financial institutions to issue debt it shall accord MFN and national treatment to foreign service suppliers established in its territory) is a welcome addition to increase the global contestability of markets – without putting into jeopardy the stability of financial systems.

Furthermore, it is important to discuss the constituent elements of a claim under the market access provision in the GATS. The Appellate Body held that a complainant in a WTO dispute is required to make its prima facie case 'by first alleging that the [respondent] has undertaken market access commitments in its GATS Schedule; and, secondly, by identifying, with supporting evidence, how the challenged laws constitute impermissible "limitations" falling within' one of the six subparagraphs of Article XVI:2.[101] In interpreting a

[97] See para B.2 of the Understanding. GATS, Art XIII(1) (Government Procurement), which provides that services purchased by governmental agencies for governmental purposes are not subject to MFN, market access and national treatment.

[98] See para B.5 of the Understanding. GATS, Art XXVIII(d), which defines 'commercial presence' as 'any type of business or professional establishment, including through (i) the constitution, acquisition or maintenance of a juridical person, or (ii) the creation or maintenance of a branch or a representative office', for the purpose of supplying a service.

[99] See para B.7. The Understanding defines a new financial services as 'a service of a financial nature, including services related to existing and new products or the manner in which a product is delivered, that is not supplied by any financial service supplier in the territory of a particular Member but which is supplied in the territory of another Member.'

[100] See para B.10 of the Understanding.

[101] Appellate Body Report, *US – Gambling*, para 143. See also Panel Reports, *China – Publications and Audiovisual Products*, para 7.1354; *China – Electronic Payment Services*, paras 7.511–7.512, *EU – Energy Package*, para 7.233 and *Argentina – Financial Services*, paras 7.391–7.392.

WTO Member's Schedule, the sectoral entries must be read together with the entries in the horizontal section of that Schedule to identify any limitations on market access.[102] In short, the WTO adjudicatory bodies have identified the two steps required for WTO complainants to show a violation of the GATS, Article XVI, namely: (i) first, by demonstrating that a WTO Member has undertaken a market access specific commitments in respect of a specific sector, subsector or activity (including a particular mode of supply); and (ii) second, by adducing evidence that the restrictive measure in question is in breach of one of the limitations listed in Article XVI(2) of the GATS.

Market access is one of the main liberalising tools endorsed in the GATS. Perhaps more notably, it enables WTO Members to open their services sectors to foreign competition by binding 'market access' commitments in their schedules. In the realm of financial services, it has been evidenced that WTO Members' commitments under the GATS lead to tangible liberalisation efforts.[103] The analysis below provides an anatomy of the national treatment provision (GATS Article XVII), which results in the liberalisation of trade in (financial) services aimed at opening markets to foreign services and ensuring that such foreign services are accorded substantially the same treatment as domestic like services.

ii. National Treatment

The national treatment provision set out in Article XVII(1) of the GATS requires each WTO Member to 'accord to services and service suppliers, of any other Member, in respect of all measures affecting the supply of services, treatment no less favourable than that it accords to its own like services and service suppliers'. The scope of application of this obligation is very broad, consisting of 'all measures affecting trade in services' but it only applies to WTO Members whose measures have indicated in their Schedules of Commitments that the obligation applies in the service at stake (such as trading derivative products). Furthermore, even if a WTO Member has made a binding commitment, the Member may still have included limitations to the commitment in its Schedule. Moreover, the national treatment obligation is only applicable to measures that impact the conditions of competition in the territory of the WTO Member adopting the measures – Article XVII does not apply to measures affecting services exports.[104]

Following this, the GATS provides flexibility to WTO Members in designing their commitments and involves only progressive liberalisation at the pace individual WTO Members deem suitable. Hence, to evaluate whether a

[102] Panel Report, *EU – Energy Package*, para 7.354.

[103] See, for example, Marchetti, 'Financial Services Liberalization in the WTO and PTAs' (n 81); Marchetti and Mavroidis, 'The Genesis of the GATS (General Agreement on Trade in Services)' (n 4).

[104] See R Adlung, 'Negotiations on Safeguards and Subsidies in Services: A Never-Ending Story?' (2007) 10 *Journal of International Economic Law* 235.

WTO Member's measure concerning financial market infrastructure services or service suppliers is consistent with Article XVII GATS, one needs to review the Member's Schedule of Commitments.

With respect to the scope of Article XVII, the WTO adjudicators held that while the scope of the market access obligation under Article XVI:2 of the GATS 'applies to six carefully defined categories of measures of a mainly quantitative nature', the scope of the national treatment obligation under Article XVII extends generally to 'all measures affecting the supply of services'.[105]

Moreover, the Understanding on Commitments in Financial Services offers a sort of a formula approach to scheduling commitments under Article XVII of the GATS in respect of financial services. It is worth examining the two specific obligations in connection with national treatment, as many WTO Members have adopted their commitments on the basis of the Understanding. First, the Understanding sets out that each WTO Member [who has undertaken commitments by reference to the Understanding] must grant to financial services providers of any other Member established in its territory, under national treatment terms and conditions, 'access to payment and clearing systems operated by public entities, and to official funding and refinancing facilities available in the normal course of ordinary business'.[106] This obligation is not intended, however, to grant access to the WTO Member's lender of last resort facilities. This is further corroborated by the fact that the Understanding does not make any mention of measures that are adopted in cases of emergency – which would in principle be outside the 'normal course of ordinary business'[107] and would be covered by the GATS prudential carve-out if its legal requirements were fulfilled (see discussion below). This obligation seeks to ensure that foreign financial services and/or financial institutions are not prevented from gaining access to the payments' processing infrastructure which is run by public entities (such as central banks) and to official funding and refinancing facilities available in the normal course of business (excluding, for example, emergency measures taken to strengthen financial stability).[108] By granting national treatment

[105] Panel Report, *China – Electronic Payment Services*, para 7.652.

[106] See para C.1 of the Understanding.

[107] See R Wolfrum et al, 'Understanding on Commitments in Financial Services' in R Wolfrum et al (eds), *WTO-Trade in Services* (Leiden, Brill Nijhoff, 2008).

[108] As to the precise scope of 'official funding and refinancing facilities' no clarity has been provided by the drafters of the Understanding. Based on definitions in the GATS we can deduct that 'official' refers to measures adopted by WTO Members (contrary to action taken by private entities). Specifically, the GATS applies only to measures stemming from 'central, regional or local governments and authorities' (GATS, Art 1(3)(a)(i)) as well as 'non-governmental bodies in the exercise of powers delegated by central, regional or local governments and authorities (GATS, Art 1(3)(a)(ii)). The author's view is that funding and refinancing facilities refers to central banks' lending and deposit facilities but this reading has not yet been confirmed or denied by WTO adjudicatory bodies. For a more detailed discussion on the matter, see B De Meester, 'The Global Financial Crisis and Government Support for Banks: What Role for the GATS?' (2010) 13 *Journal of International Economic Law* 27, 41–43.

to foreign services and or service providers in connection with those facilities, WTO Members promote the international contestability of financial markets as they reduce some of the regulatory trade barriers foreign services and service suppliers typically face when they enter third markets[109] – without putting into jeopardy the integrity of the financial system as the obligation has introduced sufficient caveats on top of the existence of the prudential carve-out.

Second, the Understanding mandates that when membership or participation in, or access to, any self-regulatory body, securities or futures exchange or market, clearing agency, or any other organisation or association, is required by a WTO Member in order for foreign financial service suppliers to supply financial services on an equal basis with national financial service suppliers, or when the WTO Member provides such entities, directly or indirectly, with privileges or advantages in supplying financial services, the WTO Member shall ensure that such entities accord national treatment to foreign financial service suppliers resident in the territory of the Member.[110] In this context, the Understanding makes reference to 'resident' financial service suppliers, and not to 'established' financial services suppliers, but no definition is given of either term. This obligation is very important for the economic integration of financial market infrastructure as it provides that where a WTO Member has put in place a requirement for membership/participation/access to, for example, a central counterparty it shall ensure that foreign service providers are not accorded less favourable treatment by such counterparty vis-à-vis domestic financial service suppliers. Such an obligation is all the more important in the context of the post-crisis regulatory frameworks in several jurisdictions for central counterparties which require clearing for certain types of derivatives.[111] In this regulatory environment, an obligation that tackles differential treatment in accessing host country financial infrastructure (such as clearing houses and trading venues) by foreign financial institutions is undoubtedly conducive to increasing the contestability

[109] By way of example, some of the issues raised in the *China – Electronic Payments Services* (DS413) dispute were pertinent to the compatibility of China's measures concerning the interoperability of bank card payments bearing certain logo with its national treatment commitments under the GATS. While China's Schedule of Commitments (GATS/SC/135) has not inscribed commitments in financial services sectors by reference to the Understanding, access to payment processing infrastructure by foreign services and service suppliers is one of the prominent issues disputed in the proceedings.

[110] See para C.2 of the Understanding.

[111] Among the measures put forward by the G20 in the aftermath of the 2008 global financial crisis, there was one according to which governments committed to ensure that all OTC derivative contracts are cleared through central-counterparties. See G20, 'G20 Leaders Statement: The Pittsburgh Summit' (G20 Information Centre, 24 September 2009) www.g20.utoronto.ca/2009/2009communique0925.html accessed 25 July 2023. The relevant part of the statement read '[a]ll standardized OTC derivative contracts should be traded on exchanges or electronic trading platforms, where appropriate, and cleared through central counterparties by end-2012 at the latest. OTC derivative contracts should be reported to trade repositories. Non-centrally cleared contracts should be subject to higher capital requirements.' For a more detailed analysis of the regulatory framework in the EU, see Chapter 3 below.

of those markets. The forthcoming analysis focuses on the requisite standard of the GATS, Article XVII.

The constituent elements of the GATS national treatment provision, as confirmed by the Panel in *EU – Energy Package*,[112] are the following: (i) whether the services at issue are inscribed in a WTO Member's Schedule of Specific Commitments; (ii) the extent of the WTO Member's national treatment commitments, including any conditions or qualifications in respect of these services entered in its Schedule; (iii) whether the measures at issue affect the supply of these services; and (iv) whether these measures accord less favourable treatment to service suppliers of other Members, in comparison with like domestic suppliers. Given the case-specific nature of WTO Members' inscribed commitments in connection with modes of supply, the discussion above suffices to explain the mechanics of Schedules of Commitments and another review is not called for. In the analysis below, we shed light on the content of 'treatment no less favourable' and the concept of likeness in the context of GATS, Article XVII, by focusing on the relevant interpretations put forward by WTO jurisprudence.

The concept of likeness in GATS, Article XVII provides that a measure will only be discriminatory in comparison to foreign services or service suppliers if the service suppliers that are treated less favourably are 'like' the domestic service suppliers of the WTO adopting the measure. However, discrimination may also exist in cases where 'unlike' services or service providers are treated exactly in the same way. This is expressly recognised in Article XVII(2) of the GATS which reads: 'A Member may meet the requirement of para 1 by according to services and service suppliers of any other member either formally identical treatment or formally different treatment to that it accords to its own like services and service suppliers'.

In *China – Publications and Audiovisual Products*, the Panel noted that when origin is the only factor on which a measure bases a difference in treatment between domestic service providers and foreign service suppliers, the 'likeness' condition is met, if there will, or can, be domestic and foreign providers that under the measure are the same in all material respects except for origin.[113]

However, in the realm of financial services the assessment of likeness between domestic and foreign services and service providers might be a more complex endeavour in view of the prominent role of regulation in those services, which aims at tackling the market failures which are intimately linked to the financial services industry.[114] In the following chapter a concrete case study is provided in which the interplay between financial regulation and the trade norms housed in the GATS is discussed. Along those lines, in *China – Electronic Payment Services* the Panel identified that the difference in treatment was 'not exclusively linked

[112] Panel Report, *EU – Energy Package*, para 7.235. See also Panel Report, *China – Publications and Audiovisual Products*, para 7.944.

[113] Panel Report, *China – Publications and Audiovisual Products*, paras 7.975–7.976.

[114] See, for example, Goodhart et al (n 86).

to the origin of service suppliers, but to other factors'. As a result, the Panel decided to carry out 'a more detailed analysis of the likeness issue'.[115] The Panel further noted that using the analytical framework on likeness developed in the context of the multilateral agreements on trade in goods for assessments on services might not be appropriate due to the 'important dissimilarities between the two areas of trade – notably the intangible nature of services, their supply through four different modes, and possible differences in how trade in services is conducted and regulated'.[116]

The Panel in the same dispute then elaborated on the ordinary meaning of the term 'like' and the context of the phrase 'like services'. The Panel deduced from the wording of Articles XVII:1 and XVII:3 that 'Article XVII seeks to ensure equal competitive opportunities for like services of other Members' and that 'like services are services that are in a competitive relationship with each other (or would be if they were allowed to be supplied in a particular market)'.[117] The Panel also said:

> 7.701 Furthermore, we note that Article XVII is applicable to all services[891], in any sector, and that services – which are intangible – may be provided through any of the four modes of supply. As well, Article XVII refers to 'like services and service suppliers'. In the light of this complexity, 'like services and service suppliers' analyses should in our view take into account the particular circumstances of each case. In other words, we consider that determinations of 'like services', and 'like service suppliers', should be made on a case-by-case basis.[892]
>
> 7.702 In the light of the above, we consider that a likeness determination should be based on arguments and evidence that pertain to the competitive relationship of the services being compared. As in goods cases where a panel assesses whether a particular product is a 'like product', the determination must be made on the basis of the evidence as a whole. If it is determined that the services in question in a particular case are essentially or generally the same in competitive terms, those services would, in our view, be 'like' for purposes of Article XVII.[895] [118]
>
> [891] Except for services supplied in the exercise of governmental authority. See Article I:3(b) of the GATS.
>
> [892] For a similar view with regard to 'like products' determinations in the context of Article III of the GATT 1994, see Appellate Body Reports, *EC – Asbestos*, para 101; and *Japan – Alcoholic Beverages II*, DSR 1996:I, 97, at p. 113.
>
> [895] It is important to note that even if relevant services are determined to be 'like' and a measure of a Member is found to result in less favourable treatment of 'like' services of another Member, it may still be possible to justify that measure under one of the general exceptions set out in Article XIV of the GATS.

[115] Panel Report, *China – Electronic Payment Services*, para 7.697.

[116] ibid, para 7.698.

[117] ibid, para 7.670.

[118] Panel Report, *China – Electronic Payment Services*, paras 7.701–7.702 (certain citations omitted).

Additionally, the Appellate Body's observations in *Argentina – Financial Services* with respect to 'like service suppliers' and the presumption of 'likeness', discussed above (in the section dealing with GATS, Article II on most favoured nation) are applicable *mutatis mutandis* in the context of national treatment. Hence, it is clear that the determinant in finding likeness is whether and to what extent the services and service suppliers in question are in a competitive relationship; by way of example, in the context of trading venues for the purposes of shares and derivatives, whether a WTO Member's exchanges dealing with shares and derivatives are in competition with foreign venues (either established in the WTO Member or providing their services in a cross-border fashion). The remainder of the GATS, Article XVII analysis sheds light on the LFT requirement.

With respect to the 'treatment no less favourable' element of GATS, Article XVII, WTO adjudicators held that:

> This treatment is to be assessed in terms of the 'conditions of competition' between like services and services suppliers, as specified in Article XVII:3 of the GATS [...]. In our view, a measure that prohibits foreign service suppliers from supplying a range of services that may, subject to satisfying certain conditions, be supplied by the like domestic supplier cannot constitute treatment 'no less favourable', since it deprives the foreign service supplier of any opportunity to compete with like domestic suppliers. In terms of paragraph 3 of Article XVII, such treatment modifies conditions of competition in the most radical way, by eliminating all competition by the foreign service supplier with respect to the service at issue.[119]

In *Argentina – Financial Services*, the Appellate Body clarified its understanding of LFT in Articles II:1 and XVII of the GATS. Regarding Article XVII of the GATS, the Appellate Body held that:

> Examining the text of these provisions, we note that the second and third paragraph of Article XVII elaborate on the meaning of a Member's obligation to grant 'treatment no less favourable' pursuant to Article XVII:1. Specifically, Article XVII:2 recognizes that a Member may meet this requirement by according to services and service suppliers 'either formally identical treatment or formally different treatment'. Article XVII:3 stipulates that '[f]ormally identical or formally different treatment shall be considered to be less favourable if it modifies the conditions of competition in favour of services or service suppliers of the Member compared to like services or service suppliers of any other Member'. In our view, while Article XVII:3 refers to the modification of conditions of competition in favour of domestic services or service suppliers, the legal standard set out in Article XVII:3 calls for an examination of whether a measure modifies the conditions of competition to the detriment of services or service suppliers of any other Member. Less favourable treatment of foreign services or service suppliers and more favourable treatment of like domestic services or service suppliers are flip-sides of the same coin.

[119] Panel Report, *China – Publications and Audiovisual Products*, paras 7.978–7.979.

> Footnote 10 to Article XVII:1 provides further insight as to the meaning of the obligation to accord 'treatment no less favourable' under Article XVII:1. Footnote 10 stipulates that specific commitments assumed under Article XVII:1 'shall not be construed to require any Member to compensate for any inherent competitive disadvantages which result from the foreign character of the relevant services or service suppliers'. As its text indicates, the 'inherent competitive disadvantages' referred to in footnote 10 result from the 'foreign character' of the relevant services or service suppliers, rather than from the contested measure adopted by the importing Member. The 'inherent competitive disadvantages' under footnote 10, therefore, must be distinguished from the measure's impact on the conditions of competition in the marketplace. By stating that a Member is not required to 'compensate for' such 'inherent competitive disadvantages', footnote 10 thus makes clear that the national treatment obligation under Article XVII:1 is not about the relative competitive advantages or disadvantages of the services and service suppliers that are not caused by the contested measure. Rather, the standard of 'treatment no less favourable' must be based on the impact on the conditions of competition that results from the contested measure.[120]

Thus, subject to all other GATS, Article XVII conditions being met, formally identical or different treatment of foreign service suppliers result in a violation of Article XVII:1 if and only if such treatment modifies the terms of competition to their detriment.

As already discussed in the context of LFT under GATS Article II, in line with the GATS architecture, the legal standard for 'treatment no less favourable' under the non-discrimination provisions in the GATS should be severed from certain regulatory aspects or concerns which should be appropriately addressed in the context of the relevant exceptions.[121] At the same time, regulatory aspects which have a bearing on the conditions of competition might need to be borne in mind by the WTO adjudicating bodies, subject to the particularities of each case.[122] Hence, for the evaluation of LFT under the GATS national treatment provision, one needs to pay particular attention to whether a WTO Member's measure modifies the conditions of competition for 'like' services and/or service providers.

All in all, the GATS principles of 'market access' and 'national treatment' have been instrumental in liberalising financial services sectors in WTO Members' jurisdictions[123] (as well as in the context of economic integration agreements).[124] While these two principles are inextricably linked to

[120] Appellate Body Report, *Argentina – Financial Services*, paras 6.103–6.104. See also Panel Report, *EU – Energy Package*, para 7.744.

[121] Appellate Body Report, *Argentina – Financial Services*, paras 6.114–6.115.

[122] ibid, para 6.127.

[123] See, for example, Marchetti, 'Financial Services Liberalization in the WTO and PTAs' (n 81); Marchetti and Mavroidis, 'The Genesis of the GATS (General Agreement on Trade in Services)' (n 4).

[124] Chapter 4 of this volume offers a detailed study on the role 'market access' and 'national treatment' principles play in the liberalisation of financial infrastructure services in the context of economic integration agreements.

WTO Members' specific commitments inscribed in their Schedules, they promote the liberalisation of financial services with tangible outcomes. Finally, these two obligations are a reflection of the 'progressive liberalisation' approach housed in the GATS Preamble.[125]

C. Domestic Regulation

Regulation is one of the main instruments that governments use to harness financial services sectors – including the areas of financial market infrastructure – and to tackle market failures (such as negative externalities and information asymmetries).[126] In doing so, governments determine the degree of liberalisation in services sectors, including the financial one, by the very design of their regulatory frameworks, which may (or may not) incorporate some legitimate non-tariff trade barriers to, for example, support the integrity of financial systems.[127] There are voices arguing that financial regulation may be subject to rent-seeking and does not always in practice deliver on the outcomes it is designed to address.[128] However, the scope of domestic regulation in the GATS is much narrower and not unacceptably intrusive focusing on certain type of trade barriers – such as transparency and procedural fairness. GATS, Article VI introduces a mechanism which requires that WTO Members' regulations are not inequitable, excessively interventionist, or inhibit trade disproportionately to the desired outcomes.[129] In particular, Article VI scrutinises how domestic regulations are designed, administered, and applied when specific commitments

[125] The 'progressive liberalisation' approach is expressed in the second paragraph of the Preamble of the GATS and reads: '*Desiring* the early achievement of progressively higher levels of liberalisation of trade in services through successive rounds of multilateral negotiations aimed at promoting the interests of all participants on a mutually advantageous basis and at securing an overall balance of rights and obligations, while giving due respect to national policy objectives.'

[126] There is vast literature on this subject. By way of example, see P Pinotti, 'Trust, Regulation and Market Failures' (2012) 94 *Review of Economics and Statistics* 650; A Schwartz, 'Regulating for Rationality' (2015) 67 *Stanford Law Review* 1373; PM Booth, 'Is 'Market Failure'a Good Justification for Financial Regulation?' [2021] Institute for International Monetary Research Discussion Paper.

[127] See, for example, B Hoekman and P Messerlin, 'Liberalizing Trade in Services: Reciprocal Negotiations and Regulatory Reform' in P Sauvé and RM Stern (eds), *GATS 2000: New Directions in Services Trade Liberalization* (Washington DC, Brookings Institution Press, 2000); B Hoekman et al, 'The Political Economy of Services Trade Liberalization: A Case for International Regulatory Cooperation?' (2007) 23 *Oxford Review of Economic Policy* 367; B Hoekman and A Mattoo, 'Services Trade Liberalization and Regulatory Reform: Re-Invigorating International Cooperation' [2011] World Bank Policy Research Working Paper.

[128] For some recent takes on rent-seeking in connection with finance, see AI Khwaja and A Mian, 'Rent Seeking and Corruption in Financial Markets' (2011) 3 *Annual Review of Economics* 579; RL Hasen, 'Lobbying, Rent-Seeking, and the Constitution' (2012) 64 *Stanford Law Review* 191; J Kidd, 'FinTech: Antidote to Rent-Seeking' (2018) 93 *Chicago-Kent Law Review* 165.

[129] For the negotiations on dmestic regulation, see P Delimatsis, 'Concluding the WTO Services Negotiations on Domestic Regulation – Hopes and Fears' (2010) 9 *World Trade Review* 643.

are undertaken. It stipulates legally binding provisions of procedural nature,[130] a mandate to deploy a multilateral discipline for licensing requirements, and a substantive obligation of transitional nature. The application of WTO Members' domestic regulatory measures shall reflect on the principles embedded in the GATS, most importantly, on fairness, as an expression of non-discrimination, openness, in the form of transparency, and on negotiated commitments.[131] The panel delineated the scope of Article VI in *US – Gambling*, and stated that WTO Members' regulatory sovereignty ceases when the GATS rights of other Members are infringed.[132] Notably, Article VI is a hybrid provision because certain of its elements are inextricably linked to WTO Members' Schedules of Commitments. Before examining the specific provisions of Article VI, it is worth noting that the term 'domestic regulation' is not defined in the GATS[133] and this provision has not been the direct subject of any WTO dispute thus far.[134] Accordingly, our understanding of this provision is relatively limited.

First, Article VI:1 calls for the 'reasonable, objective and impartial' administration of all measures of general application affecting trade in services in the particular sectors, or sub-sectors where WTO Members have scheduled GATS commitments. WTO jurisprudence has not pronounced on the mechanics of this provision.[135] From the text of this provision it is clear that 'tailor-made' measures would not fall under its purview: for example, the support granted to rescue a financial institution under a specific program which is not part of a broader policy – such as a recovery and resolution mechanism which would, in principle, qualify as a 'measure of general application'.[136] Such 'tailor-made' intervention, was witnessed earlier in March 2023 in the case of Silicon Valley Bank, where the US administration approved actions enabling the Federal Deposit Insurance

[130] Panel Report, *US – Gambling*, para 6.432.

[131] P Delimatsis, *International Trade in Services and Domestic Regulations: Necessity, Transparency, and Regulatory Diversity* (Oxford, Oxford University Press, 2007) 95.

[132] Panel Report, *US – Gambling*, para 6.316. The Appellate Body reaffirmed the panel's finding: Appellate Body Report, *US – Gambling*, para 235.

[133] The six paragraphs in GATS, Art VI might be better interpreted as obligatory 'good governance' rules. Only Art VI:3 actually makes reference to 'domestic rules and regulations'. For more information, ME Footer and C George, 'The General Agreement on Trade in Services' in PFJ Macrory et al (eds), *The World Trade Organization: Legal, Economic and Political Analysis* (New York, Springer Publishing, 2005) 836.

[134] The Panel in *US – Gambling* examined the relationship between Arts VI, XVI, XVII and XVIII of the GATS to define 'the nature and the scope of the obligations contained in Article XVI' (see para 6.300). However, the Appellate Body in the same dispute did not consider Art VI relevant to the interpretation of Art XVI (para 250).

[135] For completeness, it is worth mentioning that GATS, Art VI:1 was invoked by Antigua in the *US – Gambling* dispute. However, the Panel held that Antigua had not demonstrated the existence of a 'measure of general application', the administration of which would breach this provision. See Panel Report, *US – Gambling*, paras 6.434 and 6.437. However, it should be noted that this provision mirrors GATT, Art X(3)(a) discussed in the next chapter assessing the compatibility of EU rules with the GATS.

[136] This example is without prejudice to the application of the GATS prudential carve-out, discussed below.

Corporation (FDIC) to complete the resolution of the abovementioned bank in a way that fully protects all depositors and not only the first US$ 250,000 of deposits after rapid-fire bank run.[137] In the case of measures of general application where a WTO Member has undertaken specific commitments, evidence of unreasonable, subjective or partial administration would need to be adduced to substantiate a violation under this provision.

Next, Article VI:2 is applicable to all services sectors covered by the GATS, irrespective of whether or not a WTO Member has entered specific commitments. Specifically, Article VI:2 sets out the establishment of courts or procedures for the objective and impartial review of administrative decisions in so far as they affect trade in services.[138] To exemplify this in the context of financial infrastructure, this obligation prescribes that WTO Members' ought to have in place an objective and impartial review mechanism for administrative or judicial decisions affecting the supply of derivatives trading or clearing services (such as equivalence decisions adopted by the EU or substituted compliance orders taken by the US). This is a prominent provision housed in the GATS, as it helps to prevent arbitrary decision-making in services sectors falling within the scope of the GATS, regardless of the degree of liberalisation provided by WTO Members in their Schedules.

Furthermore, Article VI:3 is another illustration of 'good governance' as, while recognising that authorisation procedures might be key to the supply of services, it stipulates that such authorisations must be given within a 'reasonable period of time' and mandates the provision of information, upon request, in connection with the statutes of applications for authorisation. Again, this provision is contingent upon WTO Members' scheduled commitments. For example, where a WTO Member has undertaken commitments on 'settlement and clearing services for financial assets, including securities, derivative products, and other negotiable instruments' in its GATS Schedule and it has an authorisation procedure for foreign financial services providers, its competent regulatory authorities have to communicate their decision about applications from third-country financial institutions within a timely manner and, when asked, ought to share information about applications' status without undue delays.

[137] In this case, Silicon Valley Bank was shut down by regulators on 10 March 2023 as the day before (ie 9 March 2023) customers – mostly venture capital funds – had initiated withdrawals of US$ 42 billion. See FDIC, 'Press Release, Joint Statement by the Department of the Treasury, Federal Reserve, and FDIC, Sunday, March 12, 2023' (12 March 2023) www.fdic.gov/news/press-releases/2023/pr23017.html accessed 25 July 2023. For more information, see, for example, The Economist, 'What Really Went Wrong at Silicon Valley Bank' (*The Economist*, 13 March 2023) www.economist.com/leaders/2023/03/13/what-really-went-wrong-at-silicon-valley-bank?utm_content=article-link-1&etear=nl_today_1&utm_campaign=a.the-economist-today&utm_medium=email.internal-newsletter.np&utm_source=salesforce-marketing-cloud&utm_term=3%2F13%2F2023&utm_id=1522372 accessed 25 July 2023.

[138] GATS, Art VI:2(b) provides an exemption for WTO Members from this condition if it would be inconsistent with their constitutional structure or the nature of their legal systems.

Moreover, GATS, Article VI:4 was the outcome of the acknowledgement among WTO Members during the Uruguay Round that domestic regulatory measures might have potentially trade restrictive effects and as a result agreed to develop specific disciplines to ensure that such regulations in the form of: (i) licensing requirements; (ii) qualification requirements; and (iii) technical standards, are not unduly restrictive. Bearing in mind the WTO Members' 'right to regulate, and to introduce new regulations, on the supply of services within their territories in order to meet national policy objectives',[139] Article VI:4 aims to ensure that domestic regulations 'do not constitute unnecessary barriers to trade in services', thereby recognising that regulations – even when burdensome – might be legitimate. To date, this provision has not been fleshed out. Finally, GATS, Article VI:5 was designed to address the period pending the development of regulatory disciplines pursuant to Article VI:4 – which is still pending.[140] Specifically, Article VI:5 set out that in sectors where specific commitments have been entered the WTO Members concerned will not apply domestic regulations that 'nullify or impair' those commitments, unless such rules could have reasonable been foreseen at the time when the specific commitments were undertaken.

All in all, in light of the foregoing it is clear that there is much unfulfilled promise in this GATS provision to further integrate services sectors between WTO Member in the future by ensuring that their domestic regulations concerning qualification or licensing standards for services sectors are not more burdensome than necessary. However, the WTO Membership to this day has not reached a consensus on incorporating such a necessity test in the WTO acquis. At the same time, GATS, Article VI still succeeds in injecting some procedural fairness into the design of WTO Members' domestic regulatory frameworks, such as financial regulations. The next section focuses on how governments integrate their services sectors through recognition arrangements and sheds light on the GATS-specific rules in this regard.

D. Recognition Agreements

At the outset, 'recognition' may be defined as an understanding between two or more countries according to which each recognises the adequacy of the other's regulation, supervision and/or enforcement of services (such as trading derivatives provided across borders or clearing securities products) or service suppliers (eg central counterparties) as a substitute for its own.[141] As a result, services or

[139] Preamble to the GATS, fourth recital.

[140] A Mattoo, 'National Treatment in the GATS: Corner-Stone or Pandora's Box?' (1997) 31 *Journal of World Trade* 107, 129.

[141] For a detailed analysis on the concept of mutual recognition in the context of finance, see, for example, PH Verdier, 'Mutual Recognition in International Finance' (2011) 52 *Harvard International Law Journal* 55.

service suppliers who comply with the applicable home country rules may gain access to the host country in accordance with an exemption from the host country's rules.[142] The main benefits associated with recognition agreements relate to achieving market liberalisation as well as improvements in domestic regulation. Recognition agreements promote the liberalisation of financial services to the extent that they facilitate the supply of international transactions by eliminating the need to conform with several (and perhaps divergent) regulations. In addition, recognition agreements may raise regulatory standards and control international externalities insofar as they condition market access on the existence of an equivalent regulatory regime in the home country as they reduce the risk that financial regulatory failures will impact the host country – either directly or through contagion and other types of systemic risk.[143] After this succinct overview of the concept of mutual recognition agreements, the following analysis focuses on 'recognition' through the lenses of the GATS.

GATS Article VII permits a departure from the obligation under Article II (most-favoured nation treatment) in connection with unilateral or mutual recognition of 'the education or experience obtained, requirements met, or licenses or certifications granted in a particular country'. For example, a WTO Member may recognise the regulatory framework for the operation of a central counterparty from another country either through harmonisation or via recognition agreements. Recognitions agreements can be either effectuated autonomously (ie unilaterally) or can be arrangements between two WTO Members (such as Australia and the United States).[144]

GATS, Article VII fleshes out the 'recognition' principle:

1. For the purposes of the fulfilment, in whole or in part, of its standards or criteria for the authorization, licensing or certification of services suppliers, and subject

[142] See PB Griffin, 'The Delaware Effect: Keeping the Tiger in Its Cage – The European Experience on Mutual Recognition in Financial Services' (2001) 7 *Columbia Journal of European Law* 337; K Nicolaidis and G Shaffer, 'Transnational Mutual Recognition Regimes: Governance without Global Government' (2004) 68 *Law and Contemporary Problems* 263, 271; JP Trachtman, 'Embedding Mutual Recognition at the WTO' (2007) 14 *Journal of European Public Policy* 780.

[143] For a more detailed analysis, see Verdier (n 141).

[144] The EU 'equivalence' decisions are a prime example of unilateral recognition in the field of financial infrastructure. By way of example, the European Commission's equivalence decision for US exchanges supervised by the US Securities and Exchange Commission of 4 April 2022 which contributed to the EU capital markets to be better integrated with other international markets; see 'Press Release, European Commission Adopts Additional Equivalence Decisions for US Exchanges' (European Commission, 4 April 2022) https://ec.europa.eu/commission/presscorner/detail/en/ip_22_2263 accessed 25 July 2023. In contrast, a prominent example of mutual recognition through bilateral arrangement in the area of financial services is the mutual recognition arrangement hammered out between the US Securities and Exchange Commission and the government of Australia and the Australian Securities and Investments Commission, which considers applications for exemptions made by stock exchanges and broker-dealers regulated by the other; see 'Press Release, U.S. Sec. & Exch. Comm'n, SEC, Australian Authorities Sign Mutual Recognition Agreement' (US Securities and Exchange Commission, 25 August 2008) www.sec.gov/news/press/2008/2008-182.htm accessed 25 July 2023.

> to the requirements of paragraph 3, a Member may recognize the education or experience obtained, requirements met, or licenses or certifications granted in a particular country. Such recognition, which may be achieved through harmonisation or otherwise, may be based upon an agreement or arrangement with the country concerned or may be accorded autonomously.
>
> 2. A Member that is a party to an agreement or arrangement of the type referred to in paragraph 1, whether existing or future, shall afford adequate opportunity for other interested Members to negotiate their accession to such an agreement or arrangement or to negotiate comparable ones with it. Where a Member accords recognition autonomously, it shall afford adequate opportunity for any other Member to demonstrate that education, experience, licenses, or certifications obtained or requirements met in that other Member's territory should be recognised.
> 3. A Member shall not accord recognition in a manner which would constitute a means of discrimination between countries in the application of its standards or criteria for the authorization, licensing or certification of services suppliers, or a disguised restriction on trade in services.
> 4. Each Member shall:
>
>   (a) within 12 months from the date on which the WTO Agreement takes effect for it, inform the Council for Trade in Services of its existing recognition measures and state whether such measures are based on agreements or arrangements of the type referred to in paragraph 1;
>
>   (b) promptly inform the Council for Trade in Services as far in advance as possible of the opening of negotiations on an agreement or arrangement of the type referred to in paragraph 1 in order to provide adequate opportunity to any other Member to indicate their interest in participating in the negotiations before they enter a substantive phase;
>
> for a promptly inform the Council for Trade in Services when it adopts new recognition measures or significantly modifies existing ones and state whether the measures are based on an agreement or arrangement of the type referred to in paragraph 1.
>
> 5. Wherever appropriate, recognition should be based on multilaterally agreed criteria. In appropriate cases, Members shall work in cooperation with relevant intergovernmental and non-governmental organizations towards the establishment and adoption of common international standards and criteria for recognition and common international standards for the practice of relevant services trades and professions.

This 'recognition' principle entails that a WTO Member accepts that when a service can be provided in the home country in line with the applicable regulatory framework, it can also be supplied in the host country, without having to also ensure compliance with the rules in this host jurisdiction.[145] The rationale

[145] See K Nicolaidis, 'Non-Discriminatory Mutual Recognition: An Oxymoron in the New WTO Lexicon?' in PC Mavroidis and P Blatter (eds), *Non Discrimination in the WTO: Past and Present, Journal of World Trade* (Ann Arbor, University of Michigan Press, 2000) 268.

of Article VII lies in furthering trade integration through recognition, while disallowing discrimination.[146]

In addition, the Annex on Financial Services also stipulates specific provisions on recognition which, for the most part, mirror the content of GATS, Article VII. Paragraph 3(a) of the Annex reads 'A Member may recognize prudential measures of any other country in determining how the Member's measures relating to financial services shall be applied'.[147] The important difference between the two provision relates to the obligation set out in paragraph 4(b) of the GATS, Article VII relating to in advance notification of Council of Trade in Services of the opening of negotiations of mutual agreements which is not applicable for financial services.[148] These recognition provisions stipulate that agreements can be concluded either mutually or unilaterally, and spell out specific conditions that shall be respected, which are examined in detail below.

First, transparency in the form of notifying recognition measures to the Council for Trade in Services is prescribed in the GATS.[149] This obligation can potentially increase the WTO Members' understanding of what are the driving forces of recognition agreements, and ultimately contribute to further integration.[150] However, for trade in financial services, openness through transparency is not attained because Members largely abstain from notifying any of their recognition measures.[151] This does not imply that recognition in financial services sectors between Members or unilaterally is not accorded, but rather that

[146] See AB Zampetti, 'Mutual Access through Mutual Recognition: The Promise and Limits of GATS Article VII' in P Sauvé and RM Stern (eds), *GATS 2000: New Directions in Services Trade Liberalization* (Washington DC, Brookings Institution Press, 2000); K Nicolaïdis and J Trachtman, 'From Policed Regulation to Managed Recognition: Mapping the Boundary of GATS' in Sauvé and Stern (ibid); A Mattoo, 'MFN and the GATS' in T Cottier and PC Mavroidis (eds), *Regulatory Barriers and the Principle of Non-Discrimination in World Trade Law*, vol 2 (Ann Arbor, University of Michigan Press, 2000).

[147] GATS, Annex, para 3(a). The relevant provision mandates: 'A Member may recognize prudential measures of any other country in determining how the Member's measures relating to financial services shall be applied. Such recognition, which may be achieved through harmonisation or otherwise, may be based upon an agreement or arrangement with the country concerned or may be accorded autonomously.'

[148] GATS, Annex, para 3(c) reads: 'Where a Member is contemplating according recognition to prudential measures of any other country, paragraph 4(b) of Article VII shall not apply.'

[149] GATS, Art VII:4.

[150] For an analysis that argues that like-minded countries tend to conclude mutual recognition agreements (MRAs), see JA Marchetti and PC Mavroidis, 'I Now Recognize You (and Only You) as Equal: An Anatomy of (Mutual) Recognition Agreements in the GATS' in I Lianos and O Odudu (eds), *Regulating Trade in Services in the EU and the WTO: Trust, Distrust and Economic Integration* (Cambridge, Cambridge University Press, 2012).

[151] This position is premised on research conducted on the Notifications Database of the WTO. It is striking that there are only seven recognition agreements/arrangements on financial services notified to the Council, pursuant to GATS, Art VII:4, since 1995. Interestingly, only two of those notifications date after the 2008 financial crisis, namely: (i) on 12 January 2021, Switzerland and the United Kingdom notified an agreement on direct insurance other than life insurance (S/C/N/1039); (ii) on 16 June 2020, Australia notified its new regulatory framework for foreign financial services providers that wish to provide financial services to wholesale clients or professional investors in Australia.

the transparency obligation is not fulfilled. As a result, since the practice of states does not facilitate trade openness, it becomes more difficult to pursue recognition with WTO Members that are not 'like-minded' partners. Most importantly, this lack of transparency has implications on restricting future recognition agreements. The second GATS recognitions obligation requires that a Member 'shall afford adequate opportunity for other interested Members to negotiate their accession to such an agreement or arrangement or to negotiate comparable ones with it'.[152] The Annex clarifies in that regard, that equivalent regulation, supervision, and enforcement are of vital importance for financial services. It should be understood that in practice Members that lack the regulatory expertise and the supervisory and/or enforcement resources are not necessarily offered adequate opportunity to conclude recognition agreements due to the complexities involved in these processes. In the next chapter, we provide a concrete case study and evaluate its complex substantive and procedural elements as well as their conformity with WTO rules on recognition. Third, recognition agreements according to the GATS shall not be either discriminatory or constitute a disguised trade restriction.[153] This caveat is used to ensure that mutual recognition agreements are not used to favour the services and/or service providers of certain jurisdictions over others in the application of a WTO Member's standards for recognition.

At this stage, an interpretative comment on the relation between GATS, Article VII and the Annex paragraph 3 is required to shed light on the applicable provisions for the recognition of prudential measures. At first, the Annex provision on Recognition is a *lex specialis* to the GATS, Article VII. However, we should underscore that the existence of paragraph 3 of the Annex by no means leads to the inapplicability of the broader GATS provision. This can be convincingly substantiated by an *a contrario* interpretation of the Annex, paragraph 3(c) which explicitly stipulates that: 'Where a Member is contemplating according recognition to prudential measures of any other country, paragraph 4(b) of Article VII shall not apply.' Notably, the founding fathers consciously discarded only the applicability of paragraph 4(b) of Article VII for financial services sectors; namely, the Members' transparency obligation in relation to the notification of potential ongoing recognition procedures. As a result, it emanates from this reading that all the other GATS Article VII provisions still apply for financial services with the particular specificities attached to paragraphs 3(a) and (b) of the Annex.

[152] See GATS, Art VII:2 and Annex on Financial Services, para 3(b). The latter reads as follows: 'A Member that is a party to such an agreement or arrangement referred to in subparagraph (a), whether future or existing, shall afford adequate opportunity for other interested Members to negotiate their accession to such agreements or arrangements, or to negotiate comparable ones with it, under circumstances in which there would be *equivalent regulation, oversight, implementation of such regulation*, and, if appropriate, *procedures concerning the sharing of information between the parties to the agreement or arrangement*. Where a Member accords recognition autonomously, it shall afford adequate opportunity for any other Member to demonstrate that such circumstances exist' (emphasis added).

[153] GATS, Art VII:3.

Given that most GATS, Article VII obligations remain applicable for financial services, it is worthwhile briefly discussing the role of Article VII:5 in this context. This provision spells out a best-effort obligation for Members to negotiate common international standards and criteria for recognition in international fora. This provision is not excluded from the scope of financial services. In principle, WTO Members, when appropriate, must adopt the standards put forward by international standard setting organisations. Perhaps the key condition contained in this provision is 'in appropriate cases' because it leaves considerable room for manoeuvre to WTO Members. Especially, the intricacies associated with financial regulation and the stability considerations enshrined in the prudential carve-out might strip this provision of meaning for financial services recognition agreements. Arguably, it would be a long shot to claim that WTO Members have a hard obligation to adopt the standards promulgated by the Bank for International Settlements and the International Organization of Securities Commissions for clearing services[154] based on this GATS article.

Although the GATS is permissive in respect of recognitions arrangements for financial services' measures, it should be mentioned that typically financial regulatory/supervisory authorities and central banks are in the lead in consummating such recognition agreements. This is evident from the examples brought already where government agencies for financial services (such as the Securities and Exchange Commission, the Australian Securities and Investment Commission and Her Majesty's Treasury) are in charge of such negotiating and concluding such negotiation agreements.[155] This is only natural – especially given the level of expertise required for complex endeavours of this sort. However, this practice reality should not diminish the role of the GATS in promoting openness and fairness in recognition arrangements through its hard obligations.

E. Prudential Carve-Out for Financial Services

The prudential carve-out (PCO) for financial services appears to provide wide leeway to financial regulators. GATS Annex on Financial Services paragraph 2(a) stipulates that

[154] For the relevant standards, see Committee and Settlement Systems and Technical Committee of International Organization of Securities Commissions, 'Principles for Financial Market Infrastructures' (Bank for International Settlements, April 2012) www.bis.org/cpmi/publ/d101a.pdf accessed 25 July 2023.

[155] This approach is corroborated by the fact that supervisory cooperation and information sharing agreements in the realm of financial services are typically in the form of a Memorandum of Understanding (MoU), statements of cooperation or exchange of letters between authorities. See, for example, the MoU between the European Securities and Markets Authority (ESMA) and the Hong Kong counterpart in respect of the supervision of CCPs established in Hong Kong which provide their services in the EU. See European Securities and Markets Authority, 'Memorandum of Understanding between ESMA and the Securities and Futures Commission Related to CCPs Established in Hong Kong' (ESMA, 18 March 2022) www.esma.europa.eu/sites/default/files/library/revised_mou_esma-sfc_hong_kong_tc-ccps_-_final.pdf accessed 25 July 2023.

> Notwithstanding any other provisions of the Agreement, a Member shall not be prevented from taking measures for prudential reasons, including for the protection of investors, depositors, policy holders or persons to whom a fiduciary duty is owed by a financial service supplier, or to ensure the integrity and stability of the financial system. Where such measures do not conform with the provisions of the Agreement, they shall not be used as a means of avoiding the Member's commitments or obligations under the Agreement.

The autonomy to legislate prudential rules for the sake of financial stability, among other objectives, is encouraged by the PCO, even if these rules do not conform with the GATS. However, despite the broad margin offered to regulators, the provision reads in the second sentence that prudential rules must not 'be used as a means of avoiding' trade disciplines.[156] This 'anti-circumvention' clause exists to delimit the range of regulatory space of WTO Members in financial services. To date, our knowledge of what type of measures can be justified under the PCO is quite restricted as there is limited case law elaborating on the prudential exception. The prudential exception has been only interpreted once, in *Argentina – Financial Services*. In the light of this dispute's findings, we discuss the PCO requisite legal standard.

The panel dealing for the first time with the GATS prudential exception developed an analysis that employs three requirements for measures to fall under its remit.[157] Specifically, the party invoking the PCO ought to meet the following conditions: (i) the measures at issue are 'affecting the supply of financial services'; (ii) the measures at issue were adopted 'for prudential reasons'; and (iii) the measures at issue have not been used 'as a means of avoiding commitments or obligations under the GATS'.[158] The scope of the PCO constitutes the first requirement. It was hotly debated between Panama and Argentina whether all types of 'measures affecting the supply of financial services',[159] or only 'domestic regulation', in the sense of the GATS, Article VI, fall under the purview of paragraph 2(a).[160] In response to it, the Appellate Body adopted the panel's interpretation and ruled that the PCO scope comprises all the measures that affect the supply of financial services.[161]

[156] The wording of the prudential exception is in juxtaposition to the chapeau of GATS, Art XIV, which presupposes a necessity assessment of measures: P Delimatsis and B Hoekman, 'National Tax Regulation, Voluntary International Standards, and the GATS: Argentina – Financial Services' (2018) 17 *World Trade Review* 265, 272.

[157] Panel Report, *Argentina – Financial Services*, paras 7.853–7.945.

[158] Panel Report, *Argentina – Financial Services*, para 7.851.

[159] GATS, Annex para 1(a). This provision reads as follows: 'This Annex applies to measures affecting the supply of financial services. Reference to the supply of a financial service in this Annex shall mean the supply of a service as defined in paragraph 2 of Article I of the Agreement.'

[160] Both the panel and the Appellate Body sided with the argument that all measures fall within the scope of the PCO. This reasoning was adopted because it better reflects the GATS rationale, illustrated in paras 3 and 4 of the Preamble, and better captures the content of para 2(a) and the context of the Annex. See Panel Report, *Argentina – Financial Services*, paras 6.825, 7.847; Appellate Body Report, *Argentina – Financial Services*, paras 6.253–6.262.

[161] Appellate Body Report, *Argentina – Financial Services*, para 6.262.

As regards the meaning of the word 'affecting', the panel in *Argentina – Financial Services* referred to the Appellate Body's interpretation, put forward in *EC – Bananas III*, and found:

> [I]n determining whether the measure 'affects' the supply of financial services within the meaning of paragraph 1(a) of the Annex on Financial Services, the Panel can be guided by this jurisprudence of the Appellate Body. This leads us to the view that the word 'affecting' in paragraph 1(a) of the Annex on Financial Services has a broader scope than such terms as 'regulating' or 'governing' and therefore covers any measure that has 'an effect on' the supply of financial services.[162]

Further the Appellate Body in *Argentina – Financial Services* held that the fact that paragraph 2(a) covers infringements of obligations under 'any provisions of the Agreement' implies that this provision 'could be invoked to justify inconsistencies with all of a Member's obligations under the GATS'.[163] Specifically, the Appellate Body noted:

> These include, for example, a Member's most-favoured-nation treatment obligation under Article II, market access commitments under Article XVI, or national treatment obligation under Article XVII. This indicates that, for example, measures which are of the types listed in Article XVI:2, and which impose market access restrictions for prudential reasons, could potentially fall within the scope of paragraph 2(a). The type of measure taken by a Member (such as market access restrictions) and the provision of the GATS contravened by such measure (such as Article XVI) are distinct, but related, concepts.[164]

In addition, the Appellate Body observed that the introductory clause '[n]otwithstanding any other provisions of the Agreement' in the first sentence of the PCO is pertinent to the scope of the measures covered by the exception. In particular, it noted:

> The ordinary meaning of the term 'notwithstanding', on the basis of its relevant dictionary definition, is 'in spite of, without regard to or prevention by'. This means that, under paragraph 2(a), a Member shall not be prevented from taking measures for prudential reasons despite its obligations under 'any other provisions of the Agreement', provided that such measures fulfil all of the requirements of paragraph 2(a). This understanding of the meaning of the introductory clause of paragraph 2(a) is confirmed by the second sentence of paragraph 2(a). Specifically, the second sentence states that '[w]here such measures do not conform with the provisions of the Agreement, they shall not be used as a means of avoiding the Member's commitments or obligations under the Agreement.' The reference to 'the provisions of the Agreement' suggests that this sentence also relates to inconsistencies with any other provision of the GATS.[165]

[162] Panel Report, *Argentina – Financial Services*, para 7.855.
[163] Appellate Body Report, *Argentina – Financial Services*, para 6.255.
[164] ibid.
[165] Appellate Body Report, *Argentina – Financial Services*, para 6.254.

Moreover, the second requirement introduced by the panel in *Argentina – Financial Services* pertains to measures taken 'for prudential reasons'. This criterion is further divided by the panel into two separate analyses for the purposes of judicial review. First, it shall be determined whether the rationale behind Members' regulatory measures are prudential 'reasons', in the sense that the measures act to prevent a risk, injury or danger that does not necessarily have to be imminent'.[166] Second, it shall be illustrated, based on the word 'for' in paragraph 2(a), whether there is a 'rational relationship of cause and effect between the measure and the prudential reason'.[167] The rational link between the regulatory measure and the prudential reason lies with the 'adequacy' of the first, through its design, to attain the desired outcome.[168] Assuming that a rational relationship exists, the third requirement of the PCO is that the measure in question shall 'not be used as a means of avoiding the Member's commitments or obligations under the Agreement'.[169]

The WTO case law drew distinctions between the terms 'measures for prudential measures' and 'prudential measures' and did not consider them synonyms for the purposes of interpreting the PCO:

> The Panel is not convinced [...] that the two concepts – 'measures for prudential reasons' and 'prudential measures' – signify the same thing or have the same effects. Firstly, we note that the prudential exception does not speak of 'prudential measures' but of 'measures for prudential reasons'. We therefore consider that it is the reason which must be 'prudential' and not the measure per se. The meaning of the two expressions cannot be the same and, in our opinion, this is an important aspect to be borne in mind when interpreting this provision. In other words, the GATS does not seek to identify measures that could be characterized as specifically prudential, such as those usually cited in the context of the standards defined by the Basel Committee on Banking Supervision.[1073] Nor does paragraph 2(a) of the Annex on Financial Services refer to any international norm to be used as a guide when deciding on the nature of a measure in the light of the Agreement. Rather, instead of exempting a specific type of measures from the obligations and commitments under the GATS, the exception makes it possible to exempt or exonerate any measure affecting the supply of financial services that has been taken 'for prudential reasons'.[170]
>
> [1073] See the 'Core principles for effective banking supervision', established by the Basel Committee on Banking Supervision, in particular Principles 14 to 29 relating to 'prudential regulations and requirements' (September 2012 version).

Importantly, as mentioned above, the panel in *Argentina – Financial Services* concluded, in a finding not reviewed by the Appellate Body, that a measure is adopted 'for' prudential reasons when there is a 'rational relationship of

[166] Panel Report, *Argentina – Financial Services*, para 7.879; *cf* paras 7.904, 7.937, and 7.946.
[167] ibid, para 7.889.
[168] ibid, para 7.891.
[169] ibid, para 7.945.
[170] Panel Report, *Argentina – Financial Services*, para 7.861.

cause and effect' between the measure in question and the prudential reason provided:

> Hence, it seems to us that the use of the word 'for' in the phrase 'measures for prudential reasons' denotes a rational relationship of cause and effect between the measure and the prudential reason. Thus, the Member taking the measure in question must demonstrate that in its design, structure or architecture there is a rational relationship of cause and effect between the measure it seeks to justify under paragraph 2(a) and the prudential reason provided. A central aspect of this rational relationship of cause and effect is the adequacy of the measure to the prudential reason, that is, whether the measure, through its design, structure and architecture, contributes to achieving the desired effect. Whether a measure has been taken 'for prudential reasons', that is, whether there is a rational relationship of cause and effect between the measure and the reason, can only be determined on a case-by-case basis, taking account of the particular characteristics of each situation and each dispute.[171]

Furthermore, the PCO offers Members' regulators extended room for manoeuvre. In principle, measures that seek to protect the safety and soundness of financial systems fall within its purview. However, as demonstrated by recent WTO case law, certain checks and balances exist for the PCO (eg they must be adopted for prudential reasons and they shall not be used as a means of circumventing other GATS obligations and/or commitments). These filters scrutinise the measures at issue. The 'rational relationship of the cause and effect' requirement, conceptualised by the panel, limits to a substantial degree the wide scope of the prudential exception. At the same time, the PCO scope is still wider than the exceptions of GATS, Article XIV, which presupposes necessity. Thus, regulators, while crafting their prudential rules, should take into consideration that their financial regimes should not circumvent trade disciplines and should be fit for the purpose they aspire to achieve.

As an alternative to this mainstream interpretation of the PCO that understands it as a GATS exception-type provision, Cantore offers an alternative interpretation of the PCO where 'measures adopted in pursuance of prudential objectives are not covered by the discipline of the GATS, even if the Member has listed specific commitments and the new regulations may have a detrimental impact on them'.[172] This approach is put forward on the basis of: (i) the absence of a *chapeau* in the text of the PCO – which is an essential element in all the GATT and GATS exception provisions; (ii) the inclusion of a non-exhaustive list of prudential objectives – in sharp contrast to the fixed and exhaustive list of policies embedded in exception provisions; and (iii) the negotiating history of the PCO.[173]

[171] ibid, para 7.891.
[172] Cantore (n 69) 187.
[173] ibid 168–224.

All in all, while the scope of the PCO is quite broad, financial regulators still need to be mindful of the GATS when crafting their domestic legal frameworks to ensure that they satisfy the abovementioned criteria. This of course applies to domestic regulations in connection with financial market infrastructure services (such as trading and clearing derivative products). Moreover, the fact that the prudential exception has been invoked only once in the WTO dispute settlement system might imply that WTO Members may prefer to respect each other's ability to define which set of rules may be 'prudential'.[174] Such an approach appears to be consonant with the wide leeway exercised by financial regulators in addressing financial instability – by taking action which even overrides their own rulebooks specifically designed for times of financial turbulence.[175] In addition, the fact that private parties (which may have been negatively impacted by financial regulations adopted by other governments) cannot bring claims to dispute settlement in the WTO might explain the limited adjudication on the subject.[176] In the next chapter, we will investigate in a concrete case study the extent to which measures affecting the international supply of clearing services may be covered by the scope of the PCO.

F. Subsidies Discipline under the GATS

Subsidies granted by WTO Members have traditionally been assessed under the Agreement on Subsidies and Countervailing Measures Agreement (SCM Agreement).[177] In short, the SCM Agreement provides for rules which prohibit certain types of subsidies (ie prohibited subsidies)[178] and sets up a mechanism

[174] Key (n 33) 25.

[175] By way of example, the regulatory frameworks designed in response to the global financial crisis of 2008 were not used as intended by either the US or Switzerland in the recent bank failures of the Silicon Valley Bank and Credit Suisse, respectively, in March 2023. For a thoughtful take, see M Sandbu, 'Policymakers Are Bungling Their Response to Failing Banks' (*Financial Times*, 23 March 2023) www.ft.com/content/33c0d6aa-f6ac-4f2d-929f-09ba4f8f4cf1 accessed 25 July 2023.

[176] In accordance with the WTO acquis only governments may bring claims to settlement at the WTO. However, it should be noted that there are procedures for private parties to petition their governments to have recourse to the WTO dispute settlement mechanism to challenge the legality of third-country measures with the WTO agreements (in the case of the EU, see Regulation (EU) 2015/1843 of the European Parliament and of the Council of 6 October 2015 laying down Union procedures in the field of the common commercial policy in order to ensure the exercise of the Union's rights under international trade rules, in particular those established under the auspices of the World Trade Organization (the Trade Barrier Regulation)). Beyond the existing framework, scholars have argued in favour of private parties' gaining 'direct access' to the WTO dispute settlement system. See, for example, GT Schleyer, 'Power to the People: Allowing Private Parties to Raise Claims before the WTO Dispute Resolution System' (1996) 65 *Fordham Law Review* 2275; PC Mavroidis and WJ Davey, 'Is the WTO Dispute Settlement Mechanism Responsive to the Needs of the Traders? Would a System of Direct Action by Private Parties Yield Better Results?' (1998) 32(2) *Journal of World Trade* 147.

[177] WTO (n 1) 231.

[178] SCM Agreement, Art 3. Prohibited subsidies are the following: (i) export subsidies; and (ii) local content subsidies.

to deal with other types of subsidies that result in negative effects to the interest of WTO Members (ie actionable subsidies).[179] However, these provisions only apply to subsidies in the area of goods as the SCM Agreement is included in Annex 1A to the Marrakesh Agreement Establishing the WTO.

With respect to the definition of subsidies set out in Article 1 of the SCM Agreement, the Panel in *US – Large Civil Aircraft* referred to Articles XV and XIII:2[180] of the GATS. Specifically, the Panel held that transactions properly characterised as purchases of services are excluded from the scope of Article 1 of the SCM Agreement, which expressly refers to purchases of goods but omits any reference to purchases of services. During its analysis, the Panel noted that

> [w]hile the SCM Agreement was being negotiated, parallel negotiations on trade in services were also taking place. Article XIII:2 and XV of the GATS reflect the fact that the negotiators of the GATS were unable to reach agreement on disciplines regarding governmental purchases of services, or on disciplines governing the provision of subsidies to service suppliers.[181]

The Panel in the same dispute concluded that when the omission of 'purchases' of 'services' from the text of Article 1 of the SCM Agreement is read against this historical background, it offers further confirmation that the drafters of that provision could not have removed the express reference to 'purchases' of 'services' from Article 1 of the SCM Agreement on the understanding that the reference was superfluous.[182] In light of the above, it is clear that when it comes to WTO Members' subsidies flowing to suppliers of services it is the GATS that is applicable framework (and not the SCM Agreement).

In respect of subsidies granted in services sectors, there is no specific agreement. The GATS puts forward only a provision which requires WTO Members to launch negotiations for developing the 'the necessary multilateral disciplines' to prevent potential distortive effects resulting from subsidies. Regrettably, trade negotiations have not yielded any outcome until now.[183] In particular, Article XV of the GATS sets out:

> 1. Members recognize that, in certain circumstances, *subsidies may have distortive effects on trade in services*. Members shall enter into negotiations with a view to developing the necessary multilateral disciplines to avoid such trade-distortive effects.[7] The negotiations shall also address the appropriateness of countervailing procedures. Such negotiations shall recognize the role of subsidies in relation to the development programmes of developing countries and take into

[179] SCM Agreement, Art 5.

[180] GATS, Art XIII:2, entitled 'Government Procurement', mandates that '[t]here shall be multilateral negotiations on government procurement in services under this Agreement within two years from the date of entry into force of the WTO Agreement'.

[181] Panel Report, *US – Large Civil Aircraft (2nd Complaint)*, para 7.968.

[182] ibid, para 7.969.

[183] See, for example, Adlung (n 104); P Poretti, 'Waiting for Godot: Subsidy Disciplines in Services Trade' in M Panizzon et al (eds), *GATS and the Regulation of International Trade in Services* (Cambridge, Cambridge University Press, 2008).

account the needs of Members, particularly developing country Members, for flexibility in this area. For the purpose of such negotiations, *Members shall exchange information concerning all subsidies related to trade in services that they provide to their domestic service suppliers.*

2. Any Member which considers that it is adversely affected by a subsidy of another Member may *request consultations* with that Member on such matters. Such requests shall be accorded sympathetic consideration. (emphasis added)

[7] A future work programme shall determine how, and in what time-frame, negotiations on such multilateral disciplines will be conducted.

GATS, Article XV(2) indicates that in cases where a WTO Member considers that its interests are adversely affected by the subsidy granted by another Member in the services sector, it may request consultation with that Member. While the GATS stipulates that such requests should be given 'sympathetic consideration', there is a legal vacuum with regard to the outcome of such consultations and there is no clarity as to what WTO Members should do when consultations do not yield any solutions.

However, it should be noted that the GATS might not be entirely irrelevant in connection with WTO Members' subsidisation of services sectors in light of specific commitments undertaken by WTO Members in their schedules with respect to national treatment and the MFN principle. As confirmed by the WTO Secretariat,

> Article XVII applies to subsidies in the same way that it applies to all other measures. Article XV (Subsidies) merely obliges Members to 'enter into negotiations with a view to developing the necessary multilateral disciplines' to counter the distortive effects caused by subsidies and does not contain a definition of subsidy. Therefore, any subsidy which is a discriminatory measure within the meaning of Article XVII would have to be either scheduled as a limitation on national treatment or brought into conformity with that Article. Subsidies are also not excluded from the scope of Article II (MFN).[184]

At the same time, it should be noted that there is no obligation in the GATS which requires a WTO Member to adopt measures outside their jurisdiction. Following this, the national treatment under Article XVII does not require WTO Members to extend such treatment to services or service suppliers located in the territory of another WTO Member.[185] As a result, undertaken commitments under Article XVII in relation to the granting of a subsidy do not require WTO Members to provide such a subsidy to the service supplier located in the territory of another Member.

[184] See WTO, Guidelines for the Scheduling of Specific Commitments under the General Agreement on Trade in Services (GATS), Adopted by the Council for Trade in Services on 23 March 2001, S/L/92, 28 March 2001, para 16.

[185] ibid, para 15. The Appellate Body in *US – Gambling* noted that the Guidelines can be used as 'supplementary means of interpretation' (within the meaning of Art 2 of the Vienna Convention on the Law of Treaties) of the provisions in the GATS. See Appellate Body Report, *US – Gambling*, para 195.

Following this, if in theory a WTO Member which in its GATS Schedule of Specific Commitments extends full national treatment for mode 3 (ie commercial presence) without limitations in connection with 'Settlement & clearing for financial assets, including securities, derivative products, and other negotiable instruments' decides to provide subsidies to domestic central securities depositaries (CSDs) to assist them in boosting their efficiency (eg by increasing the pool of assets they service or by optimising their underlying technology to avoid settlement fails) but extends LFT to *like* foreign CSDs having commercial presence in its jurisdiction by not extending subsidies to them, there might be sufficient grounds to claim a possible violation of GATS, Article XVII. Of course, for such infringement to be established likeness of the CSDs and LFT would have to be established and the subsidy measure must affect the terms of competition in the territory of the WTO Member adopting the measures. It should be also noted that an assessment of this sort would need to factor in any financial stability considerations at play and evaluate the measure's consistency with the PCO discussed above.

In practice, such an issue of a derogation from a WTO Member's national treatment commitment enshrined in its GATS Schedule concerning subsidies has not been the subject matter of any dispute before a WTO Panel or the Appellate Body so far. Thus, the possibility of WTO law capturing subsidies granted from other WTO Members in services sectors where a national treatment binding commitment is not complied with remains a theoretical possibility for now since it has not been put to the dispute settlement test to see the extent to which the WTO judiciary would endorse or reject such an interpretation of the GATS rules. In the author's view, the GATS national treatment provision applies in its own right to subsidies which are discriminatory in accordance with Article XVII so long as they vitiate a WTO Member's undertaken commitment. This reading is further corroborated by the fact that, in contrast to the corresponding provision in the General Agreement on Tariffs and Trade (GATT),[186] which expressly excludes subsidies from the national treatment obligation,[187] the GATS has not incorporated such exclusion. Thus, WTO Members' subsidies are in principle subject to the national treatment provision housed in the GATS. Moreover, in the absence of a developed legal framework on subsidies in the area of services under WTO rules, it is all the more important to ensure that subsidisation would be at the very least be covered by other GATS provisions (such as national treatment) where the requisite legal standard is met.

From a trade angle, it is worth noting that subsidies to financial services suppliers may have an effect on competition in the financial services industry, both in domestic markets and internationally – specifically, in cases where there

[186] GATT, Art III. See WTO (n 1) 423.

[187] GATT, Art III(8)(b) stipulates that the National Treatment obligation in Art III 'shall not prevent the payment of subsidies exclusively to domestic producers [...]'.

are significant opportunities for international arbitrage.[188] Such considerations have prompted the European Commission to issue guidance on the design and implementation of state aid in favour of banks to ensure that emergency measures for financial stability ensure a 'level playing field' between banks located in different EU Member States as well as between banks which receive public support and those which do not.[189] Additionally, the EU recently enacted the Foreign Subsidies Regulation (FSR),[190] according to which the EU will have the power to impose redressive measures to financial contributions granted by foreign governments to undertakings (including, financial institutions) operating in the EU which have distortive effects in the EU internal market. The FSR's conformity with WTO rules has not been undisputed.[191]

All in all, while it is evident that the current WTO rules seem to provide limited legal restraints to WTO Members' subsidisation in services sectors (including subsidies flowing to financial infrastructure operators),[192] it cannot be excluded that in future policymakers might spearhead discussions to prevent government support from creating international distortions of competition and ensure a level playing field without putting into jeopardy measures that genuinely seek to protect the stability and integrity of the financial system.

IV. CONCLUSION

This chapter has fleshed out in concrete terms how the liberalisation of financial market infrastructure services takes place under the applicable WTO legal framework. Moreover, it has shed light on the GATS rules specific to governing

[188] In the context of the global financial crisis of 2008, the Financial Stability Board noted that '[Crisis-related] measures have distortionary effects on the allocation of capital across borders as well as within them .... The impact of the measures on cross-border flows depends on a range of characteristics such as the willingness and ability of agents to arbitrage between countries.' See Financial Stability Board, 'Improving Financial Regulation – Report of the Financial Stability Board to G20 Leaders' (2009).

[189] See 'Communication from the Commission on the Application, from 1 August 2013, of State Aid Rules to Support Measures in Favour of Banks in the Context of the Financial Crisis ('Banking Communication'), OJ C 216, 30 July 2013'; 'Communication from the Commission – The Recapitalisation of Financial Institutions in the Current Financial Crisis: Limitation of Aid to the Minimum Necessary and Safeguards against Undue Distortions of Competition, OJ C 10, 15 January 2009'; 'Communication from the Commission on the Treatment of Impaired Assets in the Community Banking Sector, OJ C 72, 26 March 2009'; 'Communication from the Commission on the Return to Viability and the Assessment of Restructuring Measures in the Financial Sector in the Current Crisis under the State Aid Rules, OJ C 195/9, 19 August 2009'.

[190] Regulation (EU) 2022/2560 of the European Parliament and of the Council of 14 December 2022 on foreign subsidies distorting the internal market [2022] OJ L 330/1.

[191] See, for example, V Crochet and M Gustafsson, 'Lawful Remedy or Illegal Response? Resolving the Issue of Foreign Subsidization under WTO Law' (2021) 20 *World Trade Review* 343.

[192] This approach has been confirmed in connection with banking services in the context of the 2008 global financial crisis. See De Meester, 'The Global Financial Crisis and Government Support for Banks: What Role for the GATS?' (n 108).

trade in financial services and has identified the prospects and limitations in their design. While the existing rulebook has since its entry into force contributed to the global integration of financial infrastructure services, there is certainly room for further liberalisation in the future that could be triggered by subsequent rounds of financial services negotiations of the GATS. By way of example, the development of international minimum regulatory standards as well as the adoption of codes of good practices to ensure the integrity of financial systems by WTO Members could further contribute to driving forward the process of international liberalisation of financial services.

The following chapter picks a robust case study to assess how a WTO Member's rulebook concerning the cross-border supply of financial infrastructure services is consistent with WTO law. Specifically, Chapter 3 investigates to what extent the EU regime for 'third-country' central counterparties is in conformity with the GATS principles discussed above. The forthcoming analysis sheds light on the pertinent questions WTO Members' legislatures, financial regulators, trade negotiators and WTO lawyers face at the stages of designing, negotiating, implementing, and enforcing regulatory frameworks impacting international trade in financial infrastructure services. In addition, it underscores potential barriers to trade in the regulatory framework under scrutiny and identifies concrete ways to overcome them while ensuring that the integrity and stability of the financial system is not jeopardised.

3

Testing the Consistency of the EU Third-Country Equivalence Regime for Clearinghouses with the GATS

I. INTRODUCTION

As discussed above, in the aftermath of the 2008 global financial crisis, the EU regulators introduced the mechanism of 'third-country equivalence' for non-European financial institutions to access the EU internal market. This chapter evaluates the GATS-consistency of the current European rules on third-country clearinghouses.[1] Through this exercise, this study sheds light on the tension between financial regulation, on the one hand, and WTO law, on the other, exploring how these two different disciplines can be reconciled. Building on the international economic law principles of non-discrimination and transparency, the analysis reveals that the European financial rulebook could negatively impact the access of smaller countries to the EU internal market. The European financial rules are selected as a case study due to the EU's prominent role as an international standard setter[2] as well as its importance as a major financial services market. The EU financial regulation in question is assessed under the GATS, Article VI (domestic regulation), Article II (most favoured nation), Article VII (recognition), and the Annex on Financial Services prudential carve-out (PCO).

The findings of this case study indicate that the vast flexibility that trade law has delegated to national regulators possibly has adverse effects on the liberalisation of financial services. The chapter concludes that if WTO Members do not derogate from their GATS obligations and commitments, the stability of the

[1] This chapter draws from an earlier study of the author in which he assessed for the first time the conformity of the applicable EU framework on 'third-country' CCPs in 2020. See GA Papaconstantinou, 'The GATS and Financial Regulation: Time to Clear-House?' (2020) 19 *World Trade Review* 379. This chapter offers an updated version of this work, reflecting the latest applicable set of rules in connection with non-EU central counterparties.

[2] For an account of how the EU influences rules globally, see A Bradford, *The Brussels Effect: How the European Union Rules the World* (Oxford, Oxford University Press, 2020); A Bradford, 'The Brussels Effect' (2012) 107 *Northwestern University Law Review* 1.

financial system would not be jeopardised, while the prospect of international integration would be increased.

The remainder of this chapter explores the interface between international economic integration of financial services and domestic regulation.[3] Financial services are traded internationally but regulated on the national level. The tension between trade integration and national sovereignty is especially hard to reconcile in the area of financial services. This comes as a result of the multiple aims financial regulation seeks to achieve: alleviate information asymmetries, market failures, and negative externalities.[4] A thin line exists between protectionist measures, which seek to stave off foreign competition, for instance, and measures that serve legitimate objectives.[5] Defining the extent to which international trade law affects domestic financial regulation and, subsequently, challenging financial regulatory measures, is a delicate exercise. This chapter aims to highlight the benefits of striking a balance between the two disciplines – financial regulation and international trade law – and uses clearinghouses of OTC derivatives as a case study.

II. EU LEGAL FRAMEWORK AND FUNCTIONS OF CCPs

At the outset, the role of clearinghouses in the financial market infrastructure landscape is set out to pave the way for the forthcoming analysis of the conformity of the EU regulation at issue with WTO law. Clearinghouses, also known as central counterparties, are entities that mitigate systemic risk and increase

[3] For general literature on the interplay between financial regulation and international economic law, see K Alexander, 'Global Financial Standard Setting, the G10 Committees, and International Economic Law' (2008) 34 *Brooklyn Journal of International Law* 861; C Brummer, 'Why Soft Law Dominates International Finance – and Not Trade' (2010) 13 *Journal of International Economic Law* 623; C Brummer, 'How International Financial Law Works (and How It Doesn't)' (2010) 99 *Georgetown Law Journal* 257; T Cottier and M Krajewski, 'What Role for Non-Discrimination and Prudential Standards in International Financial Law?' (2010) 13 *Journal of International Economic Law* 817; R Bismuth, 'Financial Sector Regulation and Financial Services Liberalization at the Crossroads: The Relevance of International Financial Standards in WTO Law' (2010) 44 *Journal of World Trade* 489; P Delimatsis and P Sauvé, 'Financial Services Trade after the Crisis: Policy and Legal Conjectures' (2010) 13 *Journal of International Economic Law* 837; B De Meester, 'The Global Financial Crisis and Government Support for Banks: What Role for the GATS?' (2010) 13 *Journal of International Economic Law* 27; P Delimatsis and N Herger, *Financial Regulation at the Crossroads: Implications for Supervision, Institutional Design and Trade* (Alphen aan den Rijn, Kluwer Law International BV, 2011); P Delimatsis, 'Financial Innovation and Prudential Regulation: The New Basel III Rules' (2012) 46 *Journal of World Trade* 1309; P Delimatsis, 'Transparent Financial Innovation in a Post-Crisis Environment' (2013) 16 *Journal of International Economic Law* 159.

[4] The objectives and mechanics of financial regulation are well developed in DT Llewellyn, *The Economic Rationale for Financial Regulation*, vol 21 (London, Financial Services Authority, 1999). See also C Goodhart et al, *Financial Regulation: Why, How and Where Now?*, 1st edn (Abingdon, Routledge, 1998); M Brunnermeier et al, *The Fundamental Principles of Financial Regulation*, vol 11 (Geneva, ICMB, 2009).

[5] See, inter alia, AO Sykes, 'Regulatory Protectionism and the Law of International Trade' (1999) 66 *The University of Chicago Law Review* 15; RE Baldwin et al, *Regulatory Protectionism, Devel-*

financial stability by inserting themselves between the parties to derivative transactions. Clearinghouses are used for the back-office processing or 'plumbing' of securities, this taking place after a trade is agreed and before it is settled.[6] In particular, CCPs clearing shifts the allocation of performance risk that is endemic to derivatives trading. Traditionally, in OTC derivative transactions, the original counterparties bear the risk of potential failure of each other to perform on their obligations for the contract's duration. Unlike such bilateral trades, when contracts are cleared by CCPs the original counterparties' contracts with one another are replaced with a pair of contracts with a CCP. The CCP acts as the buyer to every seller and as the seller to every buyer. If a buyer or seller cannot fulfil its obligations and/or becomes bust, the central counterparty is vested with the responsibility to pay all that is owed to the non-defaulting party. Clearinghouses have at their disposal a number of financial resources, including collateral pledged by those who clear via CCPs and financial commitments made by its members and owners, all of which are prescribed in regulatory frameworks in support of financial stability.

For decades clearinghouses have been widely used for options and futures traded in exchanges (or other trading venues). However, the regulatory measures that were crafted in the aftermath of the 2008 financial crisis, such as the Dodd-Frank Act in the US and the European Market Infrastructure Regulation (EMIR)[7] in the EU, significantly increase the volume of cleared transactions and require that the majority of OTC transactions be cleared. This regulatory change represents a game-changer in the functioning of financial market infrastructure.[8] Importantly, the CCPs' primary tasks are: (i) confronting counterparty credit risk;[9] (ii) reducing systemic risk;[10] and (iii) developing loss-sharing structures.[11]

Those tasks are briefly discussed in turn: clearinghouses address beyond any doubt counterparty credit risk as they interpose themselves between contractual

oping Nations, and a Two-Tier World Trade System [with Comments and Discussion] (Brookings Institution Press, 2000); F Erixon and R Sally, 'Trade, Globalisation and Emerging Protectionism since the Crisis' (2010) No 02/2010 ECIPE Working Paper.

[6] For scholarship on the role of CCPs in the aftermath of the crisis, see, for instance, C Monnet, 'Let's Make It Clear: How Central Counterparties Save(d) the Day' (2010) Q1 *Business Review, Federal Reserve Bank of Philadelphia* 1; A Rehlon and D Nixon, 'Central Counterparties: What Are They, Why Do They Matter, and How Does the Bank Supervise Them?' (2013) Q2 *Bank of England Quarterly Bulletin*; F Wendt, 'Central Counterparties: Addressing Their Too Important to Fail Nature' [2015] IMF Working Paper No 2015/021.

[7] Regulation (EU) No 648/2012 of the European Parliament and of the Council of 4 July 2012 on OTC derivatives, central counterparties, and trade repositories [2012] OJ L201/1 (EMIR).

[8] See C Pirrong, 'The Economics of Central Clearing: Theory and Practice' (2011) 1 ISDA Discusson Papers Series 5–6.

[9] Counterparty credit risk or simply counterparty risk refers to the risk of a party's default or insolvency in a derivative contract before final settlement.

[10] See FB Chang, 'The Systemic Risk Paradox: Banks and Clearninghouses under Regulation' (2014) 14 *Columbia Business Law Review* 747.

[11] See Pirrong (n 8) 6–11, 30–34.

counterparties and assume their responsibilities in case one of the two cannot fulfil their part of the deal – similar to an insurance company. Further, as to the loss-sharing features that the regulation of CCPs puts forward, a number of measures, such as member contributions to the default fund, are introduced for the members of clearinghouses in order to create a mechanism that would be capable of withstanding potential failures of entities without generating spillover effects to other market actors (and members) and endangering the efficacy of the CCP.[12] Finally, as to the issue of CCPs counteracting systemic risk, academic literature has sufficiently investigated whether clearinghouses are apt to succeed in carrying out this task. Importantly, CCPs contribute to the stability of financial systems with their functions but their potential failure could negatively impact on the integrity of financial systems. That is why financial regulators have recently devised rules in order to set the framework for the recovery and resolution of clearinghouses, which would tackle the risks that the distress of a clearinghouse itself might pose to financial stability.[13]

Following the G20 mandate to increase transparency and reduce risks in OTC derivative markets,[14] clearinghouses have emerged at the centre of policymakers' post-crisis reform agendas. With respect to the relevant context that marked the advent of clearinghouses' regulatory overhaul, in order to beef up the international financial regulatory system G20 undertook to improve the functioning of OTC derivatives markets:

> All standardized OTC derivative contracts should be traded on exchanges or electronic trading platforms, where appropriate, and cleared through central counterparties by end-2012 at the latest. OTC derivative contracts should be reported to trade repositories. Non-centrally cleared contracts should be subject to higher capital requirements. We ask the FSB and its relevant members to assess regularly implementation and whether it is sufficient to improve transparency in the derivatives markets, mitigate systemic risk, and protect against market abuse.[15]

[12] Central counterparties would still have 'skin in the game' to avoid situations of moral hazard in default waterfall situations.

[13] See, for example, Regulation (EU) No 2021/23 of the European Parliament and of the Council of 16 December 2020 on a framework for the recovery and resolution of central counterparties and amending Regulations (EU) No 1095/2010, (EU) No 648/2012, (EU) No 600/2014, (EU) No 806/2014 and (EU) 2015/2365 and Directives 2002/47/EC, 2004/25/EC, 2007/36/EC, 2014/59/EU and (EU) 2017/1132 [2021] OJ L22/1. This regulation aims to ensure that both CCPs and national authorities in the EU are appropriately equipped to act decisively if a crisis scenario were to occur. Moreover, it seeks to maintain the critical functions of CCPs while preserving financial stability and protecting taxpayers. As it is a common place in global finance, international soft bodies put forward the first guidance in respect of the recovery and resolution of CCPs. See, for example, Committee on Payments and Market Infrastructures and Board of the International Organization of Securities Commissions, 'Recovery of Financial Market Infrastructures' (Bank for International Settlements, October 2014) www.bis.org/cpmi/publ/d162.pdf accessed 25 July 2023.

[14] G20, 'G20 Leaders Statement: The Pittsburgh Summit' (G20 Information Centre, 24 September 2009) para 13 www.g20.utoronto.ca/2009/2009communique0925.html accessed 25 July 2023.

[15] ibid.

Central counterparties have been placed in the epicentre of this pledge as they are expected to harness international OTC derivative markets valued at US$ 618 trillion in the second half of 2022.[16] This is why clearinghouses have been called 'super systemically important'[17] institutions, with their role being seen as pivotal in the post-crisis financial architecture.[18]

Explaining the role of clearinghouses in global financial networks involves the consideration of international standard-setting bodies and their regulatory proposals,[19] market structure analyses for different financial products, major financial centres' legal regimes (like EU and US),[20] the operation of market participants, and WTO law among others. This chapter's contribution investigates the European clearinghouse regulation in connection with non-EU CCPs from an international economic law perspective. In addition, it touches on the surrounding issues but only to the extent that they serve its analytical framework.

The EMIR raises issues on how international integration in the field of clearing derivatives is to be achieved and we use it as a case study to test the conformity of its prudential rules with WTO law. One may wonder to what degree European financial regulation and its application encroach on the opportunities of 'third-country' clearinghouses which aim to provide their services in the European market. Additionally, the rationale behind financial regulation and international trade law often differs significantly despite the fact that they regulate the same activities. Clarifying their relationship is one of this chapter's goals.

Notably, the examination of clearinghouses is crucial due to: (i) their importance to the post-crisis reform of financial markets; (ii) the failure of existing literature to assess their role in international economic law; and (iii) the

[16] Bank for International Settlements, 'OTC Derivatives Outstanding' (Bank for International Settlements, 17 May 2023) www.bis.org/statistics/derstats.htm accessed 25 July 2023.

[17] This term was used by Benöit Coeuré (ECB) at the Federal Reserve Bank of Chicago Symposium on Central Clearing (10 April 2015).

[18] J Rennison and P Stafford, 'Reforming the Derivatives Market: An Explainer' (Financial Times, 22 September 2016) www.ft.com/content/6b5e97e0-7029-11e6-9ac1-1055824ca907 accessed 25 July 2023.

[19] International standards for the regulation of CCPs exist but fall short of generating uniformity among national regimes and facilitating international trade flows. The recognition of third countries' regimes is key to attaining market access to foreign jurisdictions. Nonetheless, these standards put forward good-governance principles for financial market infrastructure regulations. See Committee and Settlement Systems and Technical Committee of International Organization of Securities Commissions, 'Principles for Financial Market Infrastructures' (Bank for International Settlements, April 2012) www.bis.org/cpmi/publ/d101a.pdf accessed 25 July 2023. See JA Marchetti, 'Technical Standard-Setting in the Financial Sector' in P Delimatsis (ed), *The Law, Economics and Politics of International Standardisation* (Cambridge, Cambridge University Press, 2015).

[20] The regime of 'substituted-compliance' in the US is similar to the EU one: see Dodd-Frank Wall Street Reform and Consumer Protection Act of 2010, Pub L No 111-203, Title VII (codified in sections of 7 USC and 15 USC). For an analysis of the EU and US recognition regimes of equivalence and substituted compliance, see Y Yadav, 'The Problematic Case of Clearinghouses in Complex Markets' (2012) 101 *Georgetown Law Journal* 387; Y Yadav and D Turing, 'The Extraterritorial Regulation of Clearinghouses' (2016) 2 *Journal of Financial Regulation* 21.

transnational nature of clearing OTC derivatives. In practical terms, when an international clearinghouse enters a derivatives transaction with market participants from other jurisdictions, they will engage multiple sets of rules that will likely include the WTO's rules for trade in financial services. Trade in financial services constitutes a significant part of international trade (particularly for the EU and the US) and the WTO offers its own legal system that places national legislations under scrutiny, provided commitments have been assumed.

As discussed in detail above, international integration in financial services is facilitated by the GATS.[21] The research question we address in this chapter is how may international trade law scrutinise the European rules on clearinghouses. On a broader level, we question the degree to which trade has the potential means to further financial services liberalisation. Investigating this subject matter is of relevance to anyone interested in how international economic law (the GATS) and financial regulation (exemplified by the European financial rulebook) relate to each other. The analysis suggests that the two disciplines are in conflict and explores whether a closer relation that furthers the interests of both is feasible. The writer answers in the affirmative, so long as WTO Members re-evaluate their approach to trade norms.

The structure of this chapter continues as follows: Section III examines the European regulatory framework for 'third-country' clearinghouses to set the scene. Next, Section IV ventures into testing the GATS consistency of the European regime to evaluate the tension between the two disciplines. To that end, the analysis builds on the principles of non-discrimination and transparency in the light of domestic regulation (GATS, Article VI), MFN (GATS, Article II), recognition (GATS, Article VII), and the PCO (Annex on Financial Services, paragraph 2(a)). Examining the European regulation's conformity with the relevant GATS provisions is essential to establish how financial policy objectives can be reconciled with trade disciplines and, subsequently, contribute to international economic integration. Finally, Section V offers preliminary conclusions.

III. THE EUROPEAN REGIME FOR THIRD-COUNTRY CLEARINGHOUSES

In response to the G20 agreement, the European Commission drafted a proposal for regulating CCPs since they have turned into 'systemic market infrastructure' in the financial system.[22] Subsequently, EMIR came into play in 2012. EMIR was

[21] GATS, Annex 1B to the Agreement Establishing the WTO. See WTO, *The Legal Texts: The Results of the Uruguay Round of Multilateral Trade Negotiations* (Cambridge, Cambridge University Press, 2000) 357.

[22] See European Commission, 'Press Release, Capital Markets: Agreement on More Robust Supervision of Central Counterparties' (European Commission, 13 March 2019) europa.eu/rapid/press-release_IP-19-1657_en.htm accessed 25 July 2023.

amended by the EMIR 2.2,[23] which was published in the Official Journal of the EU on 12 December 2019, entered into force on 1 January 2020 and is the framework under review in this chapter. EMIR is currently again under revision.[24] Some of the newly proposed features, such as the changes concerning third-country CCPs, present interesting angles for the scope of this book. However, since the rules on third-country clearinghouses have not yet been amended, the analysis of this chapter focuses on the WTO law consistency of the existing applicable rules.

The EMIR's provisions connected to international trade in clearing derivatives are examined to set the scene for the subsequent WTO law analysis, specifically, the rules associated with a clearinghouse established outside the EU providing its service to European market participants. Not surprisingly, the European regulation and EU executive agencies exercise thorough checks and balances for assessing the eligibility of clearinghouses from third countries. This is conducted through the EU rules on equivalence. As OTC derivatives markets rely heavily on the functioning of clearinghouses, it is sensible for financial authorities to evaluate whether foreign CCPs comply with their own prudential rules. Due to the transnational nature of derivatives markets, different regulatory frameworks can generate disruptions in international trade-flows by increasing transaction costs and undermining the efficient allocation of funds.[25]

Clearinghouses from non-European countries can only provide clearing services to clearing members and trading venues set up in the EU after they have been recognised by the European Securities and Markets Authority (ESMA).[26]

[23] Regulation (EU) 2019/2099 of the European Parliament and of the Council of 23 October 2019 amending Regulation (EU) No 648/2012 as regards the procedures and authorities involved for the authorisation of CCPs and requirements for the recognition of third-country CCPs [2019] OJ L322/1.

[24] The European Commission in December 2022 put forward a proposal to amend EMIR (the so-called EMIR 3 package). According to the Commission, some of these measures seek to improve the competitiveness of EU-based clearinghouses and of EU clearing activities while reducing the reliance of EU financial institutions on third-country CCPs. Additionally, EMIR III would aim to introduce amendments in connection with clearing thresholds and mitigate some of the issues arising from energy markets – specifically the difficulties in meeting counterparties' margin obligations. For more details, see Proposal for a Regulation of the European Parliament and of the Council amending Regulations (EU) No 648/2012, (EU) No 575/2013 and (EU) 2017/1131 as regards measures to mitigate excessive exposures to third-country central counterparties and improve the efficiency of Union clearing markets, 7 December 2022, COM(2022) 697 final.

[25] For a primer on the interests at stake regarding potential disruptions by regulatory clearing rules after Brexit, see P Stafford, 'US Derivatives Regulator Warns EU over Clearing Plans' (Financial Times, 12 September 2017) www.ft.com/content/fc95e500-0172-3b00-8404-6319ebc52c69 accessed 25 July 2023.

[26] ESMA is an independent EU authority that contributes to safeguarding the stability of the EU's financial system and seeks to enhance the protection of investors and to foster stable and orderly financial markets. ESMA was established by Regulation (EU) No 1095/2010 of the European Parliament and of the Council of 24 November 2010 establishing a European Supervisory Authority (European Securities and Markets Authority), amending Decision No 716/2009/EC and repealing Commission Decision 2009/77/EC [2010] OJ L331/84. For literature on ESMA, see N Moloney, 'I. Reform or Revolution? The Financial Crisis, EU Financial Markets Law, and the European

According to the applicable rules, as part of the recognition process, ESMA is also required to categorise each third-country central-counterparty as Tier 1 or Tier 2, depending on the level of risks they pose to the financial stability of the EU or one or more of its Member States.[27] Tier 1 are the third-country CCPs which qualify as non-systemically important and that are recognised based on appropriate deference to their home state regulatory authorities.[28] Conversely, Tier 2 are the third-country clearinghouses which qualify as systemically important and are required to meet the relevant EMIR conditions in connection with capital requirements (EMIR, Article 16) as well as requirements for CCPs (EMIR, Title IV) and interoperability arrangements (EMIR, Title V) either directly or through 'comparable compliance'.[29] By this tiering, the review of EMIR (EMIR 2.2) sought to establish a progressive and risk-driven approach to the recognition of non-EU clearinghouses. Moreover, ESMA's recognition arrangements must be reviewed when third-country CCPs aim to increase or limit the range of their activities and services in the EU and in any event at least every five years. Importantly, ESMA's recognition hinges on the European Commission adopting an equivalence decision for third-countries' legal, supervisory and

Securities and Markets Authority' (2011) 60 *International & Comparative Law Quarterly* 521; P Schammo, 'The European Securities and Markets Authority: Lifting the Veil on the Allocation of Powers' (2011) 48 *Common Market Law Review* 1879; N Moloney, 'The European Securities and Markets Authority and Institutional Design for the EU Financial Market – a Tale of Two Competences: Part (1) Rule-Making' (2011) 12 *European Business Organization Law Review* 41; N Moloney, 'The European Securities and Markets Authority and Institutional Design for the EU Financial Market – a Tale of Two Competences: Part (2) Rules in Action' (2011) 12 *European Business Organization Law Review* 177.

[27] For more details on the background that gave rise to this categorisation, see Commission Staff Working Document, 'Impact Assessment Accompanying the Proposal for a Regulation of the European Parliament and of the Council Amending Regulation (EU) No 1095/2010 Establishing a European Supervisory Authority (European Securities and Markets Authority)' COM (2017) 331 final.

[28] ESMA is in charge of monitoring Tier 1 third-country CCPs on the basis of the risks attached to their EU activities by setting up a detailed information-gathering process directly by the third-country clearinghouses and through the revised Memoranda of Understanding concluded between ESMA and third-country authorities.

[29] Notably, ESMA is responsible for supervising systemically important third-country CCPs' operations and their ongoing compliance with the relevant EMIR conditions as well as carrying out a comprehensive review of key decisions, such as the extension of services or important amendments to risk models. ESMA's supervision of the Tier 2 non-EU clearinghouses is realised through regular and ad hoc reviews focusing on the potential risks associated with their connection to the EU financial system and the risks that could pose to the financial system of the EU or one of its Member States. For more details on the tiering criteria, see Commission Delegated Regulation (EU) 2020/1303 of 14 July 2020 supplementing Regulation (EU) No 648/2012 of the European Parliament and of the Council with regard to the criteria that ESMA should take into account to determine whether a central counterparty established in a third-country is systemically important or likely to become systemically important for the financial stability of the Union or of one or more of its Member States [2020] OJ L305/7. For further details on how 'comparable compliance' under Art 25a of EMIR works, see Commission Delegated Regulation (EU) 2020/1304 of 14 July 2020 supplementing Regulation (EU) No 648/2012 of the European Parliament and of the Council with regard to the minimum elements to be assessed by ESMA when assessing third-country CCPs' requests for comparable compliance and the modalities and conditions of that assessment [2020] OJ L305/13.

enforcement regimes with respect to CCPs, and ESMA striking cooperation agreements or Memoranda of Understanding with the relevant authorities to buttress supervisory cooperation and information exchange.

Specifically, pursuant to EMIR, for a CCP established in a third country to provide clearing services to clearing members or trading venues set up in the EU, a recognition decision is required.[30] ESMA may recognise a non-EU CCP where the following criteria are met:

(a) that the CCP shall be authorised in its home country, and 'is subject to effective supervision and enforcement ensuring full compliance with the prudential requirements applicable in that third country';[31]
(b) that the European Commission adopts its equivalence decision;[32]
(c) that the anti-money laundering and financing of terrorism laws in the third country are equivalent to the ones of the EU;[33]
(d) that the regulatory authority of the third country has concluded cooperation arrangements with ESMA;[34] and

[30] EMIR, Art 25(1).

[31] EMIR, Art 25(2)(b).

[32] EMIR, Art 25(2)(a). Additionally, the actual wording is of significance, see EMIR, Art 25(6): 'The Commission may adopt an implementing act under Article 5 of Regulation (EU) No 182/2011, determining that: (a) the legal and supervisory arrangements of a third country ensure that CCPs authorised in that third country comply on an ongoing basis with legally binding requirements which are equivalent to the requirements laid down in Title IV of this Regulation; (b) those CCPs are subject to effective supervision and enforcement in that third country on an ongoing basis; (c) the legal framework of that third country provides for an effective equivalent system for the recognition of CCPs authorised under third-country legal regimes.' It is deduced from that provision that the Commission's assessment of third-countries' regulatory frameworks is threefold.

[33] EMIR, Art 25(2)(d).

[34] EMIR, Art 25(2)(c). Pursuant to EMIR, Art 25(7), ESMA shall establish effective cooperation arrangements with the relevant competent authorities of third countries whose legal and supervisory frameworks have been recognised as equivalent to EMIR. Such cooperation arrangement must include the mechanism for the exchange of information between the relevant regulatory authorities, the mechanism for prompt notification of ESMA by third-country competent authorities in certain cases of relevance (eg a third-country CCP operating in breach of its authorisation conditions) and the procedures necessary for the effective monitoring of regulatory and supervisory developments in a third country, among others. ESMA and third-country securities regulatory authorities conclude Memoranda of Understanding (MoU) that establish cooperation arrangements between the signatory authorities regarding clearinghouses that are established outside the EU and have applied for recognition under EMIR. Those MoU are established under EMIR, which provides for cooperation arrangements to be established between ESMA and third-country authorities whose legal and supervisory frameworks for CCPs have been deemed equivalent to EMIR by the European Commission. The rationale behind the conclusion of MoU is to ensure compliance with EMIR, and to provide ESMA with adequate flexibility to assess the ongoing compliance by the underlying CCPs with the recognition criteria housed in EMIR. For an example of a cooperation arrangement, see European Securities and Markets Authority, 'Memorandum of Understanding between European Securities and Markets Authority and Monetary Authority of Singapore Related to Central Counterparties Established in Singapore' (ESMA, 10 February 2022) www.esma.europa.eu/sites/default/files/library/mou_esma_mas_sg_ccps.pdf accessed 25 July 2023. For ESMA's guidelines on cooperation arrangements and information exchange between competent authorities and between competent authorities and ESMA, see European Securities and Markets Authority, 'Guidelines on Cooperation Arrangements and Information Exchange' (ESMA, 27 March 2014) www.esma.europa.eu/sites/

(e) the third-country CCP has not been determined as systemically important or likely to become systemically important; thus, a Tier 1 third-country clearinghouse.[35]

The abovementioned criteria are limited for Tier 1 (non-systemically important) third-country clearinghouses. With respect to Tier 2 (systemically important) non-EU CCPs, an additional set of rules is applicable based on the EU's risk-driven approach. Specifically, ESMA must, after carrying out its own assessment and consulting with central banks, pronounce on whether a third-country CCP is systemically important; ESMA's assessment may take into consideration, for instance: the nature, size and complexity of the CCP's business in the EU and outside the EU to the degree its operations may have a systemic impact on the EU or on one of its Member States; the effect that the default of or a disruption to the CCP would have on financial stability of the EU; as well as the CCP's business relationships and profile (such as its clearing membership structure and clients set up in the EU).[36] Where ESMA determines a CCP to be Tier 2, it must only recognise that CCP if, on top of the conditions discussed in the previous paragraph, it complies with additional requirements concerning, for example, capital requirements and interoperability arrangements.[37] If those conditions are not met, ESMA may recommend that the Commission adopts a decision confirming that that CCP should not be recognised to offer certain clearing services or activities.[38]

In terms of procedure, the European Commission requests that ESMA provides technical advice with regard to third-country jurisdictions of major derivatives markets and clearinghouses that have applied for recognition. ESMA's assessments represent a factual comparison of the third-country provisions with the ones of the EU. They also provide advice to the Commission with respect to the possible effects of regulatory discrepancies and what should be incorporated in the Commission decisions. Equivalence determinations may be unilateral acts, but at the same time they are endorsed within a scheme of collaboration between the EU and third-countries. Notably, it should be underlined that there is no specific procedure under which third countries can apply to the European Commission for assessments of equivalence. Third countries, in principle, can express an interest in being assessed, which the Commission would duly consider without any further commitment.[39]

default/files/library/2015/11/2014-298_guidelines_on_cooperation_arrangements_and_information_exchange_0.pdf accessed 25 July 2023.

[35] EMIR, Art 25(2)(e).

[36] EMIR, Art 25(2a).

[37] EMIR, Art 25(2b).

[38] EMIR, Art 25(2c).

[39] No right is extended to third countries for receiving an equivalence assessment. See Commission Staff Working Document, 'EU Equivalence Decisions in Financial Services Policy: An Assessment' SWD (2017) 102 final 8, 21.

These standards ensure that recognised third-country clearinghouses do not disrupt the orderly functioning of European financial markets and do not earn a competitive advantage against European ones.[40] The rationale behind extending recognition to CCPs from foreign jurisdictions only if their regulatory frameworks are trustworthy and of similar standards to domestic regulations, is to avoid potential market failures in their own jurisdictions. During the EMIR legislative development, contentious discussions about the form of the equivalence regime took place in Brussels with WTO commitments supposedly being taken into consideration.[41] To date, 11 years after EMIR's introduction, 39 non-European clearinghouses from 21 third countries – established in Australia, Hong Kong, Japan, Singapore, South Africa, Canada, Mexico, New Zealand, Switzerland, South Korea, the US, the United Arab Emirates, Dubai, United Kingdom, Chile, Malaysia, Taiwan, Colombia, Israel, People's Republic of China and Brazil – have been recognised by ESMA.[42] Notably, and after some troublesome discussions, the US Dodd-Frank regime was deemed equivalent by the European Commission.[43] Following this, the Commission adopted additional equivalence decisions for US CCPs in 2021[44] and US exchanges in 2022.[45]

What does the number of recognised third-country regimes and clearinghouses tell us about the effectiveness of the EU equivalence regime? It implies that it is a fact-based detailed process that is very cumbersome as it lasts on average between two and four years.[46] Similarly, as the 'substituted compliance'

[40] See European Securities and Markets Authority, 'Draft Technical Standards for the Regulation on OTC Derivatives, CCPs and Trade Repositories' ESMA/2012/379 para 126.

[41] See L Quaglia, 'The Politics of "Third-country Equivalence" in Post-Crisis Financial Services Regulation in the European Union' (2015) 38 *West European Politics* 167.

[42] For the list of the 39 recognised clearinghouses, see European Securities and Markets Authority, 'List of Third-Country Central Counterparties Recognised to Offer Services and Activities in the Union' (ESMA, 30 April 2023) www.esma.europa.eu/sites/default/files/library/third-country_ccps_recognised_under_emir.pdf accessed 25 July 2023.

[43] For the Commission press release, see European Commission, 'Press Release, European Commission Adopts Equivalence Decision for CCPs in USA' (European Commission, 15 March 2016) europa.eu/rapid/press-release_IP-16-807_en.htm accessed 25 July 2023. For the Commission Implementing Decision, see Commission Implementing Decision (EU) 2016/377 of 15 March 2016 on the equivalence of the regulatory framework of the United States of America for central counterparties that are authorised and supervised by the Commodity Futures Trading Commission to the requirements of Regulation (EU) No 648/2012 of the European Parliament and of the Council [2016] OJ L70/32.

[44] European Commission, 'Press Release, Financial Services: Commission Adopts Equivalence Decision for US Central Counterparties' (European Commission, 27 January 2021) ec.europa.eu/commission/presscorner/detail/en/IP_21_205 accessed 25 July 2023.

[45] 'Press Release, European Commission Adopts Additional Equivalence Decisions for US Exchanges' (European Commission, 4 April 2022) ec.europa.eu/commission/presscorner/detail/en/ip_22_2263 accessed 25 July 2023.

[46] European Parliament, 'Briefing: Understanding Equivalence and the Single Passport in Financial Services: Third-Country Access to the Single Market' (European Parliament, February 2017) 3 www.europarl.europa.eu/RegData/etudes/BRIE/2017/599267/EPRS_BRI(2017)599267_EN.pdf accessed 1 June 2023.

regime in the US,[47] it implies that it is a rather long process that lasts a number of years. However, when it attains its *finalité*, it can provide clarity and legal certainty to the clearinghouses doing business with Europe. But what about the third countries whose regimes do not qualify as equivalent? Are their clearinghouses afforded the same opportunities to determine their equivalence and provide their services in the EU?

The forthcoming analysis filters the conformity of the European financial rules on third-country CCPs under the GATS. The EU regime permits clearing trade flows with certain jurisdictions outside Europe. Neither the European Commission nor ESMA have unlimited resources to engage in highly complex analyses of all third-countries' clearinghouse regulations. Accordingly, CCPs from 'third countries' that have not been deemed equivalent might find it more burdensome to offer their services in the European internal market.[48] For the sake of this argument, there are clearinghouses that have applied for recognition, while their domestic regime has not yet qualified as 'equivalent', and might need to wait for an undetermined number of years before they can provide their clearing services in Europe.[49]

These regulatory frameworks on OTC derivatives seem to produce a new type of asymmetric compliance that can generate disruptions in the international derivatives clearing business.[50] Equivalence regimes that safeguard clearinghouses conducting transnational business are on a level – high standard – playing field. This would imply that their costs are comparable. As such, clearinghouses from one or the other side would not need to incur inflated compliance costs in foreign jurisdictions or, conversely, reduced conditions of competition. Nevertheless, even as market certainty for cross-border OTC derivatives clearing is promoted, liquidity is injected and no market disruptions occur if a third-country CCP is recognised under EMIR. The opposite can be said when an 'equivalence' agreement is not struck. This is all the more relevant for the minor jurisdictions which do not have an equivalence deal with the EU. Next, we examine EMIR through the GATS 'looking glass' to evaluate the tension between financial regulation and international trade law.

[47] The comparability determinations by the Commodity Futures Trading Commission are even fewer than the 'equivalence' assessments. See Commodity Futures Trading Commission, 'Comparability Determinations for Substituted Compliance Purposes' (CFTC) www.cftc.gov/LawRegulation/DoddFrankAct/CDSCP/DoddFrankCDF5.html accessed 25 July 2023.

[48] As evidenced in the discussion on 'likeness' under Art II of the GATS, those clearinghouses would have to demonstrate that they are 'like suppliers'.

[49] CCPs from Argentina, Turkey, Russia and Thailand among others have applied for recognition. See ESMA's list for further details, European Securities and Markets Authority, 'List of Central Counterparties (CCPs) Established in Non-EEA Countries Which Have Applied for Recognition under Article 25 of Regulation (EU) No 648/2012 of the European Parliament and of the Council (EMIR)' (ESMA, 4 January 2021) www.esma.europa.eu/sites/default/files/library/list_of_applicants_tc-ccps.pdf accessed 25 July 2023.

[50] See J Philpott, 'Equivalence' – The Key to Global OTC Swap Reform, 11 October 2015, www.theotcspace.com/equivalence-the-key-to-global-otc-swap-reform/ accessed 25 July 2023.

The liberalisation of financial services in the multilateral trading system is affected through the GATS disciplines and WTO Members' commitments.[51] This contribution reveals the extent to which the GATS legal order challenges the European framework for conducting equivalence assessments of non-European clearinghouses. In that endeavour, I inquire whether clearinghouses from some third countries might find it more burdensome to access the European market than other non-European clearinghouses. The relevance of this exercise lies not only in examining the tension between financial regulation and WTO law, but also in finding a mutually beneficial space for third countries. The analysis builds on the concepts of non-discrimination and transparency, and the GATS relevant provisions are put in context. It should be mentioned that the limited jurisprudence on the GATS, alongside the vast flexibility that the Agreement offers for financial services, makes this exercise somewhat delicate.

Investigating how the European rules that affect international derivatives clearing may be scrutinised under this legal order contributes to understanding and challenging the balance between Members' regulatory autonomy and international economic integration norms. Furthermore, the EU is a full member of the WTO. The forthcoming analysis is limited to Tier 1 (non-systemically important) third-country CCPs, as they represent the vast majority of the non-EU clearinghouses recognised to offer their services in the European internal market (namely, 37 out of the 39 third-country CCPs recognised to offer services and activities in the Union are classified as Tier 1).[52] Additionally, the risk-driven approach put forward by the EU in connection with systemically important CCPs seems to be a textbook case covered under the GATS financial services PCO and thus of limited relevance for our assessment under the WTO framework.

IV. ASSESSING THE WTO LAW CONSISTENCY OF THE EU 'THIRD-COUNTRY' CCP REGIME

A. Analysis under the GATS Article VI on Domestic Regulation

As discussed above, domestic regulation is a GATS hybrid provision because certain of its elements are intimately linked to the Members' Schedules. GATS, Article VI introduces a mechanism that requires that Members' regulations to not be inequitable, excessively interventionist, or inhibit trade disproportionately

[51] Pursuant to GATS, Art XX:3, schedules are an integral part of the GATS.

[52] In particular, according to the European Securities and Markets Authority, 'List of Third-Country Central Counterparties Recognised to Offer Services and Activities in the Union' (n 42) out of the 39 recognised non-EU clearinghouses only LCH Limited and ICE Clear Europe Limited from the UK are classified as Tier 2.

to the desired outcomes.[53] Generally, liberalisation in services is confined by non-tariff barriers that take the form of regulations.[54] This is especially the case for financial services, which is one of the most heavily regulated industries. Nevertheless, the WTO Members' regulatory autonomy is prescribed in the fourth recital of the GATS,[55] and can serve as a valuable means of interpretation. It is assumed that governmental protectionism[56] can be entrenched in Members' regulations and subsequently can be deemed, on a case-by-case basis, unlawful under WTO law.

Article VI scrutinises how domestic regulations are designed, administered, and applied when specific commitments are undertaken. It stipulates legally binding provisions of a procedural nature,[57] a mandate to deploy a multilateral discipline for licensing requirements, and a substantive obligation of transitional nature. The application of Members' domestic regulatory measures shall reflect the principles embedded in the GATS, most importantly fairness, as an expression of non-discrimination, openness, in the form of transparency, and negotiated commitments.[58] The panel delineated the scope of Article VI in *US – Gambling*, and stated that WTO Members' regulatory sovereignty ceases when the GATS rights of other Members are infringed.[59] The analysis proceeds by testing the compatibility of the EMIR equivalence regime under Article VI:1 and VI:5.

i. EMIR's Equivalence Framework Evaluated under the GATS Article VI:1

Article VI:1 of the GATS reads as follows:

> In sectors where specific commitments are undertaken, each Member shall ensure that all measures of general application affecting trade in services are administered in a reasonable, objective and impartial manner.

[53] For the negotiations on domestic regulation, see P Delimatsis, 'Concluding the WTO Services Negotiations on Domestic Regulation – Hopes and Fears' (2010) 9 *World Trade Review* 643.

[54] For a categorisation of barriers to trade in services, see B Hoekman and CA Primo Braga, 'Protection and Trade in Services: A Survey' (1997) 8 *Open Economies Review* 285; RM Stern, 'Quantifying Barriers to Trade in Services' in *Development, Trade, and the WTO: A Handbook. Washington, DC: The World Bank* (Washington DC, World Bank Publications, 2002).

[55] The forth recital of the GATS Preamble reads as follows: 'Recognising the right of Members to regulate, and to introduce new regulations, on the supply of services within their territories in order to meet national policy objectives and, given asymmetries existing with respect to the degree of development of services regulations in different countries, the particular need of developing countries to exercise this right.'

[56] See J Bhagwati, 'The Pure Theory of International Trade: A Survey' (1964) 74 *The Economic Journal* 1.

[57] Panel Report, United States – Measures Affecting the Cross-Border Supply of Gambling and Betting Services (10 November 2004), WT/DS285/R (*US – Gambling*), para 6.432.

[58] See P Delimatsis, *International Trade in Services and Domestic Regulations: Necessity, Transparency, and Regulatory Diversity* (Oxford, Oxford University Press, 2007) 95.

[59] Panel Report, *US – Gambling*, para 6.316. The Appellate Body reaffirmed the panel's finding; Appellate Body Report, United States – Measures Affecting the Cross-Border Supply of Gambling and Betting Services (7 April 2005) WT/DS285/AB/R (*US – Gambling*), para 235.

When it comes to how the Commission conducts EMIR equivalence assessments of third-country clearinghouse regimes, it is underlined that WTO rules cover both how the measure is administered and the measure itself. The Commission's role is to examine the regulatory frameworks of third countries, using ESMA's technical advice, and to determine the regime's equivalence with EMIR. Importantly, it is a stepping stone in the recognition process and impacts greatly on the market access of third-country CCPs. Given that third countries are largely WTO Members, it is vital to evaluate the measure's GATS conformity for possible breaches.

At the outset, whether EMIR, Article 25 constitutes a measure of 'general application' in the context of Article VI:1 is examined. It is important to understand that the EMIR framework puts forward the rules that the European Commission follows while discharging its equivalence assessment tasks. Carrying out equivalence assessments qualifies as a measure of general application, first, because it affects an unidentified number of economic operators[60] – namely, all CCPs established in third countries on the one hand and all market participants within the EU receiving clearing services on the other. Second, a wide range of measures is included within Article 25 and the rules of conduct alongside the exercise of influence of certain authoritative bodies, such as the Commission, are scrutinised by this provision.[61] Consequently, the Commission's administrative conduct and decision-making function under the EMIR provision at issue can be characterised as of general application for the purposes of GATS, Article VI:1.

The application of the equivalence assessments by the European Commission can be challenged as biased against the regulatory frameworks of smaller countries that are not financial hubs because: (i) even if Members have CCP regulatory frameworks of similar quality, some Members have received equivalence decisions while others have not; and (ii) there are no guidelines or rules on the sequence in which the European Commission carries out its equivalence assessments. Overall, the Commission seems to favour CCPs from jurisdictions that have stronger 'regulatory leverage' because it is more sensible from an economic standpoint to acquire the clearing services from WTO Members with stronger financial institutions rather than the opposite. The WTO dispute settlement mechanism is at the disposal of smaller countries that can initiate consultations (and potentially litigation if an amicable solution is not reached). The argument that the European Commission's administration of equivalence assessments is discretionary is procedural in nature and the role of the

[60] Panel Report, United States – Restrictions on Imports of Cotton and Man-Made Fibre Underwear (8 November 1996), WT/DS24/R (*US – Underwear*), para 7.65.

[61] See Panel Report, European Communities and its Member States – Tariff Treatment of Certain Information Technology Products (16 August 2010), WT/DS375/R (*EC – IT Products*), paras 7.1026–7.1027.

Commission is examined to reveal whether the current state of affairs can be problematic from a WTO law perspective.

The Commission can be accused of not safeguarding the standards of due process for WTO Members. Notably, it has been characterised as inherently political.[62] This claim is substantiated by the fact that some financial rulebooks are selected to be assessed and are deemed equivalent by the European Commission, while the regulatory frameworks of other Members are not. As a result, some Members' clearinghouses cannot be recognised by ESMA to supply services to European financial institutions abroad in countries other than to those with equivalence decisions, issued by the Commission. What is political in this process is the sequencing of the equivalence assessments. In the absence of guidelines setting out the order to be followed for carrying out equivalence assessments, some Members are given priority to the detriment of others. For instance, the regimes of Singapore, Australia, Japan, and Hong Kong, countries that represent international financial centres, acquired their equivalence decisions by the European Commission in 2014. Conversely, Members such as Argentina, Turkey, and Thailand are still on the waiting list. To that end, the two specific procedural aspects – mentioned above – of the general mandate for the administration of equivalence assessments by the European Commission, enshrined in EMIR, need to be examined more closely.

The first paragraph of Article VI, similarly to Article X:3(a) of the GATT 1994,[63] stipulates the obligation of reasonable, objective, and impartial administration. This obligation hinges on Members' assumed commitments in service sectors and mirrors the GATS' asymmetric architecture. The asymmetric architecture of the GATS provides that, as it is a sovereign right of WTO Members to enter commitments, it is natural for specific services sectors that the level of liberalisation of national treatment and market access commitments would vary among WTO Members on the basis of their respective undertaken commitments.[64] Interestingly, Article VI:1 presupposes that Members, when

[62] In particular, J Hill, the former Commissioner for Financial Stability, Financial Services and Capital Markets Union, said: 'Competitive pressures and political reality influence how people think about the equivalence process': see European Parliament, 'Briefing: Understanding Equivalence and the Single Passport in Financial Services: Third-Country Access to the Single Market' (n 46), 3.

[63] Art X:3(a) of the GATT 1994 reads as follows: 'Each contracting party shall administer in a uniform, impartial and reasonable manner all its laws, regulations, decisions and rulings of the kind described in paragraph 1 of this Article ("of general application").' The line of reasoning developed by the WTO judiciary can prove a salient guide for understanding the mechanics of the GATS, Art VI:1. See P Delimatsis, 'Due Process and "Good" Regulation Embedded in the Gats – Disciplining Regulatory Behaviour in Services through Article vi of the Gats' (2007) 10 *Journal of International Economic Law* 13.

[64] For example, for 'clearing and settlement' services Country X might have entered market access and national treatment full commitment for modes of supply 1–3, which implies a high level of liberalisation, while Country Y might have undertaken no market access commitment for modes 1–3 and national treatment commitment for only mode 3, which would imply a significant lower level of liberalisation. Thus, the term asymmetric geometry/architecture of the GATS is used to express the leeway that WTO Members enjoy in entering their commitments for services sectors.

administering their domestic legal frameworks, will conform to certain minimum standards of due process,[65] which include the notions of fairness and equity.[66] This provision reinforces the norms of consistency and predictability[67] and promotes good regulation standards for Members. The scarcity of GATS case law on this provision makes its GATT counterpart a valuable guide to investigate the WTO adjudicatory bodies' stance.

Any measure that on the surface appears fair and just could come under the purview of this provision if it is de facto applied in an arbitrary, unreasonable, and biased fashion, as the Appellate Body noted in *US – Shrimp*.[68] This element of WTO judicial review is essential to avoid governmental circumvention based on the distinction between measures as applied/as such. Additionally, an infringement of the obligations mandated in Article VI:1 of the GATS can occur as the result of an omission in a case where an obligation to act in a specific manner is imposed.[69] Differential treatment over time and relating to other trade operators is disallowed as well.[70] The WTO jurisprudence reveals that the obligation laid down in Article VI:1 circumscribes the administration of such measures or how these measures are applied in practice,[71] and does not scrutinise their substantive elements.[72] The administration of measures should have a significant impact on the holistic application of a Member's regulation, and not only on the course of a particular case.[73]

EMIR has been in place since 2012. In that period, the European Commission has decided that 22 third-country CCP regimes are equivalent to the EU's.[74] Accordingly, only clearinghouses from these 22 jurisdictions can provide, once they are recognised by ESMA, their services to European markets. It should

[65] See Panel Report, European Communities – Selected Customs Matters (16 June 2006), WT/DS315/R (*EC – Selected Customs Matters*), para 7.134.

[66] G Feketekuty, 'Regulatory Reform and Trade Liberalization in Services' in P Sauvé and RM Stern (eds), *GATS 2000: New Directions in Services Trade Liberalization* (Washington DC, Brookings Institution Press, 2000) paras 7.127, 7.490.

[67] ibid paras 7.108, 7.431.

[68] Appellate Body Report, United States – Import Prohibition of Certain Shrimp and Shrimp Products (12 October 1998) WT/DS58/AB/R (*US – Shrimp*), para 160.

[69] Panel Report, Dominican Republic – Measures Affecting the Importation and Internal Sale of Cigarettes (26 November 2004), WT/DS302/R (*Dominican Republic – Import and Sale of Cigarettes*), para 7.379.

[70] Panel Report, *EC – Selected Customs Matters*, para 7.123.

[71] Appellate Body Report, European Communities – Regime for the Importation, Sale and Distribution of Bananas (9 September 1997) WT/DS27/AB/R (*EC – Bananas III*), para 200.

[72] Panel Report, *US – Gambling*, para 6.432; *cf* for the GATT perspective, Panel Report, Argentina – Measures Affecting the Export of Bovine Hides and the Import of Finished Leather (19 December 2000), WT/DS155/R (*Argentina – Hides and Leather*), paras 11.70–11.71; Appellate Body Report, *EC – Selected Customs Matters*, paras 200–201.

[73] See Panel Report, United States – Anti-Dumping Measures on Certain Hot-Rolled Steel Products from Japan (28 February 2001), WT/DS184/R (*US – Hot-Rolled Steel*), para 7.268.

[74] For the European Commission document listing the EMIR Equivalence decisions, see European Securities and Markets Authority, 'List of Third-Country Central Counterparties Recognised to Offer Services and Activities in the Union' (n 42).

be stressed that the way equivalence assessments are carried out takes time. However, less trade-restrictive alternatives that do not jeopardise stability might be available, and are discussed below. Moreover, due to financial integrity considerations and the intricacies of financial regulation, the process becomes additionally complex and cumbersome.[75] Nonetheless, the outcome limits the access of European market participants to third-country clearinghouses abroad from the abovementioned jurisdictions.

The way the Commission conducts its equivalence assessments raises questions of impartiality and objectivity. First, the European Commission seems to indulge in 'cherry-picking' of the jurisdictions that admittedly have bigger clearinghouses, such as the US, Hong Kong, Australia, and Singapore. This practice seems sensible from an economic perspective. Nevertheless, that is not the case from an international trade angle, provided that the GATS obligations and commitments are borne in mind. That is because the Commission's procedure for the assessment of equivalence appears to favour certain third countries at the expense of others, simply by not evaluating their regimes (and as a result not allowing their CCPs to offer their services to the EU market). More interestingly, although the central-clearing frameworks of South Africa, Indonesia, Russia and India are on the same regulatory implementation rating by the Financial Stability Board (FSB), only Russia has not acquired an equivalence decision by the European Commission.[76] Of course the European Commission is by no means obliged to make its decisions on the basis of the ratings published by the FSB. Yet such ratings might be a good guide for financial authorities to use in the order they carry out their equivalence evaluations in order to avoid criticism of due process by third countries. Nevertheless, an empirical study that exceeds the scope of this volume would be required to identify the patterns and consistently appraise the methodology the Commission uses to assess third-countries' financial rulebooks. Second, priority is given to the countries that have 'regulatory leverage', in the sense that countries with stronger financial centers are assumed to craft better regulations. Thus, it seems easier for Europe to proceed with the examination of their regimes.

[75] ESMA's technical advice documents are objective-based analyses which examine the non-European countries' regimes on a line-by-line basis, resulting in a thorough but cumbersome process; this can be verified by the fact that the Dodd-Frank framework got the green light from the Commission only in 2016. See, for example, the ESMA technical advice issued for the US, European Securities and Markets Authority, 'Final Report, Technical Advice on Third Country Regulatory Equivalence under EMIR – US' (ESMA, 1 September 2013) www.esma.europa.eu/sites/default/files/library/2015/11/2013-1157_technical_advice_on_third_country_regulatory_equivalence_under_emir_us.pdf accessed 25 July 2023.

[76] The FSB frequently conducts assessments of the regulatory frameworks of G20 countries on central-counterparties, trade reporting, market transparency, and exchange and electronic platform trading. For the latest report on central clearing and the regulatory implementation ratings, see Financial Stability Board, 'OTC Derivatives Market Reforms: Implementation Progress in 2022' (Financial Stability Board, 7 November 2022) www.fsb.org/wp-content/uploads/P071122.pdf accessed 25 July 2023.

Importantly, since there are no guidelines on what sequence the Commission should follow to examine foreign jurisdictions, another question of compatibility with Article VI:1 of the GATS emerges. The absence of guidelines or standards in how the Commission decides to initiate its equivalence assessments raises the question of whether the administration of EMIR, Article 25 is objective,[77] especially as CCPs from smaller Members apply, but are unable to supply their services to European financial institutions abroad due to the Commission's lack of an Implementing Act. Notably, irrespective of the CCPs' date of application for recognition at ESMA, there is no procedural rule that sets a condition to the Commission relating to the order of third-country equivalent assessments. Consequently, what might be in violation of GATS, Article VI:1 is that the Commission prioritises in its equivalence assessments some Members over others by its discretion to decide to evaluate some regimes, without providing the same opportunity to clearinghouses from other jurisdictions.

Arguably, the Commission and ESMA lack the unlimited resources to conduct simultaneously assessment of all WTO Members' financial rulebooks. Considering the complexities of such determinations and the number of third-country jurisdictions, this can be understandable. However, the Commission's discretionary behaviour in the administration of EMIR could be found to be in violation of the GATS, Article VI:1. To remedy the current state-of-play would require either: (a) provision to all Members of an equal opportunity to have their regulations evaluated for equivalence – something that is extremely difficult in practice; or (b) further harmonisation of regulatory standards among Members, or at least parts thereof, to permit trade flows.[78] On a normative note, it can be argued that to encourage trade in financial services without facing the transaction costs and market access barriers raised by regulations, such as the regimes of equivalence or substituted compliance, it is essential for the WTO to provide a venue for its Members to discuss – and if possible mitigate – their regulatory divergences.

[77] From GATT 1994 jurisprudence, the panel in *China – Raw Materials* noted that the lack of definition, guidelines, or standards in how the export quotas were allocated by local departments constituted non-uniform administration inconsistent with Art X:3(a). Panel Report, China – Measures Related to the Exportation of Various Raw Materials (5 July 2011), WT/DS394/R (*China – Raw Materials*), paras 7.751–7.752.

[78] The watering down of the excessive regulatory scrutiny in equivalence determinations and the focus solely on the regulatory provisions that matter can facilitate the international integration of clearing services. This approach is consonant with efficiency considerations of increasing liquidity and reducing transaction costs in the derivatives clearing business. The International Swaps and Derivatives Association (ISDA) put forward five principles according to which equivalence/substituted compliance frameworks should operate in order to avoid the current troublesome state-of-play: see ISDA, 'Whitepaper: Cross-Border Harmonization of Derivatives Regulatory Regimes: A Risk-Based Framework for Substituted Compliance via Cross-Border Principles' (ISDA, 2017).

ii. Assessing Transparency Elements under the EMIR Equivalence System Through the GATS Article VI:5

Transparency is one of the WTO fundamental disciplines that reflects the Members' openness towards their counterparts. It is also one of the general obligations applicable to trade in services. Transparency, as it is enshrined in GATS, Article III, relates to the Members' mandate to furnish predictability in the multilateral trading system.[79] *Lex specialis* resides in GATS, Article VI, paragraph 5(a)(i), which encounters the concept of transparency in the domain of qualification procedures, technical standards, and licensing requirements. GATS, Article VI:5 encompasses a substantive legal obligation of transitional character; this obligation is 'pending the entry into force of the disciplines developed in these sectors pursuant to paragraph 4', interestingly since 1995. This provision accommodates a minimum qualitative set of standards of market access, only for the legal orders of Members that have entered commitments.

Article VI:5 of the GATS reads:

(a) In sectors in which a Member has undertaken specific commitments, pending the entry into force of disciplines developed in these sectors pursuant to paragraph 4, the Member shall not apply licensing and qualification requirements and technical standards that nullify or impair such specific commitments in a manner which:

- i. does not comply with the criteria outlined in subparagraphs 4(a), (b) or (c); and
- ii. could not reasonably have been expected of that Member at the time the specific commitments in those sectors were made.

[79] Article III of the GATS, entitled 'Transparency' reads as follows:

1. Each Member shall publish promptly and, except in emergency situations, at the latest by the time of their entry into force, all relevant measures of general application which pertain to or affect the operation of this Agreement. International agreements pertaining to or affecting trade in services to which a Member is a signatory shall also be published.
2. Where publication as referred to in paragraph 1 is not practicable, such information shall be made otherwise publicly available.
3. Each Member shall promptly and at least annually inform the Council for Trade in Services of the introduction of any new, or any changes to existing, laws, regulations or administrative guidelines which significantly affect trade in services covered by its specific commitments under this Agreement.
4. Each Member shall respond promptly to all requests by any other Member for specific information on any of its measures of general application or international agreements within the meaning of paragraph 1. Each Member shall also establish one or more enquiry points to provide specific information to other Members, upon request, on all such matters as well as those subject to the notification requirement in paragraph 3. Such enquiry points shall be established within two years from the date of entry into force of the Agreement Establishing the WTO (referred to in this Agreement as the 'WTO Agreement'). Appropriate flexibility with respect to the time-limit within which such enquiry points are to be established may be agreed upon for individual developing country Members. Enquiry points need not be depositories of laws and regulations.
5. Any Member may notify to the Council for Trade in Services any measure, taken by any other Member, which it considers affects the operation of this Agreement.

(b) In determining whether a Member is in conformity with the obligation under paragraph 5(a), account shall be taken of international standards of relevant international organizations applied by that Member.

The criteria set by GATS, Article VI:5 are: (i) a Member has a commitment in a specific services sector; (ii) this Member imposes licensing, or qualification requirements, or technical standards in this sector; (iii) the application of the measures nullifies or impairs the specific commitments assumed; (iv) the nullification or impairment transpires in a way that is not consonant with the conditions of transparency, objectivity, and necessity stipulated in Article VI:4 (a)–(c);[80] and (v) such nullification or impairment could not have been reasonably anticipated by that Member when the specific commitment was undertaken.[81] Along these lines, the first two criteria are fulfilled because Europe has made commitments for clearing derivatives services for mode 2 pursuant to the Understanding and EMIR spells out the licensing requirements. EMIR's transparency considerations are drawn next to assess whether they could impair the EU's commitments. Surprisingly, Article VI:5, regardless of its pervasive nature, has never been interpreted by WTO adjudicatory bodies. The only time a panel had the opportunity to shed light on the provision, in *Mexico – Telecoms*, it neglected to do so for reasons of judicial economy.[82]

The EU, in its attempt to design a robust regulation for clearinghouses, has indulged in adopting measures that can be contested before WTO judiciary on the basis of transparency. WTO Members whose CCPs have not acquired a recognition and are unable to supply their services in Europe, could contend that EMIR lacks objective and transparent criteria with respect to its licensing requirements. This can be substantiated by the fact that the main criteria on which ESMA and the Commission base their assessments are not exactly clear. The third-country recognition procedure is driven by motives relating to the clearinghouse's jurisdictional 'creditworthiness'. The Implementing Acts[83] that the Commission adopts reinforce the regulatory framework's lack

[80] See GATS, Art VI:4. Article VI:5 has been defined as 'an effort to operationalize the objectives stated in VI:4, the most important of which was the necessity test', according to the WTO Secretariat, 'Report on the Meeting Held on 11 May 2001' S/WPDR/M/11, 7 June 2001, para 29.

[81] The GATS entered into force in 1995 and this category captures the measures in place before then.

[82] Panel Report, Mexico – Measures Affecting Telecommunications Services (2 April 2004), WT/DS204/R (*Mexico – Telecoms*), para 5.30.

[83] The Implementing Acts are based on Art 5 of Regulation No 182/2011 and are highly dependent upon the technical advice on third-country regimes that ESMA produces. The Commission Delegated Regulation (EU) No 153/2013 of 19 December 2012 supplementing EMIR with regard to regulatory technical standards on requirements for central counterparties, on the basis of Art 2 sets out particular conditions in respect of CCP's target member states, types of instruments cleared, its shareholders, margin and collateral, stress tests, compliance, record, outsourcing arrangements, segregation arrangements, membership criteria, and interoperability arrangements. Although numerous criteria are put forward, it is maintained that there is no transparency on the methodology by which these criteria are assessed by the EU institutions.

of transparency exactly because of the nature of their determinations regarding: (i) 'effective supervision and enforcement' that the CCPs are subject to in third countries; and (ii) third countries' 'legally binding requirements which are equivalent' to EMIR.

These criteria prescribed in EMIR are abstract. The missing determinant is the way they are assessed by the European executive agencies because the requirements themselves leave considerable room for discretion in the appraisal phase. At first glance, these criteria, as they are articulated in the text of the Regulation, seem quite transparent. However, when read in conjunction with ESMA's advice and the Commission's Acts, they generate further questions. The discrepancy among Members' financial regulatory frameworks requires further clarity with respect to how these legal aspects are assessed. The points on effective supervision and enforcement and legally binding requirements that are equivalent to EMIR are not clear because they are not benchmarks that third countries and their clearinghouses can rely on. Rather, they promulgate some criteria that the EU institutions can construe with a high margin of appreciation. Moreover, confusion can emerge from the discrepancies in the assessment of different jurisdictions.

EMIR's lack of transparency might be inconsistent with GATS, Article VI, paragraph 5(a)(i) provision because it can impair or nullify the commitments EU assumed for clearing financial instruments in accordance with the Understanding. In particular, by hindering third-countries from acquiring a clear view of the system in place for the implementation of equivalence assessments, the EU could impair its commitments for financial services. More broadly, for violation cases there is a rebuttable presumption of nullification or impairment.[84] However, the special nature of this provision links the concept of nullification or impairment to a substantive infringement of WTO rules, displaying the negotiators' reluctance in restricting their own regulatory autonomy.[85] The burden of proof of nullification/impairment rests with the Member seeking to demonstrate that the application of the equivalence assessment is in violation of Article VI:5. The application of EMIR rules can be characterised as trade restrictive in the sense that service suppliers from third countries suffer the loss of opportunity to transact with European market

[84] This presumption is housed in Art 3:8 of the Dispute Settlement Understanding (DSU) which reads 'In cases where there is an infringement of the obligations assumed under a covered agreement, the action is considered prima facie to constitute a case of nullification or impairment. This means that there is normally a presumption that a breach of the rules has an adverse impact on other Members parties to that covered agreement, and in such cases, it shall be up to the Member against whom the complaint has been brought to rebut the charge'. This has been confirmed by the WTO judiciary: Appellate Body Report, European Communities – Export Subsidies on Sugar (28 April 2005) WT/DS265/AB/R (*EC – Export Subsidies on Sugar*), para 300. The concept of nullification or impairment also accommodates non-violation complaints in services, GATS, Art XXIII:3.

[85] See WTO, Trade in Services, 'Decision on Domestic Regulation', S/L/70, 28 April 1999, para 23. For a discussion see Delimatsis, 'Due Process and "Good" Regulation Embedded in the Gats – Disciplining Regulatory Behaviour in Services through Article vi of the Gats' (n 63) 39–47.

participants abroad. The lack of transparency is evidenced in the absence of explicit guidelines that explain what third countries' effective supervision and enforcement might entail, and what would be the parameters for the equivalence assessment, given that financial regulations across the globe are inherently disparate. Conducting these analyses is not an easy task, due to the complexities of Members' financial rulebooks. Nevertheless, more transparent criteria should be put in place for the sake of predictability and in order to inform Members about the precise steps EU institutions take. Transparency is intended to furnish openness to services' trade, and the regulatory framework in question does not seem to facilitate multilateral trade in clearing derivatives.

B. Analysis under the GATS Article II on MFN Treatment for Non-European Clearinghouses

Non-discrimination constitutes the cornerstone of the multilateral trading system and MFN is the most representative GATS obligation. GATS, Article II can test the consistency of EMIR's equivalence regime and states that service providers of any Member shall not receive less favourable treatment than like services and service providers of any other Member.

To fall within the scope of MFN, two criteria must be satisfied, which are articulated for our discussion as: (i) that clearing services or clearinghouses from countries that have been deemed 'equivalent' by the EU are 'like' to CCPs from countries that have not; and (ii) if yes, that the application of the EMIR equivalence assessments extends LFT to clearinghouses with specific origin in comparison to other countries; if no, the question of LFT would not arise at all. The forthcoming analysis assesses how the GATS, Article II:1 conditions can filter EMIR, Article 25, in the light of the *Argentina – Financial Services*. This dispute elaborates on the tension between trade and regulation because differential treatment can be accorded to Members based on their regulatory frameworks.

i. 'Likeness' Assessment under the GATS Article II

As noted above, the determination of discriminatory behaviour in WTO law depends on the concept of likeness. Like service suppliers from different Members cannot be accorded differential treatment. However, if they are not considered like, they can be treated differently. Extensive WTO jurisprudence on likeness exists in trade of goods,[86] but our focus lies with services. The panel

[86] Appellate Body, European Communities – Measures Affecting Asbestos and Products Containing Asbestos (12 March 2001) WT/ DS135/AB/R (*EC – Asbestos*), para 102, refers to the requirements promulgated by the GATT working party report on Border Tax Adjustments. These criteria relate to: (i) the properties, nature, and quality of the products; (ii) the end-uses of the products;

in *Canada – Autos* held that 'to the extent that the service suppliers concerned supply the same services, they should be considered like'.[87] This statement is drafted broadly, and seems to disregard the complex nature of services and the role of regulation. Additionally, it could restrict the right of Members to regulate the supply of services on the basis of national policy preferences. The GATS likeness determination differentiates from the standards set out by WTO jurisprudence for goods. Allowances must be made for Members' regulatory framework divergences that can complicate the conditions of 'likeness'. Recently, WTO case law has broadened our understanding of how trade norms can filter WTO Members' prudential frameworks. It has also provided guidance on how 'likeness' can be established between service providers from different jurisdictions. The question I address here relates to whether non-European CCPs from Country X, which has been deemed to have an equivalent regime by the Commission, are 'like' clearinghouses from Country Y, which has not.

The Appellate Body *in Argentina – Financial Services* held in respect of 'likeness' of the GATS, Article II:1 that 'the determination of "likeness" of services and service suppliers must focus on the competitive relationship of the services and service suppliers at issue'.[88] Additionally, the Appellate Body noted:

> Thus, we consider that the concept of 'likeness' of services and service suppliers under Articles II:1 and XVII:1 of the GATS is concerned with the competitive relationship of services and service suppliers. This is consonant with the Appellate Body's understanding of 'likeness' in the ambit of trade in goods. In EC – Asbestos, the Appellate Body held that the word 'like' in Article III:4 of the GATT 1994 is to be interpreted as applying to products that are in a competitive relationship, and that therefore a determination of 'likeness' under Article III:4 is, fundamentally, a determination about the nature and extent of a competitive relationship between and among products. As the Appellate Body noted, '[i]f there is – or could be – no competitive relationship between products, a Member cannot intervene, through internal taxation or regulation, to protect domestic production.'
>
> Further, in the context of trade in goods, the Appellate Body noted that there is a spectrum of degrees of 'competitiveness' or 'substitutability' of products in the marketplace. The assessment of such a competitive relationship requires a market-based analysis. The Appellate Body also stated that not all products that are in some competitive relationship are 'like products', and that it is difficult, if not impossible,

(iii) consumers' tastes and habits or consumers' perceptions and behaviour in respect of the products; and (iv) the tariff classification of the products; *cf* Appellate Body Report, Argentina – Measures Relating to Trade in Goods and Services (14 April 2016), WT/DS453/AB/R (*Argentina – Financial Services*), para 6.30.

[87] Appellate Body Report, Canada – Certain Measures Affecting the Automotive Industry (31 May 2000) WT/DS139/AB/R (*Canada – Autos*), para 10.248; *cf* Panel Report, *EC – Bananas III*, para 7.322.

[88] Appellate Body Report, *Argentina – Financial Services*, para 6.24; *cf* Appellate Body Report, European Communities – Measures Prohibiting the Importation and Marketing of Seal Products (22 May 2014) WT/DS401/AB/R (*EC – Seals Products*), para 5.82, Appellate Body Report, *EC – Asbestos*, para 99.

> in the abstract, to indicate precisely where on this spectrum the word 'like' falls. In our view, the same is true with respect to 'like services and service suppliers', and, thus, the likeness of services and service suppliers can only be determined on a case-by-case basis, taking into account the specific circumstances of the particular case.[89]

Notably, the competition concept is adopted from the GATS, Article XVII, and can prove to be a useful guide in the process of assessing whether service suppliers are like. Although the *China – Electronic Payment Services* panel queries the determination of likeness for both services and service suppliers,[90] the Appellate Body understands these terms *in tandem*, and suggests they should not be examined in isolation.[91] Furthermore, the presumption approach refers to the case where the complainant can establish 'likeliness' by merely illustrating that the measure in question distinguishes between services and service suppliers based exclusively on origin. This 'presumption' has been accepted by numerous panels for trade in goods,[92] and recently adopted by the Appellate Body.[93] Nevertheless, the perimeter of the 'likeness' presumption is narrower for trade in services; this is due to inherent complexities of services sectors, distinctions between services and service suppliers, varying modes of supply,[94] and domestic regulations, which define the realm of operation of service suppliers alongside with consumers' preferences, that all need to be borne in mind.[95] Interestingly, in *Argentina – Financial Services* the panel concluded that 'it is not the origin per se which determines … but the regulatory framework inextricably linked to such origin'.[96] The Appellate Body reversed the panel's finding because its analysis erred in fulfilling the presumption of 'likeness' criteria.[97]

The Appellate Body in *Argentina – Financial Services* held that, with respect to the applicability of the presumption approach in the context of trade in services:

> While these complexities do not, as a matter of principle, render the presumption approach inapplicable in the context of trade in services, the scope of this presumption is more limited than in trade in goods. Whether and to what extent such complexities have an impact on the determination of whether a distinction is based exclusively on origin in a particular case will depend on the nature, configuration, and operation of the measure at issue and the particular claims raised.[98]

[89] Appellate Body Report, *Argentina – Financial Services*, paras 6.25–6.26.
[90] Panel Report, *China – Electronic Payment Services*, paras 7.698–7.709.
[91] Appellate Body Report, *Argentina – Financial Services*, para 6.29.
[92] Panel Report, Colombia – Indicative Prices and Restrictions on Ports of Entry (27 April 2009) WT/DS366/R (*Columbia – Ports of Entry*), paras 7.355–7.356; Panel Report, United States – Certain Measures Affecting Imports of Poultry from China (29 September 2010) WT/DS392/R (*US – Poultry (China)*), paras 7.424–7.432.
[93] Appellate Body Report, *Argentina – Financial Services*, paras 6.38, 6.52, 6.61.
[94] Panel Report, *China – Electronic Payment Services*, para 7.704.
[95] ibid paras 6.38–6.41.
[96] Panel Report, *Argentina – Financial Services*, para 7.166.
[97] Appellate Body Report, *Argentina – Financial Services*, para 6.61.
[98] Appellate Body Report, *Argentina – Financial Services*, para 6.40. See also para 6.52 of the Appellate Body Report.

Moreover, the Appellate Body stated that 'in keeping with the general rule that the burden of proof rests upon the party that asserts the affirmative of a particular claim, the complainant bears the burden of making a prima facie case that a measure draws a distinction between services and service suppliers based exclusively on origin'.[99] According to the Appellate Body:

> if a panel finds that the complainant has failed to make a prima facie case that a measure provides for differential treatment based exclusively on origin, then the panel must engage in an analysis of 'likeness' of services and service suppliers on the basis of the relevant criteria adapted to trade in services, as addressed above, before it may proceed to the analysis of less favourable treatment.[100]

These benchmarks for determining 'likeness' between service providers furnish clear filters for evaluating whether clearinghouses from third countries are like or not. However, case-by-case analysis is required to establish if the conditions are met. It should be mentioned that the burden of proof always lies with the party that asserts an affirmative claim.[101] The role of regulatory frameworks has been stressed by WTO judiciary in the determination of 'likeness' for services/service suppliers. Potential complainants who would challenge an EMIR equivalence mechanism should either illustrate that differential treatment is extended between the clearinghouses of Countries X and Y exclusively on the basis of origin to adhere to the condition of the presumption approach, or query whether the regulatory divergence between CCP regulation does not alter the conditions of competition in the traditional 'likeness' determination. If it does not and the regulatory frameworks of X and Y follow the same standards and implementation,[102] then their clearinghouses should be considered 'like'. In the case where there are fundamental discrepancies between the countries' clearing-derivatives regimes, then 'likeness' would be more challenging to prove.

ii. 'LFT' Assessment under the GATS Article II

LFT is embedded in both GATS, Articles II:1 and XVII and the WTO judiciary holds that both provisions employ the same standard.[103] The Appellate Body in *Argentina – Financial Services* offered its appraisal on the nature of 'treatment no less favourable' housed in those two articles of the GATS. As regards Article II:1 of the GATS, it noted:

> 6.105 Turning to Article II:1 of the GATS, we note that this provision does not further define the term 'treatment no less favourable'. Furthermore, we recall that

[99] Appellate Body Report, *Argentina – Financial Services*, para 6.42.

[100] ibid para 6.43.

[101] Appellate Body Report, United States – Measures Affecting Imports of Woven Wool Shirts and Blouses from India (25 April 1997) WT/DS33/AB/R (*US – Wool Shirts and Blouses*), paras 14, 335.

[102] See, for example, Financial Stability Board (n 76).

[103] Appellate Body Report, *Argentina – Financial Services*, paras 6.105, 6.106; *cf* Appellate Body Report, *EC – Bananas III*, para 233.

> Article XVII:1 contains a national treatment obligation, whereas Article II:1 contains a most-favoured-nation obligation. Nonetheless, the operative parts of these provisions are similarly worded, in that a Member is required to accord 'treatment no less favourable' to 'services and service suppliers of any other Member'. Both provisions serve the function of prohibiting discrimination against foreign services and service suppliers vis-à-vis like services and service suppliers. Although the immediate context of this term in Articles II:1 and XVII:1 is not expressed in identical words, and Article II does not contain the elaboration of the 'less favourable treatment' standard found in Articles XVII:2 and 3, the Appellate Body has found that both provisions share the essential nature of anti- discrimination provisions, and cover both de jure and de facto discrimination.[290] Thus, the elaboration on the meaning of the term 'treatment no less favourable' contained in Article XVII, and in particular in Article XVII:3, should also be pertinent context to the meaning of the same term in Article II:1.
>
> We note that, in EC – Bananas III, the Appellate Body upheld the panel's finding that the EC licensing procedures in that dispute conferred less favourable treatment under both Article II and Article XVII of the GATS. In so doing, the Appellate Body based its findings under both provisions on the same notion of 'less favourable treatment'. Specifically, the Appellate Body agreed with the panel that various aspects of the EC licensing procedures at issue created less favourable conditions of competition for service suppliers of the complainants' origin.[291] The Appellate Body's findings indicate that, on substance, the concept of 'treatment no less favourable' under both the most-favoured-nation and national treatment provisions of the GATS is focused on a measure's modification of the conditions of competition. This legal standard does not contemplate a separate and additional inquiry into the regulatory objective of, or the regulatory concerns underlying, the contested measure. Indeed, in prior disputes, the fact that a measure modified the conditions of competition to the detriment of services or service suppliers of any other Member was, in itself, sufficient for a finding of less favourable treatment under Articles II:1 and XVII of the GATS.[104]
>
> [290] Appellate Body Report, *EC – Bananas III*, para 233.
>
> [291] Appellate Body Report, *EC – Bananas III*, paras 240–248 [remainder of footnote not reproduced]

The Appellate Body in *Argentina – Financial Services* crystallised the notion of LFT. It underlined that both de jure and de facto discrimination are covered by the scope of Article II and it made clear that Article II is informed in determining the notion of 'less favourable treatment' by the more elaborate language included in Article XVII of the GATS. Most importantly, for both provisions the crucial element that qualifies whether certain measures extend LFT is based on the modification of the conditions of competition to the benefit of services or service suppliers of a Member in comparison to like services or service suppliers of another Member – as stipulated in Article XVII:3.[105]

[104] Appellate Body Report, *Argentina – Financial Services*, paras 6.105–6.106. See also Panel Report, *EU – Energy Package*, para 7.489.

[105] Art XVII reads: 'Formally identical or formally different treatment shall be considered to be less favourable if it modifies the conditions of competition in favour of services or service suppliers of the Member compared to the like services or services suppliers of any other Member.'

Jurisprudence developed for goods agreements does not always chime with the mechanics of the GATS due to their structural differences.[106] Nevertheless, the GATS legal requirement for establishing LFT has been recently delineated by the Appellate Body for trade in financial services, as noted. A measure fails to confer 'treatment no less favourable' if it modifies the conditions of competition to the detriment of services or service suppliers of any other Member in comparison to like services or service suppliers of, respectively, any other country or the Member imposing the contested measure.[107] Thus, the driving force of LFT is the relation between the measure in question and whether that measure alters the conditions of competition between like service suppliers.[108]

Regulatory frameworks admittedly affect trade in services. Indeed, it all depends on the standard of review for LFT to determine whether differential treatment is extended or not. Evaluating whether a measure leads to a modification of the conditions of competition at the expense of like service suppliers 'must begin with scrutiny of the measure, including consideration of the design, structure, and expected operation of the measure at issue'.[109] However, this type of regulatory assessment will not go beyond the content of the GATS, and change its internal balances. The panel in *Argentina – Financial Services* attempted an alternative to the text of the GATS treaty interpretation of the LFT, which resembles the approach devised by the Agreement on Technical Barriers to Trade (also known as the TBT Agreement). The panel's analysis went beyond just taking account of the regulatory aspects relating to services that may affect the conditions of competition, and attempted to justify LFT on 'certain regulatory distinctions'.[110] This stance disregards the broader GATS taxonomy, which favours Members pursuing their national policies and at the same time provides the prudential exception under which financial regulations can be justified.[111] Conversely, the TBT Agreement has this regulatory distinction in the determination of LFT, but does not furnish exceptions as the GATS does. Ultimately, the Appellate Body did not endorse the panel's interpretation.[112] It stated that to the degree that evidence pertaining to the regulatory aspects has a bearing on

[106] The LFT standard in the GATT is identical to the one in the GATS; see Appellate Body Report, *EC – Seals Products*, para 5.90. The TBT Agreement does not employ the same LFT legal standard because it requires an additional step that is not justifiable in the GATS geometry, namely the 'legitimate regulatory distinction': see Appellate Body Report, United States – Measures Affecting the Production and Sale of Clove Cigarettes (4 April 2012) WT/DS406/AB/R (*US – Clove Cigarettes*), para 182.

[107] Appellate Body Report, *Argentina – Financial Services*, para 6.151.

[108] See Appellate Body Report, *EC – Bananas III*, paras 244, 246; Panel Report, *China – Electronic Payment Services*, paras 7.712, 7.714.

[109] Appellate Body Report, Thailand – Customs and Fiscal Measures on Cigarettes from the Philippines (17 June 2011) WT/DS371/AB/R (*Thailand – Cigarettes (Philippines)*), para 134.

[110] Panel Report, *Argentina – Financial Services*, paras 7.212, 7.232.

[111] The GATS prudential exception is discussed below. See CM Cantore, *The Prudential Carve-out for Financial Services: Rationale and Practice in the GATS and Preferential Trade Agreements* (Cambridge, Cambridge University Press, 2018).

[112] Appellate Body Report, *Argentina – Financial Services*, paras 6.151–6.153.

the conditions of competition, it might be taken into consideration, subject to the specific characteristics of the case.[113]

The GATS, Article II:1 LFT status quo provides clarity as to how like service suppliers are to be treated. If national regulatory frameworks impact on the conditions of competition between like service suppliers, then differential treatment at odds with the MFN principle is extended. The 'less favourable treatment' test does not bear in mind the regulatory intent and/or objectives but rather gravitates around the real effects as the result of the modification of the conditions of competition for third country 'like' services or service suppliers. One may wonder to what degree the European clearinghouse regulation affects the opportunities of third-country CCPs planning to provide their services in the EU market. Applying the stated two-pronged test presupposes that the clearinghouses of Country X, which has been deemed to have an 'equivalent' regulatory framework by the Commission, are 'like' clearinghouses from Country Y, which has not. Then as soon as 'likeness' is established, LFT is extended by the EU because CCPs from Country X can supply their services to European financial institutions, while CCPs from Country Y cannot. To illustrate, we first assume that the central clearing regime of India, which has been deemed equivalent by the EU, and the regulatory framework of Argentina, which has not, are considered to provide similar standards. Accordingly, their clearinghouses would be deemed 'like' by the WTO judiciary. Then, establishing LFT would only rely on proving that the EU regulation changes the terms of competition between the CCPs of India and Argentina, by disallowing the latter from providing their services in Europe. The EMIR regime affects the conditions of competition because it favours clearinghouses from certain jurisdictions and forecloses the European market to others. Consequently, the EMIR regime might result in violation of the GATS, Article II. Nevertheless, the GATS provides regulatory flexibility and Article VII, along with the Annex on Financial Services, paragraph 3, furnishes a safe harbour from MFN, as long as their conditions are satisfied.

C. Analysis under GATS Article VII on Recognition Agreements for Financial Services

In response to the G20 accord,[114] regulators have devised their frameworks for clearinghouses. Subsequently, they carry out their own evaluations of

[113] ibid para 6.127.

[114] See G20 (n 13). The G20 explicitly committed to improving the OTC derivatives markets by the following mechanism, 'All standardized OTC derivative contracts should be traded on exchanges or electronic trading platforms, where appropriate, and cleared through central counterparties by end-2012 at the latest. OTC derivative contracts should be reported to trade repositories. Non-centrally cleared contracts should be subject to higher capital requirements. We ask the FSB and its relevant members to assess regularly implementation and whether it is sufficient to improve transparency in the derivatives markets, mitigate systemic risk, and protect against market abuse.'

third-country CCP rules to determine whether the regimes are equivalent to theirs. These assessments determine whether other Members' clearinghouses can furnish their services or not. In a similar vein, EMIR promulgates that the Commission publishes equivalence decisions of third-country CCP frameworks. Accordingly, some jurisdictions are deemed equivalent while others are not. The clearinghouses of Members that are extended recognition of their regimes find it less burdensome to offer their services in Europe than clearinghouses from Members that are not. However, the GATS states that 'a Member may recognise … requirements met, or licenses or certifications granted in a particular country'.[115] The rationale of Article VII lies in furthering trade integration through recognition, while disallowing discrimination.[116] In addition to Article VII and closer to our analysis, the Annex on Financial Services reads: 'A Member may recognise prudential measures of any other country in determining how the Member's measures relating to financial services shall be applied.'[117] These recognition provisions stipulate that agreements can be concluded either mutually or unilaterally, and spell out specific conditions that shall be respected.

First, transparency in the form of notifying recognition measures to the Council for Trade in Services is prescribed in the GATS.[118] This obligation can potentially increase the WTO Members' understanding of what are the driving forces of recognition agreements, and ultimately contribute to further

[115] GATS, Art VII:1. The entire GATS provision reads as follows: 'For the purposes of the fulfilment, in whole or in part, of its standards or criteria for the authorization, licensing or certification of services suppliers, and subject to the requirements of paragraph 3, a Member may recognize the education or experience obtained, requirements met, or licenses or certifications granted in a particular country. Such recognition, which may be achieved through harmonization or otherwise, may be based upon an agreement or arrangement with the country concerned or may be accorded autonomously.'

[116] See AB Zampetti, 'Mutual Access through Mutual Recognition: The Promise and Limits of GATS Article VII' in P Sauvé and RM Stern (eds), *GATS 2000: New Directions in Services Trade Liberalization* (Washington DC, Brookings Institution Press, 2000). See also K Nicolaïdis and J Trachtman, 'From Policed Regulation to Managed Recognition: Mapping the Boundary of GATS' in Sauvé and Stern (ibid) 315.

[117] GATS, Annex, para 3(a). The relevant provision mandates: 'A Member may recognize prudential measures of any other country in determining how the Member's measures relating to financial services shall be applied. Such recognition, which may be achieved through harmonization or otherwise, may be based upon an agreement or arrangement with the country concerned or may be accorded autonomously.'

[118] GATS, Art VII:4. The relevant paragraph reads as follows: 'Each Member shall:

(a) within 12 months from the date on which the WTO Agreement takes effect for it, inform the Council for Trade in Services of its existing recognition measures and state whether such measures are based on agreements or arrangements of the type referred to in paragraph 1;
(b) promptly inform the Council for Trade in Services as far in advance as possible of the opening of negotiations on an agreement or arrangement of the type referred to in paragraph 1 in order to provide adequate opportunity to any other Member to indicate their interest in participating in the negotiations before they enter a substantive phase;
(c) promptly inform the Council for Trade in Services when it adopts new recognition measures or significantly modifies existing ones and state whether the measures are based on an agreement or arrangement of the type referred to in paragraph 1.'

integration.[119] However, for trade in financial services, openness through transparency is not attained because Members do not notify the WTO of any of their recognition measures.[120] This does not imply that recognition in financial services sectors between Members is not accorded, but rather that the transparency obligation is not fulfilled. As a result, since the practice of states does not facilitate trade openness, it becomes more difficult to pursue recognition with WTO Members that are not 'like-minded' partners. Most importantly, this lack of transparency has implications for restricting future recognition agreements. The second obligation requires that a Member 'shall afford adequate opportunity for other interested Members to negotiate their accession to such an agreement or arrangement or to negotiate comparable ones with it'.[121] The Annex clarifies, in that regard, that equivalent regulation, supervision, and enforcement are of vital importance for financial services. It should be understood that in practice Members that lack the regulatory expertise and the supervisory and/or enforcement resources are not necessarily offered adequate opportunity to conclude recognition agreements due to the complexities involved in these processes, as discussed above. Third, recognition agreements shall not either be discriminatory or constitute a disguised trade restriction.[122]

[119] For an analysis that argues that like-minded countries tend to conclude mutual recognition agreements (MRAs), see JA Marchetti and PC Mavroidis, 'I Now Recognize You (and Only You) as Equal: An Anatomy of (Mutual) Recognition Agreements in the GATS' in I Lianos and O Odudu (eds), *Regulating Trade in Services in the EU and the WTO: Trust, Distrust and Economic Integration* (Cambridge, Cambridge University Press, 2012) 415.

[120] This position is premised on research conducted on the Notifications Database of the WTO. It is striking that only two recognition agreements on financial services have been notified to the Council, pursuant to GATS, Art VII:4, since the 2008 financial crisis; specifically: (i) on 12 January 2021, Switzerland and the UK notified an agreement on direct insurance other than life insurance (S/C/N/1039); (ii) on 16 June 2020, Australia notified its new regulatory framework for foreign financial services providers that wish to provide financial services to wholesale clients or professional investors in Australia.

[121] See GATS, Art VII:2, Annex on Financial Services para 3(b). These provisions read as follows: 'A Member that is a party to an agreement or arrangement of the type referred to in paragraph 1, whether existing or future, shall afford adequate opportunity for other interested Members to negotiate their accession to such an agreement or arrangement or to negotiate comparable ones with it. Where a Member accords recognition autonomously, it shall afford adequate opportunity for any other Member to demonstrate that education, experience, licenses, or certifications obtained or requirements met in that other Member's territory should be recognized'; and 'A Member that is a party to such an agreement or arrangement referred to in subparagraph (a), whether future or existing, shall afford adequate opportunity for other interested Members to negotiate their accession to such agreements or arrangements, or to negotiate comparable ones with it, under circumstances in which there would be equivalent regulation, oversight, implementation of such regulation, and, if appropriate, procedures concerning the sharing of information between the parties to the agreement or arrangement. Where a Member accords recognition autonomously, it shall afford adequate opportunity for any other Member to demonstrate that such circumstances exist', respectively.

[122] GATS, Art VII:3. This provision stipulates that 'A Member shall not accord recognition in a manner which would constitute a means of discrimination between countries in the application of its standards or criteria for the authorization, licensing or certification of services suppliers, or a disguised restriction on trade in services.'

At this stage, an interpretative comment on the relation between GATS, Article VII and the Annex, paragraph 3 is required to shed light on the applicable provisions for the recognition of prudential measures. First, the Annex provision on recognition is a *lex specialis* to the GATS, Article VII. However, we should underscore that the existence of paragraph 3 of the Annex by no means leads to the inapplicability of the broader GATS provision. This can be convincingly substantiated by an *a contrario* interpretation of paragraph 3(c) of the Annex, which explicitly stipulates that: 'Where a Member is contemplating according recognition to prudential measures of any other country, paragraph 4(b) of Article VII shall not apply'. Notably, the founding fathers consciously discarded only the applicability of paragraph 4(b) of Article VII for financial services sectors; namely, the Members' transparency obligation in relation to the notification of potential ongoing recognition procedures. As a result, the implication of this reading is that all the other GATS, Article VII provisions still apply for financial services with the particular specificities attached to paragraphs 3(a) and (b) of the Annex.

Given that most GATS, Article VII obligations remain applicable for financial services, it is worthwhile briefly discussing the role of Article VII:5 in this context.[123] This provision spells out a best-effort obligation for Members to negotiate common international standards and criteria for recognition in international fora. This provision is not excluded from the scope of financial services. In principle, Members, when appropriate, must adopt the standards put forward by international standard-setting organisations. Perhaps the key condition enclosed to this provision is 'in appropriate cases', because it leaves considerable room for manoeuvre to WTO Members. Especially, the intricacies associated with financial regulation and the stability considerations enshrined in the prudential carve-out might strip this provision of meaning for financial services recognition agreements. Arguably, it would be a long shot to claim that WTO Members have a hard obligation to adopt the standards promulgated by the BIS and the IOSCO for clearing services[124] based on this GATS article.

EMIR equivalence assessments should fall under the unilateral recognition category of Article VII. Nevertheless, the collaboration between regulatory agencies should not be underestimated, as cooperation arrangements between ESMA and third-country regulators are required. In the light of the GATS, Article VII obligations, clearinghouses from Argentina, for example, should, in

[123] GATS, Art VII:5. The provision reads as follows: 'Wherever appropriate, recognition should be based on multilaterally agreed criteria. In appropriate cases, Members shall work in cooperation with relevant intergovernmental and non-governmental organizations towards the establishment and adoption of common international standards and criteria for recognition and common international standards for the practice of relevant services trades and professions.'

[124] For the relevant standards, see Committee and Settlement Systems and Technical Committee of International Organization of Securities Commissions (n 19).

principle, be afforded equal opportunity to negotiate a recognition procedure as CCPs from India. However, problematic features regarding the process followed by the European Commission in the conclusion of equivalence decisions must be underscored. First, the transparency obligation to notify recognition agreements in accordance with Article VII:1 is not fulfilled. Second, the potential discretionary nature of the equivalence assessments' application in favour of Members with higher regulatory leverage and bigger clearinghouses seems to suggest that adequate opportunity to negotiate recognition agreements has not been evenly extended to Members. In the absence of formal criteria, the European Commission chooses on a discretionary basis the WTO Members with which it conducts equivalence assessments, irrespective of similar equivalent standards between third countries.[125] Nonetheless, it would be for WTO judiciary to decide whether EMIR's possible GATS inconsistencies could be justified under Article VII on a case-by-case basis.

D. Analysis under the GATS Prudential Carve-Out for Financial Services

The PCO appears to provide wide leeway to financial regulators.[126] The autonomy to legislate prudential rules for the sake of financial stability, among other objectives, is encouraged by the PCO, even if these rules do not conform with the GATS. However, despite the broad margin offered to regulators, the provision reads in the second sentence that prudential rules must not 'be used as a means of avoiding' trade disciplines.[127] This 'anti-circumvention' clause exists to delimit the range of regulatory space of Members in financial services. To date, our knowledge of what type of measures can be justified under the PCO is quite restricted as there is limited case law elaborating on the prudential exception. The prudential exception has been only interpreted once, in *Argentina – Financial Services*. In the light of this dispute's findings, we discuss the PCO legal standards while investigating whether EMIR's possible GATS inconsistencies can fall within its scope.

[125] See, for example, Financial Stability Board, 'OTC Derivatives Market Reforms: Implementation Progress in 2022' (Financial Stability Board, 7 November 2022) and discussion above.

[126] GATS, Annex para 2(a). The text of this provision stipulates that 'Notwithstanding any other provisions of the Agreement, a Member shall not be prevented from taking measures for prudential reasons, including for the protection of investors, depositors, policy holders or persons to whom a fiduciary duty is owed by a financial service supplier, or to ensure the integrity and stability of the financial system. Where such measures do not conform with the provisions of the Agreement, they shall not be used as a means of avoiding the Member's commitments or obligations under the Agreement.'

[127] The wording of the prudential exception is in juxtaposition to the chapeau of GATS, Art XIV which presupposes a necessity assessment of measures: see P Delimatsis and B Hoekman, 'National Tax Regulation, Voluntary International Standards, and the GATS: Argentina – Financial Services' (2018) 17 *World Trade Review* 265.

The panel dealing for the first time with the prudential exception developed an analysis that employs three requirements for measures to fall under its remit.[128] The scope of the PCO constitutes the first requirement. It was hotly debated between Panama and Argentina whether all types of 'measures affecting the supply of financial services',[129] or only 'domestic regulation', in the sense of the GATS, Article VI, fall within the purview of paragraph 2(a).[130] In response to it, the Appellate Body adopted the panel's interpretation and ruled that the PCO scope comprises all the measures that affect the supply of financial services.[131]

As regards the meaning of the word 'affecting', the panel in *Argentina – Financial Services* referred to the Appellate Body's interpretation, put forward in *EC – Bananas III*, and found:

> [I]n determining whether the measure 'affects' the supply of financial services within the meaning of paragraph 1(a) of the Annex on Financial Services, the Panel can be guided by this jurisprudence of the Appellate Body. This leads us to the view that the word 'affecting' in paragraph 1(a) of the Annex on Financial Services has a broader scope than such terms as 'regulating' or 'governing' and therefore covers any measure that has 'an effect on' the supply of financial services.[132]

Further the Appellate Body in *Argentina – Financial Services* held that the fact that paragraph 2(a) covers infringements of obligations under 'any provisions of the Agreement' implies that this provision 'could be invoked to justify inconsistencies with all of a Member's obligations under the GATS'.[133] Specifically, the Appellate Body noted:

> These include, for example, a Member's most-favoured-nation treatment obligation under Article II, market access commitments under Article XVI, or national treatment obligation under Article XVII. This indicates that, for example, measures which are of the types listed in Article XVI:2, and which impose market access restrictions for prudential reasons, could potentially fall within the scope of paragraph 2(a). The type of measure taken by a Member (such as market access restrictions) and the provision of the GATS contravened by such measure (such as Article XVI) are distinct, but related, concepts.[134]

[128] Panel Report, *Argentina – Financial Services*, paras 7.853–7.945.

[129] GATS, Annex, para 1(a). This provision reads as follows: 'This Annex applies to measures affecting the supply of financial services. Reference to the supply of a financial service in this Annex shall mean the supply of a service as defined in paragraph 2 of Article I of the Agreement.'

[130] Both the panel and the Appellate Body sided with the argument that all measures fall within the scope of the PCO. This reasoning was adopted because it better reflects the GATS rationale, illustrated in paras 3 and 4 of the Preamble, and better captures the content of para 2(a) and the context of the Annex. See Panel Report, *Argentina – Financial Services*, paras 6.825, 7.847; Appellate Body Report, *Argentina – Financial Services*, paras 6.253–6.262.

[131] ibid para 6.262.

[132] Panel Report, *Argentina – Financial Services*, para 7.855.

[133] Appellate Body Report, *Argentina – Financial Services*, para 6.255.

[134] ibid.

Additionally, the second condition put forward by the panel relates to measures taken 'for prudential reasons'. This requirement is further split by the panel into two separate analyses for reasons of judicial scrutiny. Firstly, it shall be defined whether the reasoning behind Members' regulatory measures concerns prudential 'reasons', meaning that the measures aim 'to prevent a risk, injury or danger that does not necessarily have to be imminent'.[135] Secondly, it must be shown, based on the word 'for' in paragraph 2(a), whether there is a 'rational relationship of cause and effect between the measure and the prudential reason'.[136] The rational link between the regulatory measure and the prudential reason concerns the 'adequacy' of the first, through its design, to attain the desired outcome.[137] Under the assumption that a rational relationship is in place, the third condition of the prudential carve-out is that the measure at issue must 'not be used as a means of avoiding the Member's commitments or obligations under the Agreement'.[138]

The WTO jurisprudence distinguished between the terms 'measures for prudential reasons' and 'prudential measures' and did not consider them synonyms for the purposes of interpreting the PCO. In particular, the panel in *Argentina – Financial Services* noted that it had not been convincingly argued that the two concepts concern the same thing or result in the same effects. It further held that that the text of the PCO provision does not speak of 'prudential measures' but instead of 'measures for prudential reasons'. In light of the above, it concluded that that the reason behind the measure must be 'prudential' and not the measure in itself. The panel further clarified that the GATS does not aim to identify measures that could be characterized as specifically prudential (such as those usually referred to in the context of the standards defined by the Basel Committee on Banking Supervision.[139] Contrary to this, paragraph 2(a) of the Annex on Financial Services enables WTO Members to exempt or exonerate any measures affecting the supply of trade in financial services that has been adopted 'for prudential reasons'.[140]

Notably, as stated above, the panel in *Argentina – Financial Services* concluded, in a finding not reviewed by the Appellate Body, that a measure is taken 'for' prudential reasons where a 'rational relationship of cause and effect' exists between the measure at issue and the prudential reason provided. In particular, the panel observed that the use of the word 'for' in the phrase

[135] Panel Report, *Argentina – Financial Services*, para 7.879; *cf* paras 7.904, 7.937, and 7.946.

[136] ibid para 7.889.

[137] ibid para 7.891.

[138] ibid para 7.945.

[139] See the 'Core principles for effective banking supervision', established by the Basel Committee on Banking Supervision, in particular Principles 14 to 29 relating to 'prudential regulations and requirements' (September 2012 version, Spanish text can be viewed at: http://www.bis.org/publ/bcbs230_es.pdf).

[140] Panel Report, *Argentina – Financial Services*, para 7.861.

'measures for prudential reasons' appears to concern a rational relationship of cause and affect between the measure and the prudential reason. Following this, the panel held that Members must show that in the measure's design, structure or architecture there is a rational relationship of cause and effect between the measure it seeks to justify under the GATS prudential exception and the prudential reason set out. According to the panel, a crucial element of this rational relationship of cause and effect is the adequacy of the measure to the prudential reason, which begs the question whether the measure – through its design, structure and architecture – plays its part in achieving the desired outcome. Finally, the panel noted that whether a measure has been adopted 'for prudential reasons' (meaning whether there is a rational relationship of cause and effect between the measure and the reason) can only be decided on a case-by-case basis, taking into consideration the particular characteristics of each situation and each dispute.[141]

Moreover, the PCO provides Members' regulatory authorities large room for manoeuvre. Principally, measures aiming to safeguard the safety and soundness of financial systems are covered by its remit. Yet, as demonstrated by recent WTO case law, certain checks and balances are in place for the prudential carve-out (eg they must be adopted for prudential reasons and they must not be used as a way to circumvent other GATS obligations and/or commitments). These filters assess the WTO consistency of the measures at issue. The 'rational relationship of the cause and effect' requirement, put forward by the panel, restricts to a significant degree the wide scope of the prudential exception. Having said that, the PCO scope is still wider than the exceptions of GATS, Article XIV, which requires necessity. Therefore, regulators, while designing their prudential regulations, should take into account that their financial framework should not circumvent trade disciplines and should be fit for the purpose they seek to achieve.

Contrary to this interpretation of the PCO, Cantore develops an alternative narrative of the prudential carve-out according to which measures adopted in the pursuit of prudential objectives do not fall under the purview of the GATS, even if the Member has listed specific commitments and the new regulations may have a detrimental effect on them.[142] The reasoning of this approach is informed by: (i) the absence of a *chapeau* in the text of the PCO (which is a pivotal element in all the GATT and GATS exception provisions); (ii) the inclusion of a non-exhaustive list of prudential objectives (which is in contrast to the fixed and exhaustive list of policies incorporated in exception provisions); and (iii) the negotiating history of the prudential carve-out.[143]

[141] Panel Report, *Argentina – Financial Services*, para 7.891.
[142] Cantore (n 111) 187.
[143] ibid 168–224.

The following analysis proceeds with the ordinary interpretation of the PCO. Notably, if the European equivalence regime for third-country clearinghouses was found to be in breach of a GATS provision, one would wonder if it could be justified under the prudential exception. The first step is to ascertain whether the measures for recognising non-EU CCPs fall under the scope of the PCO. The discussion above verifies that the European regulatory measures undoubtedly affect the supply of financial services and the first PCO requirement is fulfilled. Unlike the first, the second requirement is quite tricky. With regard to the first prong, the fact that the EMIR equivalence regime is crafted to promote OTC derivatives market stability is well known. Accordingly, it would not be a problem for this regulatory measure to argue that it serves prudential reasons.[144] Nevertheless, the challenging task would be to demonstrate that there is a 'rational relationship' between the equivalence mechanism, the application of which might be characterised as discriminatory or ill-transparent, and the prudential objective. A case-by-case qualitative evaluation is necessitated to determine whether such a relationship exists and the WTO judiciary would have to address this issue based on the parties' submitted evidence. The writer's view is that it would be difficult for the EU to draw a cause and effect link between this type of trade barrier and the rationale of financial stability. Although the EMIR equivalence regime undoubtedly safeguards the integrity of financial systems, it is contestable whether the application of equivalence assessments is the adequate instrument to meet this end. In principle, the design of regimes such as equivalence or substituted compliance promotes financial stability but their implementation might not be appropriate to achieve their goals.

That said, if the European regulatory measure in question is found to be discriminatory or lacking in transparency by the WTO judiciary, it would be challenging to substantiate the existence of a rational link between the application of equivalence rules and financial stability. Furthermore, even if this relationship is established, the non-circumvention criterion is the last stop before the PCO conditions are satisfied. This requirement also heavily relies on a case-by-case analysis, and a conclusive answer cannot be given in respect of the EMIR measures at issue. Given that the prudential exception has never been invoked in relation to regulatory measures touching on financial stability, it is very difficult to predict how the WTO judiciary would conduct its analysis in that regard. Consequently, the PCO is still an uncharted territory – *terra incognita*.

[144] The panel in *Argentina – Financial Services* underlined that the concept of 'prudential reasons' is an evolving one (para 7.870), while the 'stability of the financial system' is an overarching prudential consideration enshrined in the PCO.

V. CONCLUSION

This chapter has sought to evaluate the tension between financial regulation and WTO law by taking the EU's clearinghouse regulation as a case study. Completion of this exercise allows for three significant deductions with respect to the future liberalisation of financial services within the GATS legal architecture. First, the analysis demonstrates that regulatory equivalence assessments of financial services' foreign jurisdictions can negatively impact on the terms of trade and conditions of competition between WTO Members. Second, the findings indicate that smaller countries without regulatory leverage are less likely to gain access to the European market because of the structural problems of the rules on equivalence. Third, and perhaps more interestingly, this contribution has found that the Members' vast flexibility to regulate financial services (provided by the GATS) does not make use of all avenues provided by the multilateral trading system to achieve further integration.

In all these cases, this study has evidenced that the most problematic issues arise with respect to the GATS principle of non-discrimination and transparency. Namely, in terms of transparency, problems arise not only in publishing substantial elements of the regulatory frameworks per se but also in disclosing recognition agreements. With respect to non-discrimination, both procedural and substantive GATS legal disciplines are potentially disregarded by EMIR equivalence rules and the application thereof. Specifically, the discretionary and politically driven application of rules seems to advantage some countries over others.

These findings can be explained by the absence of coordination and synergies between the trade and finance administrations of Members, such as the EU in our case study. In the aftermath of the crisis, it became clear that regulation of financial services, including that of clearinghouses, was crucial to safeguard the integrity of global financial systems. That said, our example challenges whether the means employed by financial regulators always justify the end sought. As a result, the conformity with the GATS rulebook by domestic financial regulators is put in question. The outcome of the tension between financial services regulation and liberalisation seems hard to reconcile.

The importance of a correct balance between financial regulation and liberalisation extends far beyond a pure legal argument. Ultimately, combining financial regulatory capacity with the benefits of trade in financial services could and should translate into more integration for WTO Members.

A starting point towards this goal could be to explore less trade-restrictive means available at the WTO, such as the application of non-differential treatment in financial rulebooks. Additionally, international standards for the harmonisation of transnational derivatives clearing frameworks, in parallel with monitoring by international standard-setting organisations and supervisory cooperation by regulators could be even more effective. These may usefully boost the unfulfilled potential of financial services liberalisation and at the same time achieve the legitimate objectives set by financial regulators. By using these tools, WTO Members do not derogate from their GATS financial services obligations and they re-start using the avenues available at the WTO.

This chapter did not intend to exhaust the question of available WTO tools capable of striking a fair balance between financial services liberalisation and regulation. Rather, its purpose was to start a much-needed debate on an increasingly important, but scarcely discussed subject: the relationship between financial services regulation and WTO rules. We have demonstrated that the current system of financial regulation leaves important gaps on the road to trade liberalisation. In addition, we have also suggested that important avenues for tackling these gaps may be found within the WTO legal framework itself. The questions that remain are when and under which conditions these avenues will reach their full potential.

Part II

Financial Regulation and the Plurilateral Trading System

4

The Liberalisation of Financial Market Infrastructure Services in Economic Integration Agreements

I. INTRODUCTION

UNDERSTANDING HOW FINANCIAL services liberalisation works in trade agreements is crucial to gain a broader perspective on the international supply of financial services. Financial markets are so interconnected that regulation of one state fundamentally impacts on other jurisdictions and they affect trade flows as well. Thus, the regional integration of financial services through preferential trade agreements is crucial for the operation of financial market infrastructure. Shedding light on the liberalisation of regionalism and explaining its elements are this study's purpose. This chapter aims to map out how financial services' regionalism, illustrated by Economic Integration Agreements (EIAs),[1] compares and contrasts with the liberalisation of financial services at the multilateral trading system, and to investigate the role of financial regulations in that context. The increasing importance of regionalism in international trade, while multilateral negotiations under the World Trade Organization have stalemate effects, makes this exercise highly relevant.[2] One of the EIAs' objectives is to decrease or eliminate the barriers to trade in services and investment among their Members. This study assesses the liberalisation depth of financial securities' clearing and settlement services in EIAs. To that end, we evaluate how the regulation of international trade contributes to the

[1] This chapter has opted to use the term EIA, as employed in Art V of the General Agreement on Trade in Services (GATS), because securities' clearing and settlement services are embedded in international trade agreements regulating trade in services. However, the terms Preferential Trade Agreement (PTA), Free Trade Agreement (FTA) or Regional Trade Agreement (RTA) can be used interchangeably since they refer to the same type of agreements. This study draws from an author's earlier study, see GA Papaconstantinou, *Financial Services Liberalization Under EU FTAs: The Case of Clearing and Settlement Services* (Yearbook of International Economic Law, Springer International Publishing, 2020) 65–87.

[2] See, for example, RV Fiorentino and JA Crawford, 'The Changing Landscape of Regional Trade Agreements' [2005] WTO Discussion Paper No 8; M Roy et al, 'Services Liberalization in the New Generation of Preferential Trade Agreements (PTAs): How Much Further than the GATS?' (2007) 6 *World Trade Review* 155.

integration of financial services, on the one hand, and explore the transnational dynamics and trends that explain the integration of the service's sector in question, on the other. The recent proliferation of concluded EIAs on trade in services underscores their importance for international trade and policy, and at the same time brings into the spotlight the need for a better understanding of the plurilateral trading system's ramifications in the liberalisation of services.

Carrying out this exercise is crucial to delineate the relationship between trade in services under disparate legal orders, namely under the WTO and under EIAs. The mechanics and asymmetric architecture of the GATS[3] have been examined thoroughly by literature and by the previous chapters in relation to the liberalisation of financial market infrastructure under WTO law. However, it is worth highlighting that the liberalisation of trade in services is principally contingent on WTO Members' GATS commitments under Articles XVI and XVII on market access and national treatment respectively.[4] This chapter is not concerned with the GATS levels of liberalisation per se, but rather the liberalisation depth achieved in EIAs. In that endeavour, the WTO Members' commitments under the GATS are used as the benchmark to measure how much beyond them the undertaken commitments in EIAs extend.[5] The methodology of this study is developed in detail in the next section. The following paragraphs summarise the importance of clearing and settlement services for the integrity of financial systems, and their regulatory evolution as of today.

Financial instruments' clearing and settlement services were regulated by international trade for the first time in late 1990s, when the GATS Annex in Financial Services entered into force.[6] Since then, a lot has changed in terms of the services' prominence in world economics' financial market infrastructure. In particular, the industry itself has been subject to numerous changes driven by the force of regulation across the globe. Regardless of the economic model followed by WTO Members and the underlying competition structures of clearing and settlement service suppliers, whether monopolistic or oligopolistic, the interconnectedness of international finance cannot permit major operational

[3] General Agreement on Trade in Services, Annex 1B to the Agreement Establishing the World Trade Organization, done at Marrakesh on 15 April 1994, UNTS No 31874. The text is available in WTO, *The Legal Texts: The Results of the Uruguay Round of Multilateral Trade Negotiations* (Cambridge, Cambridge University Press, 2000) 357.

[4] WTO Members voluntarily enter commitments on market access (Art XVI), national treatment (Art XVII), and additional commitments (Art XVIII) in their GATS Schedules, which constitute treaty text, on the basis of their national preferences. Liberalisation is attained in the multilateral trading system in accordance to these specific commitments. As long as WTO Members decide to open more services sectors to international competition from other WTO Members, more liberalisation is achieved. Accordingly, there is a positive relation between the process of entering commitments and the liberalisation of services.

[5] In limited instances, we have identified that certain EIA parties' commitments go below their GATS binding commitments. For more information, see below.

[6] The GATS Annex on Financial Services explicitly refers in its indicative list to clearing services in para 5(a)(xiv): 'settlement and clearing services for financial assets, including securities, derivative products, and other negotiable instruments'.

discrepancies that can result in financial market disruptions, and potentially place the whole system's financial stability into jeopardy. Importantly, clearing and settlement services are traditionally tasked with addressing the risks associated with the trading of financial instruments, such as the failure of a counterparty to fulfil its part of the deal in a derivatives transaction or even the 'loss' of a security due to its high exchangeability, being the 'back-office' activity of trading securities.[7] That said, clearing and settlement services have been part of the financial markets since late nineteenth century,[8] but their relevance today has been shaped due to the regulatory shift responding to the 2007–2009 global financial crisis.

In the aftermath of the crisis, and in accordance with the G20 mandate, financial regulations that place the functioning of clearinghouses in the epicentre of OTC derivative markets were crafted. The new role attributed to clearinghouses sets out the mandatory clearing of certain types of OTC derivatives[9] that can potentially have a systemic spill-over effect should one of the counterparties to the transaction go bust.[10] This regulatory change aspires to reduce the perils posed by derivative markets, while taking into consideration the additional costs levied to trading parties, by the posting of collateral. This regulatory trend is in sharp contrast to what used to occur, where financial institutions were free to choose whether they wanted to employ clearing services or proceed the transaction without. Accordingly, the whole business of clearing has developed since then and, interestingly, this study seeks to investigate if this regulatory change has impacted on the liberalisation of clearing services, traced in EIAs. The GATS commitments on clearing services are ubiquitous in the multilateral trading system. Nonetheless, they are not apt to capture regulatory evolution because they are not updated by WTO Members. This chapter seeks to identify whether EIAs are better placed to respond to these regulatory challenges.

Investigating the commitments undertaken by WTO Members for clearing and settlement services in EIAs leads to measuring the depth of their liberalisation, while aiming to grasp the underlying dynamics that are the driving forces of the observed integration model. Some of the questions to be addressed are: What are the geographical trends that contribute to the liberalisation of international clearing trade flows? What types of restrictions on the integration of these services are placed on EIAs? This chapter is structured as follows: Section II sets out the methodology of the study. Section III sheds light on the descriptive statistics and observations drawn by the study to deploy a comprehensive analysis

[7] For general literature on financial instruments clearing and settlement services in the EU see D Turing, *Clearing and Settlement* (Oxford, Bloomsbury Publishing, 2016).

[8] For a historical narrative of clearinghouses see NL Wolkoff and JB Werner, 'The History of Regulation of Clearing in the Securities and Futures Markets, and Its Impact on Competition' (2010) 30 *Review of Banking and Financial Law* 313.

[9] Such as interest rate swaps, foreign exchange, and credit default swaps among others.

[10] This regulatory trend can be identified in all major global economies, and its efficacy on the basis of the G20 standards is measured by the Financial Stability Board annually.

of the stakes involved. Section IV adopts a line of argument with regard to the relationship between the regulation of financial services and the law of international trade based on the findings of the paper. Finally, Section V concludes.

II. METHODOLOGY

Besides establishing a comprehensive typology of the commitments pertinent to clearing and settlement services in EIAs, this chapter's principal objective is to measure the liberalisation of financial market infrastructure services in the plurilateral trading system. Our analysis covers 152 EIAs currently in force,[11] which have been notified to the WTO up to September 2018 under Article V (economic integration) of the GATS, under Article XXIV (territorial application – frontier traffic – customs inions and free-trade areas) of the General Agreement on Tariffs and Trade (GATT 1994), and the Enabling Clause (decision on differential and more favourable treatment, reciprocity and fuller participation on developing countries).[12] The scope of this chapter is limited to the agreements whose level of integration utilises the trade liberalising toolkit provided by the GATS. Deeply integrated economic unions are not examined, because their inclusion would not add any value, as the tools employed to further integrate these markets: (i) deviate from the traditional trade instruments and as a result cannot serve the purposes of this empirical study because they are not comparable; and (ii) represent a small fraction (12/152) of the number of agreements notified to the WTO.[13] The two main set of documents that this analysis relies on are undoubtedly the Schedules of Commitments, and the List of Reservations of the parties to the EIAs, which are usually in the form of annexes attached to the main agreement.[14] Nonetheless, on several occasions recourse to the

[11] The WTO Regional Trade Agreements (RTAs) database has been used as the main source to collect the data for this study. All EIAs that are reviewed here, along with the text of the agreements, the annexes and other related documents, can be found in the linked database, WTO, 'Regional Trade Agreements Database' (WTO, last updated 16 June 2023) rtais.wto.org/UI/PublicMaintainRTAHome.aspx accessed 25 July 2023.

[12] Those EIAs were notified to the WTO up to November 2018. Since then, the majority of EIAs notified to the WTO concern agreements concluded between the UK and third countries following the UK's withdrawal from the EU. Thus, although the UK is a new international actor of relevance for trade in financial services, the findings of this study and trends identified hold true and remain valid as the UK was – until 31 January 2020 – a full member of the EU and was covered by all the EIAs concluded by the EU.

[13] The 12 EIAs notified to the WTO that are not covered by this study are the following: EC (15) Enlargement, EC (25) Enlargement, EC (27) Enlargement, EC Treaty, EU (28) Enlargement, Eurasian Economic Union (EAEU), Eurasian Economic Union (EAEU) – Accession of Armenia, Eurasian Economic Union (EAEU) – Accession of Kyrgyz Republic, European Economic Area (EEA), European Free Trade Association (EFTA), Southern Common Market (MERCOSUR), Caribbean Community and Common Market (CARICOM).

[14] For all the undertaken commitments and/or reservations on clearing and settlement services in Economic Integration Agreements, see the Appendix: Clearing & Settlement Commitments in Economic Integration Agreements at the end of this volume.

agreements' chapters and side documents, such as protocols, communication letters, understandings, and other documents associated with the EIAs, is necessary to obtain a holistic perspective of this study's subject matter.

Henceforth, since the nature of this inquiry is to measure the liberalisation of clearing and settlement services in EIAs, it is essential to clarify the tools that are employed to that end. Traditionally, trade in services is supplied through the GATS four modes of supply: namely, cross-border supply (mode 1), consumption abroad (mode 2), commercial presence (mode 3), and movement of persons (mode 4).[15] When it comes to wholesale financial services, such as the ones of clearing and settlement, mode 4 immediately becomes redundant, because these types of services are provided by large financial institutions rather than by individuals. Therefore, this study examines the liberalisation of clearing and settlement services for modes 1, 2, and 3. Furthermore, the same as in the multilateral trading system, in EIAs the liberalisation of financial services is effectuated through undertaken commitments on market access, and national treatment, which are contingent upon specific mode of supply. Thus, the modes of supply and the entered commitments on market access and national treatment are the existing variables that define the level of liberalisation of clearing and settlement services in EIAs.

For the sake of clarity, it must be underlined that when evaluating the level of liberalisation of clearing and settlement services in EIAs on the basis of the abovementioned landmarks (modes of supply, and market access/national treatment commitments), challenges emerge due to the different approaches that countries adopt in scheduling their commitments.[16] The three most frequently met methods are: (i) positive lists, which mirror the scheduling approach put forward in the GATS. Specifically, countries list in their Schedules of Commitments all the services sectors and subsectors, and indicate whether they undertake particular commitments for market access and national treatment for the particular modes of supply; (ii) *negative lists* follow the approach used for the first time in North Atlantic Free Trade Agreement (NAFTA). The negative list approach, instead

[15] It is well documented that the evolution of technological means by which financial services are supplied transnationally has created a legal problem in the interpretation of undertaken commitments for modes 1 (cross-border supply) and 2 (consumption abroad), whether under the multilateral trading system, through the GATS schedules, or under EIAs. For analyses on this issue, and the possible problematic implications, see WTO, Council for Trade in Services, Committee on Trade in Financial Services, S/C/W/312, S/FIN/W/73, 3 February 2010, para 36, p 10; JO Berkey, 'A Framework Agreement for Electronic Commerce Regulation Under the GATS 1-2' (Institution of International Finance, 2001); GA Papaconstantinou, 'The GATS and Financial Regulation: Time to Clear-House?' (2020) 19 *World Trade Review* 379, 385–88.

[16] For thorough analyses with regard to the different approaches that parties to EIAs use in opening their services sectors see M Roy et al, 'The Race towards Preferential Trade Agreements in Services: How Much Market Access Is Really Achieved?' in M Panizzon et al (eds), *GATS and the Regulation of International Trade in Services: World Trade Forum* (Cambridge, Cambridge University Press, 2008); JA Marchetti, 'Do PTAs Actually Increase Parties' Services Trade?' in KW Bagwell and PC Mavroidis (eds), *Preferential Trade Agreements: A Law and Economics Analysis* (Cambridge, Cambridge University Press, 2011).

of schedules of commitments, has lists of reservations which strictly refer to the measures that are not subject to full commitment (complete liberalisation); (iii) *hybrid lists* have emerged as a model that combines characteristics of the two other methods. For instance, hybrid lists use a positive list for cross-border supply and negative lists for establishment. Traditionally, negative listing is closer than its positive counterpart to the objective of trade liberalisation because it forces states to scrutinise their regulatory frameworks and check their compatibility with trade disciplines, before concluding their trade agreements, where they have to specifically include these measures in their List of Reservations. The challenges encountered in the process of collecting the empirical data for this study lie in the inherent differences of the two approaches. To produce a comprehensive dataset that measures the level of liberalisation of EIAs it is necessary to first compile and structure the data in a uniform fashion. To that end, in the process of compiling the data from EIAs with negative lists, I translated them into positive commitments so that the contribution could be more thorough and provide for a clearer picture of the overall EIAs' state of play.

The question that next comes to mind relates to the methodology adopted to gauge the 'depth' of the just-described liberalisation. For starters, WTO Members have undertaken commitments in their GATS Schedules for clearing and settlement services. These commitments naturally mirror the GATS asymmetric geometry, and are different for each and every WTO Member. Notably, this chapter investigates the clearing and settlement services' commitments of parties to EIAs. Once the commitments of EIA parties are mapped out, they are juxtaposed to the ones entered by the same countries in their GATS Schedules. The outcome of the juxtaposition between the countries' commitments in EIAs, and their commitments under the GATS defines the liberalisation depth. More specifically, there are three possible scenarios in that score: first, if Country X's undertaken commitments in an EIA fall below the GATS threshold, then this is a *GATS-minus* result (however, due to the existence of the GATS, Article II on MFN, this category constitutes nothing but a legal fiction as long as the conditions of Article II of the GATS are fulfilled); second, if Country X has entered in an EIA exactly the same commitments as the ones under the GATS, then there is a *GATS* liberalisation depth; third, if the commitments of Country X in an EIA go beyond the ones in the GATS, then this constitutes a *GATS(+)*.[17]

This chapter aims first to empirically assess the liberalisation levels of clearing and settlement services in EIAs, and second to explore the underlying dynamics and trends that spearhead the surveyed liberalisation. For instance, an essential query that this study seeks to address relates to which geographical regions

[17] For the sake of completeness, *GATS(+)*, as a category, can be further narrowed down toL (i) *GATS-plus* when the undertaken commitments go beyond the entered commitments in the relevant GATS Schedules; and (ii) *GATS-extra* if Country X has not undertaken any commitments in the GATS, but it does in the context of the EIA. For the purposes of some figures and tables in this chapter, those two categories are merged under the *GATS(+)* term.

put forward the liberalisation agenda for these financial market infrastructure services and, if possible, interpret the reasons behind this. The recent history of the GATS has taught us that it was the US and its industry, along with the European Community at the time, which aspired and managed to introduce an international rulebook for the trade in financial services.[18] Has something changed in the course of the following decades, or are the same regions now the net exporters of financial services? The case study of clearing and settlement services is going to be a helpful guide in addressing such queries. Next, other trends in terms of the specific services sector are discerned based on the data, such as negative or positive listing and which is more prone to foster liberalisation. Additionally, new regulatory frameworks for clearinghouses across the globe, in the aftermath of the crisis, started being enacted around 2010. How does this regulatory trend blend with the liberalisation of clearing services in EIAs? This study will try to give an answer to that as well.

After having contextualised the features of this chapter and explained the methodological steps that the analysis undertakes, it is time to venture into the empirical data of this study in order to engage in the subject matter and put forward the arguments of this contribution. To start with, the study's scope and main findings are presented. Following this the trends that have been identified in the EIAs' commitments on clearing and settlement services are discussed.

III. EMPIRICAL ANALYSIS

A. Findings

Before delving into the more granular aspects of this chapter, it is essential to introduce its precise scope, and main features. To start with, as mentioned above, this study covers the EIAs, included in Table 1, which regulate securities' clearing and settlement services, and at least one party has made commitments.[19] Additionally, the timeframes of their conclusions are detailed in the next two columns so that the chronological trends in terms of the scheduling approaches (either through positive, negative or hybrid lists), and liberalisation levels that exceed the GATS state of play can be initially drawn, before we further shed light on them in the course of the analysis. Out of the 102 EIAs, 49 use Schedules

[18] Admittedly, it was American Express that put forward the agenda of incorporating financial services under the negotiations of the WTO. For analyses on the dynamics that led to the inclusion of financial services in the GATS, see JA Marchetti and PC Mavroidis, 'The Genesis of the GATS (General Agreement on Trade in Services)' (2011) 22 *European Journal of International Law* 689; see also SJ Key, *The Doha Round and Financial Services Negotiations* (Washington DC, American Enterprise Institute, 2003).

[19] In subsection C below, the 38 preferential trade agreements that either do not regulate trade in financial services or do not provide specific set of commitments for clearing and settlement services are examined. Behavioural patterns and geographical trends are discerned.

of Commitments (positive lists) and 48 lists of reservations (negative lists), while three are hybrids. The fifth column observes whether at least one party to the EIA in question enters commitments on clearing and settlement services that are more trade liberalising than the ones it has undertaken in the multilateral trading system, under the GATS. Interestingly, 64 EIAs extend greater commitments than the ones under the GATS regime.

Table 1 EIAs under Review

EIA	Entry into force	WTO notification	Positive or Negative list?	EIA's commitments on clearing and settlement going beyond the GATS?
ASEAN – Australia– New Zealand	Jan 2010	Apr 2010	Positive list	No
ASEAN – China	Jul 2007	Jun 2008	Positive list	No
ASEAN – India	Jul 2015	Aug 2015	Positive list	No
ASEAN – Korea, Republic of	Oct 2010	Jul 2010	Positive list	No
Australia – Chile	Mar 2009	Mar 2009	Negative list	Yes
Australia – China	Dec 2015	Jan 2016	Negative list	Yes
Australia – New Zealand	Jan 1989	Nov 1995	Negative list	Yes
Brunei Darussalam – Japan	Jul 2008	Jul 2008	Positive list	Yes
Canada – Colombia	Aug 2011	Oct 2011	Negative list	Yes
Canada – Honduras	Oct 2014	Feb 2015	Negative list	Yes
Canada – Panama	Apr 2013	Apr 2013	Negative list	Yes
Canada – Peru	Aug 2009	Jul 2009	Negative list	Yes
Canada –Korea, Republic of	Jan 2015	Jan 2015	Negative list	Yes
Chile – Japan	Sep 2007	Aug 2007	Positive list	Yes
Chile – Thailand	Nov 2015	Sep 2017	Positive list	Yes
China – Georgia	Jan 2018	Apr 2018	Positive list	Yes
China – Korea, Republic of	Dec 2015	Mar 2016	Positive list	No
China – New Zealand	Oct 2008	Apr 2009	Positive list	No
China – Singapore	Jan 2009	Mar 2009	Positive list	No
Costa Rica – Colombia	Aug 2016	Oct 2016	Negative list	Yes

(continued)

Table 1 *(Continued)*

EIA	Entry into force	WTO notification	Positive or Negative list?	EIA's commitments on clearing and settlement going beyond the GATS?
Dominican Republic – Central America – United States Free Trade Agreement (CAFTADR)	Mar 2006	Mar 2006	Negative list	Yes
EFTA – Central America (Costa Rica and Panama)	Aug 2014	Nov 2014	Positive list	Yes
EFTA – Colombia	Jul 2011	Sep 2011	Positive list	Yes
EFTA – Georgia	Sep 2017	Aug 2017	Positive list	Yes
EFTA – Hong Kong, China	Oct 2012	Sep 2012	Negative list	Yes
EFTA – Korea, Republic of	Sep 2006	Aug 2006	Positive list	Yes
EFTA – Mexico	Jul 2001	Jul 2001	Negative list	Yes
EFTA – Singapore	Jan 2003	Jan 2003	Positive list	No
EFTA – Ukraine	Jun 2012	Jun 2012	Positive list	Yes
EU – Canada	Sep 2017	Sep 2017	Negative list	No
EU – CARIFORUM	Dec 2008	Oct 2008	Positive/ Negative	No
EU – Central America	Aug 2013	Feb 2013	Negative list	Yes
EU – Chile	Mar 2005	Oct 2005	Positive list	Yes
EU – Colombia and Peru	Mar 2013	Feb 2013	Negative list	Yes
EU – Colombia, Peru – Accession of Equador	Jan 2017	Mar 2017	Positive/ Negative	Yes
EU – Georgia	Sep 2014	Jul 2014	Hybrid	No
EU – Korea, Republic of	Jul 2011	Jul 2011	Positive list	No
EU – Mexico	Oct 2002	Jun 2002	Negative list	Yes
EU – Moldova, Republic of	Sep 2014	Jun 2014	Hybrid	No

(continued)

Table 1 *(Continued)*

EIA	Entry into force	WTO notification	Positive or Negative list?	EIA's commitments on clearing and settlement going beyond the GATS?
EU – Ukraine	Apr 2014	Jul 2014	Hybrid	No
Gulf Cooperation Council (GCC) – Singapore	Sep 2013	Jun 2015	Positive list	Yes
Hong Kong, China – Chile	Oct 2014	Oct 2014	Positive list	Yes
Hong Kong, China – Macao, China	Oct 2017	Dec 2017	Positive list	No
Hong Kong, China – New Zealand	Jan 2011	Jan 2011	Negative list	No
Iceland – China	Jul 2014	Oct 2014	Positive list	No
India – Japan	Aug 2011	Sep 2011	Positive list	Yes
India – Malaysia	Jul 2011	Sep 2011	Positive list	No
India – Singapore	Aug 2005	May 2007	Positive list	No
Japan – Australia	Jan 2015	Jan 2015	Negative list	Yes
Japan – Indonesia	Jul 2008	Jun 2008	Positive list	Yes
Japan – Malaysia	Jul 2006	Jul 2006	Positive list	Yes
Japan – Mexico	Apr 2005	Mar 2005	Negative list	No
Japan – Mongolia	Jun 2016	Jun 2016	Positive list	No
Japan – Peru	Mar 2012	Feb 2012	Negative list	Yes
Japan – Philippines	Dec 2008	Dec 2008	Positive list	Yes
Japan – Singapore	Nov 2002	Nov 2002	Positive list	No
Japan – Switzerland	Sep 2009	Sep 2009	Negative list	Yes
Japan – Thailand	Nov 2007	Oct 2007	Positive list	Yes
Japan – Viet Nam	Oct 2009	Oct 2009	Positive list	Yes
Jordan – Singapore	Aug 2005	Jul 2006	Positive list	No
Korea, Republic of – Australia	Dec 2014	Dec 2014	Negative list	Yes
Korea, Republic of – India	Jan 2010	Jul 2010	Positive list	No
Korea, Republic of – Singapore	Mar 2006	Feb 2006	Positive list	No

(continued)

Table 1 *(Continued)*

EIA	Entry into force	WTO notification	Positive or Negative list?	EIA's commitments on clearing and settlement going beyond the GATS?
Korea, Republic of – US	Mar 2012	Mar 2012	Negative list	Yes
Korea, Republic of – Viet Nam	Dec 2015	Mar 2016	Positive list	No
Malaysia – Australia	Jan 2013	May 2013	Positive list	No
Mexico – Panama	Jul 2015	Jun 2016	Negative list	Yes
New Zealand – Chinese Taipei	Dec 2013	Nov 2013	Negative list	Yes
New Zealand – Malaysia	Aug 2010	Feb 2012	Positive list	No
New Zealand – Singapore	Jan 2001	Sep 2001	Positive list	No
Nicaragua – Chinese Taipei	Jan 2008	Jul 2009	Negative list	Yes
North American Free Trade Agreement (NAFTA)	Jan 1994	Mar 1995	Negative list	Yes
Pacific Alliance	May 2016	Nov 2016	Negative list	Yes
Pakistan – China	Oct 2009	May 2010	Positive list	No
Pakistan – Malaysia	Jan 2008	Feb 2008	Positive list	No
Panama – Chinese Taipei	Jan 2004	Jul 2009	Negative list	Yes
Panama – Costa Rica (Panama – Central America)	Nov 2008	Apr 2009	Negative list	Yes
Panama – El Salvador (Panama – Central America)	Apr 2003	Feb 2005	Negative list	Yes
Panama – Guatemala (Panama – Central America)	Jun 2009	Apr 2013	Negative list	Yes

(continued)

Table 1 *(Continued)*

EIA	Entry into force	WTO notification	Positive or Negative list?	EIA's commitments on clearing and settlement going beyond the GATS?
Panama – Honduras (Panama – Central America)	Jan 2009	Dec 2009	Negative list	Yes
Panama – Nicaragua (Panama – Central America)	Nov 2009	Feb 2013	Negative list	Yes
Panama – Peru	May 2012	Apr 2012	Negative list	Yes
Panama – Singapore	Jul 2006	Apr 2007	Negative list	Yes
Peru – China	Mar 2010	Mar 2010	Positive list	Yes
Peru – Korea, Republic of	Aug 2011	Aug 2011	Negative list	Yes
Peru – Mexico	Feb 2012	Feb 2012	Negative list	Yes
Peru – Singapore	Aug 2009	Jul 2009	Positive list	No
Singapore – Australia	Jul 2003	Sep 2003	Negative list	Yes
Singapore – Chinese Taipei	Apr 2014	Apr 2014	Positive list	No
Switzerland – China	Jul 2014	Jun 2014	Positive list	No
Thailand – Australia	Jan 2005	Dec 2004	Positive list	Yes
Ukraine – Montenegro	Jan 2013	Apr 2013	Positive list	No
US – Australia	Jan 2005	Dec 2004	Negative list	Yes
US – Bahrain	Aug 2006	Sep 2006	Negative list	Yes
US – Chile	Jan 2004	Dec 2003	Negative list	Yes
US – Colombia	May 2012	May 2012	Negative list	Yes
US – Jordan	Dec 2001	Jan 2002	Positive list	No
US – Morocco	Jan 2006	Dec 2005	Negative list	Yes
US – Oman	Jan 2009	Jan 2009	Negative list	No
US – Panama	Oct 2012	Oct 2012	Negative list	Yes
US – Peru	Feb 2009	Feb 2009	Negative list	Yes
US – Singapore	Jan 2004	Dec 2003	Negative list	No

Source: Own analysis, WTO RTA database.

B. Comments on EIAs' Commitments: Stability and Competition Considerations

This subsection investigates the *comments* that parties to EIAs have attached to their commitments on financial instruments' clearing and settlement services. The importance of this exercise principally lies, on the one hand, in discovering different countries' perceptions/intentions over the underlying services, and discerning potential trends on the other. Regardless of the major differences between the two financial market infrastructure services sectors, due to their CPC classification they are always examined hand in hand in all plurilateral trade agreements, the same as in the GATS. Nonetheless, such categorisation brings complexity to trade negotiators charged with bargaining over trade in financial services issues because it links two significantly different industries under the same roof. We contend that the boundaries that exist between the trade and finance teams of most countries administrations is to blame for the lack of convergence of the two disciplines. This dichotomy between trade and finance administrations is exemplified strikingly by the content of PTAs, whereby no reflections of the financial industry's evolution in terms of commitments or specific provisions are recorded.

Below, Table 2 sheds light on the comments pertinent to the subject matter of the study and later we discuss the way these comments explain the state of play of international clearing and settlement trade flows, as at the same time we attempt to interpret the relation between trade commitments and international finance.

Table 2 EIA Comments on Commitments in Clearing and Settlement Services

Country	EIA comments on commitments limiting liberalisation in clearing and settlement services	In EIAs with
Singapore	*Market Access and National Treatment*: (Mode 1): unbound, except for the provision of settlement and clearing services for financial assets which are listed on overseas exchanges only. (Mode 3): these measures are also limitations on *national treatment*. Settlement and clearing services for exchange traded securities and financial futures can only be provided by Central Depository (Pte) Limited and Singapore Exchange Derivatives Clearing Ltd (SGX-DT) respectively. Only one clearing house established under the Banking Act may provide clearing services for Singapore dollar cheques and inter-bank fund transfer.	AESEAN – Australia – New Zealand, AESEAN – China, AESEAN – India, AESEAN – Korea, China, EFTA, GCC, India, Japan, Jordan, Korea, New Zealand, Panama, Peru, Chinese Taipei and US

(continued)

Table 2 *(Continued)*

Country	EIA comments on commitments limiting liberalisation in clearing and settlement services	In EIAs with
Singapore	*Market Access Reservation*: Singapore reserves the right to adopt or maintain any measure affecting the supply of clearing and settlement services for exchange traded securities, financial futures and interbank transfers. *National Treatment and Market Access Reservation*: Singapore reserves the right to adopt or maintain any measure in the form of subsidies or grants provided by Singapore in connection with the supply of any financial service involving what Singapore deems as systemically important financial markets infrastructure, including: (a) exchanges; (b) central depositories; (c) repositories; (d) clearing and settlement facilities; and (e) market operators.	Australia
Cambodia	*Market Access*: (Mode 3): unbound until the Government of Cambodia determines what types of entities can conduct these services, the related laws and regulation are established, and such business is authorised by the government or other relevant designated authority.	AESEAN – India and AESEAN – Korea
Jordan	*Market Access*: (Mode 3): access restricted to the depository centre at the Amman Bourse for securities, and to the Central Bank of Jordan for all other financial instruments.	Singapore and US
Montenegro	*Market Access*: (Mode 3): this type of service may be provided by the central depository of scurities only	Ukraine
Bahrain	*Market Access*: (Mode 1): unbound, except for cross-listed equities that may be cleared on exchanges offering reciprocal privileges and that meet Bahrain information requirements. (Mode 3): unbound. Bahraini Dinar (BD) clearing must be through the Central Bank of Bahrain. Bahrain Stock Exchange listed equities and securities must be cleared through the BSE.	GCC – Singapore
Saudi Arabia	*Market Access and National Treatment*: (Modes 2 and 3): unbound for all domestic settlement and clearing services provided exclusively by Saudi Arabian Monetary Agency (SAMA) under 'j.' This also limits national treatment.	GCC – Singapore

(continued)

Table 2 *(Continued)*

Country	EIA comments on commitments limiting liberalisation in clearing and settlement services	In EIAs with
Romania	*Market Access*: (Mode 1): unbound for financial leasing, for trading of money market instruments, foreign exchange, derivative products, exchange rate and interest rate instruments, transferable securities and other negotiable instruments and financial assets, for participation in issues of all kinds of securities, for asset management and for settlement and clearing services for financial assets. Payments and money transmission services are allowed only through a resident bank.	EU – Ukraine, EU – Moldova, EU – Korea, EU – Georgia, EU – Colombia – Peru – Ecuador, EU – Colombia – Peru, EUCentral America and EU – CARIFORUM
Croatia	*Market Access*: (Mode 3): none, except for settlement and clearing services where the Central Depositary Agency (CDA) is the sole supplier in Croatia. Access to the services of the CDA will be granted to non-residents on a non-discriminatory basis.	EU – Ukraine and EU– Colombia – Peru – Ecuador
Italy	*Market Access*: (Mode 3): clearing and settlement of securities may be conducted only by the official clearing system. A company authorised by the Bank of Italy in agreement with Consob could be entrusted with the activity of clearing, up to the final settlement of securities.	EU – Mexico
Italy	*Market Access*: (Mode 3): clearing services including the phase of final settlement may be conducted only by entities duly authorised and supervised by the Bank of Italy in agreement with Consob.	EU – Chile
Honduras	*Market Access*: (Mode 3): depositories for the custody, compensation and liquidation of shares in Honduras must be constituted as public corporations.	CAFTA – DR
Dominican Republic	*Market Access:* (Mode 3): the following entities must be incorporated under the laws of the Dominican Republic: (a) stock exchanges; (b) commodities exchanges; (c) brokers; (d) dealers; (e) clearing houses; (f) centralised depositories of securities; (g) investment fund managers; and (h) securities underwriters.	CAFTA– DR

(continued)

Table 2 *(Continued)*

Country	EIA comments on commitments limiting liberalisation in clearing and settlement services	In EIAs with
Chile	*Market Access:* (Mode 3): clearing houses for futures contracts and options on securities must be constituted in Chile as corporations for that sole purpose and with an authorisation from the Superintendencia de Valores y Seguros (SVS). They may only be constituted by stock exchanges and their stockbrokers.	Japan, Thailand, EU, Hong Kong and Pacific Alliance
Chile	*Market Access:* (Mode 3): clearing houses of futures, options and other contracts of similar nature that the SVS may authorise, must be established as special purpose corporations (sociedades anónimas especiales) under Chilean law. Only stock exchanges established in Chile and stock brokers who are members of those exchanges can be shareholders of clearing houses. Clearing houses of futures and options on cattle and agricultural commodities must be established as special purpose corporations (sociedades anónimas especiales) under Chilean law.	Australia and US
Korea, Republic of	*Market Access*: only the Korea Securities Depository and the Korea Exchange may perform liquidation and settlement of securities and derivatives listed or traded on the Korea Exchange.	Australia and US

Source: Own analysis, WTO RTA database.

The comments attached to the commitments on financial assets' clearing and settlement services can serve as a good indicator of how the trade negotiating teams of some states understand this sector of high relevance for the integrity of international financial systems. In addition, while identifying some patterns in the process for entering commitments in EIAs, the study indicates that the existing boundaries between financial regulators and trade negotiators do not facilitate their much-needed interaction. Specifically, the absence of such interaction is at odds with the liberalisation of financial services and the promotion of international competition. Let us first review the prevalent trends before we commence the discussion on their implications in the transnational regulatory framework.

First, the common denominator for Singapore, in all the EIAs it has concluded, alongside the Republic of Korea, in its preferential agreements with Australia and the US, Bahrain and Saudi Arabia, in their commitments under GCC – Singapore, is that they all limit market access of clearing and settlement services for domestically listed securities.[20] The clear-cut rationale behind this barrier to trade is none other than financial stability considerations. The economy's financial integrity constitutes an overarching priority for regulators. Especially in the wake of the 2008 global financial crisis, States have ostensibly paid much attention to restructuring their regulatory architecture in ways that can potentially address perilous scenarios. The services provided by clearinghouses for OTC derivatives have been at the forefront of financial rulebooks' revisions, to mitigate the systemic risks involved in these transactions. Nonetheless, financial stability considerations are not only met in the context of financial regulatory standards and supervisory boards' list of priorities; they are additionally encountered in the GATS Annex on Financial Services,[21] and in most of the concluded EIAs.[22] The prudential exemption embedded in trade agreements is designed to offer to regulators all the regulatory space they need to address situations of emerging financial instability, while filtering whether the 'corresponding measures' are fit for the purpose, without providing for unnecessary trade barriers. The next paragraph attempts to appraise to what extent the limitation met at the abovementioned EIAs' commitments can be justified under financial stability considerations. This is of particular relevance as states enjoy wide discretion in entering their services commitments, following the model developed in the GATS era.

The recent crisis illustrated the interconnectedness of national financial markets, which was evidenced by the proliferation effects of securitised financial instruments in derivative markets around the world.[23] Clearing and settlement are the so-called 'back-office' services which are designed to support the trading of financial instruments. The whole business of financial market infrastructure is international in nature because it mirrors the way financial market transactions occur in parallel to the operations of multinational financial institutions.

[20] For instance, the Republic of Korea in its EIA with the US states that: 'only the Korea Securities Depository and the Korea Exchange may perform liquidation and settlement of securities and derivatives listed or traded on the Korea Exchange'. And Singapore, for the provision of cross-border (mode 1) services, always mandates that the services are: 'unbound except for the provision of settlement and clearing services for financial assets which are listed on overseas exchanges only'.

[21] For thorough analysis of the role of the GATS prudential carve-out, see above Chapters 2 and 3.

[22] For an empirical approach and a comprehensive analysis of the role of the PCO in EIAs, and its negotiating history in the GATS see CM Cantore, *The Prudential Carve-out for Financial Services: Rationale and Practice in the GATS and Preferential Trade Agreements* (Cambridge, Cambridge University Press, 2018) 102–67.

[23] For a great narrative of the unfolding of the crisis, see M Lewis, *The Big Short: Inside the Doomsday Machine* (London, Penguin Books, 2011). *cf* J Crotty, 'Structural Causes of the Global Financial Crisis: A Critical Assessment of the "New Financial Architecture"' (2009) 33 *Cambridge Journal of Economics* 563; S Claessens et al, 'Lessons and Policy Implications from the Global Financial Crisis' [2010] IMF Working Paper No 2010/044; RJ Shiller, *The Subprime Solution: How Today's Global Financial Crisis Happened, and What to Do about It* (Princeton, Princeton University Press, 2012).

Additionally, it should be clarified that, especially after the regulatory overhaul based on the G20 mandate, international competition for the clearing of OTC derivatives is omnipresent. However, foreign competition in clearing services is contingent upon equivalence or substituted compliance regimes,[24] whereby a state can test whether the rules of other states and the supervision and enforcement of clearinghouses are on the same page as their own. Hence, one observation that can be made at the outset about the limitation of clearing and settlement of home listed securities from foreign entities is that it does not encourage competition in the respective sectors. The conundrum in striking the right balance between financial stability and competition in financial services is not yet resolved,[25] and accordingly there is no established path along which states may steer their national regulatory policies.

Additionally, these services sectors have been traditionally subject to monopolistic competition structures, and only within the most recent decades has competition started to emerge in certain states. Another observation to be made is that the countries that decide to have their home listed securities cleared and settled within their own jurisdiction do so on the premise that the integrity of their capital markets would not be affected by possible malfunction of a foreign financial institution. This rationale seems absolutely legitimate and in line with the prudential carve-out provision embedded not only in the GATS, but also in most of the EIAs examined here. Nevertheless, financial instruments' clearing and settlement from foreign service suppliers, which currently becomes increasingly relevant, does not seem to pose any systemic stability problem, as long as the institutions themselves are robust and well managed. The shift to international competition in the relevant financial market infrastructure services, such as clearing and settlement, is gradual.[26] Nonetheless, liberalisation in the sector does not seem to pose any risk for the integrity of financial markets.[27]

Moreover, it is worth examining one of the reservations that Singapore listed in its EIA with Australia, which was signed and entered into force in 2003, because it brings into the spotlight the discourse between competition and

[24] For an analysis of the EU/US financial regimes see Y Yadav and D Turing, 'The Extraterritorial Regulation of Clearinghouses' (2016) 2 *Journal of Financial Regulation* 21. For the interaction between financial regulation and WTO law, see Papaconstantinou (n 15) 1–23.

[25] See, respectively, for example, contributions in economics and law literature addressing the intense relation between financial stability and competition: X Vives, *Competition and Stability in Banking* (Princeton, Princeton University Press, 2016); B De Meester, *Liberalization of Trade in Banking Services: An International and European Perspective* (Cambridge, Cambridge University Press, 2014).

[26] For example the US Intercontinental group (ICE) started operating a clearing house in Europe in 2014: see P Stafford, 'ICE Clear Europe Wins European CDS Approval' (*Financial Times*, 14 April 2014) www.ft.com/content/09a08298-c3f6-11e3-870b-00144feabdc0 accessed 25 July 2023.

[27] However, it should be clarified that even if liberalisation, in the sense of international trade flows, does not pose any perils to financial systems, problems could potentially arise due to the way industries evolve and the way regulatory frameworks adapt (or not). Examples pertinent to clearing are the absence both in the US and in the EU of resolution mechanisms of central counterparties (also called derivatives clearing organisations (DCOs) on the other side of the water).

stability in financial services: Singapore reserves the right to adopt or maintain any measure in the form of subsidies or grants it provides in connection with the supply of any financial service involving what Singapore deems as systemically important financial markets infrastructure, including: (a) exchanges; (b) central depositories; (c) repositories; (d) clearing and settlement facilities; and (e) market operators. This national treatment and market access reservation circumscribes possible subsidies measures destined for systemically important financial institutions (SIFIs). The reservation thereto seems to be prophetic in a number of ways. At first sight, it should be explored whether the potential provision of subsidies to SIFIs in the absence of the national treatment discipline would give rise to any MFN issues. The answer relies heavily on whether the SIFIs would be from Singapore or not. In the former case, no MFN issue seems to arise, while in the latter an assessment of the requirements of the MFN provision in the respective EIA would be warranted. Further, this reservation captures what happened in the banking sectors of Europe and the US, as a response to the 2008 crisis vicious cycle when banks had to be rescued with public money (taxpayers' contributions). These regulatory options are not prima facie consistent with the rules of international economic law and domestic EU competition law,[28] and thus, this reservation explicitly provides for the necessary latitude to Singaporean authorities. Furthermore, it highlights the systemic importance of financial market infrastructure, something that today more than ever is true for the functioning of clearinghouses and their international trade-flows.

In the aftermath of the 2008 crisis, no WTO law litigation arose with regard to states' support of the banking industry. Nevertheless, one may wonder to what degree these bailout practices, both in the EU and the US, distorted competition in relevant markets, encouraged good practices, and promoted national champions. Such a discourse is all the more relevant today, after Credit Suisse's demise.[29] The discussion over banks' bailouts exceeds the scope of this book, but it suffices to say that the considerations that led to such course of action involved the extent to which market failures of international financial institutions could result in negative externalities for domestic financial systems, in addition to those institutions' role in buying and holding sovereign debt. In the same vein, what

[28] For a contribution that examines the role of injecting capital into the banking sector of the EU and the law of the WTO, see B De Meester, 'The Global Financial Crisis and Government Support for Banks: What Role for the GATS?' (2010) 13 *Journal of International Economic Law* 27.

[29] In March 2023, Swiss authorities engineered a deal under which UBS agreed to buy Credit Suisse following the latter's collapse. This resulted in a merger of Switzerland's largest banks. For a narrative of Credit Suisse's demise, see G Steer, 'The Inside Story of Credit Suisse's Collapse, by Credit Suisse' (*Financial Times*, 24 April 2023) www.ft.com/content/857567b8-775c-496a-8578-c7b6419c9c96 accessed 25 July 2023. Reportedly, a case against Switzerland might be lodged by Singaporean investors under the Singapore –European Free Trade Agreement. Those investors' Credit Suisse AT1 bonds' were written down as the result of a decision by the Swiss government. For more information, see M Ruehl, 'Singapore Bondholders Prepare to Sue Switzerland over Credit Suisse' (*Financial Times*, 20 April 2023) www.ft.com/content/438fa6de-92f8-4d41-a169-c7e9ecada1bd accessed 25 July 2023.

is special about Singapore's reservation is that it caters for a treaty provision in a trade agreement that reflects on the considerations of the financial industry and the state itself, while the majority of WTO Members when concluding trade agreements tend to overlook financial services' intricacies. This reservation does not solely rely on the existence of the PCO for rainy days. It, rather, represents a well considered expression of domestic protection from third countries' judicial scrutiny in the case of turmoil in Singapore's domestic financial market infrastructure. Thus Singapore, with this reservation, sets a good precedent on meaningful considerations of financial services included in EIAs, regardless the possible anticompetitive effects of such provision.

Not surprisingly, it is impossible to foresee all the potential competition and stability evolutions of the financial services industry. Nonetheless, states should at least strive to explain and communicate to their trade delegations all the issues of relevance for international trade and accordingly support them in the challenging task of liberalising these markets through international agreements. Therefore, the Singaporean reservation at issue, although potentially trade-restrictive, constitutes a great example of interaction between the trade and finance teams of its government and attempts to strike a fair balance between competition and stability in an international trade agreement.

C. EIAs not Regulating Trade in Securities Clearing and Settlement Services and International Finance

The forthcoming analysis sheds light on the EIAs that do not promulgate the liberalisation of financial services, and explores the underlying reasons behind this approach. To address this issue, a review of the EIAs' legal texts, as well as political economy considerations is required. The clearing and settlement of securities is a part of the broader realm of financial services, and that is why this study is necessary before we delve into their specific commitments undertaken for this services sector. In terms of sheer numbers, out of the 152 preferential trade agreements notified to the WTO, 37 either do not capture trade in financial services at all, or even if they do, their commitments are set out *in abstracto*, either in the form of future rounds of negotiations or in vague or weak commitments that do not even rise to the WTO threshold. This exercise can serve as a useful guide to highlight the parts of the world that do not seem to be eager proponents of financial services integration, and to provide explanations for why this is the case, while underscoring some observed patterns on the basis of the collected data. Additionally, trade agreements are not only about the promotion of economic interests; political considerations and zones of influence also play a major role in their conclusion. First, Table 3 records the 37 EIAs that are observed not to be financial services liberalisation proponents, with the legal justification traced in the content of these trade treaties. Following this, an analysis that underscores and elaborates on the most important aspects is developed.

Table 3 EIAs Excluding Financial Services

EIA	Entry into force	Provisions that exclude financial services from the scope of the EIA
Canada – Chile	5 Jul 97	Pursuant to Articles G-01(2) and H-01(2)(a), the Agreement does not cover trade in financial services for either investment purposes or cross-border supply, respectively.
Chile – China	1 Aug 10	Pursuant to Article 2(a) of the Supplementary Agreement on Trade in Services, financial services are not covered by the scope of the Free Trade Agreement between Chile and China.
Chile – Colombia	8 May 09	Pursuant to Articles 9.1(4) and 10.1(4)(a) the Agreement does not cover financial services for either investment or cross-border supply, respectively.
Chile – Costa Rica	15 Feb 02	Pursuant to Article 11.02(3)(d) of the Agreement, financial services are not covered by the scope of the Free Trade Agreement.
Chile – El Salvador	1 Jun 02	Pursuant to Article 11.02(3)(d) of the Agreement, financial services are not covered by the scope of the Free Trade Agreement.
Chile – Guatemala	23 Mar 10	Pursuant to Article 11.02(3)(d) of the Agreement, financial services are not covered by the scope of the Free Trade Agreement.
Chile – Honduras	19 Jul 08	Pursuant to Article 11.02(3)(d) of the Agreement, financial services are not covered by the scope of the Free Trade Agreement.
Chile – Mexico	1 Aug 99	Pursuant to Articles 9-02(3) and 10-02(3)(a), the Agreement does not cover financial services for either investment or cross-border supply, respectively.
Chile – Nicaragua	19 Oct 12	Pursuant to Article 11.02(3)(d) of the Agreement, financial services are not covered by the scope of the Free Trade Agreement.
China – Costa Rica	1 Aug 11	Pursuant to Article 91(3)(e), the Agreement does not cover financial services.
China – Hong Kong, China	29 Jun 03	This Closer Economic Partnership, although regulating financial services, is not comprehensive and its trade disciplines are not fully developed. When it comes to MA it is absent from the Agreement text and it is not implicitly existent in either commercial presence (only NT & MFN) or cross-border supply, which is three lines about further liberalisation discussions.

(continued)

Table 3 *(Continued)*

EIA	Entry into force	Provisions that exclude financial services from the scope of the EIA
China – Macao, China	13 Oct 03	This Closer Economic Partnership, although regulating financial services, is not comprehensive and its trade disciplines are not fully developed. When it comes to MA it is absent from the Agreement text and it is not implicitly existent in either commercial presence (only NT & MFN) or cross-border supply, which is three lines about further liberalisation discussions.
Colombia – Mexico	1 Jan 95	The Parties, according to Articles 12–15, shall submit their reservations to FS sectors. [NB: this has not yet happened at the last date of checking (25 July 2023)]
Colombia – Northern Triangle (El Salvador, Guatemala, Honduras)	12 Nov 09	Pursuant to Articles 12.2(5) and 13.2(4)(a), the Agreement does not cover financial services for either investment or cross-border supply, respectively.
Costa Rica – Peru	1 Jun 13	Pursuant to Articles 12.1(8) and 13.1(8), the Agreement does not cover financial services for either investment or cross-border supply, respectively.
Costa Rica – Singapore	1 Jul 13	Pursuant to Articles 11(3) and 10.2(7), the Agreement does not cover financial services for either investment or cross-border supply, respectively.
EFTA – Chile	1 Dec 04	Pursuant to Article 45 of the Agreement, no commitments have been undertaken by the Parties in relation to trade in financial services.
El Salvador – Honduras – Chinese Taipei	1 Mar 08	Pursuant to Articles 10.02(2)(a) and 11.02(3)(d), the Agreement does not cover financial services for either investment or cross-border supply, respectively.
EU – Albania	1 Apr 09	Financial services are covered by the scope of the Stabilization and Association Agreement to the extent that progressive liberalisation between the Parties shall occur in the coming years. MFN treatment is only explicitly extended for mode 3 of trade in services. There are no concrete MA and NT commitments, and that is reaffirmed by the absence of Schedules.

(continued)

Table 3 *(Continued)*

EIA	Entry into force	Provisions that exclude financial services from the scope of the EIA
EU – Bosnia Herzegovina	1 Jun 15	Financial services are covered by the scope of the Stabilization and Association Agreement to the extent that progressive liberalisation between the Parties shall occur in the coming years. MFN treatment is only explicitly extended for mode 3 of trade in services. There are no concrete MA and NT commitments, and that is reaffirmed by the absence of Schedules.
EU – Montenegro	1 May 10	Financial services are covered by the scope of the Stabilization and Association Agreement to the extent that progressive liberalisation between the Parties shall occur in the coming years. MFN treatment is only explicitly extended for mode 3 of trade in services. There are no concrete MA and NT commitments, and that is reaffirmed by the absence of Schedules.
EU – Serbia	1 Sep 13	Financial services are covered by the scope of the Stabilization and Association Agreement to the extent that progressive liberalisation between the Parties shall occur in the coming years. MFN treatment is only explicitly extended for mode 3 of trade in services. There are no concrete MA and NT commitments, and that is reaffirmed by the absence of Schedules.
EU – FYROM	1 Apr 04	Financial services are covered by the scope of the Stabilization and Association Agreement to the extent that progressive liberalisation between the Parties shall occur in the coming years. MFN treatment is only explicitly extended for mode 3 of trade in services. There are no concrete MA and NT commitments, and that is reaffirmed by the absence of Schedules.
Guatemala – Chinese Taipei	1 Jul 06	Pursuant to Articles 10.02(2)(a) and 11.02(3)(d) the Agreement does not cover financial services for either investment or cross-border supply, respectively.
Korea, Republic of – Colombia	15 Jul 16	Pursuant to Articles 8.1(4) and 9.1(4)(a), the Agreement does not cover trade in financial services for either investment purposes or cross-border supply, respectively.
Korea, Republic of – Chile	1 Apr 04	Pursuant to Articles 10.2(3)(a) and 11.2(3)(a), the Agreement does not cover trade in financial services for either investment purposes or cross-border supply, respectively.

(continued)

Table 3 *(Continued)*

EIA	Entry into force	Provisions that exclude financial services from the scope of the EIA
Korea, Republic of – New Zealand	20 Dec 15	Pursuant to Articles 10.3(4) and 8.3(3)(a), the Agreement does not cover trade in financial services for either investment purposes or cross-border supply, respectively.
Mexico – Central America	1 Sep 12	Pursuant to Articles 11.2(3)(a) and 12.2(2)(b), the Agreement does not cover trade in financial services for either investment purposes or cross-border supply, respectively.
Mexico – Uruguay	15 Jul 04	Pursuant to Articles 13–02(4) and 10-02(2)(a), the Agreement does not cover trade in financial services for either investment purposes or cross-border supply, respectively.
Panama – Chile	7 Mar 08	Pursuant to Article 10.1(3)(a), the Agreement does not cover financial services.
Peru – Chile	1 Mar 09	Pursuant to Articles 11.1(4)(a) and 12.1(3)(a), the Agreement does not cover trade in financial services for either investment purposes or cross-border supply, respectively.
Thailand – New Zealand	1 Jul 05	Pursuant to Article 8.1, trade in services is not captured by the scope of the current Agreement. Services trade is regulated by ASEAN – Australia – NZ.
Trans-Pacific Strategic Economic Partnership	28 May 06	Pursuant to Article 12.3(2)(a), the Agreement does not cover trade in financial services.
GUAM	10 Dec 03	Pursuant to Article 17 of the FTA, trade in services liberalisation is in a primary stage, and accordingly no specific commitments on financial services have been entered.
Iceland – Faroe Islands	1 Nov 06	No commitments have been entered for financial services, and it is unclear from the Treaty text whether trade in services is covered at all.
East African Community (EAC)	1 Jul 10	Neither in the Treaty for the establishment of the East African Community, nor in the Protocol for the establishment of the EAC Common Market, have commitments for financial services been entered, but rather proclamations for regulatory cooperation are set out.

(continued)

Table 3 *(Continued)*

EIA	Entry into force	Provisions that exclude financial services from the scope of the EIA
Dominican Republic – Central America	4 Oct 01	Although trade and investment in financial services is covered by the content of the FTA, no country has undertaken any commitments pursuant to the provisions of the Treaty, and following the wording of Article 10.15 future liberalisation is awaited. Due to CAFTA – DR agreement and the role of the US, this liberalisation has been achieved in the context of another agreement.

Source: Own analysis, WTO RTA database.

The content of Table 3 above illustrates those EIAs that do not regulate trade in financial services. To start with, the common denominator among these regional trade agreements is that their participating countries, on average, seem to be financial services net importers, rather than exporters. This means that since their financial industries do not have the capacity to export, and as a result generate revenues through trade in financial services, the inclusion of financial services chapters or commitments is hardly of any relevance to them. On the contrary, it can only hinder the course of the EIA negotiations. To substantiate this claim it suffices to show in the table that most of the parties to these EIAs are Latin American and Caribbean countries which, with the exception of Panama,[30] are not interested in exporting financial services, because of the nature of their economies.[31]

However, as demonstrated by Stephanou, trade in financial services liberalisation in EIAs is, inter alia, highly contingent upon the bargaining power of the parties to the agreement. The three well-known categories are: (i) the so-called 'North-South' EIAs, which refer to the agreements that are concluded between developing and developed countries; (ii) the 'South-South' EIAs, signed between developing countries; and (iii) the ones between developed countries, characterised as 'North-North'. Unsurprisingly, when it comes to the first category (North-South), due to the existing strong and asymmetric bargaining power between the concluding parties, it is observed that the liberalisation of financial

[30] Panama is an off-shore financial hub which constitutes an important financial services exporter, especially given its size. For general literature, see JL Moreno-Villalaz, 'Financial Integration and Dollarization: The Case of Panama' (2005) 25 *Cato Journal* 127.

[31] Specific studies have devoted their attention to how Latin American and Caribbean countries have liberalised their financial services sectors, and how they have proceeded with the conclusion of EIAs. See, for example, MA Marconini, 'Services in Regional Agreements Between Latin American and Developed Countries' (2006) serie 71 *Comercio Internacional*; MP Goncalves and C Stephanou, 'Financial Services and Trade Agreements in Latin America and the Caribbean: An Overview' (2007) 4181 *World Bank Policy Research Working Paper*.

services is at the top of the agenda.[32] Conversely, states in the second category (South-South) do not seem to be concerned about capturing financial services, or liberalising them, although they are of vital importance for the growth and development of the contracting states. This pattern is predominantly evidenced in this study, and the content of Table 3: 21 EIAs between developing countries do not cover the trade in financial services, and Latin and Caribbean countries are the main participants.[33]

Consequently, it is clear that when developing countries conclude trade agreements with one another they do not necessarily include financial services, because it is not an area of special interest to their economies. The inclusion of financial services' sectors to their trade agreement does not contribute to their growth, while the negotiating costs would surge. It is efficient from their perspective to leave them out of their EIAs. Nonetheless, when developing states negotiate EIAs with 'North' states, then they are leveraged into the inclusion of financial services in the agreements. That comes as a natural consequence, since bigger and economically robust countries are more prone to exert pressure and achieve their goals in the conclusion of EIAs. As a result, the same 'South' states when they conclude trade agreements with 'North' states, not only include financial services in their agreements, but they tend to offer higher commitments than the ones entered in their GATS Schedule. The analysis that follows examines the 'depth' of the undertaken clearing and settlement services commitments in EIAs.

Before discussing this topic, it is intriguing to succinctly underline another trend observed in the absence of firm commitments on financial services in EIAs. The analysis so far examines trade agreements as contracts that reflect the rational economic behaviour of the participating states. This approach represents the general norm, but the existence of additional means and rationales that are not solely economic and according to which EIAs are designed and implemented should not be disregarded. An example of an alternative course of action is the EU in the EIAs concluded with Western Balkans, namely, Albania, Montenegro, North Macedonia, Serbia, and Bosnia and Herzegovina.[34] These

[32] This has been observed in the literature, especially with regard to the EIAs that the US and the EU have concluded, and it is brought into the spotlight empirically in the context of clearing and settlement commitments below.

[33] The 'South-South' EIAs that do not cover trade in financial services are the following: Chile – Colombia, Chile – Costa Rica, Chile – El Salvador, Chile – Guatemala, Chile – Honduras, Chile – Mexico, Chile – Nicaragua, Colombia – Mexico, Colombia – El Salvador – Guatemala – Honduras, Costa Rica – Peru, El Salvador – Chinese Taipei, Guatemala – Chinese Taipei, Mexico – Central America, Panama – Chile, Peru – Chile, GUAM, Iceland – Faroe Islands, Dominican Republic – Central America, East African Community (EAC), and Trans-Pacific Strategic Economic Partnership.

[34] These agreements fall under the Stabilization and Association Agreements that the EU concludes in order to promote peace, freedom, stability, and economic prosperity through trade to the region. For more information, see https://neighbourhood-enlargement.ec.europa.eu/enlargement-policy/glossary/stabilisation-and-association-agreement_en accessed 25 July 2023.

agreements regulate both trade in goods and in services, including financial services, but their primary goal is not to liberalise financial markets of Western Balkans and accrue the associated benefit of free trade, but to stabilise the region and encourage its economic growth.

Indeed, an analysis of the EU's position in the region demonstrates that the liberalisation of financial services is far from being one of the main EU priorities for the Western Balkans. As emphasised in the Thessaloniki European Council conclusions of 2003, that confirm the enlargement perspective of the Western Balkan countries, the EU's priorities in the area remain focused on stabilisation of the region and fulfilment of the political criteria for membership. Specifically, EU actions are primarily focused on building lasting peace and preserving good neighbourly relations in the region, as well as building resilient institutions, capable of upholding democracy, rule of law and fundamental rights.[35] These essential pre-conditions are first required before a credible commitment for any future liberalisation of financial services is extended.

Economic consideration criteria are also included in the Agreements, but they come largely at the second stage of integration, and serve mainly as conditional incentives for the above-mentioned political commitments.[36] Financial services are only partially covered by the Stabilization and Association Agreements. They are only liberalised for the purposes of MFN for mode 3.[37] The soft language in the text of the Agreements ('developing a suitable framework for the encouragement' of financial services[38]) reveals that there are many steps to be taken before firm commitments are undertaken for the financial services sectors. In particular, the liberalisation of financial services – in the sense of extending concrete commitments for cross-border supply (mode 1) and consumption abroad (mode 2) services – will only start as the second stage of the transition period of the services acquis chapters under these FTAs,[39] something that has not yet happened for any of the Western Balkan countries. In this respect, for instance, the Commission's Report on North Macedonia clearly indicates that the country's financial services sectors are moderately prepared for further integration with the EU,[40] a common reality for the whole region. Notably, problems such as weak regulatory systems, incomplete anti-money laundering frameworks and high risks of terrorist financing are commonly reported by the Commission.[41] Thus, further integration of the Western

[35] See Council of the European Union, Thessaloniki European Council of 19 and 20 June 2003, Presidency Conclusions, 1 October 2003, 11638/03.

[36] See, for example, Art 5 of the Stabilisation and Association Agreement between the EU and North Macedonia.

[37] ibid, Arts 49–51.

[38] ibid, Art 83(1).

[39] ibid, Art 55.

[40] See European Commission, North Macedonia 2019 Report (Staff Working Paper SWD(2019) 218 final, Brussels, 29 May 2019, 65–66.

[41] See European Commission, Communication on the EU Enlargement Policy SWD(2019) 260 final, Brussels, 29 May 2019, 4.

Balkan's financial systems with the EU would occur only once the essential pre-conditions are in place, which would in turn credibly guarantee the resilience and integrity of the EU financial markets.

Another facet of international trade is pertinent to establishing relations between states and promoting their peace and prosperity. The EU through these agreements does exactly that, and meanwhile it extends its geopolitical influence on the territories of the Western Balkans' contracting countries. These Stabilization and Association Agreements are not comprehensive in terms of the commitments inscribed for the liberalisation of financial services, but that is exactly because that is not the reason behind the conclusion of these treaties. By signing these treaties, the EU seeks to distribute the benefits of trade to these states, in order for them to grow economically while transacting with EU Member States. The next subsection starts to address how commitments on financial securities' clearing and settlement services are entered in preferential trade agreements. Specifically, the 'depth' of these commitments is investigated, using the ones undertaken under the GATS as the benchmark.

D. Clearing and Settlement Commitments in EIAs: The Countries that Lead the Way and the Playbook of International Dynamics for Financial Services

i. Aggregate Number of Clearing and Settlement Commitments in EIAs

We first investigate the mere number of clearing and settlement commitments that have been entered and received by WTO Members in the context of the unravelling effects of the exponential spike of regionalism. At the outset, this study illustrates the intentions of EIA parties to further integrate this particular financial services sector with their trading partners. The countries that are financial services net exporters, as shown in Figure 1 below, are the ones that strive for higher levels of trade in financial services liberalisation, through the preferential trade agreements they conclude. As a result, their trade policy agenda is oriented around the premise of acquiring commitments to that end. By receiving market access (MA), and national treatment (NT) commitments from their trade agreement partners, the principal challenges (in the form of qualitative and discretionary barriers to trade) that their home suppliers can encounter in providing financial services in the respective foreign markets are limited.

Next, after having set out the primary information collected in terms of clearing and settlement commitments,[42] a more detailed analysis proceeds

[42] Clearing and settlement commitments for the purpose of this figure amount to at least either a national treatment or a market access commitment of a party to an EIA for one of the three modes of supply (cross-border supply, consumption abroad, and commercial presence) that constitute the scope of this study.

which factors in the specific level of liberalisation observed in EIAs, using as benchmark the GATS standard at the multilateral trading field. Additionally, the international dynamics are put into context through a network analysis, whereby the countries with higher leverage are able to steer the behaviour of smaller countries into opening their financial services markets to international competition. Geographical and chronological observations come into play later on.

First, Figure 1 below depicts in an aggregate fashion the number of commitments for securities' clearing and settlement services that parties to EIAs have entered for their trading partners, and accordingly, have *received* from them.

Figure 1 Aggregate Clearing and Settlement Commitments in EIAs

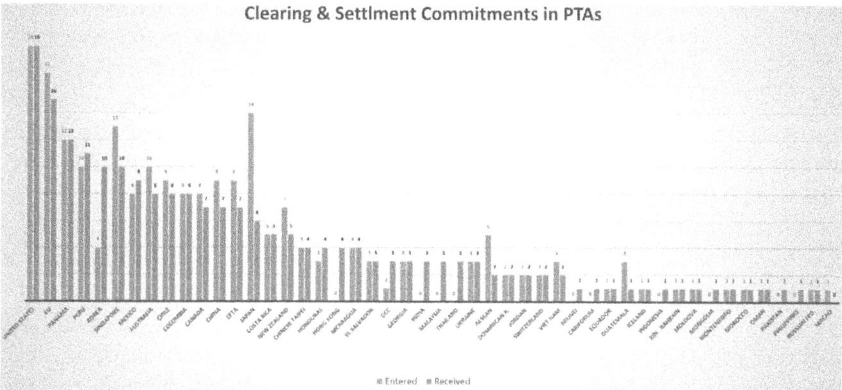

Source: Own analysis and computations based on WTO RTA database.

Figure 1 reveals that the countries that are the major financial services net exporters, such as the EU Member States, the US, Singapore, Switzerland and Hong Kong among others,[43] are the ones that have the tendency: (i) to provide for commitments in clearing and settlement services, since they have already very advanced financial industries, and they are not afraid of foreign competition; and accordingly (ii) to receive commitments on this service sector from their EIA partners.

[43] The data of International Trade Center (ITC), United Nations Conference on Trade and Development (UNCTAD) and WTO trade in services database on exports of financial services, computed on the basis of the balance of payments (BOPs), indicate that the countries that were the principal financial services exporters for 2021 were the US (approximately US$ 172 billion), the UK (approximately US$ 84 billion), Luxembourg (approximately US$ 77 billion), followed by Singapore, Germany, Ireland, Switzerland, Hong Kong, France, Netherlands, Japan, Canada and Belgium among others. For detailed data on the imports and exports of trade in financial services see ITC, 'List of Exporters for the Selected Service' (ITC) www.trademap.org/tradestat/Country_SelService_TS.aspx?nvpm=1|||||||S07|1|3|1|2|2|1|2|1| accessed 25 July 2023.

The US financial industry has been traditionally 'offensive' in acquiring access to its trading partners' jurisdictions, while having the bargaining power to leverage its own terms in trade agreements.[44] As the figure shows, the US comes first in the aggregate number of EIA commitments, having undertaken and received 19 commitments, followed by the EU, which has entered 17 commitments on clearing and settlement services, and has received 15. Panama, Singapore, and Australia are also high on the list. The analysis that follows in subsection ii, investigates the specific commitments and their intrinsic characteristics.[45]

To embark on explaining Figure 1, the observations have to be examined in parallel with the simple fact that economically robust countries and big regional powers – such as the US and the EU respectively – have concluded the highest number of preferential trade agreements. Thus, since they have been parties to numerous economic integration agreements, it is not surprising that these developed economies have acquired a high number of commitments on securities' clearing and settlement services. However, it should be highlighted that out of the 152 EIAs on services, only 100 comprise commitments on clearing and settlement services. Consequently, the fact that these countries have participated in many EIAs is a crucial indicator but it is not self-evident that their trading partners will liberalise their financial services sectors. At the same time, it should not be disregarded that the parties to EIAs cannot be forced to enter commitments on financial services in their EIAs, but rather trade negotiations tend to play a tit-for-tat game.

To gain a better understanding of the reasons why WTO Members and parties to EIAs negotiate and conclude international trade agreements, it is imperative to realise what triggers them to be at the negotiating table in the first place. One of the dominant answers is their belief in the benefits of free trade. Free trade, first, urges economic actors to seek and exploit their comparative advantage.[46] Subsequently, free trade opens markets and incentivises

[44] For a narrative of the liberalisation of financial services and the role of the industry, see CZ Wagner, 'The New WTO Agreement on Financial Services and Chapter 14 of NAFTA: Has Free Trade in Banking Finally Arrived' (1999) 5 *NAFTA: Law and Business Review of the Americas* 5, 5.

[45] Since commitments can differ significantly from one another, the analysis below specifically examines the type of commitments that have been undertaken in the realm of preferential trade agreements, and measures their legal trade-liberalising traits.

[46] The theory of the comparative advantage was conceptualised for the first time at the beginning of the nineteenth century by a British political economist: see D Ricardo, *Principles of Political Economy and Taxation* (London, G Bell and Sons, 1891). More recently, the traditional economic approach to trade agreements has been criticised due to its unrealistic hypothesis on governments' national welfare maximisation. For the modern account, so called political-economy approach, that factors in the distributional consequences of trade policies, including rent-seeking, see RE Baldwin, *The Political Economy of US Import Policy* (Cambridge, MIT Press, 1985); K Bagwell and RW Staiger, 'An Economic Theory of GATT' (1999) 89 *American Economic Review* 215; K Bagwell and RW Staiger, 'Reciprocity, Non-Discrimination and Preferential Agreements in the Multilateral Trading System' (2001) 17 *European Journal of Political Economy* 281. See also, for a comprehensive account of the economic theories behind trade, K Bagwell and RW Staiger, *The Economics of the World Trading System* (Cambridge, MIT Press, 2002) 13–42.

firms to be more productive and innovative in order to acquire a better share of the expanded pie; this comes with more competition at the international level. In addition to these economic rationales, it is also free trade that grants peace and prosperity to the nations that play by its rules, as the EU experiment has proven since the end of World War II. These general benefits of free trade happen to materialise in tangible commitments when it comes to trade in services agreements, either in the context of the WTO or preferential trade agreements.[47]

The general principle is that since countries care to boost their economic growth they are prone to negotiate trade agreements that are suitable for allowing them to export the goods or services sectors in which they have a comparative advantage. For countries to acquire market access to the sectors they wish, they have to offer for something in return. Most of the time, they have to provide for favourable treatment to the contracting parties' areas of interest. For a trade agreement hypothetical, assuming that Country X has a very strong financial services industry, that represents 13 per cent of its GDP, while Country Y's economy is largely based on tourism, a win-win deal would be for Countries X and Y to negotiate a trade agreement that would open the financial services market of Y to the service providers of X, and at the same time would incentivise tourism trade-flows towards Y. On that premise, trade negotiations are carried out, but on some occasions it is not only rational economic thinking that dictates the terms of negotiations, but also the influence that big countries exert over smaller ones.

That has traditionally been the case for trade in financial services, since the first time they were regulated multilaterally under the GATS. The US financial industry lobbied for that to increase its share of the pie, and WTO Members followed up for their own reasons. For the purposes of this book, it is essential to realise who are the main players in the international financial services arena, in order to develop a comprehensive analysis of the clearing and settlement services in EIAs in the first place, and to proceed by assessing how these countries conclude their EIAs, and under which terms and conditions. By now, it is clear that it is the EU and the US who internationally pull the strings of financial liberalisation,[48] and it is this study's mission to witness how this trend is effectuated in the context of the financial service in question in EIAs. Accordingly,

[47] For a contribution that captures the intricacies and particularities of services trade and its negotiations see B Hoekman and A Mattoo, 'Services Trade and Growth' (2008) 4461 Policy Research Working Paper; JA Marchetti, 'Financial Services Liberalization in the WTO and PTAs' in JA Marchetti and M Roy (eds), *Opening Markets for Trade in Services, Countries and Sectors in Bilateral and WTO Negotiations* (Cambridge, Cambridge University Press, 2009).

[48] The difference between financial liberalisation and the liberalisation of financial services lies in the fact that the first constitutes the broader category and the second is a subset of it. On the one hand, financial liberalisation refers to the elimination of distortions in domestic financial systems which impede the efficient allocation of capital and the functioning of competition. On the other, the liberalisation of financial services, as has been demonstrated in this chapter, pertains to the

the analysis proceeds by measuring the 'depth' of liberalisation on clearing and settlement services in EIAs, and furthermore, scrutinises the state of play of the EIAs that the US and the EU have concluded.

ii. Measuring the Depth of Clearing and Settlement Commitments in EIAs

The objective of this subsection is to shed light on the depth of the undertaken commitments on financial securities' clearing and settlement services in preferential trade agreements, and at the same time investigate the driving factors and relevant parameters that are of importance in that endeavour. At the outset, this study denotes, as described above, the level of liberalisation on the basis of the status quo of WTO Members at the multilateral trading system, namely WTO Members' GATS commitments. Specifically: (i) GATS, where the level of liberalisation is the same as in the Members' GATS Schedule; (ii) GATS plus, where the Member provides for commitments in addition to its GATS Schedule; and (iii) GATS extra, where the Member enters commitments for clearing and settlement services for the first time in EIAs. Categories (ii) and (iii) are together compounded as GATS+, for the sake of simplicity as the analysis of this empirical study unfolds. As a first step, Figure 2 sets out the whole aggregate clearing and settlement services commitments in EIAs, which are 226 in total, charted in the *y* axis of time. This chronological illustration indicates whether the depth of liberalisation (either at the same level as in the WTO (GATS) or going beyond (GATS+)) evolves. The value of this graph lies in offering a holistic view of the way commitments in this financial services sector are entered in international trade and investment agreements over time.

Figure 2 Level of Liberalisation of Clearing and Settlement Commitments in EIAs over Time

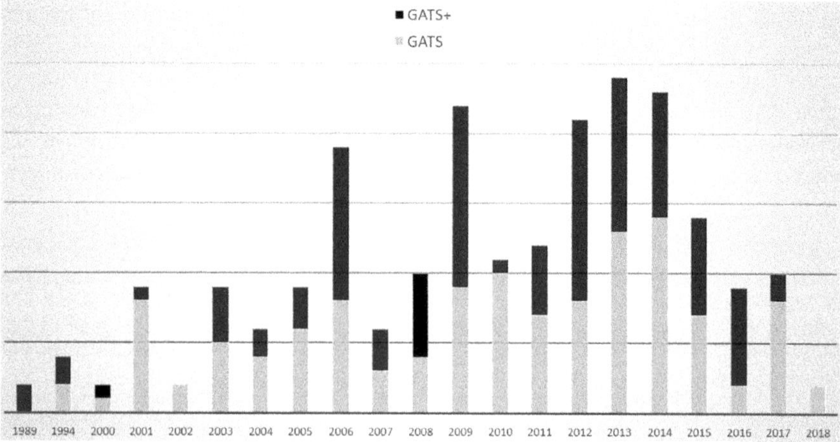

Source: Own analysis and computations based on WTO RTA database.

To interpret this figure accurately, it is imperative to understand first that out of the total number of commitments entered in EIAs for clearing and settlement services, half of them have adopted the GATS standard, whereas the other half has exceeded the GATS threshold.[49] What can also be discerned by the bars of the graph is that, although in general there is an equilibrium between the GATS and the GATS+ commitments over the years, in 2006, 2009, 2012, and 2016 higher level of liberalisation for clearing and settlement services has been effectuated in EIAs. It is extremely difficult to distinguish the determinants that drive these EIAs' GATS+ commitments, but the analysis proceeds by tracing the route these commitments follow, in order to reveal which countries open their clearing and settlement markets at first and, as a second consideration, to whom through the conclusion of the economic integration agreements.

Subsequently, the empirical analysis focuses on the GATS+ commitments on financial securities' clearing and settlement services in international trade treaties. By exclusively examining this set of commitments it is easier to discern the factors that result in furthering the liberalisation of financial services. To that end, the EIAs that liberalise clearing and settlement services beyond the GATS threshold are put under the microscope, Figures 3 and 4 set out the route that these commitments follow, and ultimately, their intrinsic characteristics are investigated below. Pursuing the objective of delineating which are the contributing factors in the liberalisation of clearing and settlement services, Figures 3 and 4 underscore which are the countries that enter GATS+ commitments in EIAs, and which are the states that reap the benefits of this liberalisation, respectively.

Figures 3 and 4 are very intuitive because they demonstrate the state of play of the liberalisation of clearing and settlement services in economic integration agreements. Essentially these two graphs show how GATS+ commitments on the services in question are distributed in EIAs. They explicitly indicate which countries are the net contributors and which are the net beneficiaries.

elimination of quantitative restrictions in the access of foreign financial services suppliers, in the form of the principle of market access, and to the elimination of discriminatory treatment through the national treatment principle. For literature on financial liberalisation see, for example, BR Johnston, 'Sequencing Capital Account Liberalizations and Financial Sector Reform' (1998) 98 IMF Paper on Policy Analysis and Assessment; S Claessens and M Jansen, *The Internationalization of Financial Services: Issues and Lessons for Developing Countries* (Heidelberg, Springer Netherlands, 2000); GL Kaminsky and SL Schmukler, 'Short-Run Pain, Long-Run Gain: The Effects of Financial Liberalization' [2003] IMF Working Paper No 2003/034; GL Kaminsky and SL Schmukler, 'Short-Run Pain, Long-Run Gain: The Effects of Financial Liberalization' [2003] NBER Working Paper 9787.

[49] To be precise, computations based on the WTO RTA database reveal that 54.42%, until 23 May 2018, have used their GATS level of liberalisation for financial securities' clearing and settlement services, whereas 45.58% have opted for deeper liberalisation in the services sector in question. It should be reiterated that the figures here represent the commitments that provide for this services liberalisation in EIAs, and not the ones that do not ('unbound' for example), although this lack of commitment would represent the same level of liberalisation as the one inscribed in some countries' GATS Schedules.

Figure 3 WTO Members Entering GATS+ Clearing and Settlement Commitments in EIAs

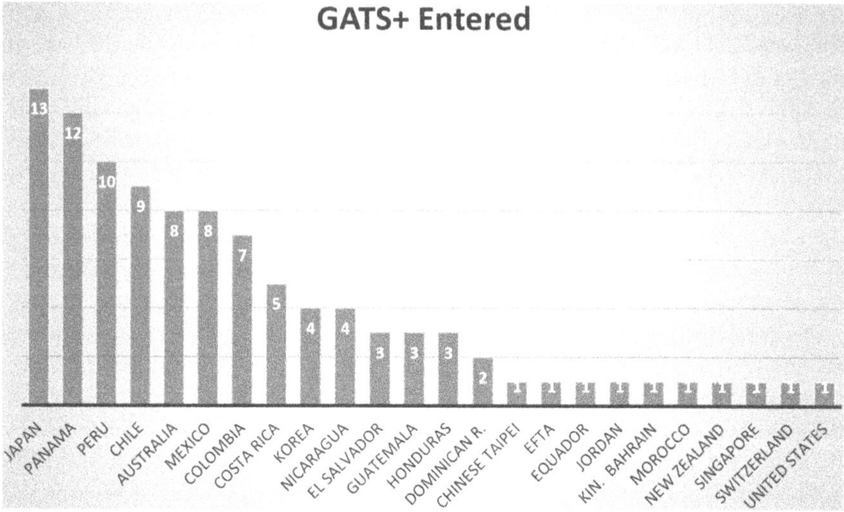

Figure 4 WTO Members Receiving GATS+ Clearing and Settlement Commitments in EIAs

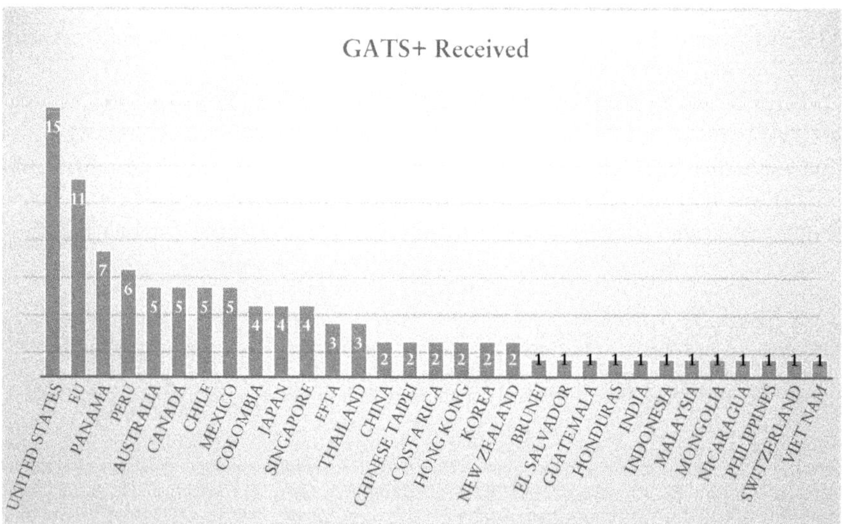

Source: Own analysis and computations based on WTO RTA database.

The results speak for themselves, but in this volume we try to contextualise these liberalisation features, in order to make some sense out of them. The analysis first touches on the issues pertinent to the WTO Members that liberalise their financial services, in addition to the GATS status quo.

To understand what goes beyond the GATS it is essential to understand first that the legal architecture of trade in services at the WTO is inherently asymmetric. This comes as the result of the political compromise that WTO Members struck during the Uruguay Round in order to incorporate the regulation of trade in services into the text of the Marrakesh Agreements.[50] Trade in services – unlike trade in goods, which is easier to engage in for developing economies – requires high levels of expertise and is not inclusive in terms of the capacities that states and their industries have to achieve growth through its mechanics. By default, advanced economies have a comparative advantage in trading services. To compensate for that and for the developing states to be persuaded in a consensus at the multilateral trading system, the provisions under the title 'Commitments' had to be introduced. These commitments allow WTO Members to provide for progressive liberalisation to their services sectors, through market access and national treatment principally, as they please. Consequently, referring to the GATS asymmetric architecture means that each WTO Member has defined its own depth of liberalisation in its GATS Schedule of Commitments, and as a result there is no homogeneity. This context accentuates the fact that not all countries share the same starting point in liberalising their services' sectors in the GATS, and financial services are no exception to the rule.

When it comes to EIAs, the same principle applies with the difference that the liberalisation attained under these agreements does not extend to all WTO Members, but only to the ones that are parties to the specific preferential trade agreement, which is in accordance with the GATS, Article V.[51] The rationale of this provision is to encourage further liberalisation of services, even this integration extends its benefits only to parts of the WTO system, assuming the conditions of the GATS Article V are fulfilled. For the purposes of this study, it should be mentioned that the existence of the GATS' immense discretion in scheduling commitments has produced divergences in the liberalisation of services among WTO Members. As a result, some countries have far more ground to cover to reach the levels of other countries. Additionally, financial services is a sector that traditionally protectionist policies are attached to, and clearing and settlement services do not seem to deviate from this pattern.

Not surprisingly, the vast majority of WTO Members that go deeper than their GATS commitments on securities' clearing and settlement services while concluding EIAs are developing states, such as Panama, Peru, Chile, Colombia, Costa Rica etc. This can partially be explained by the fact that these states have lots of ground to cover to liberalise their financial market infrastructure to the levels of developed WTO Members. This divergence on

[50] See Marchetti and Mavroidis (n 18).

[51] GATS, Art V, under the title 'economic integration', provides for the legal basis on which preferential trade agreements on services are concluded.

the liberalisation of financial services can be easily exemplified by looking at the 20 states that have adopted the Understanding on the Commitments on Financial Services in contrast with the remaining WTO Members. In addition to that, some developed states also opt to further open their clearing markets, such as Japan, Australia, and Korea. To fully capture the dynamics that drive these states to the underlying policy decisions in EIAs, it is essential to investigate Graphs 3 and 4 in tandem, in order to see which are the countries on the other side of the table, who accordingly – potentially – reap the benefits of such liberalisation effects.

Figure 4 very clearly illustrates that it is the EU and the US that secure better liberalisation conditions for clearing and settlement services through the conclusion of EIAs, in terms of market access and national treatment commitments. This is a ramification of their asymmetric bargaining power and strong interest in exporting financial services. As a result, their EIAs reflect these two contributing factors, and this is bluntly portrayed in the GATS+ commitments the EU and the US receive for the financial services sector in question. The next subsection explicitly monitors which WTO Members offer these GATS+ commitments to the EU and the US, to complete the picture of the regulation of international financial instruments' clearing and settlement trade flows in economic integration agreements.

iii. The Roadmap of GATS+ Commitments for the EU and the US

This subsection indicates which are the countries that offer GATS+ commitments to the EU and the US through the regional trade agreements they have concluded. As Figures 5 and 6 show, the countries that inscribe GATS+ commitments in their Schedules of Commitments or lists of reservations with the US and the EU are very similar, with Latin American and Caribbean countries being the common denominator for the EIAs that both states have concluded.

These graphs show how securities' clearing and settlement services are regulated and liberalised in EIAs. Nonetheless, the liberalisation of financial services is not only contingent on commitments undertaken under either the WTO or preferential trade agreements, but most importantly it is dependent on the regulation of financial services by WTO Members. In a perfect world, trade provides the norms and principles – such as non-discrimination and transparency – on which regulatory standards are constructed, assuming that market access and national treatment commitments have been inscribed for particular services sectors. Allowances must be made that trade sets out the general liberalising patterns for services sectors, but it is the regulation of these sectors that prescribes the details, and the specific terms and conditions that domestic and foreign service providers must comply with to ply their services. Thus, the trade of financial services is such a delicate field of law because the regulation of the services in question must be calibrated with the international commitments of states under the GATS and other regional trade agreements. The next section

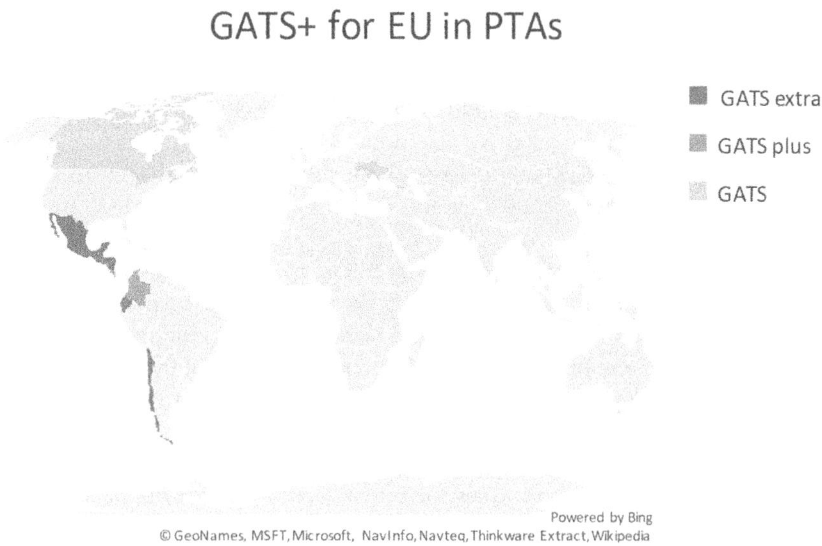

Figure 5 EIAs with the EU

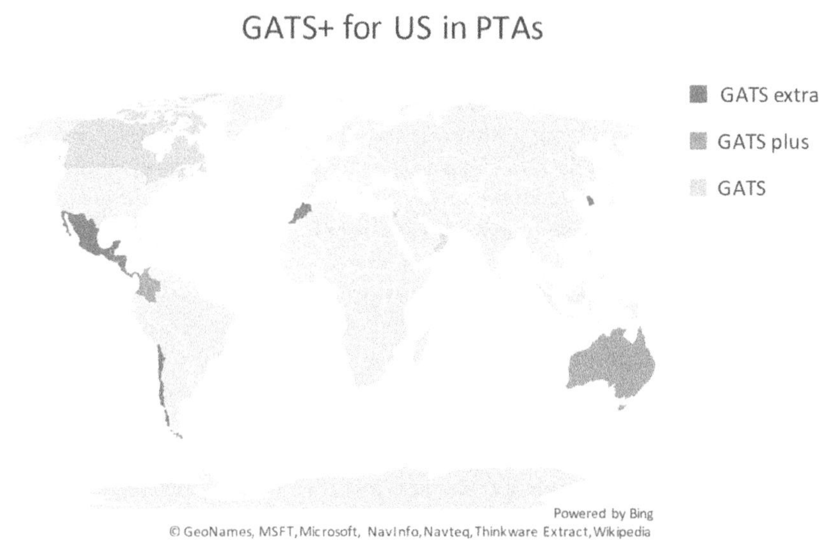

Figure 6 EIAs with the US

Source: Own analysis and computations based on WTO RTA database.

ventures into an examination of the general patterns of the regulation of clearinghouses in the aftermath of the 2007–2009 global financial crisis and serves as a way to navigate around the interaction between financial regulatory standards and regionalism.

IV. FINANCIAL MARKET INFRASTRUCTURE REGULATION AND THE STATES' SILOS IN NEGOTIATING TRADE AGREEMENTS

This section aims to illustrate how the regulation of clearing services after the global financial crisis has changed the industry immensely and has provided for the international standard on the basis of which the international clearing flows are effectuated, and to reveal that EIAs that have been concluded after 2010 do not seem to either mirror or adapt their scope to the twists and turns that industry has followed. Yet, international trade law and financial regulation are disparate legal disciplines, with different mechanics and points of reference. However, since they both prescribe legal norms for the regulation of the financial services' sector in question, one would reasonably expect that synergies exist between the two legal orders to promulgate a coherent set of rules, rather than having two systems that do not interconnect at all. The analysis underscores an absence of coordination between the trade and finance teams of WTO Members' administration, and raises the question of the degree to which this deficiency can be mitigated either domestically – through convergence – and/or via constant exchange of information between the financial regulatory and supervisory authorities and the trade teams tasked with trade in financial services responsibilities, including the negotiation of economic integration agreements.[52]

In response to the G20 accord, states started heavily regulating the clearing of OTC derivatives around the world. Prudential regulations of clearinghouses seek to mitigate the risks associated with the trading of derivatives that can have a seismic impact from a financial stability perspective. To that end, financial rulebooks around the world have been very comprehensive in regulating the industry and all its specific characteristics. One of the aspects of these regulatory standards pertains to how clearinghouses from foreign jurisdictions can provide their services in domestic markets, to domestic entities or even have a substantial effect on them. The sets of rules that permit foreign clearinghouses market access fall in general under the category of regulation called 'third-country equivalence' or 'substituted compliance' in the EU and the US, respectively.[53] Therefore, for foreign clearinghouses to offer their services in other jurisdictions the key is to comply with the abovementioned regimes.

Nonetheless, the regulation of international trade either under the WTO or under preferential trade agreements provides for its own set of rules for financial services, either in the form of market access or national treatment commitments, or in the form of recognition provisions. Due to the intricacies

[52] For example, while negotiating international trade treaties government officials vested with negotiations of trade in financial services should be aware of all the regulatory developments in their own jurisdiction and the country with which they are negotiating commitments/reservations for financial services sectors in order to achieve more efficient outcomes.

[53] For an analysis of the European regulatory framework and the examination of its consistency under WTO law see Papaconstantinou (n 15).

of financial regulation and the existing gaps between trade and finance administrations, trade delegations at the WTO and the trade agreements' negotiating teams do not seem to take account of the challenges ahead relevant to the regulation of financial market infrastructure. This claim is substantiated by the fact that the regulatory change on the role of clearinghouses globally is not reflected in anyway in the content of EIAs. To corroborate this view, it suffices to say that when a financial sector is subjected to major shifts of that scale – as in the case of clearinghouses – which heavily impact on the terms of trade, it is only for international economic law to react accordingly in order to adjust to new realities. Therefore, by closely following the evolution of financial services, international economic law should utilise its toolkit so that it not only keeps up with the financial industry's progress, but also facilitates the integration of these services through encouraging international trade flows. Nevertheless, this approach does not reflect the reality.

The drastic change in the regulation of the financial industry described above is not captured by the regionalism of trade agreements. Specifically, neither the lists of reservations nor the Schedules of Commitments of the parties to EIAs concluded after 2009 keep pace with the changes. Alternatively, EIAs parties – simply by noting next to the clearing and settlement category of their commitments that the supply of the services at issue hinges on specific provisions of their financial rulebooks which translate the substituted compliance/third-country equivalence frameworks – could have made a difference because at least then the content of the trade agreement would provide for legal certainty with regard to the treatment of the financial sectors in question and would be consistent with the legal practices promulgated by states' financial regulatory/supervisory authorities. However, this is emphatically not the case in EIAs, as evidenced by this study. Interestingly there is no mention of OTC derivatives as such in the content of preferential trade agreements in general, despite their importance for many financial services sectors, and for securities' clearing and settlement *in concreto*, which are vested with harnessing it. Thus, the absence of coordination evidenced in this study brings into the spotlight the existing internal boundariesin WTO Members' administrative structures for finance and international trade.

An additional dimension that trade delegations seem to disregard relates to the fact that financial services industries develop rapidly due to either the impetus of technology,[54] or the role of regulation in financial markets. Thus, it is

[54] Technological progress tends to challenge the traditional forms of banking and finance and, accordingly, change the financial industry as we know it. Innovations such as artificial intelligence or block chain technologies nowadays spearhead the emergence of maverick companies and as a result many traditional financial services providers have started to face more competition. See, for example, P Yeoh, 'Regulatory Issues in Blockchain Technology' (2017) 25(2) *Journal of Financial Regulation and Compliance* 196; W Song, 'Bullish on Blockchain: Examining Delaware's Approach to Distributed Ledger Technology in Corporate Governance Law and Beyond' (2017) 8 *Harvard Business Law Review Online* 9; M Arnold, 'How Finance Is Being Taken over by Tech'

imperative to devise a mechanism in preferential trade agreements to revise the inscribed commitments or lists of reservations, on the basis of impact assessments that calibrate the existing legal texts to the new realities. Allowances should be made in respect of countries' specific procedures for updating their undertaken Commitments or List of Reservations. Countries should regularly revise their Commitments/List of Reservations to reflect the latest regulatory standards affecting trade in financial services so that that transparency on the terms of trade is increased and abusive practices are prevented. It is doubtful that such a scheme could be created under the WTO, since negotiation rounds have been stagnant for a long period. However, under EIAs one would expect that there is much room for improvement on that score, as the parties to international trade agreements are more flexible and, on average, they are homogeneous.

Ultimately, this study suggests that if there were more efficient synergies between the trade and finance teams of WTO Members, the associated benefits for the liberalisation of trade in financial services would be greater. First, because financial rulebooks would have transparent standards that can only promote trade openness and liberalisation. This would contribute to reducing or eliminating non-discriminatory structural barriers to trade in financial services generated by unfair and opaque regulatory procedures and would ensure that parties to economic integration agreements do not use their regulatory processes to undermine the market access and national treatment commitments that have been undertaken (both at the multilateral and at the plurilateral trading system level). Second, because the content of EIAs would be better informed about reflecting financial services sectors legal state of play, and as a result would enhance the plurilateral trading relations and deepen their markets. This trade liberalising outcome would emanate from EIA parties' willingness to tackle non-qualitative and non-discriminatory structural barriers to trade in order to open their respective markets and achieve more development and growth.[55] Third, because trade liberalisation and financial regulation need to work in parallel in order to tame financial innovation and to achieve financial stability, while at the same time eliminate anticompetitive barriers to trade that cannot be justified on prudential justifications and serve to limit market access to service suppliers from third countries.

(*Financial Times*, 17 January 2017) www.ft.com/content/2f6f5ba4-dc97-11e6-86ac-f253db7791c6 accessed 27 May 2023; K Johnson et al, 'Artificial Intelligence, Machine Learning, and Bias in Finance: Toward Responsible Innovation' (2019) 88 *Fordham Law Review* 499; K Werbach, 'Trust, but Verify: Why the Blockchain Needs the Law' (2018) 33 *Berkeley Technology Law Journal* 487; I Lianos et al, *Regulating Blockchain: Techno-Social and Legal Challenges* (Oxford, Oxford University Press, 2019).

[55] This would only happen subject to states' willingness to achieve those results. It is important to bear in mind that, beyond the market integration principles embedded in the GATS and in EIAs, there are more efficient liberalising tools, discussed in the next chapter (eg harmonisation, application of competition/antitrust rules), that could be utilised by EIA parties to the extent that there is political appetite to do so.

V. CONCLUSION

This chapter comprehensively evaluates in an empirical analysis the depth of liberalisation attained in the plurilateral trading system for the financial services of securities' clearing and settlement in the aftermath of the global financial crisis. This endeavour is driven by the need to examine the regulation of international trade and the one of financial services *in parallel* in order to attain legal certainty for the provision of the services in question, and to avoid situations under which the regulation of the one discipline does not capture the legal intricacies promulgated by the other, as is argued by this study.

The findings of this chapter indicate that the integration of international financial market infrastructure services in economic integration agreements goes significantly beyond the threshold achieved in the WTO system by the GATS Schedules of Commitments. More importantly, it is observed that the beneficiaries of financial services liberalisation traced in the clearing and settlement services of securities are principally the EU and the US. The main explanations for this trend put forward by this study are associated with the two trade powerhouses' high bargaining power along with their strong interest in opening third countries' markets to their own financial service providers.

Ultimately, we evaluate how the regulation of financial market infrastructure, and in particular the one on clearinghouses crafted after the 2008 financial crisis, comes to grips with the way preferential trade agreements are structured and deal with the services in question. We find that the internal boundaries in WTO Members' administrations between trade and finance teams are striking and that is substantiated by the mere fact that there is no indication in the content of EIAs that something has changed in terms of this financial services sector since 2009, even for the trade agreements concluded thereafter. This is problematic mainly for two reasons: first, because international trade law does not reflect and factor in the legal realities and regulatory standards that represent the most important hurdles to trade in services. Such a situation does not promote legal certainty for the financial industry seeking to provide its services abroad; second, given that both legal disciplines set out the rules for the operation of financial services it is essential to update EIAs in accordance with the mandates of financial regulation and not over-rely on provisions such as the PCO, so that further integration of financial services is attained. Finally, this study argues that in order to remedy the mismatch between the evolving regulation of financial services and the static content of international economic agreements a frequent updating process of the economic integration agreements is required.

The next chapter assesses the tension between the regulation of financial market infrastructure and economic integration in the context of the EU – the most integrated economic system of different states there is. The EU single market is effectively an endeavour to attain 'EU contestability of markets'[56] by meeting comprehensive liberalisation patterns, including, inter alia, national treatment and market access, removal of non-discriminatory structural barriers through the harmonisation of regulatory frameworks and the principle of mutual recognition, freedom of capital movements and – last but not least – the application and enforcement of EU competition law. The following analysis focuses on the role of financial regulation and the application of EU competition law in integrating the European internal market due to their prominence as trade liberalising tools. The qualitative methodology put forward by this study, as demonstrated below, takes into consideration the seminal role of financial regulation and competition law in liberalising the EU market – both to internal and external competition – while at the same time accounting for the EU industry's global competitiveness.

[56] For an interesting take on the notion of 'international contestability of markets' and, specifically, the comparative advantages embedded in the EU model, see Key (n 18) 53–54.

Part III

Financial Regulation and EU Competition Law

5

EU Financial Regulation and Competition Law Promoting the Trade Liberalisation of Financial Market Infrastructure

I. INTRODUCTION

THIS CHAPTER SEEKS to further shed light on this book's inquiry on how the regulation of financial infrastructure interacts with different economic integration settings. To this end, the interface between financial regulation and competition/antitrust law is investigated in order to assess how the tension plays out in the case study at hand. So far, the integration models explored in the previous chapters (ie WTO in Chapters 2 and 3 and EIAs in Chapter 4) do not provide for as much liberalisation as the EU model does. The rules that define the functioning of the EU internal market result in a more integrated outcome for EU Member States in comparison with other integration models (either in the form of the multilateral trading system or in the form of plurilateral trade agreements that solely rely on the traditional trade-liberalising instruments described above – such as market access, national treatment) for several important reasons.

Most importantly, the EU model achieves a higher degree of integration of the financial market infrastructure of its Member States because it manages to tackle non-discriminatory and non-qualitative structural barriers. Specifically, the EU rulebook goes above and beyond in terms of integration due to the harmonisation of specific sets of rules across jurisdictions for the provision of financial services, the intra-EU mutual recognition,[1] and the application of competition/antitrust law. The role of both harmonisation/mutual recognition

[1] The principle of mutual recognition in the EU legal order was introduced in 1979 with the *Cassis de Dijon* ruling of the European Court of Justice. For literature emanating from this judgment, see, for example, JHH Weiler, 'Mutual Recognition, Functional Equivalence and Harmonization in the Evolution of the European Common Market and the WTO' in FK Padoa Schioppa (ed), *The Principle of Mutual Recognition in the European Integration Process* (London, Palgrave Macmillan UK, 2005); C Janssens, *The Principle of Mutual Recognition in EU Law* (Oxford, Oxford University

and competition law in achieving the integration of the EU internal market have been thoroughly explored by the literature.[2] In light of this, this chapter focuses solely on deciphering the current tension between the EU financial regulation and competition/antitrust law. Thus, the EU is selected as a case study due to its liberal economic integration model – which is arguably the most integrated one globally – driven by the forces of a harmonised financial rulebook and competition law and policy. The interaction between financial regulation, exemplified by the EU regulation of clearinghouses, on the one hand and EU competition law, on the other, is evaluated to draw conclusions about the relationship between the two.

In particular, the EU is an indispensable case study for the endeavour of this book to investigate the tension between the regulation of clearinghouses and separate economic integration models for the following reasons: (i) the EU financial regulation at issue has implemented the standards promulgated by G20 and therefore is one of the most developed financial regulatory frameworks at the global level; (ii) the case study raises financial stability and supervision considerations in the context of cross-border clearing of specific financial instruments; (iii) the EU Clearinghouses Regulation has in itself procompetitive elements that seek to increase competition in the EU internal market; (iv) EU competition/antitrust law has consistently resisted and targeted monopolisation in financial market infrastructure; (v) EU competition law and enforcement, through the European Commission, are global standard setters as national competition authorities (NCAs) draw inspiration on how rules are to be applied; and (vi) the EU Clearinghouses Regulation in conjunction with antitrust law define to a great extent the terms of trade of international clearing flows, as this chapter demonstrates.

One of the most prominent driving forces of the EU's internal market is none other than competition. From an EU law perspective, referring to EU economic law includes the four fundamental freedoms and competition law. For the

Press, 2013); K Nicolaïdis, 'The Cassis Legacy: Kir, Banks, Plumbers, Drugs, Criminals and Refugees' in B Davies and F Nicola (eds), *EU Law Stories: Contextual and Critical Histories of European Jurisprudence* (Cambridge, Cambridge University Press, 2017). Additionally, Nicolaidis provides a thought-provoking examination of the current state of play of the principle of mutual recognition in the context of the first example of disintegration in the EU: K Nicolaidis, 'Mutual Recognition: Promise and Denial, from Sapiens to Brexit' (2017) 70 *Current Legal Problems* 227.

[2] See, for example, LPP Maduro, *We the Court: The European Court of Justice and the European Economic Constitution* (Oxford, Bloomsbury Publishing, 1998); S Estrin and P Holmes, *Competition and Economic Integration in Europe* (Cheltenham, Edward Elgar, 1998); S Deakin, *Regulatory Competition versus Harmonisation in European Company Law* (ESRC Centre for Business Research, Department of Applied Economics, 2000); E Avgouleas, 'The Harmonisation of Rules of Conduct in EU Financial Markets: Economic Analysis, Subsidiarity and Investor Protection' (2000) 6 *European Law Journal* 72; G Falkner et al, *Complying with Europe: EU Harmonisation and Soft Law in the Member States* (Cambridge, Cambridge University Press, 2005); C Twigg-Flesner, '"Good-Bye Harmonisation by Directives, Hello Cross-Border Only Regulation?" – A Way Forward for EU Consumer Contract Law' (2011) 7 *European Review of Contract Law* 235.

purposes of this chapter, the covered scope includes the analysis of EU competition law in financial market infrastructure due to its prominence in liberalising financial services *in tandem* with financial regulation. An additional reason why competition law is selected as the most instrumental economic integration paradigm in the EU is because over the last decade it has – in multiple cases – sought to integrate the financial market infrastructure of EU Member States either through the decisions of competition authorities or through the judgments of EU courts.

As to the nature of this inquiry, it is important to understand from the outset that this chapter evaluates EU financial regulation and competition law together. The two fields of law are in constant tension, and we seek to extrapolate how they together contribute to liberalising the financial market infrastructure in the EU. To that end, the following analysis evaluates how specific financial regulatory measures and competition decisions and judgments rendered by the EU Courts foster liberalisation in the financial market infrastructure. In doing this, I take account of three parameters: (i) the competitive landscape in the EU; (ii) the global competitive landscape; (iii) the EU industry's international competitiveness. These indicators are selected because they can clearly demonstrate the benefits for the liberalisation of financial market infrastructure services and the advantages of the EU integration model.

The following analysis on the importance of competition law in liberalising the EU market of financial infrastructure is not limited to back-end infrastructure services (ie financial instruments' clearing and settlement) unlike the case studies of the multilateral and the plurilateral trading system. It also covers trading of financial instruments because: (i) the EU regulatory frameworks for clearing and for trading are intimately connected in their attempt to open the EU financial market infrastructure – as demonstrated below; (ii) those two financial services sectors tend to be provided by the very same institutions (eg trading venues that also provide clearing and settlement services) and if they were to be examined separately – by only focusing on one or the other – we would miss the whole picture of how the application of competition law fosters the integration of financial market infrastructure; and (iii) in order to provide a comprehensive account of how EU competition law contributes to the liberalisation of financial market infrastructure, the examination of the prominent body of case law and practice on trading cannot be disregarded.

Overall, the findings of this study indicate that the EU rulebook on financial infrastructure and EU competition/antitrust law have a positive effect on the terms of trade in financial market infrastructure services. They both contribute to increasing competition in the provision of those services both at the EU and at the global level. Also, they do not seem to favour the European industry's big players and thus they do not boost the EU's global competitiveness.

This chapter develops as follows: Section II elaborates on the EU financial regulatory elements that aim to increase competition in the EU financial infrastructure for clearing services. The antitrust elements of this study are included in Section III, which delves into how competition law liberalises financial market infrastructure in the EU and its efficacy is evaluated. Finally, Section IV supplements the discussion with the relevant international trade law elements that are of the essence for the application of competition in financial services and draws conclusions as to the relationship between the regulation of financial infrastructure and competition law and policy.

II. REGULATION AS A COMPETITION STIMULUS IN THE EU FINANCIAL MARKET INFRASTRUCTURE

A. Financial Regulation in the Pursuit of Breaking-up Silos

The EU Regulation on OTC derivatives, CCPs and trade repositories (also referred to as EMIR) along with the Markets in Financial Instruments Regulation[3] (MIFIR) aim to get rid of commercial barriers that could prevent competition in the clearing of securities. Importantly, those financial regulatory frameworks require: (i) central counterparties to accept securities for clearing irrespective of the trading venue; (ii) trading venues to offer trade feeds to clearinghouses; and (iii) benchmark owners to provide central counterparties and trading venues with the possibility of acquiring licences. In doing this, non-discriminatory and transparent standards should be applied by the financial market infrastructure economic actors. The following analysis sheds light on the most relevant regulatory elements that boost competition in the EU clearing markets.

It is important to note that the financial industry is integrated vertically to a very great extent. As a result, the use of services from competing firms represents the exception rather than the norm in many sectors. In the same vein, financial market infrastructure has been traditionally vertically integrated, and most clearinghouses are usually part of groups with regulated markets – such

[3] See Regulation (EU) No 600/2014 of the European Parliament and of the Council of 15 May 2014 on markets in financial instruments [2014] OJ L173/84, being part of the MiFID II regulatory package. For literature on the reforms brought by MiFID II see, for example, G Ferrarini and N Moloney, 'Reshaping Order Execution in the EU and the Role of Interest Groups: From MiFID I to MiFID II' (2012) 13 *European Business Organization Law Review* 557; S Grundmann, 'The Bankinter Case on MIFID Regulation and Contract Law' (2013) 9 *European Review of Contract Law* 267; D Busch, 'MiFID II: Regulating High Frequency Trading, Other Forms of Algorithmic Trading and Direct Electronic Market Access' (2016) 10 *Law and Financial Markets Review* 72; GA Papaconstantinou, 'Investment Bankers in Conflict: The Regime of Inducements in MiFID II and the Member States' Struggle for Fairness' (2016) 12 *European Review of Contract Law* 356; I Sheridan, 'MiFID II in the Context of Financial Technology and Regulatory Technology' (2017) 12 *Capital Markets Law Journal* 417; S Grundmann, 'Das Grundlegend Reformierte Wertpapierhandelsgesetz–Umsetzung von MiFID II (Conduct of Business Im Kundenverhältnis)' (2018) 30 *Zeitschrift für Bankrecht und Bankwirtschaft* 1; F Della Negra, *MiFID II and Private Law: Enforcing EU Conduct of Business Rules* (Oxford, Bloomsbury, 2019).

as stock exchanges. Understanding that these silos are likely to culminate in the creation of barriers to entry for the purposes of the supply of financial infrastructure services within the EU internal market, the EU financial regulation at hand seeks to tackle this situation. As CCPs and trading venues are deeply integrated structures – as also evidenced in the merger control section of this chapter – the Markets in Financial Instruments Regulation (MiFIR) and EMIR seek to break up these silos by prescribing access rights for CCPs as well as access rights for trading venues.

The two graphs in Figures 7 and 8 illustrate how the two financial regulatory frameworks seek to achieve further integration of the financial market infrastructure industry in the EU:

Figure 7 Silo Structure between CCPs and Trading Venues

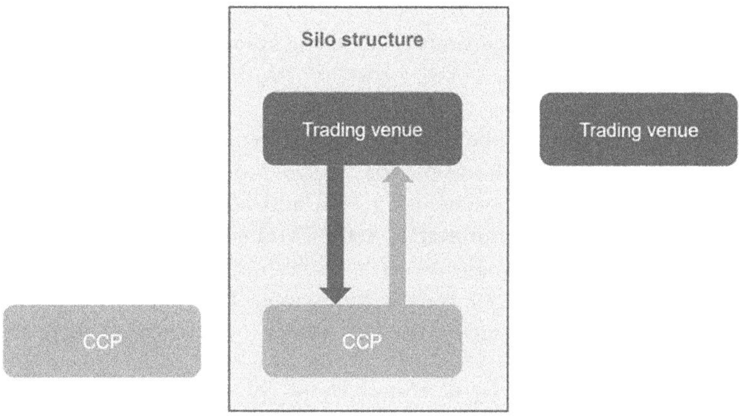

Figure 8 EMIR and MiFIR Addressing the Silo

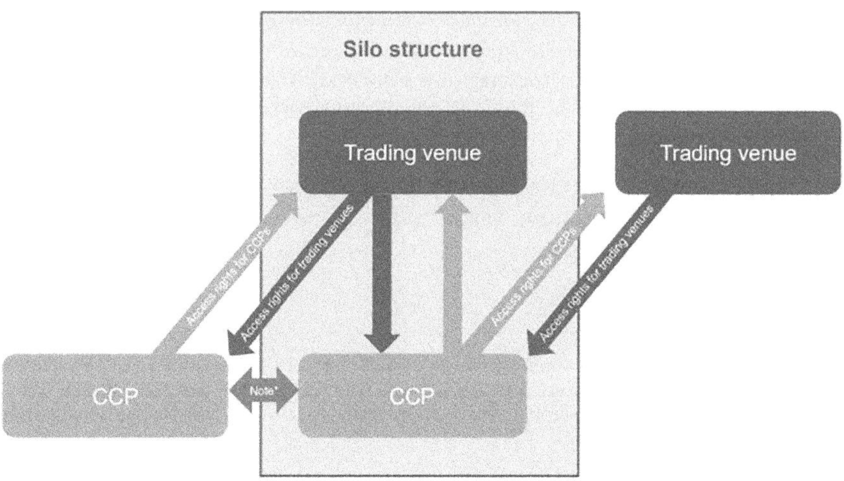

Notably, the key principle that underpins the EU's approach to the integration of the financial market infrastructure – including the services of clearinghouses – is open access.[4] Open access implies that unrestricted access to financial institutions is expected to make competition flourish in the relevant markets. As a result, open access seeks to offer lower prices, higher quality of services and lower cost structures to the market participants of the financial market infrastructure. Following this, open access would result in non-discriminatory access to all trading and clearing infrastructures. In the absence of discriminatory conditions on gaining access to trading venues for clearinghouses, the parties using the services of CCPs can reduce or net against their clearing margins through aggregated and enhanced liquidity pools as they would have access to the most efficient service providers.

B. Financial Regulatory Provisions Liberalising Financial Infrastructure Services

When it comes to the specific provisions that spell out those financial infrastructure liberalising mechanisms for central counterparties, it is worth examining their precise idiosyncrasy. EMIR and MiFIR's relevant provisions are put into context to extrapolate how the EU financial frameworks regulating the operation of clearinghouses aim to flesh out competition-flourishing principles. The following analysis demonstrates how these provisions can contribute to further integrating the EU market infrastructure; their efficacy is discussed next.

At the outset, EMIR Article 7 provides for the terms and conditions for accessing a central counterparty. Article 7 (access to a CCP) stipulates that a:

> CCP that has been authorised to clear OTC derivative contracts shall accept clearing such contracts on a *non-discriminatory* and *transparent* basis, including as regards collateral requirements and fees related to access, regardless of the trading venue. [...] A CCP may require that a trading venue comply with the operational and technical requirements established by the CCP, including the risk-management requirements.[5] (emphasis added)

The rest of the article prescribes the terms under which a CCP may refuse a formal request by a trading venue and elaborates on the role of national

[4] For a primer on the operational aspects associated with open access, see FIA, 'FIA Europe Special Report Series: Open Access: CCPs, Trading Venues and Benchmarks' (FIA, 10 June 2014) www.fia.org/fia/articles/fia-fia-europe-special-report-series-open-access-ccps-trading-venues-and-benchmarks accessed 25 July 2023.

[5] EMIR, Art 7(1).

supervisory authorities (NSAs) and ESMA throughout this process.[6] In addition, NSAs have the capacity to:

> refuse access to the CCP following a formal request by the trading venue only where such access would *threaten the smooth and orderly functioning of the markets or would adversely affect systemic risk*.[7] (emphasis added)

This provision is in line with the general principle of open access. It also strikes a fair balance between fostering the integration of the relevant markets, on the one hand, and preserving the integrity of the financial system, on the other. By providing access on a non-discriminatory and transparent basis to trading venues, the EU financial rulebook seeks to level the playing field for central counterparties in this segment of financial infrastructure. Importantly, this provision aims to break up the silos existing in the industry as, unsurprisingly, most central counterparties are in the same corporate group as the major trading venues and stock exchanges. In particular, by prohibiting discriminatory terms in accessing CCPs, EMIR envisages that trading venues irrespective of their ownership structure will start using the CCPs that are more efficient in clearing specific securities rather than simply transacting with their own vertically integrated clearinghouses. Indeed, such initiative is undoubtedly towards the further integration of financial market infrastructure.

Further, EMIR, Article 8 (access to a trading venue) sets out the framework for the reverse scenario where central counterparties require access to a trading venue. The relevant parts in Article 8 are as follows: paragraph 1 stipulates that 'A trading venue shall provide trade feeds on *a non-discriminatory* and *transparent* basis to any CCP that has been authorised to clear OTC derivative contracts traded on that trading venue upon request by the CCP' (emphasis added); and paragraph 4 sets out that:

> [a]ccess of the CCP to the trading venue shall be granted only where such access would not require interoperability or *threaten the smooth and orderly functioning of markets* in particular due to liquidity fragmentation and the trading venue has put in place adequate mechanisms to prevent such fragmentation.[8] (emphasis added)

Similar to the previous provision, Article 8 seeks to increase competition in the EU financial market infrastructure by prescribing the rules for non-discriminatory and transparent access to exchanges' trading fees by central-counterparties. Despite the silos in the industry described above, financial regulation takes account of the potential perils that may arise in the absence of liquidity and

[6] EMIR, Art 7(2)–(5).
[7] EMIR, Art 7(4).
[8] EMIR, Art 8(1), 8(4).

could put at risk the financial system's stability and, subsequently, set out the appropriate carve-outs.

In a similar vein, MiFIR seeks to increase competition in the EU financial market infrastructure. MiFIR's recital 40 reads in the relevant parts:

> Trading venues should be required to provide access including data feeds on a *transparent* and *non-discriminatory* basis to CCPs that wish to clear transactions executed on a trading venue. However, this should not necessitate the use of interoperability arrangements for clearing transactions in derivatives or create liquidity fragmentation in a way that would *threaten the smooth and orderly functioning of markets.* (emphasis added).

The content of this part of the recital is closely aligned with the obligations stipulated in EMIR and has the same rationale of increasing competition in financial market infrastructure while not putting in jeopardy the stability and integrity of the financial system.

In addition, in another relevant part in recital 40 provides that

> where commercial and intellectual property rights relate to financial services related to derivative contracts, licenses should be available on *proportionate, fair, reasonable* and *non-discriminatory* terms. Therefore, access to licences of, and information relating to, benchmarks that are used to determine the value of financial instruments should be provided to CCPs and other trading venues on a *proportionate, fair, reasonable* and *non-discriminatory* basis and any license should be on reasonable commercial terms. (emphasis added).

Again, these terms facilitate the liberalisation of the underlying financial services and at the same time they discourage monopolisation.[9] Thus, they are procompetitive. Further,

> The removal of barriers and discriminatory practices is intended to *increase competition for clearing and trading of financial instruments in order to lower investment and borrowing costs, eliminate inefficiencies and foster innovation in Union markets.* The Commission should continue to closely monitor the evolution of post-trade infrastructure and should, where necessary, intervene in order to *prevent competitive*

[9] It can be observed that such terms are aligned with the antitrust notion of 'fair, reasonable and non-discriminatory' (FRAND). Notably, EU courts have provided guidance in respect of the remedies that patent owners may seek against one that encroaches on FRAND committed patents. Specifically, the Court of Justice without excluding an antitrust liability held that if a patent owner takes certain steps to claim her right (eg notifying the one implementing the patent of an infringement), a request for an injunction will not raise concerns under competition law. See *Huawei Technologies Co Ltd v ZTE Corp, ZTE Deutschland GmbH*, Case C-170/13, ECLI:EU:C:2015:477. For literature on the subject, see N Petit, 'EU Competition Law Analysis of FRAND Disputes' in J Contreras (ed), *The Cambridge Handbook of Technical Standardization Law: Competition, Antitrust, and Patents* (Cambridge, Cambridge University Press, 2017) 290. Moreover, it should be noted that the European Commission proposed a new regulation on the licensing of standard essential patents and FRAND: see European Commission, Proposal for a Regulation of the European Parliament and of the Countil on standard essential patents and amending Regulation (EU)2017/1001, 27 April 2023.

> *distortions from occurring in the internal market*, in particular where *the refusal of access to infrastructure or to benchmarks contravenes Articles 101 or 102 TFEU.*[10] (emphasis added).

MiFIR recital 40 makes it crystal clear that the EU financial regulators seek to make competition flourish in the relevant EU markets by getting rid of trade barriers and preventing discriminatory practices that could support monopolisation. Ultimately, regulators have the objective of maximising efficiencies and promoting innovation. The role of healthy competition in these markets is underscored and the relevant provisions of the Treaty on the Functioning of the European Union (TFEU),[11] discussed in detail below, are expressly referred to in the text of the recital. Moreover, it is notable that MiFIR pinpoints specific types of conduct that are likely to fall foul of antitrust rules; namely, refusals to access infrastructure or benchmarks in the financial market infrastructure are identified as potential anti-competitive triggers. Interestingly, this chapter's analysis below on competition concretely explains why refusals to supply constitute a valid concern for regulators in the financial services industry. Despite the application of competition rules, the dominance of certain market actors in financial infrastructure might increase the likelihood of potentially abusive conduct by dominant companies – pertinent to Article 102 TFEU.

With respect to the substantive MiFIR provisions, Title VI (that goes under the title 'Non-discriminatory clearing access for financial instruments') puts forward specific provisions that aim at increasing the liberalisation of clearing services in the European internal market by imposing a specific set of obligation on financial infrastructure market participants. The relevant parts included in Articles 35 and 36 follow.

First, Article 35 (titled as 'Non-discriminatory access to a CCP') reads at the relevant parts:

> Without prejudice to Article 7 of Regulation (EU) No 648/2012, a CCP shall accept to clear financial instruments on a *non-discriminatory* and *transparent* basis, including as regards collateral requirements and fees relating to access, regardless of the trading venue on which a transaction is executed. This in particular shall ensure that a trading venue has the right to *non-discriminatory treatment* of contracts traded on that trading venue in terms of: (a) collateral requirements and netting of economically equivalent contracts, where the inclusion of such contracts in the close-out and other netting procedures of a CCP based on the applicable insolvency law would not endanger the smooth and orderly functioning, the validity or enforceability of such procedures; and (b) cross-margining with correlated contracts cleared by the same CCP under a risk model that complies with Article 41 of Regulation (EU) No 648/2012.[12] (emphasis added).

[10] MiFIR, Recital 40.
[11] Consolidated Version of Treaty on the Functioning of the European Union [2012] OJ C326/47.
[12] MiFIR, Art 35(1).

These obligations reflect the regulatory considerations of opening up the silos in the EU financial market infrastructure industry. Through that competition in the relevant markets concrete benefits can result for the market participants, and that is why the text explicitly counters the terms in contracts that might be prone to non-discriminatory treatment by clearinghouses.

Given that the EU financial regulatory frameworks are closely interwoven, paragraphs 3 and 4 of MiFIR Article 35 mirror the EMIR, Article 7 provisions, which stipulate how the procedures for requests for access are to be carried out and the reasons why competent authorities can deny access to trading venues.

Second, Article 36 (under the title 'Non-discriminatory access to a trading venue') stipulates at the relevant passages:

> Without prejudice to Article 8 of Regulation (EU) No 648/2012, a trading venue shall provide trade feeds on a *nondiscriminatory* and *transparent* basis, including as regards fees related to access, upon request to any CCP authorised or recognised by Regulation (EU) No 648/2012 that wishes to clear transactions in financial instruments that are concluded on that trading venue. That requirement does not apply to any derivative contract that is already subject to the access obligations under Article 8 of Regulation (EU) No 648/2012.[13] (emphasis added).

Following the principles enshrined in the above-described provisions, the non-discriminatory and transparent access to trading venues is laid down for clearinghouses authorised in the EU or the ones recognised through the equivalence procedure.

In a similar vein as in EMIR Article 8, the rest of Article 36 elaborates on the provisions for the assessment of requests to access a trading venue by a CCP[14] and the conditions under which the competent authorities shall not grant a CCP access to a trading venue.[15]

Consequently, the EU financial regulatory regimes at issue have promulgated explicit provisions prescribing concrete obligations that can meaningfully contribute to the further integration of the EU financial market infrastructure. Increasing competition in the financial services industry is a legitimate objective given the European Commission's increased scrutiny of cartel-like and monopolisation behaviour over the last decade – indicating that there is significant anti-competitive conduct in the financial industry. However, measuring the efficacy of these policies and specifically assessing how they translate in the actual liberalisation of the financial services in question goes beyond the scope of this volume, and would require empirical investigation.

Following this section on the procompetitive elements of EU financial regulation in the realm of clearing services, we discuss a judgment rendered by the

[13] MiFIR, Art 36(1).
[14] ibid Art 36(2)–(3).
[15] ibid Art 36(4).

EU General Court in connection with clearing services which further fostered competition in the EU market.[16]

C. General Court Judgment in Case T-496/11, *UK v ECB (Location Policy)*

In Case T-496/11, *UK v ECB (Location Policy)*, decided in March 2015, the General Court held that the European Central Bank (ECB) does not have the competence to put forward regulations concerning clearinghouses. In particular, the EU General Court annulled an ECB policy that sought to restrict access to the euro area of certain central counterparties originating in the non-euro area. The following analysis examines the more prominent elements of this judgment and assesses the relevant regulatory environment and supervisory context.

The ECB's 'location policy', formulated in 2001, triggered the case at hand. This policy was formulated as follows:

> The natural geographical scope for any 'domestic' market infrastructure (including central counterparty clearing) for securities and derivatives denominated in euro is the euro area. Given the potential systemic importance of securities clearing and settlement systems, this infrastructure should be located within the euro area.[17]

The ECB's interest in clearinghouses is justified as every securities transaction consists of two parts: a securities part; and a cash part. Accordingly, there is a direct relationship between financial market infrastructure and payment systems. Thus, disruptions in the transfer of financial instruments might 'spill over to disruptions of the payment systems that are used by the securities settlement systems'.[18] Although this policy was never used in practice,[19] the UK challenged its legality in view of the possibility of pressure being exerted on London-based clearinghouses to migrate their euro activities to within the euro area. The overarching principle behind this policy was at the epicentre of regulatory debate preceding Brexit. Interestingly, in this case the General Court sided with the UK, noting that 'the ECB does not have the competence necessary to regulate the activity of securities clearing systems'.[20]

As background to this dispute, the reasoning put forward by the ECB indicated that the term 'oversight' is not part of the EU treaties' *acquis* and this should be well borne in mind as at the time EU treaties were contemplated 'the

[16] The judgment was rendered at a time when the UK was a Member State of the EU.

[17] European Central Bank, 'The Eurosystem's Policy Line with Regard to Consolidation in Central Counterparty Clearing' (ECB, 27 September 2001) www.ecb.europa.eu/press/pr/date/2001/html/pr010927_2.en.html accessed 25 July 2023.

[18] ECB, 'Eurosystem Oversight Policy Framework', 5 July 2011, 5.

[19] Although EMIR II seems to have incorporated some considerations along those lines, as discussed above.

[20] *United Kingdom of Great Britain and Northern Ireland v European Central Bank (ECB)* Case T-496/11, ECLI:EU:T:2015:133, para 110.

understanding of oversight as a separate function was only just developing'.[21] As a result, this omission at stake must have been without intention. In addition, at that time 'clearing and settlement systems had not yet gained the size and relevance that they subsequently acquired, particularly on a cross-border context'.[22] Notably, the ECB admitted that it lacked an explicit mandate to oversee securities settlement systems. However, it claimed that such powers should be interpreted as consequential to its other tasks stipulated in Article 127 TFEU,[23] and the ECB/ESCB Statute. In particular, the ECB premised its views on Articles 127(1) and 127(2) TFEU as well as on Article 22 of the ECB/ESCB Statute.[24]

As to the content of these provisions, the overarching goal of the European System of Central Banks (ESCB) is to maintain price stability (Article 127(1) TFEU), whereas Article 127(2) TFEU sets out that the ESCB's core tasks also include the promotion of the smooth operation of payment systems. Moreover, Article 22 of the ECB Statute further clarifies that 'the ECB and national central banks may provide facilities, and the ECB may make regulations, to ensure efficient and sound clearing and payment systems within the Union and with other countries'. The ECB claimed that the above legal basis, coupled with the task of contributing to the stability of the financial system (Article 127(5) TFEU) also grants it supervisory and regulatory powers over all types of clearing systems, including central counterparties.[25]

The General Court was not persuaded by the ECB's claims and sided with the UK. Nevertheless, what is of the essence in this debate is to comprehend the competing points of view expressed in the dispute. On the one hand, the ECB insisted that the supervision of entities with a systemic importance for the Euro currency should be carried by it and such entities should be established within the Euro area. This consideration has a stability raison d'être but the extent to which it makes sense from an economic standpoint, and whether its proposal is necessary or proportionate are completely different questions. On the other

[21] ibid para 68.

[22] ibid para 74.

[23] Art 127(2) reads as follows: 'The basic tasks to be carried out through the ESCB shall be: to define and implement the monetary policy of the Union; to conduct foreign-exchange operations consistent with the provisions of Article 219; to hold and manage the official foreign reserves of the Member States.'

[24] Article 22 reads as follows: 'The ECB and national central banks may provide facilities, and the ECB may make regulations, to ensure efficient and sound clearing and payment systems within the Union and with other countries'; TFEU Protocol (No 4) on the Statute of the European System of Central Banks and of the European Central Bank [2016] OJ C202/230.

[25] See Opinion of the European Central Bank of 27 November 2012 on a proposal for a Council regulation conferring specific tasks on the European Central Bank concerning policies relating to the prudential supervision of credit institutions and a proposal for a regulation of the European Parliament and of the Council amending Regulation (EU) No 1093/2010 establishing a European Supervisory Authority (European Banking Authority) (CON/2012/96) [2013] OJ C30/6 2, where it expressly states the Eurosystem's supervisory 'competence over clearing and payment systems derives from these provisions'.

hand, the liberalisation of financial infrastructure in the EU would favour the freedom of establishment and freedom to provide services, irrespective of any systemic considerations. Finding the right balance between competition and systemic stability in financial services sectors is a conundrum, and no convincing answers have yet been put forward.[26] This study does not purport to contribute to this debate, but rather underlines its existence in passing. The remainder of this section evaluates how the pro-competitive provisions described above and the court ruling score against the three indicators affecting completion inside the EU internal market and internationally.

D. Competition Assessment of the EU Financial Regulation

There is economic and legal literature on the competition landscape in clearing services markets in the EU and the US.[27] However, the nature of the above-examined financial regulation provisions together with the General Court's ruling have not been evaluated from a competition standpoint. For the purposes of this inquiry, we use the indicators identified in this chapter's introduction – namely: (i) the competitive landscape in the EU; (ii) the global competitive landscape; (iii) the EU industry's international competitiveness – to determine to what extent the financial regulation at issue has a pro-competitive footprint.

Naturally, with respect to the first parameter it is maintained that the EU regulation of financial market infrastructure has the potential to increase competition in the EU internal market as it lays out the rules that require clearinghouses and trading venues to break up their silos and start transacting with other entities on a non-discriminatory and transparent basis. Non-discrimination within this context of EU competition law does not necessarily require likeness determinations, unlike WTO law, and it seeks to open markets that have been subjected to dominant players due to the special nature of financial market infrastructure. In a similar vein, the General Court's judgment in *UK v ECB (Location Policy)* rejected the more protectionist line of reasoning promoted by the ECB and favoured the further liberalisation of clearing services in the EU. As a result,

[26] For literature elaborating on the relationship between stability and competition in financial services, see, for example, B De Meester, *Liberalization of Trade in Banking Services: An International and European Perspective* (Cambridge, Cambridge University Press, 2014); X Vives, *Competition and Stability in Banking* (Princeton, Princeton University Press, 2016).

[27] See, for example, EG Kazarian, 'Integration of the Securities Market Infrastructure in the European Union: Policy and Regulatory Issues' [2006] IMF Working Paper No 2006/241; M Szpringer and W Szpringer, 'Law and Economics of Central Counterparties (CCP) – Selected Issues of Regulation and Competition Concerning Financial Market Infrastructure' (2016) 27 *European Business Law Review* 587; S Li, *Financial Institutions in the Global Financial Crisis* (Singapore, Springer, 2018) 105–67; D Turing, *Clearing and Settlement* (Oxford, Bloomsbury, 2016) Chapter 11; and for a commentary on the latter, see GA Papaconstantinou, '"Clearing & Settlement" by D Turing, Book Review' (2018) 42 *European Law Review* 131.

this regulatory development and General Court ruling can only contribute to the further integration of the EU financial market infrastructure.

As to the second indicator, at the outset it must be borne in mind that the EU – even after Brexit – is one of the important financial hubs at the global level. Therefore, its rules directly impact on the liberalisation of clearing services due to the interconnectedness of financial markets. In addition, given that third-country clearinghouses or trading venues which are either established in the EU or are recognised by the EU as providing their services in the EU internal market benefit from the content of these provisions similar to the European ones. Thus, as above, the financial regulation in question here can only be pro-competitive for global competition in financial infrastructure services.

Finally, regarding the third indicator, when it comes to whether the EU financial regulation at issue provides a competitive advantage to the EU industry to increase its global edge, it is inferred that this is not the case. That is because the financial regulation in question injects pro-competitive elements (such as transparency and non-discrimination in accessing trading venues) in the EU financial infrastructure markets which would provide a level playing field to domestic and foreign firms alike – so long as the latter meet the equivalence conditions which would enable them to provide their services in the EU internal market (as discussed above). Thus, if anything, the financial rulebook in question offers better terms to potential market entrants by reducing barriers to entry and hence promotes further competition in the markets in question. The next section delves into how the EU has scrutinised the financial market infrastructure from a competition perspective and draws conclusions as to how this scrutiny has contributed to the liberalisation of those markets.

III. THE APPLICATION OF COMPETITION LAW IN THE EU FINANCIAL MARKET INFRASTRUCTURE: TOWARDS FURTHER LIBERALISATION IN FINANCIAL SERVICES

A. Introductory Remarks on Competition in Financial Services

Financial services sectors and the industry have, traditionally, been consolidated due to the required economies of scope and scale required to achieve projected margins. However, financial services are by no means exempt from the application of competition law and policy. This is even more the case when it comes to financial market infrastructure, as most institutions used to be run by states not so long ago. As explained, this liberalisation is realised through regulatory reforms at the EU level alongside the application of competition law. The following analysis investigates the extent to which the enforcement of antitrust law and merger control have contributed to liberalising the EU internal market for financial market infrastructure, namely clearing and settlement together with trading. The latter is capture by the scope of this chapter due to the market structure of the industry and the prominence of antitrust enforcement in countering anti-competitive conduct in the trading sector, which therefore contributes to the liberalisation of financial market infrastructure in the EU. To this end, we seek to assess the efficacy of competition law in integrating markets and, further, attaining the benefits of such liberalisation – without disregarding the importance of financial stability considerations along the way.

B. EU Antitrust Law (Articles 101 and 102 TFEU): Scrutinising Financial Market Infrastructure

Due to state participation and the prominent role of EU Member States in the financial market infrastructure until the emergence of the Investment Services Directive (ISD),[28] competition law enforcement did not used to be as invasive in these markets as in others until recently. However, over the last decade, competition enforcers have started becoming more and more present in assessing the consistency of financial services markets in general, and financial market infrastructure in particular, with EU antitrust law. Indeed, there have recently been many studies in which scholars discuss competition law in financial services more broadly.[29] Here, we shed light on the antitrust cases that serve this chapter's analytical framework and do not exhaustively refer to all competition in financial services cases.

In particular, the following analysis focuses on competition cases germane to financial market infrastructure – defined as including the financial services relating to: (i) trading; (ii) clearing; and (iii) settlement of financial instruments – in order to draw useful conclusions about how competition/antitrust law and its enforcement contribute to the integration of financial infrastructure services in the EU.

This section's objective is to bring into the spotlight the relevant financial services cases that have been under the scrutiny of EU antitrust law. Accordingly,

[28] Council Directive of 10 May 1993 on investment services in the securities field [1993] OJ L141/27 was the predecessor of MiFID and was the first EU law attempting to liberalise financial market infrastructure in the internal market through harmonisation. For relevant literature, see NS Poser, 'Automation of Securities Markets and the European Community's Proposed Investment Services Directive' (1992) 55 *Law and Contemporary Problems* 29; MG Warren III , 'The European Union's Investment Services Directive' (1994) 15 *University of Pennsylvania Journal of Business Law* 181; G Ferrarini, *European Securities Markets: The Investment Services Directive and Beyond* (Alphen aan den Rijn, Kluwer Law International BV, 1998).

[29] See, inter alia, D Gerard, 'Managing the Financial Crisis in Europe: Why Competition Law Is Part of the Solution, Not of the Problem' (2008) December *Global Competiton Review*; M Reynolds et al, 'EU Competition Policy in the Financial Crisis: Extraordinary Measures' (2009) 33 *Fordham International Law Journal* 1670; I Kapsis, 'Competition Law and Policy for the EU Banking Sector in a Period of Increased Economic Uncertainty' (2012) 54 *International Journal of Law and Management* 284; A Lista, *EU Competition Law and the Financial Services Sector* (Abingdon, Taylor & Francis, 2013); F Ferretti, *EU Competition Law, the Consumer Interest and Data Protection: The Exchange of Consumer Information in the Retail Financial Sector* (New York, Springer, 2014).

the cases where financial market infrastructure has been assessed for potential violations of Articles 101 TFEU and 102 TFEU are this study's focal point. The discussion on concentration control in financial market infrastructure is reserved for the next sub-section.

The scope of Article 101 TFEU[30] covers anti-competitive agreements between economic market participants that restrict competition in the relevant markets. Examples of such conduct for the purposes of financial market infrastructure could include price-fixing for the provision of specific securities' trading, clearing or settlement activities. Next, as to Article 102 TFEU[31] (also referred to as 'monopolisation' in the US, regulated under the Sherman Act 1890 §2), financial market infrastructure entities can fall within the ambit of EU antitrust rules when there is evidence of an abuse of dominant position. Conduct by a dominant entity that can be characterised as anti-competitive includes predatory

[30] Art 101 TFEU reads as follows:

1. The following shall be prohibited as incompatible with the internal market: all agreements between undertakings, decisions by associations of undertakings and concerted practices which may affect trade between Member States and which have as their object or effect the prevention, restriction or distortion of competition within the internal market, and in particular those which:
   (a) directly or indirectly fix purchase or selling prices or any other trading conditions;
   (b) limit or control production, markets, technical development, or investment;
   (c) share markets or sources of supply;
   (d) apply dissimilar conditions to equivalent transactions with other trading parties, thereby placing them at a competitive disadvantage;
   (e) make the conclusion of contracts subject to acceptance by the other parties of supplementary obligations which, by their nature or according to commercial usage, have no connection with the subject of such contracts.
2. Any agreements or decisions prohibited pursuant to this Article shall be automatically void.
3. The provisions of paragraph 1 may, however, be declared inapplicable in the case of: – any agreement or category of agreements between undertakings, – any decision or category of decisions by associations of undertakings, – any concerted practice or category of concerted practices, which contributes to improving the production or distribution of goods or to promoting technical or economic progress, while allowing consumers a fair share of the resulting benefit, and which does not:
   (a) impose on the undertakings concerned restrictions which are not indispensable to the attainment of these objectives;
   (b) afford such undertakings the possibility of eliminating competition in respect of a substantial part of the products in question.

[31] Article 102 TFEU reads as follows: 'Any abuse by one or more undertakings of a dominant position within the internal market or in a substantial part of it shall be prohibited as incompatible with the internal market in so far as it may affect trade between Member States. Such abuse may, in particular, consist in:

(a) directly or indirectly imposing unfair purchase or selling prices or other unfair trading conditions;
(b) limiting production, markets or technical development to the prejudice of consumers;
(c) applying dissimilar conditions to equivalent transactions with other trading parties, thereby placing them at a competitive disadvantage;
(d) making the conclusion of contracts subject to acceptance by the other parties of supplementary obligations which, by their nature or according to commercial usage, have no connection with the subject of such contracts.'

pricing, exclusivity rebates, and refusals to supply so long as they result in negative effects in the relevant markets.[32]

Traditionally, the objectives behind antitrust law are the following: to preserve the process of competition for the benefit of consumers (also known as consumer welfare[33]); to ensure that there are strong incentives in place for businesses to operate efficiently; to keep prices down, and keep the quality of the products or services as high as possible.[34] Importantly, the objective functions of competition law include among others: (i) consumer protection from companies' potentially anti-competitive conduct; (ii) the redistribution of wealth through the promotion of economic equity rather than economic efficiency;[35] (iii) the protection of competitors; and, last but not least, (iv) the integration of the single market.[36] The following subsections pinpoint the relevant cases pertinent to financial market infrastructure and discuss the potential anticompetitive triggers that would be able to jeopardise the integration of the services in question in the EU internal market.

i. Clearstream: A Case of Dominance Impeding Competition in Financial Market Infrastructure

In September 2009 the General Court – called Court of First Instance at the time – dismissed the action for annulment[37] brought by Clearstream Banking AG – also referred to as Clearstream Banking Frankfurt – and Clearstream International SA (together called 'Clearstream' for convenience when there is no need for separation) against the 2 June 2004 Commission Decision in the

[32] The '*effects-based*' analysis of Art 102 TFEU is currently a hot topic for competition enforcing agencies and academic literature. For the relevant debates, see, for example, LH Röller and O Stehmann, 'The Year 2005 at DG Competition: The Trend towards a More Effects-Based Approach' (2006) 29 *Review of Industrial Organization* 281; G Monti, 'Article 82 EC: What Future for the Effects-Based Approach?' (2010) 1 *Journal of European Competition Law & Practice* 2; A Jones, 'The Journey toward an Effects-Based Approach under Article 101 TFEU – The Case of Hardcore Restraints' (2010) 55 *The Antitrust Bulletin* 783; P Nihoul, 'The Ruling of the General Court in Intel: Towards the End of an Effect-Based Approach in European Competition Law?' (2014) 5 *Journal of European Competition Law & Practice* 521; WPJ Wils, 'The Judgment of the EU General Court in Intel and the So-Called More Economic Approach to Abuse of Dominance' (2014) 37 *World Competition* 405.

[33] For discussion, see, inter alia, J Farrell and ML Katz, 'The Economics of Welfare Standards in Antitrust' (2006) 15 *Competition Policy International.*

[34] See R Whish and D Bailey, *Competition Law*, 9th edn (Oxford, Oxford University Press, 2018) 3–15. For a thought-provoking discussion, see WE Kovacic and C Shapiro, 'Antitrust Policy: A Century of Economic and Legal Thinking' (2000) 14 *Journal of Economic Perspectives* 43.

[35] O Odudu, 'The Distributional Consequences of Antitrust' in P Marsden (ed), *Handbook of Research in Trans-Atlantic Antitrust* (Cheltenham, Edward Elgar, 2006).

[36] Notably, the European Commissioner for competition policy, Margrethe Vestager, explained that 'The founding fathers of Europe understood that there would be no genuine integration without a Single Market – and no functioning Single Market without a strong competition policy enforced by a central competition authority' in her 'The values of competition policy' speech of 13 October 2015.

[37] Based on Art 263 TFEU.

Clearstream case. The Commission Decision had found that Clearstream infringed Article 102 TFEU by: (i) refusing to supply certain clearing and settlement services to Euroclear Bank SA, one of its customers; and (ii) applying discriminatory prices to Euroclear Bank SA (referred to as Euroclear Bank). The following paragraphs analyse the Commission Decision and the General Court's ruling in order to delineate which anticompetitive triggers are identified in the conduct of Clearstream and to underscore how this antitrust scrutiny constitutes a lesson for all financial market infrastructure providers in Europe.

a. Commission Decision in Case COMP/38.096

The Commission Decision[38] found that Clearstream Banking AG had a dominant position in the market for the provision of 'primary' clearing and settlement services for securities issued pursuant to German law to central securities depositories (CSDs) in other EU Member States and to international central securities depositories (ICSDs).[39] The Commission noted that Clearstream had a dominant position on the relevant market because the vast majority of financial instruments issued under German legislation were kept in collective safe custody, and only a *Wertpapiersammelbank* (a securites collection bank) was authorised to keep securities in custody within Germany. Interestingly, Clearstream was the only *Wertpapiersammelbank* in Germany and thus its dominant position was established.

As to specific abuses that the Commission found against Clearstream, its behaviour consisted of: (i) 'refusing to supply primary clearing and settlement services for registered shares by denying direct access to CASCADE RS, and discriminating against Euroclear Bank in relation to the supply of those services. The refusal to supply and the unjustified discrimination in relation to direct access to CASCADE RS are not two separate infringements, but rather two manifestations of the same behaviour, as the unjustified discrimination exists because CBF refused to supply Euroclear Bank with the same or similar services it was supplying to other comparable customers'; and (ii) 'applying discriminatory prices for the primary clearing and settlement services compared to such services it was providing to other comparable customers'.[40]

With respect to the first violation, it is settled case law of EU courts that undertakings holding a dominant position bear a special responsibility and, as such, in certain occasions refusals to supply (either in the form of refusals to

[38] Commission Decision of 2 June 2004 relating to a proceeding under Article 82 of the EC Treaty (Case COMP/38.096 – Clearstream (Clearing and Settlement)) [2009] OJ C165/7.

[39] See paras (205)–(215) of the Commission Decision. As to the business that ICSDs engage in, it relates to the clearing and settlement of Eurobonds mainly in international commercial environments. At the time, there were two ICSDs in the EU: Euroclear Bank, based in Belgium, and Clearstream Banking Luxembourg. ICSDs also provide other auxiliary services, such as intermediary services for equities: see para (19) of the Commission Decision.

[40] See para (216) of the Commission Decision.

start supplying or withdrawals to supply) might infringe Article 102 TFEU.[41] For completeness, US case law differs significantly on this score.[42] Notably, the Commission held that as Clearstream is a 'de facto monopolist' in the provision of primary clearing and settlement services in the market at issue; no other valid alternatives were available for Euroclear due to the high barriers to entry that amounted to making Clearstream the only option to supply those services.[43] In addition, Clearstream's refusal to provide services was at the expense of innovation and competition in the downstream market and, subsequently, to the detriment of the consumers of the EU internal market.

b. The Court's Judgment in Case T-301/04

Notably, the Court judgment confirmed both the Commission's delineation of the market and the existence of abusive conduct against Euroclear Bank, a direct competitor to Clearstream Luxembourg SA. Concerning the definition of the relevant market for services in the case at issue, the Commission and Clearstream had opposing views as to what the appropriate definition should be. On the one hand, the Commission claimed that a distinction between primary and secondary post-transaction securities processing services was crucial because of the particular market structure and the role of intermediaries vis-à-vis financial market infrastructure institutions. On the other hand, Clearstream contested this definition and, in consequence, the dominance held by it.

Specifically, Clearstream considered that the Commission's definition was artificial and underlined that 'post-transaction processing is carried out only once and for the benefit of the parties to the transaction alone', as intermediary depositories were not a part of this relationship.[44] Clearstream maintained that there was only one market in clearing and settlement services for German

[41] See, for example, the judgments in *Deutsche Post AG v GZS and Citicorp Kartenservice GmbH* Cases C-147/97 and C-148/97, ECLI:EU:C:2000:74 [2000] ECR I-825; *United Brands Company and United Brands Continentaal BV v Commission* Case 27/76, ECLI:EU:C:1978:22 [1978] ECR 207, para 182.

[42] Interestingly, one of the most unsettled domains of US antitrust law pertains to the duty of a monopolist to deal with its competitors. Generally, firms have no duty to deal with their competitors. In fact, imposing an obligation on a firm to carry out business with its rivals is not consonant with other antitrust rules that discourage agreements between competitors. For refusals to supply, case law in the US acknowledged that they are in the clear as long as there is a legitimate business reason behind this. The US Supreme Court in *Aspen Skiing Company v Aspen Highlands Skiing Corporation*, 472 US 585 (1985) came up with the concept of 'essential facilities' but it did not decide the case on the basis of this doctrine. Perhaps more interestingly, the Supreme Court in the 2004 case of *Verizon Communications, Inc v Law Offices of Curtis V Trinko, LLP*, 540 US 398 (2004) reaffirmed the general rule that businesses can refuse to deal with their competitors and made clear that it was not going to use the abovementioned doctrine as Courts are not supposed to become 'central planners' of the economy. For literature on the essential facilities doctrine in the US see, for example, R Pitofsky et al, 'The Essential Facilities Doctrine under Us Antitrust Law' (2002) 70 *Antitrust Law Journal* 443.

[43] See Commission Decision of 2 June 2004 (Clearing and Settlement) para (224).

[44] *Clearstream Banking AG and Clearstream International SA v Commission* Case T-301/04, ECLI:EU:T:2009:317, [2009] ECR II-03155 (*Clearstream v Commission*), para 36.

securities, in which Clearstream was in competition with Euroclear for the same final customers.[45]

On this score, the Court of First Instance acknowledged, at the outset, that the definition of product markets involved complex economic evaluations on the part of the European Commission and it was 'subject only to limited review by the Community judicature'.[46] The Court rejected Clearstream's argument that there was a general market in clearing and settlement services, in which those seeking services were the parties to the transaction (including the intermediary depositories when they acted on their own behalf) because by acting on behalf of parties to the transaction, the intermediary depositories were carrying on an independent business of providing services.[47]

As to the abuse, the Court's judgment addressed Clearstream's discriminatory behaviour against Euroclear Bank in comparison with other clients regarding refusal to supply services in the form of delaying the process of connecting Euroclear Bank to Clearstream's data processing system, and Clearstream charging Euroclear higher fees than it charged other clients for equivalent clearing and settlement services.[48]

With respect to Clearstream's refusal to supply, the arguments put forward by the applicant before the Court related to the complexity of the connection between Euroclear Baml and Clearstream,[49] and technical deficiencies at the end of Euroclear[50] that resulted in delaying the process of connecting the latter to the Clearstream's data processing system. In its judgment, the Court of First Instance found that Clearstream abused its dominant position by not offering Euroclear Bank access to the data processing services it had requested for over two years, while it provided access to other companies only within a few months.[51] It also reiterated that the concept of abuse is an objective concept pertinent to the behaviour of undertakings enjoying a dominant position.[52]

Regarding the application of discriminatory pricing at the expense of Euroclear Bank, Clearstream alleged that the Commission's decision had not taken into account a number of factors. Namely, that the services requested by Euroclear Bank were significantly different (including different transaction volumes, varying ranges of standardisation and automation, different insurance policies against civil liability and night services) vis-à-vis the ones offered to

[45] ibid para 38.

[46] ibid para 47. Such review would occur in cases of 'manifest error of assessment' on behalf of the Commission.

[47] ibid para 54. See to that effect, *British Airways plc v Commission* Case C-95/04 P, ECLI:EU:C:2007:166 [2007] ECR I-02331, para 93.

[48] ibid para 64.

[49] ibid para 80.

[50] ibid para 81.

[51] ibid paras 155–58.

[52] See, for example, *Hoffmann-La Roche & Co AG v Commission* Case 85/76, ECLI:EU:C:1979:36 [1979] ECR 461, para 91; and *Manufacture française des pneumatiques Michelin v Commission* Case T-203/01, ECLI:EU:T:2003:250 [2003] ECR II-04071, para 54.

Clearstream Banking Luxembourg SA, irrespective of the fact that they were both ICSDs.[53] Discriminatory pricing by a dominant undertaking is disallowed by subparagraph (c) of Article 102 TFEU. Importantly, in accordance with case law, dominant undertakings may not apply artificial price differences, such as to place its customers at a disadvantage and to distort competition.[54]

On the merits of the case, the Court held that the application to a trading partner of different prices for equivalent services – continuously over a period of five years – and by an undertaking having a de facto monopoly on the upstream market could not fail to cause that partner a competitive disadvantage and rejected Clearstream's argument. The Court dismissed Clearstream's arguments due to the higher per transaction fees charged to Euroclear in comparison to equivalent companies.[55]

For those reasons, Clearstream's behaviour amounted to abusive behaviour at odds with Article 102 TFEU. This case makes evident that abusive conduct in the form of discriminatory pricing and refusal to supply in financial market infrastructure is captured by EU antitrust law. Perhaps more importantly, this ruling sets a good precedent that underscores that the EU internal market may not permit anti-competitive conduct that would impede the integration prospects of its financial markets. Thus, it is held that the *Clearstream* case is a good example of how antitrust law as well as its enforcement and judicial review contribute to the liberalisation of financial markets by fighting against monopolisation in specific financial market infrastructure segments.

c. The CDS Cases: The Commission Investigations Relating to CDS Clearing and Information Market that, Finally, did not Hit the Target

The CDS clearing investigation was officially announced in April 2011.[56] The Commission was investigating whether the conditions of certain agreements concluded between ICE's CDS clearinghouse, ICE Clear, and nine banks prevented other clearing houses from competing in the relevant market or was discriminatory against other financial institutions. In the absence of sufficient evidence to substantiate an infringement, the Commission terminated its proceedings against ICE and the banks in December 2015.

Similarly, in April 2011 the Commission also initiated an investigation into the CDS information market, which related to an alleged concerted refusal by 16 banks to offer CDS price data to information service providers other than Markit.[57]

[53] *Clearstream v Commission*, paras 160–67.

[54] For the relevant jurisprudence, see *Tetra Pak International SA v Commission* Case T-83/91, ECLI:EU:T:1994:246 [1994] ECR II-755, para 160; and *Deutsche Bahn AG v Commission* Case T-229/94, ECLI:EU:T:1997:155 [1997] ECR II-01689, para 78.

[55] *Clearstream v Commission*, paras 194–95.

[56] See Case COMP/39.730; European Commission, 'Press Release, Antitrust: Commission Probes Credit Default Swaps Market' (European Commission, 29 April 2011) ec.europa.eu/commission/presscorner/detail/en/IP_11_509 accessed 25 July 2023.

[57] See Case COMP/39.745; ibid.

Interestingly, by July 2013 the Commission's theory of harm was modified, claiming that the banks, Markit and ISDA foreclosed entry to the market for exchange-traded unfunded credit derivatives. The Commission issued a statement of objections but, again, because of lack of evidence the proceedings were closed,[58] similar to the CDS clearing case. In 2016, Markit and ISDA offered commitments aiming to facilitate access to their respective intellectual property and data for exchange trading purposes that the Commission accepted.[59]

ii. The Manipulation of Interest Rate Derivatives: Anti-Competitive Trading under the EU Competition Enforcer's Scrutiny

The Commission's interest rate derivatives (IRDs) investigations were driven by immunity applications and were announced over a 14-month period: Euro IRDs were announced in October 2011; Japanese Yen IRDs were announced in March 2012; and Swiss Franc IRDs were announced in February 2013. These three investigations have led to the imposition of fines in the majority of cases according to the Commission's settlement procedure.[60]

As regards the Euro IRDs, in December 2013 – in the aftermath of settlement discussions – the Commission imposed fines amounting to €824m against four banks for discussions taking place among traders of those banks about their Euro Interbank Offered Rates (EURIBOR) submissions and, more broadly, their trading and pricing strategies.[61] Notably, Société General in February 2014 lodged an appeal against the calculation of its settlement fine[62] but it subsequently withdrew its appeal once the Commission dropped the fine to €227.7m, as the result of revised sales data. Three other banks did not settle and in December 2016, the Commission issued a decision imposing fines of €485m.[63] Those three banks have since appealed the Commission's decision before the EU General Court.[64]

[58] See European Commission, 'Press Release, Antitrust: Commission Closes Proceedings against 13 Investment Banks in Credit Default Swaps Case' (European Commission, 4 December 2015) ec.europa.eu/competition/antitrust/cases/dec_docs/39745/39745_13719_14.pdf accessed 25 July 2023.

[59] See European Commission, 'Press Release, Antitrust: Commission Accepts Commitments by ISDA and Markit on Credit Default Swaps' (European Commission, 20 July 2016) ec.europa.eu/commission/presscorner/detail/en/IP_16_2586 accessed 25 July 2023.

[60] See Art 10a of Commission Regulation (EC) No 773/2004 of 7 April 2004 relating to the conduct of proceedings by the Commission pursuant to Articles 81 and 82 of the EC Treaty [2004] OJ L123/18.

[61] See Commission Decision of 4 December 2013 relating to a proceeding under Article 101 of the Treaty on the Functioning of the European Union and Article 53 of the EEA Agreement (Case AT.39914 – Euro Interest Rate Derivatives) [2017] OJ C206/17. The four charged banks were Barclays, Deutsche Bank, Royal Bank of Scotland, and Société Generale.

[62] See *Société Generale v Commission* Case T-98/14, ECLI:EU:T:2016:131 (withdrawn).

[63] See European Commission, 'Press Release, Antitrust: Commission Accepts Commitments by ISDA and Markit on Credit Default Swaps' (n 59).

[64] For the appeals against the Commission Decision lodged by HSBC, JPMorgan Chase, and Credit Agricole, see respectively, *HSBC Holdings plc and Others v Commission* Case T-105/17, ECLI:EU:T:2019:675; *JPMorgan Chase v Commission* Case T-106/17, [2017] OJ C112/47; *Crédit*

By Orders, the President of the second Chamber of the General Court removed Cases T-419/18 and T-420/18 from the register of the General Court in view of the applicants' (ie Crédit Agricole and JPMorgan and Chase, respectively) wish to discontinue the judicial proceedings.[65] In respect of the proceedings lodged by HSBC, the General Court in its judgment of 24 September 2019 confirmed that the Commission had not committed a procedural error and confirmed on substance that HSBC had participated in a cartel. However, the General Court annulled the 2016 Commission Decision for insufficient justifications on the fine imposed and on the reduction factor that the Commission had used with the banks that settled in 2013.[66] In spite of the annulment of its fine, HSBC appealed to the Court of Justice on the elements that it did not win. Thus, the Court's judgment of 23 January 2023 deals only with the bank's appeal of the General Court judgment concerning the applied procedure (ie the presumption of innocence principle and its applications to the staggered hybrid settlement cases) and the substance of the case (namely, the notion of single and continuous infringement as well as the by object nature of the infringement and the possibility to bear pro-competitive elements in mind as part of the Commission's assessment under Article 101(1) TFEU).[67] In its judgment, the Court of Justice held that the General Court erred in applying the correct test regarding the presumption of innocence and in failing to evaluate the pro-competitive effects of the bank's conduct. Nevertheless, the Court ultimately found that the Commission did not breach the presumption of innocence and it was correct to qualify the bank's conduct as a by object infringement of Article 101 TFEU. With respect to the fines, the Commission re-adopted the fine for HSBC on 28 June 2021[68] and that decision is subject to separate actions for annulment that are currently pending before the Court of Justice.[69]

In respect of the Japanese Yen IRDs, during December 2013 and following discussions about settlement the Commission fined five banks and one broker firm the sum of €670m for discussions among traders of those financial institutions pertinent to their Japanese Yen London Interbank Offered Rate (LIBOR)

Agricole and Crédit Agricole Corporate and Investment Bank v Commission Case T-113/17 [2017] OJ C231/27.

[65] See Order of the President of the Second Chamber of the General Court of 6 June 2019 in Case T-420/18, ECLI:EU:T:2019:40 and Order of the President of the Second Chamber of the General Court of 7 May 2019 in Case T-419/18, ECLI:EU:T:2019:320.

[66] *HSBC Holdings plc and Others v Commission* Case T-105/17, ECLI:EU:T:2019:675, judgment of 24 September 2019.

[67] *HSBC Holdings plc and Others v Commission* Case C-883/19 P, ECLI:EU:C:2023:11, judgment of 12 January 2023.

[68] See Commission Decision C(2021) 4600 of 28.06.2021 which slightly reduced the amount of the fine of HSBC to €31.7m and improved the justification of that fine. At the same time, Commission Decision C(2021) 4610 28.06.2021 amended and improved the motivation of the 2016 Decision for *Crédit Agricole* and *JPMorgan Chase*.

[69] Case T-561/21, *HSBC v Commission*.

submissions and trading patterns.[70] In contrast with the abovementioned institutions, ICAP did not settle with the Commission and it was fined €15m in February 2015.[71] Subsequently, ICAP appealed the Commission's decision to the General Court that in November 2017 annulled part of the Commission's decision against ICAP with respect to the extent of its participation in the cartel.[72] The Commission has appealed this General Court judgment to the Court of Justice of the European Union.[73] In its judgment, the Court of Justice endorsed the General Court's reasoning in connection with the calculation of the fine and dismissed the Commission's appeal.[74]

As to the Swiss Franc IRDs, in October 2014 – once settlement agreements were reached – the Commission imposed fines totalling €94m against four financial institutions. The grounds for the fines were that they: (i) concluded agreements to quote wider bid-offer spreads to the market on certain types of Swiss Franc IRDs, while keeping narrower bid-offer spreads between themselves; and (ii) exchanged sensitive intelligence regarding specific trading positions and intended pricing strategies for future Swiss Franc LIBOR submissions.[75]

These antitrust investigations into collusive behaviour in the trading of financial instruments reveals that the enforcement of competition law does scrutinise and sanction the potentially anti-competitive conduct of entities participating in financial market infrastructure. The impact of the EU competition scrutiny in the financial infrastructure field is evaluated below in connection with its prospects of furthering the economic integration in the relevant markets.

[70] See Commission Decision of 4 December 2013 (Case AT.39861 – Yen Interest Rate Derivatives) (notified under document C(2013) 8602) [2016] OJ C348/14. The financial institutions under investigation were UBS, Royal Bank of Scotland, Deutsche Bank, JP Morgan, Citibank and broker RP Martin.

[71] See European Commission, 'Press Release, Antitrust: Commission Fines Broker ICAP €14.9 Million for Participation in Several Cartels in Yen Interest Rate Derivatives Sector' (European Commission, 4 February 2015) ec.europa.eu/commission/presscorner/detail/en/IP_15_4104 accessed 25 July 2023.

[72] See *ICAP and Others v Commission* Case T-180/15, ECLI:EU:T:2017:795, judgment of 10 November 2017.

[73] See the Commission appeal in *Commission v NEX International Limited, formerly Icap plc, Icap Management Services Ltd, Icap New Zealand Ltd* Case C-39/18 P, ECLI:EU:C:2019:584.

[74] See *Commission v ICAP and Others* Case C-39/18 P, ECLI:EU:C:2019:584, judgment of 10 July 2019. It is worth noting that the Court of Justice endorsed the Advocate General's views on the matter. See Opinion of Advocate General Tanchev delivered on 2 May 2019.

[75] See Comp/39924 Commission Decision of 21 October 2014 (Case AT.39924 – Swiss Franc Interest Rate Derivatives) (CHF LIBOR) (notified under document C(2014) 7605) [2015] OJ C72/9, and Comp/39924 Commission Decision of 21 October 2014 (Case AT.39924 – Swiss Franc Interest Rate Derivatives) (Bid Ask Spread Infringement) (notified under document C(2014) 7602) [2015] OJ C72/14. The banks in question were RBS, JP Morgan, Credit Suisse, and UBS. See also European Commission, 'Press Release, Antitrust: Commission Fines Broker ICAP €14.9 Million for Participation in Several Cartels in Yen Interest Rate Derivatives Sector' (n 71).

iii. Parallel Antitrust and Financial Regulatory Investigations and the Importance of Private Enforcement

In parallel to the general proliferation of competition scrutiny in financial services cases by the Commission, it is worth mentioning that investigations in the finance sector often involve concurrent investigations carried out by financial regulators. The raison d'être behind this is that the conduct under investigation that might be found in breach of EU competition laws might also be most commonly in violation of specific sets of financial regulations. For the sake of clarity, a few examples follow that illustrate how antitrust investigations may be coupled with the procedures lodged by financial regulators.

The LIBOR scandal in addition to the antitrust aspect was probed by financial regulators around the globe, such as the Department of Justice, the US Commodity Futures Trading Commission and the UK Financial Conduct Authority. The EU has coupled its efforts in addressing manipulation by various financial institutions of benchmarks used in trading with regulatory measures. In particular, on 16 April 2014 Market Abuse Regulation (MAR) (No 596/2014) and Market Abuse Directive (MAD) (2014/57/EU) on criminal sanctions were adopted.[76] Further, in June 2016 a Regulation on indices used as benchmarks in securities and financial contracts or measuring the performance of investment funds was adopted (No 2016/1011, also referred to as the Benchmarks Regulation).[77] Notably, the Benchmarks Regulation categorises the manipulation of benchmarks, such as EURIBOR, as a capital markets infringement and bolsters the investigative and sanctioning powers of financial regulators.[78]

For the sake of completeness, to gain a comprehensive understanding of the whole picture surrounding how antitrust in financial services works, it is necessary to bear in mind the role of private enforcement. With the advent of the

[76] For the legislative texts, see Directive 2014/57/EU of the European Parliament and of the Council of 16 April 2014 on criminal sanctions for market abuse (market abuse directive) [2014] OJ L173/179, and Regulation (EU) No 596/2014 of the European Parliament and of the Council of 16 April 2014 on market abuse (market abuse regulation) [2014] OJ L173/1. For literature on the subject of market abuse more broadly, see, for example, B Rider et al, *Market Abuse and Insider Dealing* (Oxford, Bloomsbury Publishing, 2016); JL Hansen, 'Market Abuse Case Law – Where Do We Stand With MAR?' (2017) 14 *European Company and Financial Law Review* 367; K Shahzad and G Mertens, 'The European Market Abuse Directive: Has It Worked?' (2017) 28 *Journal of International Financial Management & Accounting* 27.

[77] Regulation (EU) 2016/1011 of the European Parliament and of the Council of 8 June 2016 on indices used as benchmarks in financial instruments and financial contracts or to measure the performance of investment funds [2016] OJ L171/1. For general academic literature on benchmarks, see G-GS Fletcher, 'Benchmark Regulation' (2016) 102 *Iowa Law Review* 1929.

[78] For instance, the French Autorité de la Concurrence imposed fines of €384.9m on French banks that reached an agreement concerning interbank fees for processing cheques in the wake of the transition to a new digital clearing system. In a similar vein, the UK national competent authority found that two UK banks had unlawfully exchanged confidential pricing information with respect to commercial loans.

Damages Directive,[79] private actions for damages have significantly increased for financial services cases. As the result of the IRD investigation's fines imposed by the Commission, private claims have started to emerge. In January 2017, the US FDIC lodged a standalone claim in the UK, accusing the traders of a number of banks of colluding and misrepresenting their LIBOR submissions.[80]

iv. Competition Assessment of Antitrust Cases in Financial Market Infrastructure

On the basis of the first indicator for evaluating the pro-competitive elements of the EU integration model – ie the competitive landscape in the EU – the preceding analysis makes clear that the enforcement of EU antitrust law actively pursues the liberalisation of the European financial market infrastructure by countering monopolisation and tackling anti-competitive conduct. As discussed, companies that either have a tendency to abuse their dominant position in market segments of the financial infrastructure (eg the case of Clearstream) or they exchange sensitive information, carrying out cartel-like behaviour (namely, the banks in the EURIBOR and LIBOR cases) are scrutinised by the European Commission in order to avoid negative effects that can harm competition, consumers and innovation. Thus, there is no doubt that competition law contributes to further liberalising the financial market infrastructure of the EU.

As regards the second criterion on how EU antitrust impacts on the global competitive field, in a similar vein, it is maintained that once anti-competitive behaviours at the EU level are sanctioned by EU competition watchdogs, then international competition is more likely to flourish thanks to such interventions. In a counterfactual scenario under which European monopolists' conduct was not scrutinised and fined by the European Commission, it is obvious that international competition in the relevant markets would be foreclosed. Therefore, with higher barriers to entry, fewer (if any) international competitors would be willing to compete in those markets. Consequently, international competition in financial

[79] Council Directive 2014/104/EU of the European Parliament and of the Council of 26 November 2014 on certain rules governing actions for damages under national law for infringements of the competition law provisions of the Member States and of the European Union [2014] OJ L349/1. By now, all EU Member States have implemented the Damages Directive. For literature reflecting on the Directive in competition law literature see, for instance, FP Maier-Rigaud, 'Toward a European Directive on Damages Actions' (2014) 10 *Journal of Competition Law and Economics* 341; A Piszcz, 'Piecemeal Harmonisation Through the Damages Directive? Remarks on What Received Too Little Attention in Relation to Private Enforcement of EU Competition Law' (2015) 8 *Yearbook of Antitrust and Regulatory Studies* 79; N Dunne, 'Courage and Compromise: The Directive on Antitrust Damages' (2015) 40(4) *European Law Review* 581; M Driessen-Reilly, 'Private Damages in EU Competition Law and Arbitration: A Changing Landscape' (2015) 31 *Arbitration International* 567; S Peyer, 'Compensation and the Damages Directive' (2016) 12 *European Competition Journal* 87.

[80] See Particulars of Claim in *The Federal Deposit Insurance Corporation (as receiver for Amcore Bank NA and others) v Barclays Bank PLC and Others* [2020] EWHC 2001 (Ch).

market infrastructure is fostered by the application of EU antitrust law targeting unfair monopolisation as well as concerted practices.

With respect to the extent to which the competitiveness of the EU industry is affected by how EU antitrust law enforcement occurs, it suffices to say that in the above-named cases brought by the European Commission the companies that were scrutinised were in their majority either EU monopolists (ie Clearstream) or EU Member States' banks or subsidiaries of third-country financial institutions. Thus, the international competitiveness of the EU industry is not by any means supported by way EU antitrust law has been applied and the above-mentioned examples show why.

To conclude, this analysis has shown how EU antitrust law has contributed to the liberalisation of particular market segments of the EU internal financial market infrastructure. The following analysis elucidates how merger control has been instrumental in promoting the integration of financial market infrastructure in the EU internal market.

C. EU Merger Control: A Mechanism Preventing Monopolistic Concentration Structures in Financial Market Infrastructure

As the liberalisation of financial infrastructure in the EU started to increase as a response to regulatory frameworks' mandates, which sought to turn the EU internal market into a truly liberalised area for trading financial services, and the traditionally monopolistic financial market infrastructure started to become subject to competitive market forces, concentration ventures came into play. The rationale behind merger control is to prevent concentration structures that could be capable of independently making market decisions without bearing in mind competitors' business models and pricing strategies – and ultimately amounting to monopoly powers or, more generally, ensure that rivalry in the market will not be upset because of a merger. It should be underlined that merger control is a forward-looking exercise, hence uncertainty is factored into any concentration control investigation by competition authorities. To that end, EU concentration control[81] acts in favour of preserving markets' competitive forces when there are valid concerns that a proposed merger would lead to monopolistic outcomes for specific market segments.

In the same vein, the European Commission evaluates financial infrastructure mergers in relation to their potential anti-competitive effects. It is crucial for this study to investigate how the EU competition watchdog argues in favour of maintaining competition in segments of the European Economic Area (EEA) financial market infrastructures in order to understand how the liberalisation of

[81] See Council Regulation (EC) No 139/2004 of 20 January 2004 on the control of concentrations between undertakings (the EC Merger Regulation) [2004] OJ L24/1.

those financial services in the EU is promoted. Importantly, the forces of financial regulation, in parallel with the mechanics of concentration control, foster the liberalisation of the financial infrastructure in the EU. The following analysis demonstrates how the EU regime on merger control has promoted the liberalisation of the financial infrastructure by not clearing two proposed mega mergers for the European financial infrastructure industry and by approving another merger of importance for financial data products in the financial market infrastructure subject to certain commitments.

As case studies, Section III.C.i focuses on the New York Stock Exchange (NYSE), Euronext and Deutsche Börse (DB) proposed deal that the Commission prohibited in 2012; Section III.C.ii analyses the London Stock Exchange (LSE) and DB proposed merger that was blocked by the Commission in 2017, in the aftermath of the Brexit referendum; and Section III.C.iii discusses the LSE and Refinitiv merger clearance of 2021 conditional of full compliance with certain commitments, bringing financial data considerations to the fore.

i. NYSE EURONEXT/DB Failed Merger: A Powerhouse in Trading and Clearing Benchmark Exchange-Traded Derivatives that Never Happened

A sensitive balance that policymakers have to strike relates to preserving competition in the EEA without, at the same time, jeopardising EU industries' global competitiveness. That is precisely the point where the interface lies between antitrust and international trade law. On the one hand, European markets should not be foreclosed by the anti-competitive conduct of one[82] – or more than one[83] – economic actors or potential mergers[84] because companies have to compete on their merits for competition to flourish; efficiency arguments are factored into all the above assessments carried out by competition authorities. On the other hand, to preserve the Union's interest and for the EU's economy to grow it is essential that the European industry is able to compete head-to-head with the other global players, and as such, it should be sufficiently competitive.

There are trade defence instruments that cater for the latter when it comes to trade in goods.[85] However, for trade in services, and specifically financial services, it is regulators – together with competition authorities – that have

[82] In the form of unilateral abusive behaviour by a dominant company at odds with Art 102 TFEU, as discussed above.

[83] In the form of competition violations set forth in Art 101 TFEU.

[84] Merger control is the focal point of the following analysis.

[85] Nevertheless, these trade defence instruments are applicable only on trade in goods, and their scope does not include trade in services or intellectual property. For general literature on trade remedies see, for example, BM Hoekman and PC Mavroidis, 'Dumping, Antidumping and Antitrust' (1996) 30 *Journal of World Trade* 27; AO Sykes, 'International Trade: Trade Remedies' in AT Guzman and AO Sykes (eds), *Research Handbook in International Economic Law* (Cheltenham, Edward Elgar, 2007); CP Bown, 'The Global Resort to Antidumping, Safeguards, and Other Trade Remedies amidst the Economic Crisis' (2009) 5051 The World Bank Policy Research Working Paper Series; KW Bagwell et al (eds), *Law and Economics of Contingent Protection in International Trade* (Cambridge, Cambridge University Press, 2009).

the first and the last word on how the services in question are to be supplied in and out of their respective jurisdictions, assuming that the trade disciplines and commitments discussed in Chapter 2 and Chapter 3 are respected. Notably, the divergence in the economic models of global powers' (notably the US and China) brings into the spotlight the fact that the relationship between global competition and international trade needs to be re-evaluated in order to achieve predictability, fairness, and certainty as to how the terms of trade are determined for global players active in the major markets.

Following this, to preserve competition in on-exchange derivatives clearing activities, the Commission in February 2012 did not clear the proposed merger between DB and NYSE Euronext.[86] In the Commission's words, the merger would have led to a 'quasi-monopoly in the area of European financial derivatives traded globally on exchanges'.[87] The combined control of European derivatives traded on exchanges – as opposed to the ones traded OTC – of the two stock exchanges would have exceeded 90 per cent of the global trade in these financial instruments. The Commission identified in its Decision the differences between OTC and exchange-traded derivatives (ETDs).[88] Importantly, the Commission investigation concluded that significant barriers to entry would be raised if the entities were to merge, as new competitors would be unlikely to enter the market successfully enough to be a credible competitive threat.

At the time, Eurex[89] (operated by DB) and Life[90] (operated by NYSE Euronext) had globally the largest market shares for derivatives based on European underlying assets. They used to 'compete fiercely to attract and maintain liquidity', 'compete on fees, in technology and in product and market design' and were each other's 'closest actual and potential competitors'. In terms of fees, for derivative contracts where directly comparable alternatives were available on

[86] A Barker, 'D Börse and NYSE Challenge to Block Merger' (*Financial Times*, 30 January 2012) www.ft.com/content/d3caa948-4b41-11e1-88a3-00144feabdc0 accessed 25 July 2023.

[87] European Commission, 'Press Release, Mergers: Commission Blocks Proposed Merger between Deutsche Börse and NYSE Euronext' (European Commission, 1 February 2012) europa.eu/rapid/press-release_IP-12-94_en.htm accessed 25 July 2023.

[88] See Commission Decision of 1 February 2012 addressed to Deutsche Börse AG and NYSE Euronext declaring a concentration to be incompatible with the internal market and the functioning of the EEA Agreement (Case No COMP/M.6166 – DEUTSCHE BÖRSE / NYSE EURONEXT) COM (2012) 440 final, paras 328, 543. Most importantly, ETDs and OTC derivatives are destined for different type of trading strategies. While ETDs are suitable for short-term holding of positions, OTC markets, conversely, more adequately cater for longer-term strategies. This is because ETDs, due to their high liquidity, as a rule trade at narrow bid-ask spreads in a fully straight-through processing electronic manner with fast electronic matching for price discovery, while OTC markets have generally wider bid-ask spreads and still include broking for price discovery, at least for highly customised agreements. Therefore, it is generally more difficult to get out of a position in the OTC market as compared to the more liquid on-exchange environment.

[89] For more information on Eurex, see Eurex, 'About Us' (Eurex) www.eurex.com/ex-en/find/about-us accessed 25 July 2023.

[90] For more information on Liffe, see CFI Team, 'What Is the London International Financial Futures and Options Exchange (LIFFE)?' (Corporate Finance Institute, 25 January 2018) corporatefinanceinstitute.com/resources/derivatives/london-international-financial-futures-exchange-liffe/ accessed 25 July 2023.

other trading platforms, price competition existed between exchanges. Within this framework, the challenger prices at a considerable discount to the incumbent to attempt to overcome the latter's liquidity advantage, and is also in a position to do so because of the fact that he faces only fixed costs of entry. In a similar vein, the incumbent's capacity to respond with aggressive price cuts itself is restrained primarily by a concern to avoid undercutting its own future revenues once it has addressed the competitive threat.[91]

With respect to the market definition, the relevant market for the purposes of the Commission's analysis was the European financial derivatives market, narrowed down to European single stock, interest rate, and equity index derivatives traded on exchanges.

The Horizontal Merger Guidelines identify the situations where a potential concentration can affect the competition in the relevant markets. Specifically:

> a merger may significantly impede effective competition in a market by removing important competitive constraints on one or more sellers or service providers, who consequently have increased market power. The most direct effect of the merger will be the loss of competition between the merging firms. For example, if prior to the merger one of the merging firms had raised its prices, it would have lost some sales to the other merging firm. The merger removes this particular constraint.[92]

As part of the competitive assessment of the trading and clearing of exchange-traded derivatives, general parameters – such as the cost of trading, attracting liquidity, technology, innovation, and process and market design – were borne in mind.[93] In particular, according to the European Commission, the outcome of the proposed merger would have substantially eliminated global competition and would have resulted in important harm to parties to derivatives contracts and the European economy more broadly. In the absence of effective competitive constraint left in the market, the benefits of price competition would be taken away from the relevant market. Notably, the Commission investigation demonstrated that the high barriers to entry would discourage any other players from developing trading in European financial derivatives on a sufficient scale to keep the market competitive. Importantly, the Merger Control Regulation makes clear that all mergers that generate such non-coordinated effects shall be declared incompatible with the internal market.[94]

For a general overview of the players involved in derivatives based on European financial underlying and key parameters of their services, see the Commission's table produced for the purposes of the merger at issue:

[91] Commission Decision of 1 February 2012 addressed to Deutsche Börse AG and NYSE Euronext, paras 543–44.

[92] Guidelines on the assessment of horizontal mergers under the Council Regulation on the control of concentrations between undertakings [2004] OJ C31/5, para 24.

[93] Commission Decision of 1 February 2012 addressed to Deutsche Börse AG and NYSE Euronext, paras 500–34.

[94] EC Merger Regulation, recital 25.

Figure 9 Commission's Market Overview[95]

Company	Product offerings			Significant volumes			Sizable European Membership base	Sizable margin pool in European underlyings	Margin offset possibilities between European underlyings
	IR	EI	SE	IR	EQ	SE			
DB	•	•	•	•	•	•	•	•	•
NYX	•	•	•	•	•	•	•	•	•
CME	•	X	X	X	X	X	X	X	X
Turquoise	X	•	X	X	X	X	X	X	X
Nasdaq OMX	•	•	•	X	X	X	X	X	•
TOM	X	X	•	X	X	X	X	X	X
ELX	X	X	X	X	X	X	X	X	X

a. Barriers to Entry in the Relevant Markets

As regards barriers to entry, pursuant to the Horizontal Merger Guidelines:

> when entering a market is sufficiently easy, a merger is unlikely to pose any significant anti-competitive risk. Therefore, entry analysis constitutes an important element of the overall competitive assessment. For entry to be considered a sufficient competitive constraint on the merging parties, it must be shown to be likely, timely and sufficient to deter or defeat any potential anticompetitive effects of the merger.[96]

The General Court has held that 'the mere "threat" of an entry is not sufficient [...] What counts is the prospect of an entrant which offsets the anti-competitive effects specifically established in the contested decision at the stage of the assessment'.[97]

Barriers to entry can be defined as features of the market which give the incumbent firms an advantage over potential competitors.[98]

[95] Commission Decision of 1 February 2012 addressed to Deutsche Börse AG and NYSE Euronext, para 134.

[96] Horizontal Merger Guidelines, para 68.

[97] *Ryanair Holdings plc v Commission* Case T-342/07, ECLI:EU:T:2010:280 [2010] ECR II-03457, Recital 239.

[98] Horizontal Merger Guidelines, para 70.

In a similar vein, according to the EU General Court, barriers to entry:

> may consist in elements of various natures, in particular economic, commercial or financial elements, which are likely to expose potential competitors of the established undertakings to risks and costs sufficiently high to deter them from entering the market within a reasonable time or to make it particularly difficult for them to enter the market, thus depriving them of the capacity to exercise a competitive constraint on the conduct of the established undertakings.[99]

It follows from the above that competition authorities shall persuasively establish that entry is not only a theoretical and unlikely possibility, but will be an existing and actual threat for the merged entity, thereby placing a competitive constraint on competitors to such an extent that they would refrain from any merger-induced anti-competitive behaviour, if they seek to block a concentration.[100]

On this score, the Commission concluded that European interest rate and equity derivatives were characterised by high barriers to entry. Incumbent firms enjoyed considerable advantages over rival trading platforms because of the netting and cross-margining benefits available to incumbent firms and closed clearing margin pools.[101] Specifically, barriers to entry in European equity index derivatives were particularly high because the popular equity indices were IP protected and the IP was controlled by DB and NYSE Euronext – who had made it clear that they were not motivated to, and would not, license these indices to competing exchanges. Any replication of indices would be difficult and susceptible to be challenged legally. Given the popularity and the correlation with European single stock derivatives and desire of customers to trade these in tandem, the inability to obtain a licence to list derivatives on these benchmark indices may also deter entry into these neighbouring markets.[102] In addition, the membership base and the associated distribution network constituted a barrier to entry into European derivatives markets, especially for *de novo* players.[103]

b. Analysis on Countervailing Buying Power

As to the countervailing buying power of the contemplated transaction, it should be taken into consideration that in accordance with the Horizontal Merger Guidelines:

> countervailing buyer power in this context should be understood as the bargaining strength that the buyer has vis-à-vis the seller in commercial negotiations due to its

[99] *Cementbouw Handel & Industrie BV v Commission* Case T-282/02, ECLI:EU:T:2006:64 [2006] ECR II-319, Recital 219.

[100] See *Ryanair Holdings plc v Commission* Case T-342/07, ECLI:EU:T:2010:280 [2010] ECR II-03457, recital 547.

[101] Commission Decision of 1 February 2012 addressed to Deutsche Börse AG and NYSE Euronext, para 964. In addition to the Merger Control Regulation and its enforcement, the financial regulation discussed above, namely EMIR and MiFID II, has played an eminent role in opening up these silos to allow further liberalisation of the relevant markets, see above.

[102] ibid para 977.

[103] ibid para 983.

size, its commercial significance to the seller and its ability to switch to alternative suppliers.[104]

No evidence of buyer power on the markets in question has been substantiated. In particular, a specific dealer taking its business elsewhere would not exercise any countervailing power, as customers are not the ones dictating terms in the relevant markets. Notably, liquidity is the determinant factor[105] and, therefore, again not much leverage from the buyer's side had been evidenced in the proposed merger.[106]

Accordingly, in view of the absence of countervailing factors, the Commission concluded for the purpose of this Decision that the notified transaction was likely to result in a significant impediment to effective competition. This would occur by eliminating the closest actual and potential competitor and creating a dominant or quasi-monopoly position in the following markets, irrespective of the precise geographic market definition and for all categories of customers: the market for trading and clearing of existing and new European exchange-traded interest rate futures and options, independently of whether or not this market were to be divided between short- and long-term interest rate derivatives and/or on the basis of the currency of the underlying; and the market for trading and clearing of existing and new European exchange-traded single stock futures and options, independently of whether or not this market were to be defined at the basis of single underlyings, all underlyings of a given nationality, or all EEA underlyings.[107]

Additionally, the notified transaction would have resulted in a significant impediment of effective competition in the area of new exchange-traded European equity index futures and options by eliminating the closest competitor. The Commission found that given that it was unlikely that a timely entry would occur and sufficiently constrain the merged entity in its market behaviour, and in the absence of countervailing buyer power, the Notifying Parties' customers would have likely faced higher fees, less product innovation and would de facto have had no choice of trading platform for these products.[108]

Ultimately, the notified transaction would have combined the two leading European derivatives exchanges that are de facto the only relevant players in

[104] Horizontal Merger Guidelines, para 64.

[105] In securities regulation, the existence of the 'best execution' rule determines how trading flows are to chosen in order to, similarly, promote liquidity and offer to investors the best choice in terms of executing the trade order at the lowest available price. For literature on the principle of best execution in the US and the EU, see, for example, DA Lipton, 'Best Execution: The National Market System's Missing Ingredient' (1982) 57 *Notre Dame Law Review* 449; KD Garbade and WL Silber, 'Best Execution in Securities Markets: An Application of Signaling and Agency Theory' (1982) 37 *The Journal of Finance* 493; G Ferrarini, 'Best Execution and Competition between Trading Venues – MiFID's Likely Impact' (2007) 2 *Capital Markets Law Journal* 404; S Grundmann, 'The Fault Principle as the Chameleon of Contract Law: A Market Function Approach' (2009) 107 *Michigan Law Review* 1583.

[106] Commission Decision of 1 February 2012 addressed to Deutsche Börse AG and NYSE Euronext, paras 1013–21.

[107] ibid para 1022.

[108] ibid paras 1023–24.

the markets for European derivatives. On this score, the proposed merger, if it had been cleared, would have eliminated actual and potential competition in a number of derivatives products areas, namely existing and new European interest rate and single stock equity derivatives, irrespective of the precise product and geographic market definitions. Similarly, competition in the area of new European equity index derivatives would have been eliminated as a consequence of the notified transaction.

c. Other Final Considerations that Drove the Commission Decision

Competition between the NYSE Euronext and DB in technology, processes, service and market design would have also been eliminated, as the barriers to entry into these markets were high and countervailing buyer power weak. The Commission concluded that, given the elimination of the only credible constraint that currently exists in these markets, the merged entity would most likely have been able to impose higher trading and clearing fees to customers in the EEA and engage in less product and technology innovation. The de facto choice of derivatives trading platforms in the relevant product areas would have gone from two to one, and a ramification of this would be that customers would see a reduction in the quality of service.[109]

Moreover, the Commission found that the contemplated transaction between DB and NYSE Euronext was likely to harm competition and innovation in European interest rate and single stock equity derivatives markets at a moment when regulatory initiatives were expected to lead to significantly greater volumes of derivatives being traded and/or cleared on exchange.[110] As to the greater impact of the notified transaction, exchange traded derivatives are very important for the economy because they 'serve as insurance against price movements and reduce the volatility of companies' cash flows, which in turn results in more reliable forecasting, lower capital requirements, and higher capital productivity'.[111] Exchange-traded derivatives also contribute to creating a more liquid financial market for raising capital, which benefits both small and medium enterprises and larger firms. With no disciplining force left in the market, the merger was most likely to remove the benefits of price competition from retail and institutional investors and lead to less innovation in these markets where companies and financial institutions constantly look for new alternatives for their risk transfer solutions.

On the basis of its assessment, the Commission found that the proposed merger was likely to result in a significant impediment of effective competition

[109] ibid para 1028.

[110] The regulatory measures of this Commission conclusion are pertinent to the MiFID II/MiFIR and EMIR attempts to foster competition in the relevant financial market infrastructure, discussed above.

[111] Commission Decision of 1 February 2012 addressed to Deutsche Börse AG and NYSE Euronext, para 1029.

by creating a dominant or near-monopoly position and eliminating the closest actual and potential competitor in the markets for: existing and new European exchange-traded interest rate futures and options, independently of whether or not this market were to be divided between short- and long-term interest rate derivatives and/or on the basis of the currency of the underlying; existing and new European exchange-traded single stock futures and options, independently of whether or not this market were to be defined as the basis of single underlyings, all underlyings of a given nationality, or all EEA underlyings; off-order book services for block size European ETD contracts (irrespective of whether this market is further divided on any of the lines considered for on-book trading); and trade registration, confirmation and CCP clearing services for flexible versions of European equity futures and options traded OTC.[112]

Ultimately, the Commission's evaluation of the proposed merger between NYSE Euronext and DB that culminated in a blocking decision represents a good illustration of some of the conflicts competition authorities face. Had the Commission cleared this merger, the EU's financial market infrastructure global competitiveness would have been reinforced. Nevertheless, the European trustbuster chose to further the objectives of the internal market and, therefore, blocked the notified transaction. By allowing the European financial market infrastructure to continue growing and building capacity without facing captive markets for the trading and clearing of on-exchange derivatives, the Commission followed its mandate stipulated in the Merger Control Regulation. In a similar vein, the following analysis focuses on how the Commission assessed the proposed merger between DB and LSE in a much more turbulent regulatory and trade environment due to the aftermath of the Brexit vote.

ii. LSE/DB: Third Time was not the Charm for the Merger between LSE and Deutsche Börse

On 29 March 2017, the European Commission blocked the proposed merger – and the third attempt in 17 years for the two entities to come together– between LSE and DB after the two financial exchange groups refused to meet the Commission's requests to offset concerns about the creation of 'a de facto' monopoly in the clearing services of fixed income. As in the previous case study, the creation of an EU champion capable of challenging the top US and Asian competitors, such as CME and ICE, never occurred.[113]

For the purposes of reviewing the notified transaction in question, the Commission carried out an investigation that concluded that the proposed

[112] ibid para 1031.

[113] For more information about the story behind the merger in question, see R Toplensky and P Stafford, 'Brussels Blocks London Stock Exchange-Deutsche Börse Merger' (*Financial Times*, 29 March 2017) www.ft.com/content/8c582e2a-13d0-11e7-80f4-13e067d5072c accessed 25 July 2023; *cf* P Stafford, 'How the LSE and Deutsche Börse's Merger Unraveled' (*Financial Times*, 3 March 2017) www.ft.com/content/80053cd0-ff5d-11e6-8d8e-a5e3738f9ae4 accessed 25 July 2023. For the

merger would have produced a de facto monopoly in the markets for clearing fixed income financial instruments, by combining the businesses of the two largest European stock exchange operators. Together LSE and DB owned the stock exchanges of Germany, the UK, Italy, and also several of the largest European clearing houses. Notably, as the parties failed to offer the remedies required to alleviate the watchdog's competition concerns, in the form of divestiture or behavioural commitments, the Commission decided not to clear the merger.[114] This was the key in this case. If remedies had been accepted by the parties, the merger would have been cleared. It should be borne in mind that structural remedies are routinely recommended in merger control but only sparingly in 101 and 102 antitrust cases because they are perceived to be disproportional for the latter.[115]

In a telling table, the Commission demonstrates how the legal entities through which DB and LSE were actively participating in the relevant financial services markets complemented one another:

Figure 10 LSE and DB Presence in Various Product Classes along the EU Financial Infrastructure Value Chain[116]

Asset classes →

Value chain ↓

	Equities		Bonds		Repos		Derivatives	
Listing	• DBAG (FWB)	• LSE • Borsa Italiana	• FWB	• LSE • Borsa Italiana				
Trading	• Xetra • FWB • Trade Gate	• LSE • Borsa Italiana • Turquoise	• Eurex Bonds • FWB	• MTS • Borsa Italiana • EuroTXL	• Eurex Repo	• MTS	• Eurex • EEX	• LSE DM
Clearing	• Eurex Clearing	• LCH Ltd • LCH SA • CC&G	• Eurex Clearing	• LCH Ltd • LCH SA • CC&G	• Eurex Clearing	• LCH Ltd • LCH SA • CC&G	• Eurex Clearing • OTCClear • ECC	• LCH Ltd • LCH SA • CC&G
Custody, settlement, and collateral management	• Clear-stream	• Monte Titoli • (globe Settle)	• Clear-stream	• Monte Titoli	• Clear-stream	• Monte Titoli	• Clearstream	• Monte Titoli

Decision, see Commission Decision of 29 March 2017 declaring a concentration to be incompatible with the internal market and the functioning of the EEA Agreement (Case M.7995 – Deutsche Börse / London Stock Exchange).

[114] European Commission, 'Press Release, Mergers: Commission Blocks Proposed Merger between Deutsche Börse and London Stock Exchange' (European Commission, 29 March 2017) https://ec.europa.eu/commission/presscorner/detail/en/IP_17_789 accessed 2 August 2023.

[115] For the body of literature discussing structural and behavioural remedies, see, among others, WE Kovacic, 'Designing Antitrust Remedies for Dominant Firm Misconduct' (1998) 31 *Connecticut Law Review* 1285; PL Joskow, 'Transaction Cost Economics, Antitrust Rules, and Remedies' (2002) 18 *Journal of Law, Economics, and Organization* 95; T Sullivan, 'Antitrust Remedies in the US and EU: Advancing a Standard of Proportionality' (2003) 48 *The Antitrust Bulletin* 377; P Hellström et al, 'Remedies in European Antitrust Law' (2009) 76 *Antitrust Law Journal* 43; W Wang, 'Structural Remedies in EU Antitrust and Merger Control' (2011) 34 *World Competition* 571; JE Kwoka and DL Moss, 'Behavioral Merger Remedies: Evaluation and Implications for Antitrust Enforcement' (2012) 57 *The Antitrust Bulletin* 979.

[116] Commission Decision of 29 March 2017, Deutsche Börse / London Stock Exchange (Case COMP/M.7995), para 24.

Additionally, it is worth highlighting that there is strong vertical integration in the infrastructure of DB and LSE for the trading and clearing of financial exchange-traded derivatives.[117] Since MiFID II and MiFIR came into force[118] and the clearing of ETDs is required through EMIR for specific transactions, bundle-to-bundle competition for trading and clearing services has increased significantly.

In Chapter 2, we discussed how the EU financial regulatory terms-of-trade for the recognition of third-country clearinghouses comply with WTO norms of non-discrimination and good administration in the international economic law context. In the private sphere under competition law, similar standards apply when companies are dominant in specific markets of the EU. In this context, the notifying parties' underlined how LCH.Clearnet's commitment to provide open access on fair, reasonable, and non-discriminatory (FRAND) terms prevents it from engaging in any type of foreclosure strategy.[119]

a. Commission's Main Concerns Relating to the Proposed Merger

As to the specific objections expressed by the European Commission, the services that raised red flags from a competition standpoint were the clearing of fixed income instruments – specifically, the markets for bonds and repurchase agreements (repos) – as the parties were the only relevant providers of these services in Europe. Notably, the barriers to entry into financial infrastructure markets are high, due to strong network effects and economies of scale and scope. In order to successfully enter the market, a new player would have to: (i) overcome high investments; and (ii) overcome high regulatory requirements; (iii) achieve low costs; (iv) position itself to offer innovative product offerings to challenge what existing CCPs are able to offer; and (v) obtain the support of a sufficient number of market participants.[120]

In paragraph 200 of its Decision, the Commission concluded 'the Transaction would lead to a significant impediment of effective competition through the strengthening of a dominant position and creation of a de facto monopoly in the market for CCP clearing of bonds in the EEA'.

The Commission took account of the following factors in its evaluation: (i) the fact that the proposed merger would result in eliminating the only other player active in the clearing of automated trading system (ATS) of non-triparty repos; (ii) the importance of clearing for customers trading non-triparty repos

[117] ibid para 42.

[118] Directive 2004/39/EC of the European Parliament and of the Council of 21 April 2004 on markets in financial instruments amending Council Directives 85/611/EEC and 93/6/EEC and Directive 2000/12/EC of the European Parliament and of the Council and repealing Council Directive 93/22/EEC [2004] OJ L145/1; Regulation (EU) No 600/2014 of the European Parliament and of the Council of 15 May 2014 on markets in financial instruments [2014] OJ L173/84 (MiFIR).

[119] Commission Decision of 29 March 2017, Deutsche Börse / London Stock Exchange (Case COMP/M.7995), para 78.

[120] ibid 196–97.

on ATS; and (iii) the lack of likely entry. The Commission found that the LSE and DB proposed merger would lead to a significant impediment of effective competition through the strengthening of a dominant position on the market for ATS traded and CCP cleared non-triparty repos in the EEA. This finding is irrespective of the precise market definition.[121]

Further, having borne in mind the high market shares of LSE and DB, the elimination of DBAG's sole competitor, the likely intensification of competition that was expected to occur absent the contemplated transaction and the lack of likely market entry, the Commission noted that the proposed merger would result in an important restraint of effective competition on the same markets.[122]

The Commission analysis delved into specific aspects of the proposed merger concerning vertical foreclosure. Broadly, with respect to vertical foreclosure, two types of foreclosure can arise: (i) restriction of access to an important input (input foreclosure); or (ii) restriction of access to a sufficient customer base (customer foreclosure).[123] Importantly, 'A merger is said to result in foreclosure where actual or potential rivals' access to supplies or markets is hampered or eliminated as a result of the merger, thereby reducing these companies' ability and/or incentive to compete'.[124] Furthermore, the Commission guidelines on the assessment of non-horizontal mergers stipulate, 'significant harm to effective competition normally requires that the foreclosed firms play a sufficiently important role in the competitive process on the downstream market'.[125] They also mandate, 'for input foreclosure to lead to consumer harm, it is not necessary that the merged firm's rivals are forced to exit the market'.[126]

On this score, the Commission's assessment drew the conclusion that there would be no market player able to replace the competitive pressure exercised by Euroclear on Clearstream had the merger gone through. In addition, the contemplated transaction between DB and LSE would result in an important impediment to effective competition by offering the merged company the capacity and the incentive to foreclose competitors from the markets for international and custody services for fixed income.[127] As a general note, it is important to highlight that the more thorough the Commission's analysis is, and the more market segments it takes into consideration, the higher the likelihood that its findings do not miss any relevant factor.

[121] ibid 381–418. In particular, the Commission reached this finding irrespective of whether the markets are defined as a combined market for the trading and clearing of ATS traded non-triparty repos or a market for clearing of ATS traded non-triparty repos that is separate from trading of ATS non-triparty repos that are CCP cleared.

[122] ibid 465.

[123] ibid 570.

[124] Guidelines on the assessment of non-horizontal mergers under the Council Regulation on the control of concentrations between undertakings [2008] OJ C265/6, para 29.

[125] ibid para 48.

[126] ibid para 31.

[127] Commission Decision of 29 March 2017, Deutsche Börse / London Stock Exchange (Case COMP/M.7995), paras 653, 669.

Moreover, as to the role of regulation to alleviate anti-competitive conduct, the Commission concluded that the regulation on CSDs[128] and Target-2-Securities (T2S)[129] were not able to prevent the harm to competition.[130] On this score, the Commission concluded that the proposed merger between DB and LSE would lead to a significant impediment of effective competition in the markets for settlement and custody services provided in relation to fixed income by ICSDs and global custodians. By virtue of the parties':

> de facto monopoly in the market for ATS traded and CCP cleared non-triparty repo clearing, the market for ATS traded and CCP cleared triparty repo clearing and to a lesser extent, the market for CCP clearing of bonds, the merged entity would have the ability and incentive to partially foreclose competitors, and more particularly its closest competitor Euroclear, by diverting cleared repo transaction feeds to Clearstream, which would prevent competitors from being able to effectively compete.[131]

As financial market infrastructure is intimately interconnected, it is very likely that the effects of a contemplated merger extend beyond the narrowly-defined markets that the notifying parties promulgate, as pointed out by the Commission in this passage.

In the same vein, regarding the efficacy of MiFID II and MIFIR in promoting competition among trading venues and stock exchanges, the Commission noted that despite the important role of those regimes in promoting competition in trading, MiFID II and MIFIR would not fully prevent foreclosure of trading venues that would have been generated by the proposed merger.[132]

In respect of collateral management services concerning the relevant markets, the Commission noted that the proposed merger would lead to a significant impediment of effective competition. In light of DB and LSE's de facto monopoly in the above-mentioned markets, the foreclosure of Euroclear would lead to 'diverting cleared repo transaction feeds and requiring customers to post collateral at Clearstream, which would prevent competitors from being able to effectively compete in the market'.[133] As Euroclear was Clearstream's

[128] Regulation (EU) No 909/2014 of the European Parliament and of the Council of 23 July 2014 on improving the securities settlement in the European Union and on central securities depositories [2014] OJ L257/1. D Nougayrède, 'Towards a Global Financial Register? The Case for End Investor Transparency in Central Securities Depositories' (2018) 4 *Journal of Financial Regulation* 276; D Martin et al, 'The Consolidation of TARGET2 and TARGET2-Securities: How Is the Eurosystem Exploring Synergies across Its Infrastructures, and How Will This Impact Day-to-Day Operations?' (2019) 11 *Journal of Securities Operations & Custody* 198.

[129] For more information on the T2S platform put forward by the ECB, see European Central Bank, 'What Is TARGET2-Securities (T2S)?' (European Central Bank) www.ecb.europa.eu/paym/target/t2s/html/index.en.html accessed 25 July 2023.

[130] Commission Decision of 29 March 2017, Deutsche Börse / London Stock Exchange (Case COMP/M.7995), paras 670–77.

[131] ibid para 678.

[132] ibid paras 877–80. Interestingly, the specific provisions promoting 'open-access' among trading venues and their clearinghouses would not have been implemented by all EU Member States until 2020, something that holds true to date.

[133] ibid para 709.

closer competitor and only other existing ICSD, it had a prevalent role in the competitive landscape of the relevant markets. The potential foreclosure of Euroclear would have had a significant effect on competition on the relevant markets. This is an additional consideration that played a role in the Commission's decision.

As to the implications of the proposed merger in derivatives markets, the Commission held that Eurex and Euronext were close competitors in the potential market for single stock equity derivatives based on Belgian, French, and Dutch underlying securities and, therefore, that the merged entity would have been in a position to control pricing of both of them.[134] In particular, the Commission considered that the contemplated transaction would:

> lead to a significant impediment of effective competition in a potential market for single stock equity derivatives based on Dutch, French, and Belgium underlyings as it would eliminate competition for combined trading and clearing of exchange traded derivatives in a number of underlyings where Eurex competes with Euronext relying on merchant clearing services from LCH.Clearnet SA.[135]

Furthermore, the Commission's evaluation underlined that the proposed merger would have led to a significant barrier to competition in the market for single stock equity derivatives because: (i) it would have eliminated the horizontal bundle-to-bundle competition between Eurex and Euronext; and (ii) it would have foreclosed Euronext (fully or partially) relying on clearing services provided by LCH SA.[136] Those reasons explain why the Commission was hesitant with proceeding with clearance of the proposed merger.

b. Final Considerations

Overall, the merger would have combined the capacities of DB's Eurex with LSE's LCH.Clearnet (comprising the London-based LCH.Clearnet Ltd. and the Paris-based LCH.Clearnet SA) and Rome-based Cassa di Compensazione e Garanzia. The outcome of such a merger would have resulted in a monopoly in the clearing of fixed-income securities sector. In addition, this monopoly would impact on the downstream markets for settlement, custody, and collateral management, as service providers in these markets depended on transaction feeds from central counterparties. As DB's Clearstream competed with these service providers, the merged entity would have had the ability and the incentive to divert transaction feeds to Clearstream and foreclose the other competitors.

[134] ibid para 837.
[135] ibid para 838.
[136] ibid paras 881–82.

Further, the proposed merger would have foreclosed horizontal competition for the trading and clearing of single stock equity derivatives (based on shares of French, Dutch and Belgian corporations). At the time, Eurex competed with a bundled product (combining trading and clearing services) provided by Euronext and LCH.Clearnet SA. Had the merger been cleared, LCH.Clearnet – which had important pricing power over the bundled service – would have had less motive to compete with Eurex. It should be noted that the economics of bundling are highly complicated.[137] Ultimately, such high market power could potentially be used to squeeze out Euronext.

As the European Commission spelled out these concerns in a Statement of Objections it issued in December 2016, the parties proposed a remedy to address them consisting of the divestment of LCH.Clearnet SA.[138] The Commission noted that this divestment would have resolved the concerns pertinent to single stock equity derivatives but it would not have been effective to remedy the concerns emanating from the creation of the de facto monopoly in fixed-income clearing. On that score, the fixed-income clearing leg of LCH.Clearnet SA was dependent upon the trading feeds from LSE's fixed-income trading platform, MTS. In the absence of these feeds, the prospects of this business line would be severely compromised. The divestment of MTS would have been sufficient to alleviate the Commission's competition considerations but the set of behavioural remedies offered by the parties did not persuade the Commission, which ultimately decided to block this merger.

From a helicopter view, the timing of the proposed merger between LSE and DB, coupled with the Commission's anti-competitive concerns, culminated in this outcome. The prospect and uncertainties of Brexit tempered the parties' willingness to conclude the deal. As evidenced, in the structural remedies discussion with the Commission DB and LSE were not prepared to go the extra mile and, therefore, the deal was bound to fail for the third consecutive time. In the counterfactual scenario, where Brexit was not on the table and there was certainty about the business environment between the EU and the UK,[139] things might have evolved differently.

Indeed, the Commission's conclusions are premised on valid concerns regarding effective competition in the relevant EEA markets. However, given that

[137] For relevant literature elaborating on the economics of bundling, see, inter alia, B Nalebuff, 'Bundling as an Entry Barrier' (2004) 119 *The Quarterly Journal of Economics* 159; BH Kobayashi, 'Does Economics Provide a Reliable Guide to Regulating Commodity Bundling by Firms? A Survey of the Economic Literature' (2005) 1 *Journal of Competition Law & Economics* 707.

[138] Commission Decision of 29 March 2017, Deutsche Börse / London Stock Exchange (Case COMP/M.7995), paras 924–1027.

[139] To date, the trading and regulatory systems under which the EU and the UK businesses would be carried out have not been deciphered. As such, legal uncertainty reigns and the next section attempts to shed light on the aspects pertinent to the clearing of financial instruments between the EU and the UK.

financial services and specifically derivatives are traded internationally, perhaps it would have been favourable from a policy perspective to reflect on the prospect of creating international champions capable of challenging the strongest international market infrastructure.[140] In any event, a debate on whether merger control should remain as is or it should be subjected to political influence is bound to take place at the highest political level. The writer advocates in favour of legal certainty, and as such endorses the application of clear rules that do not permit atate interference in concentration control proceedings. The following section discusses Refinitiv's acquisition by the LSE Group, which was subject to certain conditions.

iii. LSE/Refinitiv: A Data-Driven Merger Cleared Conditional on Commitments

a. Commission's Main Concerns and Proposed Remedies

On 13 January 2021, the Commission conditionally approved the acquisition of Refinitiv by the LSE Group, following an in-depth phase II investigation.[141] In its opening decision, the Commission flagged concerns relating to both horizontal overlaps in the market for electronic trading for European Government Bonds (EGBs) as well as vertical concerns in connection with the markets for trading OTC IRDs, indices licensing, and consolidated real-time datafeeds (CRTDs) and desktop services. The merging parties provided both structural and behavioural remedies to dispel those doubts and secure the Commission's clearance in line with Article 8(2) of the Merger Regulation.

In respect of the Commission's horizontal concerns, the LSE Group and Refinitiv both own and operate electronic trading venues (MTS and Tradeweb, respectively) for EEA, UK and Swiss sovereign bonds. These trading venues are in close competition and have leading market positions. The Commission found that the proposed transaction would have resulted in the creation or strengthening of dominance in the market for electronic trading of EGBs and its potential sub-segments – in particular regarding the trading between dealers and investors. The market investigation also suggested that it would be challenging to attract clients in sufficient numbers and become a viable alternative to incumbent venues.

[140] Commission Decision of 6 February 2019 declaring a concentration to be incompatible with the internal market and the functioning of the EEA Agreement (Case M.8677 — Siemens/Alstom) (notified under document C(2019) 921) [2019] OJ C300/14. For background discussion of this argument in the context of the French and German reactions to the Commission's blockage of the proposed merger between Alstom/Siemens, see, for instance, K Efstathiou, 'The Alstom-Siemens Merger and the Need for European Champions' (Bruegel, 11 March 2019) www.bruegel.org/blog-post/alstom-siemens-merger-and-need-european-champions accessed 2 August 2023; R Lough, 'Explainer: Why Alstom-Siemens Rail Merger Is Creating European Tensions' (Reuters, 17 January 2019) www.reuters.com/article/us-alstom-m-a-siemens-politics/explainer-why-siemens-alstom-rail-merger-is-creating-european-tensions-idUSKCN1PB216 accessed 25 July 2023.

[141] Commission Decision of 13 January 2021, London Stock Exchange Group/Refinitiv (Case COMP/M.9564).

To dispel this concern, the LSE Group proposed the divestiture of its 99.9 per cent stake in the Borsa Italiana group, which includes MTS. Following this, on 9 October 2020 the LSE Group and Euronext signed a definitive and binding sale and purchase agreement.[142] Following this, the Commission approved Euronext as a suitable purchaser of the divestment business and concluded that the divestment business was being sold in a manner consistent with the above-mentioned commitment.[143] This commitment fully removed the horizontal overlap between the companies' activities in EGB electronic trading services.

The following analysis focuses on the Commission's vertical concerns.

As to the market for trading and clearing of OTC interest rate derivatives, Refinitiv's Traeweb is a venue for trading OTC IRDs, while the LSE Group offers clearing services of OTC IRDs which is carried out by the London Clearing House Swapclear. Notably, the Commission's investigation found that the proposed merger would have led to a combined entity which would enjoy significant market power in both upstream (namely, trading) and downstream (namely, clearing) services of OTC IRDs. It should be noted that OTC IRDs represent the largest category of traded derivatives globally and they are important not only for investors but also for companies which need to hedge risks associated with interest rates linked to case flows and payment obligations. In addition, there are important network effects in this market as the appeal of both trading venues and clearinghouses in OTC IRDs increase with the proportion of customers using their services. The Commission's investigation further indicated that the barriers to entry are high and customers rarely switch trading venues or clearinghouses. Following this, the LSE Group would have both the ability and the incentive to foreclose competing trading venues and related software providers in the upstream market.

To allay the Commission's foreclosure considerations, the LSE Group committed to continue providing its global OTC IRD clearing services (operated by LCH Swapclear) on an open access and non-discriminatory basis.[144] Specifically, the LSE Group undertook to observe compliance with the provisions of EMIR in connection with non-discriminatory and transparent clearing of OTC IRDs in spite of Brexit and comply with these conditions vis-à-vis trading venues as well as middleware providers. In particular, the LSE Group committed to:

> continue to comply with all regulatory requirements set out in EMIR (as may be amended from time to time) to the extent applicable to the non-discriminatory and

[142] ibid Annex I.

[143] For more details on the Borsa Italiana group divestiture commitment and the extent to which the divestment business is being sold in a manner consistent with those commitments, see Commission Decision on the implementation of the commitments – Purchaser approval of 26 February 2023, London Stock Exchange Group/Refinitiv (Case COMP/M.9564), paras 161–62.

[144] Commission Decision of 13 January 2021, London Stock Exchange Group/Refinitiv (Case COMP/M.9564), Annex III.

> transparent clearing of OTC IRDs, including Article 7 EMIR provisions that would otherwise apply to EU-recognised CCPs only. These Commitments will continue in full force and effect for the Commitment Period, irrespective of the nature and scope of any future trade agreement concluded between the European Union and the United Kingdom (or the absence thereof).[145]

LSE Group also said that it:

> will apply all regulatory requirements set out in EMIR (as may be amended from time to time) to the extent applicable to the non-discriminatory and transparent Clearing of OTC IRDs to any Middleware Provider in the same manner as they are applicable to Trading Venues, again irrespective of the nature and scope of any future trade agreement concluded between the European Union and the United Kingdom (or the absence thereof.[146]

In addition, the LSE Group committed to not granting preferential treatment to – or discriminating against – clients based on the source (namely, whether from Refinitiv's Tradeweb or other third-parties' trading venues and middleware providers) of the OTC interest rate derivate trade they submit for clearing. The LSE Group also stated that it would not engage in discrimination that could be in form of clearing charges for equivalent trades, in terms of the overall service quality (including technical specifications and operational standards) or the introduction of new products. The LSE Group offered this access remedy for ten years.

Furthermore, with respect to the market for index licensing, CRTDs and desktop services, Refinitiv aggregates financial information from various sources in the form of CRTDs and desktop services, which it offers in packages to traders, asset managers and other financial data users. The difference between datafeeds and desktop services is that the former enable the transmission of data from computer to computer while the latter offer display of data on the screen. The Commission identified three types of data offered by the LSE Group that are an important input for Refinitiv's CRTDs and desktop services, which are often without an alternative, namely: the LSE venue data; the UK Equity Indices through FTSE Russell; and security identifies called SEDOLs. In its assessment, the Commission found that following the proposed merger, the combined entity could deny competing CRTDs and desktop service providers access to the LSE group's necessary input data.

In addition, Refinitiv via its WM/R FX benchmarks provides foreign exchange indices which are among the most valuable inputs for index design and calculation. The Commission's investigation found that Refinitiv's benchmarks and CRTDs constitute necessary input for financial indices providers and that there

[145] ibid Annex III, para 3(a).
[146] ibid Annex III, para 3(b).

is no viable alternative in the market. Thus, Refinitiv's foreign exchange indices are widely used by most financial indices service providers globally. In light of the above, the Commission found that as a result of the proposed transaction, the combined entity could have the ability to deny competitors in index licensing access to Refinitiv's necessary input data.

In response to the Commission's concerns about access to essential inputs, the LSE Group offered data access remedies in respect of CRTDs and desktop services as well as index licensing.[147] In particular, the LSE Group made a commitment to provide access on non-discriminatory terms to the LSE venue data, FTSE Russell Indices as well as Refinitiv's WM/R FX benchmarks to all existing and future downstream competitors. More specifically, the LSE Group said that it would not degrade technology, quality or service in comparison with that provided intragroup. Further, the LSE Group undertook to construct information barriers to ensure that confidential information the Group receives from its customers is not shared with the competing Refinitiv CRTDs and desktop service operations.

Finally, the commitments offered by the LSE Group also included an accelerated and binding dispute resolution mechanism that can be relied upon by third parties who claim that the Group does not observe its commitments.[148] A trustee will monitor the implementation of the commitments and act as a contact point for possible complaints, including in the context of the fast-track dispute resolution mechanism.[149]

b. Final Considerations

The Commission cleared this merger subject to a combination of structural (namely, divestiture) and behavioural remedies (ie offering access and licensing on non- discriminatory terms). In accordance with the principles of the Remedies Notice, the Commission in principle prefers to choose structural remedies in merger cases because they provide permanent solutions without calling for additional monitoring. In addition, structural remedies may also dispel the concerns of national competition authorities in other jurisdictions.[150] On the other hand, while behavioural remedies are more common in antitrust cases, the Commission may accept them in merger decisions in cases where it seeks to ensure interoperability and access for competing entities and customers to essential inputs. Notably, the Commission seems willing to accept behavioural

[147] Commission Decision of 13 January 2021, London Stock Exchange Group/Refinitiv (Case COMP/M.9564), Annex II.

[148] ibid see, for example, Annex III, paras 27–54.

[149] ibid see, for example, Annex III, paras 8–26.

[150] Commission Notice on remedies acceptable under the Council Regulation (EC) No 139/2004 and under Commission Regulation, OJ C267/1 (Remedies Notice), paras 13 and 80.

remedies in vertical mergers where its doubts concern foreclosure risks instead of increased market power.[151]

Interestingly, the remedies accepted by the Commission – although not identical – share some commonalities with the commitments approved by the Competition and Consumer Commission of Singapore (CCCS) for the same transaction.[152] The CCCS identified competition concerns about third parties' continued access to Refinitiv's foreign exchange benchmarks, which constitute critical inputs with no reasonable substitutes for competing providers of index licensing and derivatives clearing services.[153] In accordance with these commitments, the LSE Group pledged, among others, to make WM/R FX benchmarks available to all existing and future customers for the purpose of providing index licensing services and clearinghouses for providing clearing services in Singapore and to ensure that the pricing and other commercial terms applied to those benchmarks would not be amended in such a fashion as to constitute a de facto failure to make those benchmarks available to the abovementioned customers. Those commitments showcase that antitrust agencies can be faced with similar issues but the approved commitments need to be adjusted to address jurisdiction-specific elements.

All in all, the approved remedies in the LSE/Refinitiv merger show the EU's commitment to open, fair, non-discriminatory and contestable financial infrastructure covering specifically the financial data segment. The fact that the EMIR 'open access' principles have been incorporated in the LSE Group's commitments – even after the UK's withdrawal from the EU – further demonstrates that the EU is serious about limiting trade barriers and promoting the economic integration of its financial market infrastructure.

iv. Competition Assessment of the EU Merger Control in Financial Market Infrastructure

The same as in the assessment on the effects of EU antitrust law in the liberalisation of financial infrastructure in the EU internal market, the EU merger control system and its application by the Commission works to the benefit of competition dynamics both at the EU and the global level. This is in accordance

[151] See, for instance, Commission decision of January 18, 2018, *Qualcomm/NXP* (Case COMP/M.8306); Commission decision of December 6, 2016, *Microsoft/LinkedIn* (Case COMP/M.8124).

[152] See CCCS, 'Grants Conditional Approval for Acquisition of Certain Subsidiaries and Assets of Refinitiv Holdings Limited by London Stock Exchange Group plc' (CCCS, 24 May 2021) www.cccs.gov.sg/media-and-consultation/newsroom/media-releases/conditional-approval-for-acquisition-of-refinitiv-holdings-limited-by-london-stock-exchange-group accessed 25 July 2023.

[153] The access commitment accepted in Singapore also covered clearinghouses while the one in the EU was, for regulatory reasons, limited to index suppliers. In particular, MiFID in the EU ensures the non-discriminatory access to critical benchmarks for clearinghouses.

with the first and second requirements identified above. Specifically, it is obvious that by blocking the proposed merger in the first two instances and by approving the abovementioned commitments in the third case the competitive landscape in the EU – and internationally as well – is better off, as competitors from the EU internal market and from outside the EU can either enter or continue providing their services in the Union without having to face monopolistic forces against them. That would have been the case in the counterfactual scenario under which the mergers would have been cleared and the dominant companies in the specific financial market infrastructure segments would be able to exercise considerable pressure to any market participant in the first two cases and in the absence of the adopted commitment in the third case we evaluated.

As to the third requirement of the competition assessment on the EU industry's global competitiveness, it is clear that EU concentration control does not favour the European financial market infrastructure and it prioritises the application of effective competition in the EU internal market.[154] This explains the blocking of the two mega-mergers that would have created EU champions in the provision of financial market infrastructure services at the global level. Thus, there should be no doubt that the EU merger control system contributes to the liberalisation of financial market infrastructure in the EEA.

v. Broader Political Economy Considerations

The two case studies discussed in the section above reveal that merger control plays a pivotal role in how competition in financial market infrastructure flourishes in the EU, and (to a great extent) how the industry is formed at the international level. Unlike the case of anti-competitive conduct being – softly – regulated at the international level,[155] merger control so far solely relies on the regimes of national and regional jurisdictions. Thus, it is very challenging for homogeneity to be present both in the substance and in the enforcement of those national or regional rules. As a direct consequence of diverging merger control regimes, the way financial market infrastructure develop and consolidate worldwide might vary significantly.

[154] In support of this view, Bradford, Jackson and Zytnick demonstrate in an empirical study that the EU merger control system does not promote the agendas of the EU industry: A Bradford et al, 'Is EU Merger Control Used for Protectionism? An Empirical Analysis' (2018) 15 *Journal of Empirical Legal Studies* 165.

[155] Notably, Art XIII (monopolies and exclusive service suppliers) and Art IX (business practices) of the GATS set forth soft law rules for the application of antitrust rules. The consistency of those provisions has never been the subject of a dispute at the WTO. Nevertheless, the only time a WTO Panel was called to interpret the legality of competition rules associated with telecommunication services was in *Mexico – Measures Affecting Telecommunication Services* in DS204, where the outcome has been contested for its legal rigour. For literature opining on the validity of the panel report, see DJ Neven and PC Mavroidis, 'El Mess in TELMEX: A Comment on Mexico-Measures Affecting Telecommunications Services' (2006) 5 *World Trade Review* 271.

The comment above paves the way to a broader concern on how the liberal global economic model in its current shape fails to capture important global actors' activities, such as China's, that generate asymmetries and competitive advantages that do not strictly rely on the international economic order as we know it. The example of *China – Electronic Payment Systems*, discussed in Chapter 2, is illustrative of how China's financial system directly challenges worldwide competitors by disregarding international trade law rules and China's own commitments under the GATS.[156]

All in all, from a political economy standpoint for the terms-of-trade of financial services to be on an equal footing, the consolidation of financial institutions and market infrastructure and, accordingly, their concentration control regimes, need to be harmonised to a great extent. The practical difficulties of such an endeavour are vast, as many WTO Members have not adopted national merger control rules or have done so very recently.[157]

For the sake of completeness, given that the financial sector is predominantly exposed to crises for a series of reasons, it is only natural for merger control rules to be ignored, as they have been,[158] on occasions when the integrity of financial systems is in question. In the same vein, the international economic legal order either at the WTO or at the regional level provides specific set of rules, discussed in Chapters 1 and 3, respectively, which directly provide prudential carve-outs in times of financial turbulence.[159] The next section draws together the lessons learnt from investigating the interplay between the European regulation of clearinghouses and EU competition law.

IV. CONCLUSION: IS IT TIME FOR AN INTERNATIONAL COMPETITION LAW SYSTEM AT THE WTO?

This chapter has assessed, in a qualitative fashion, the liberalisation of financial infrastructure and specifically clearing services in the context of the EU economic integration model. In carrying out this study, we, first, evaluated the degree to

[156] For more details, see the analysis above, in Chapter 2.

[157] See, for instance, J Wilson, *Globalization and the Limits of National Merger Control Laws* (Alphen aan den Rijn, Kluwer Law International BV, 2003); D Holbrook, 'International Merger Control Convergence: Resolving Multijurisdictional Review Problems' (2002) 7 *UCLA Journal of International Law and Foreign Affairs* 345; N Levy et al, 'Global Merger Control – Where to Now?' (2020) 8 *Journal of Antitrust Enforcement* 319.

[158] For instance, in June 2017, the ECB held Spanish Bank, Banco Popular, to be 'failing or likely to fail' and, consequently, the Commission permitted Banco Santander to complete its acquisition of Banco Popular prior to obtaining formal merger clearance. For more details, see Commission Decision of 8 August 2017 (Case Case M.8553 – BANCO SANTANDER / BANCO POPULAR GROUP) COM (2017) 5659 final.

[159] For a thorough and insightful analysis on the nature of the prudential-carve out under the GATS and regional trade agreements, see CM Cantore, *The Prudential Carve-out for Financial Services: Rationale and Practice in the GATS and Preferential Trade Agreements* (Cambridge, Cambridge University Press, 2018).

which the relevant EU financial regulation and EU antitrust and competition law contribute to the integration of the EU internal market and increase competition in the relevant markets, and, second, whether those two legal instruments pose any unwarranted barriers to the international liberalisation of the financial services in question.

Importantly, the main findings of this study are summarised as follows: (i) the EU financial regulation setting out the rules for the operation of financial market infrastructure, namely EMIR together with MiFID II, alongside the application of EU competition law, have consistently promoted the integration of the financial market infrastructure in the EU; and (ii) due to the interconnectedness of financial markets and the inherent characteristics and structure of EU financial regulation and competition law, the trade-liberalising effect is not limited to the EU internal market but it, further, extends to global financial institution supplying their services in the EU as a more competitive and open EU market also works to their benefit.

Perhaps more interestingly, this chapter's analysis raises the question of what are the comparative advantages that the EU integration model presents in comparison to the multilateral and the plurilateral trading systems (discussed in Parts I and II of this book). We argue that the two most important elements that drive the deeper liberalisation of financial market infrastructure in general, and securities clearing services in particular, in the EU internal market are: (i) the harmonised regulatory environment that seeks to attain a level playing field for market actors and to increase competition; and (ii) the application of competition law in the specific industries via enforcement by the European Commission and judicial review by EU courts. Such application of competition rules aims to address the effects of monopolisation as well as tackle concerted practices.

Moreover, the foregoing analysis has shown that the application of EU competition law has significantly contributed to the integration of financial market infrastructure not only in the EU but also at the global level – as the EEA is a market of great interest to third-country financial services players who benefit from the enforcement of the Commission's decision and the rulings of the Court of Justice of the European Union. There is literature and case law discussing the extra-territorial reach of EU competition law but, nevertheless, justifiably there are certain limits that restrict its universal application.[160] Notably, on the ground there are more than 130 competition law systems and, accordingly, antitrust authorities charged with reviewing merger filings and investigating potentially

[160] For literature on the subject, see, inter alia, JP Griffin, 'Extraterritoriality in US and EU Antitrust Enforcement' (1999) 67 *Antitrust Law Journal* 159; F Wagner-von Papp, 'Competition Law and Extraterritoriality' in A Ezrachi (ed), *Research Handbook on International Competition Law* (Cheltenham, Edward Elgar, 2012); L Prete, 'On Implementation and Effects: The Recent Case-Law on the Territorial (or Extraterritorial?) Application of EU Competition Rules' (2018) 9 *Journal of European Competition Law & Practice* 487.

anti-competitive conduct. Inevitably, even if the rules across those jurisdictions are fairly similar, the likelihood of coherent application thereof is relatively low. Therefore, in order to grasp in full the benefits and potential of competition law in integrating financial services – and other sectors of the economy – across the globe a uniform system (in the form of an international treaty) accompanied by an international competition authority – to supervise and coordinate with the workings of national ones – would be preferable, assuming that there is sufficient political appetite for this from states.

The WTO, as discussed above, has mildly attempted to scrutinise anti-competitive conduct (with a focus on the telecommunications sector). However, the existing competition-related provisions housed in the GATS do not by any means qualify as a sufficient framework able to tackle anti-competitive conduct. A drastic shift, driven by WTO Member States' willingness, would be required to initiate discussions on harmonising Members' competition rulebooks under the WTO. This is quite a farfetched scenario, given the existing scepticism that the multilateral trading system is facing. An expression of such scepticism against the world trading system is the US stance with regard to the appointment of Appellate Body Members.[161] In view of the current non-functioning of the Appellate Body, alternative dispute settlement mechanisms have emerged.[162]

Nevertheless, competition law as a discipline is applicable to economic actors' trade transactions. At the international level, there is not a more adequate institution that could host potential discussions regarding the codification of international competition law rules than the WTO, due to its prominence as an organisation regulating international economic law and having an efficient dispute settlement mechanism for the scrutiny of those rules.

Consequently, although the WTO is currently facing an identity crisis as the negotiations are stagnant and the Appellate Body is currently understaffed and falling short of having the minimum number of judges (ie three) to deliver reports, the fact remains that due to the scope of WTO's mandate it would still be the most competent international actor to lead negotiation on an international competition treaty, should WTO Members again decide to put their faith back into the multilateral trading system and seek to attain further integration of global markets through the benefits of competition law.

[161] For academic discourse on this subject matter see, for example, J Hillman, 'Three Approaches to Fixing the World Trade Organization's Appellate Body: The Good, the Bad and the Ugly?' [2018] IIEL Working Paper; R Brewster, 'The Trump Administration and the Future of the WTO' (2018) *Yale Journal of International Law Online* 9; B Hoekman and PC Mavroidis, 'Burning down the House? The Appellate Body in the Centre of the WTO Crisis' (2019) 56 Robert Schuman Centre for Advanced Studies Research Paper No RSCAS.

[162] For a take on the possible impact of adjudication through the Multiparty Interim Appeal Arbitration Arrangement and preferential trade agreements on the jurisprudential legacy of the WTO, see GA Papaconstantinou and L Pedreschi, 'Alternative Dispute Settlement and the Jurisprudential Legacy of the World Trade Organization's Appellate Body' (2022) 56(2) *Journal of World Trade* 261.

All in all, the foregoing analysis has shed light on the most prominent driving forces of liberalisation of financial market infrastructure services in the EU. So far, this volume has elucidated how the liberalisation of financial services is attained in three different economic integration models (namely, the multilateral trading system, the plurilateral trading system and EU law) and has concretely identified the existing barriers and the potentially beneficial aspects that can be utilised if more integration is needed. The next chapter offers policy recommendations and summarises the main arguments promulgated in this study.

6

Conclusions and Policy Recommendations

THIS BOOK HAS comprehensively evaluated the interface between financial regulation and economic integration. It did so by bringing forward an in-depth analysis of three case studies investigating the intersection between the regulation of financial market infrastructure and certain economic integration settings – namely, the WTO, Economic Integration Agreements, and EU competition law. The conclusions drawn relate primarily to: (i) how the liberalisation of financial market infrastructure is realised; (ii) the existing barriers to trade that may impede the further integration of the markets at issue; and (iii) from a normative perspective, the tools through which more liberalisation of the financial market infrastructure can be delivered without jeopardising the stability and integrity of the financial system. The following paragraphs summarise the essential findings of this study.

As evidenced above, the regulatory systems that determine the operations and the integration of financial market infrastructure are by no means one dimensional. Accordingly, the regulatory and legal disciplines that define how the supply of financial services (and of financial market infrastructure, in particular) is to occur, and the extent of their integration, are operating at multiple levels. Financial regulation is principally the discipline that lies at the core, setting out the rules for the operation of the financial institutions of market infrastructure in parallel with international standard setting bodies (such as the Basel Committee or IOSCO). Nevertheless, the conduct of such institutions is also scrutinised by competition/antitrust law for the purposes of merger review or when there are concerns of anti-competitive conduct (either through cartel-like behaviour or through monopolisation, as discussed in Part III). Moreover, due to the prominence of the internationalisation of finance, as evidenced by the analysis of this volume, financial regulation is not only concerned with putting forward the rules for purely domestic transactions; it also expands its reach on business with a transnational element. That is the point where the boundaries set by international economic law – either at the multilateral level by WTO law or at the plurilateral level by EIAs – kick in (as investigated in Parts I and II, respectively).

Furthermore, this book has demonstrated that financial regulation is seminal in liberalising financial market infrastructure. With respect to how the liberalisation of financial market infrastructure is achieved, each one of the above-stated disciplines plays its own unique role on this score.

First, financial regulation has several tools with which to liberalise financial market infrastructure services (such as equivalence/substituted compliance mechanisms enabling foreign financial institutions to provide their services in home markets as well as competition-enabling provisions for both domestic and foreign service suppliers). At the EU level, financial regulation over the last decade has consistently and systematically put forward provisions in the legislation for financial market infrastructure to increase competition in the provision of such services and to explicitly break up the silos that exist in the industry (as discussed in Part III). In doing so, financial regulation decisively contributes to the integration of the EU market of financial market infrastructure by inserting explicit provisions in legislation serving this end. Moreover, at the international level financial regulators hold the key to allowing third-country financial institutions to supply their services in the respective jurisdictions, as the case study in Part II has clearly demonstrated. To this end, financial regulation promotes the international integration of financial market infrastructure. This mainly materialises through equivalence or substituted compliance assessments carried out by financial supervisory authorities. In addition, mutual recognition agreements between financial regulatory authorities in relation to the efficacy of financial supervision and enforcement in the relevant states are also vital.

Second, the findings of this book clearly indicate that there is a positive correlation between the application of competition law (through its enforcement by trustbusters and judicial review) and the integration of those markets. As to how competition law and policy foster the liberalisation of financial market infrastructure, it is clear from the analysis carried out in Part III that, through the application and enforcement of antitrust and competition law, monopolisation and cartel-like conduct are directly tackled. In particular, by implementing an efficient concentration control system the EU maintains a – relatively – liberalised financial market infrastructure. As the result of the application of EU merger control system, there is no single champion that has such a market share that it would be enabled to foreclose the EU market and provide disincentives for foreign financial institutions to supply their services in the EU internal market. The examples of the two mega mergers that were blocked by the European Commission makes evident that the preservation of integrated markets for financial market infrastructure is a priority of EU competition law. In the same vein, when it comes to antitrust law that could negatively impact on the competitive landscape of financial market infrastructure and would deteriorate the levels of the market's integration, the EU has consistently countered anti-competitive behaviours. The analysis in Part III offers specific benchmarks to measure how the application of competition law in the EU contributes to the liberalisation of financial market infrastructure both in the EU and globally. Those benchmarks evaluate how the specific application of competition law impacts: (i) international competitiveness; (ii) competition in the EU domestic landscape; and (iii) competition at the global level.

Third, this work provides a comprehensive framework of the ways in which the liberalisation of financial market infrastructure occurs under international economic law. The cases of WTO law and Economic Integration Agreements are developed in Part I and Part II, respectively. Most importantly, the liberalisation of financial market infrastructure in the multilateral trading system is realised through the disciplines housed in the GATS. In particular, the most-favourable treatment provision (GATS, Article II), together with prudential carve-out of the GATS Annex on Financial Services, are key in the liberalisation of such financial services. In this context, the driving factor that determines the extent to which those markets are liberalised by each WTO Member is the specific commitments entered in their Schedules. Therefore, the empirical analysis on Economic Integration Agreements (in Part II) offers an in-depth look at how, precisely, the liberalisation of financial market infrastructure services is effectuated by the plurilateral trading system. Such liberalisation principally occurs through countries' commitments for market access (GATS, Article XVI) and national treatment (GATS, Article XVII), both in the multilateral and the plurilateral trading systems.

Moreover, on the basis of this book's findings, we have identified concrete existing barriers to the further integration of financial market infrastructure. Below, we offer an account of the most important barriers to trade in relation to the supply of financial market infrastructure services flowing from the three international economic integration settings evaluated under this study.

At the outset, barriers to trade in financial services can be very different in nature but, broadly speaking, they can be separated between: (i) market access and national treatment barriers (for example, by extending differential treatment to third-country clearinghouses only on the basis of their origin or setting a minimum number of regulated markets operating in a jurisdiction); and (ii) non-discriminatory and non-quantitative restrictions (such as impeding the equality of competitive opportunities for third-country suppliers vis-à-vis domestic institutions by permitting anti-competitive conduct or by adopting regulatory frameworks that foster the fragmentation of global financial markets without necessarily serving prudential reasons). The former category is directly addressed by the obligations and commitments entered under WTO law and Economic Integration Agreements, which are designed to capture trade barriers of this nature, while the latter category is purely contingent on the political appetite of states in the absence of any internationally binding legal framework. As a result, whether more or less liberalisation is extended to foreign financial institutions hinges on the states' design of financial market infrastructure regulation and their internal market rules.

While this monograph has shed light on both trade barriers, its focal point principally lies with the second category, which, inter alia, includes barriers to trade embedded in financial regulatory frameworks. Even if such barriers might escape the scrutiny of international trade law disciplines, they still pose obstacles that impede the further international economic integration of financial market infrastructure. The next paragraphs underscore the specific barriers highlighted by the findings of the case studies of this book together with their ways of discouraging further integration of international trade flows for financial market infrastructure services.

The first case study examining the intersection between domestic financial regulation and WTO law (Chapter 3) found that the EU rules on the unilateral recognition of 'third-country' CCPs through the mechanism of the 'equivalence' assessments pose certain procedural fairness and non-discriminatory structural trade barriers in the way of integrating third-country clearinghouses. Specifically, in respect of procedural fairness, discussed in the context of GATS, Article VI on domestic regulation and GATS, Article VII on mutual recognition, the analysis highlighted that the fact that the third-country regimes of certain countries are assessed for the purposes of evaluating equivalence while the regime of other third-countries are not offered an adequate opportunity to be assessed and, accordingly, their clearinghouses cannot gain access to the EU internal market as their regulatory frameworks have not yet been assessed by the relevant EU authorities. The most problematic aspects of this pertains to the fact that third countries with similar levels of efficacy in adopting international standards on the basis of the FSB assessment receive different treatment from EU regulators. With regard to non-discriminatory structural barriers relating to the EU equivalence regimes, this book has illustrated that there are problems of regulatory transparency that might also be inconsistent with GATS, Articles VI and VII. In particular, the fact that the European Commission does not explain the precise way it opts to assess some third-country regimes while it does not evaluate others is problematic, as in the absence of an objective methodology potential biases or political steering might be entailed. Those trade barriers can significantly impede effective market access by third-country clearinghouses into the EU single market.

The second case study evaluated the underlying characteristics of the liberalisation of financial market infrastructure in the context of Economic Integration Agreements (Chapter 4). This empirical study showed that financial market infrastructure services achieved deeper liberalisation in the plurilateral trading system in comparison to the WTO framework. Nevertheless, certain impediments were identified in relation to the extent to which financial regulation is borne in mind by trade negotiators in the negotiation rounds. Specifically, this study raised the issue of whether the latest financial regulatory state of play is reflected in the content of international trade agreements and the commitments undertaken by the signatories, and its findings were in the negative. In particular, the analysis highlighted that: (i) the fact that financial rulebooks that limit cross-border trade flows in financial market infrastructure are not included in EIA parties' List of Reservations and/or Schedules of Commitments raises problems in terms of the international trade agreements' transparency and, more broadly, exemplifies states' overreliance on the prudential carve-out – also included in EIAs; and (ii) the absence of a mechanism of regularly updating the content and undertaken commitments and/or reservations under EIAs on the basis of the evolution of financial regulatory rulebooks does not foster the global integration of financial market infrastructure services.

The third case study delved into the economic integration tools of the most liberalised system of countries there is – the intra-EU approach. The analysis shed light on the benefits associated with: (i) the efficient application and enforcement of competition law rules; and (ii) the importance of harmonisation in achieving integrated financial markets. As to the first element, it is maintained that the majority of WTO Members' legal systems have their own domestic set of competition rules that are not intertwined in the same way that competition law is structured within the EU. The flip side of this is that, in addition to substantive deviations in the text of antitrust laws, the enforcement of competition law is dispersed among national competition authorities which do not defer to a central trustbuster as the EU Member States do to the European Commission for prominent cases extending beyond the borders of a single state. Consequently, the lack of a uniform rulebook for the application of competition rules in the international arena, coupled with the existence of numerous enforcers investigating international anti-competitive conduct (with limited coordination) creates an impediment to the liberalisation of financial market infrastructure, which is by definition international due to global financial markets' high degree of interconnectedness. Thus, the non-centralisation of competition law at the global level represents a structural barrier to the integration of financial market infrastructure.

The absence of harmonisation of financial regulation at the international level is well-known and the prominence and rationale behind the dominance of soft law in international finance has been accentuated by the literature. Nevertheless, the fact remains that since states' rules differ with regard to the substantive rules on the operation of financial market infrastructure institutions and, by extension, the rules on the recognition of third-country institutions, the integration of financial market infrastructure is impeded. As a result, inevitably financial rulebooks constitute barriers to trade – irrespective of whether or not they are discriminatory towards financial service providers of foreign states.

The remainder of this concluding chapter seeks to develop a normative framework for the further integration of financial market infrastructure at the international level. With the lessons learned from this book borne in mind, we probe into the existing barriers to trade and offer policy recommendations that can be conducive to further liberalising trade in financial market infrastructure services globally without putting the financial market's integrity at risk should states willingly decide to move in this direction.

As this book has identified certain obstacles in the way of further liberalising financial market infrastructure in the economic integration settings covered by its analytical framework, we propose a number of policy recommendations that would be apt to achieve more integration of financial market infrastructure without at the same time putting at risk the stability and soundness of the financial system. The recommendations at hand are of a substantive and procedural nature and would potentially contribute to the global integration of financial services should policy makers decide to commit themselves to this objective. The following recommendations offer solutions both at the national level (eg review of national financial regulatory regimes) and at the international level (eg reform proposals at the WTO level or recommendations in the context of plurilateral trade agreements). Finally, we should note that the following proposals are indicative and emanate from the lessons learned from the findings of this study.

The proposals of substantive nature at the international level have the objective of increasing the liberalisation of financial services without jeopardising the stability of the financial system by utilising the resources of the WTO. In particular, the substantive recommendations pertain to: (i) the establishment of a harmonisation forum for certain technical financial regulatory rules (eg regimes on equivalence/substituted compliance) under the premises of the WTO; and (ii) the adoption of an international treaty on the application of competition/antitrust rules and the centralisation of national competition authorities under a mega-enforcer (such as, potentially, the WTO).

As to the first recommendation, we believe that serious harmonisation efforts of key financial regulatory provisions that extend 'effective market access', such as the rules on equivalence or substituted compliance, at the multilateral level would contribute to more integration for financial services sectors. Therefore, as long as WTO Members are interested in discussing together certain rules of their domestic rulebooks with a view to reaching a collective outcome, then further liberalisation of the financial market infrastructure would be warranted, as financial regulation and global markets' fragmentation would decrease, international competitiveness would increase and there would be more liquidity in global markets as a result of those efforts. Of course, financial stability considerations would be borne in mind during those discussions, as the persons at the negotiating table would be WTO Members' representatives from the respective financial regulatory and supervisory authorities dealing with the cross-border supply of financial infrastructure services.

With respect to the second proposal, as discussed in Chapter 5, this book has demonstrated that there is a positive correlation between the application and enforcement of competition law and the international integration of financial market infrastructure in the context of the EU. Thus, assuming that this model could be replicated at the global level, we maintain that the positive effects of competition evidenced in the EU could extend at the international level and have a global reach. A common rulebook in the form of an international treaty on antitrust and deference of national competition authorities to an international enforcing agency is put forward as a normative framework. A common set of antitrust rules under an international treaty would provide clarity at the international level and would prevent instances of companies cherry-picking their conduct depending on the jurisdictions in which they operate. As to making competition enforcement more efficient, this study takes account of the important role of national competition authorities, which would continue to carry out their tasks, but advocates in favour of an international enforcer because of global markets' interconnectedness and the international nature of business. The WTO would be a good candidate to host such discussions due to its prominence in safeguarding the common set of rules on international trade for nearly three decades and its developed expertise on economic law matters (such as safeguards, anti-dumping measures and countervailing duties as well as cases on intellectual property). Overall, should there be political willingness to promote the internationalisation of competition law, the further integration of global markets would be a natural consequence.

At the domestic level, to avoid situations where due process considerations are not observed and, therefore, the integration of financial services is not fostered (as discussed, for example, in the context of EMIR's equivalence assessments), we recommend that financial regulators, when adopting certain rules that affect the cross-border flows of financial services, accompany them with a publication of a methodology note of how they are to apply those sets of rules. In the case raised in Chapter 3 above, had the Commission published a note indicating the methodology followed in the assessment of third-country regimes, which should put forward objective criteria (based, for instance, on the order of applications for the respective order of evaluating foreign regulatory frameworks), then due process concerns might have been kept to a minimum.

At the international level, in order to ensure that the content of financial regulatory frameworks is constantly updated and reflected in the obligations and the set of Schedules of Commitments and/or lists of reservations under economic integration agreements, a mechanism of regularly reviewing and updating such agreements is promulgated. This would maximise the potential for integrating the international markets for financial infrastructure by providing regulatory transparency and by offering clarity to trading counterparts as to the specific terms of trade and trade barriers currently in place in relation to the supply of financial services.

Appendix: Clearing and Settlement Services Commitments in EIAs

RTA No	RTA Name	Parties	Listing approach		FS Coverage	Entry into force	Commitments			Commitments' depth	Comments on MA, NT, AC
							Mode (1) MA	Mode (2) NT	Mode (3) AC		
1	ASEAN – Australia – New Zealand		P/N	UFS	Yes	1-Jan-10					
		Australia	P	U			None (2),(3)			GATS	
		New Zealand	P	U			None (2),(3)	None (2),(3)		GATS	
		Singapore	P	X			None (2)	None (2)		GATS	MA: (1) Unbound, except for the provision of settlement and clearing services for financial assets which are listed on overseas exchanges only. (3) These measures are also limitations on national treatment. Settlement and clearing services for exchange traded securities and financial futures can only be provided by Central Depository

(continued)

(Continued)

RTA No	RTA Name	Parties	Listing approach		FS Coverage	Entry into force	Commitments: Mode (1) MA	Commitments: Mode (2) NT	Commitments: Mode (3) AC	Commitments' depth	Comments on MA, NT, AC
											(Pte) Limited and SGX-DT respectively. Only one clearing house established under the Banking Act may provide clearing services for Singapore dollar cheques and inter-bank fund transfer.
		Cambodia	P	X			None (2)	None (1),(2),(3)		GATS	
		Burma	P	X			No commitments on clearing services			GATS	
		Philippines	P	X			No commitments on clearing services			GATS	
		Viet Nam	P	X			None (2),(3)	None (2),(3)		GATS	
		Thailand	P	X			No commitments on clearing services			GATS	
		Malaysia	P	X			No commitments on clearing services			GATS	
		Indonesia	P	X			No commitments on clearing services			GATS	
		Brunei	P	X			No commitments on clearing services			GATS	

		LAOS	P	X			No commitments on clearing services			GATS	
2	ASEAN – China				Yes	1-Jul-07					
		China	P	X			No commitments on clearing services			GATS minus	
		Singapore	P	X			None (2)	None (2)		GATS	MA: (1) Unbound, except for the provision of settlement and clearing services for financial assets which are listed on overseas exchanges only. (3) These measures are also limitations on national treatment. Settlement and clearing services for exchange traded securities and financial futures can only be provided by Central Depository (Pte) Limited and SGX-DT respectively. Only one clearing house established under the Banking Act may provide clearing services for Singapore dollar cheques and inter-bank fund transfer.
		Cambodia	P	X			None (2)	None (1),(2),(3)		GATS	
		Burma	P	X			No commitments on clearing services			GATS	
		Philippines	P	X			No commitments on clearing services			GATS	

(continued)

(Continued)

RTA No	RTA Name	Parties	Listing approach		FS Coverage	Entry into force	Commitments			Commitments' depth	Comments on MA, NT, AC
							Mode (1) MA	Mode (2) NT	Mode (3) AC		
		Viet Nam	P	X			None (2),(3)	None (2),(3)		GATS	
		Thailand	P	X			No commitments on clearing services			GATS	
		Malaysia	P	X			No commitments on clearing services			GATS	
		Indonesia	P	X			No commitments on clearing services			GATS	
		Brunei	P	X			No commitments on clearing services			GATS	
		LAOS	P	X			No commitments on clearing services			GATS	
3	ASEAN – India				Yes	1-Jul-15					
		India (–2)	P	X			No commitments on clearing services			GATS	
		India – Indo	P	X			No commitments on clearing services			GATS	
		India – Phil	P	X			No commitments on clearing services			GATS	

		Singapore	P	X			None (2)	None (2)		GATS	MA: (1) Unbound, except for the provision of settlement and clearing services for financial assets which are listed on overseas exchanges only. (3) These measures are also limitations on national treatment. Settlement and clearing services for exchange traded securities and financial futures can only be provided by Central Depository (Pte) Limited and SGX-DT respectively. Only one clearing house established under the Banking Act may provide clearing services for Singapore dollar cheques and inter-bank fund transfer.
		Cambodia	P	X			None (2)	None (1),(2),(3)		GATS	MA: (3) Unbound until the Government of Cambodia determines what types of entities can conduct these services, the related laws and regulation are established, and such business is authorised by the government or other relevant designated authority.
		Burma	P	X			No commitments on clearing services			GATS	
		Philippines	P	X			No commitments on clearing services			GATS	

(continued)

(Continued)

RTA No	RTA Name	Parties	Listing approach		FS Coverage	Entry into force	Commitments			Commitments' depth	Comments on MA, NT, AC
							Mode (1) MA	Mode (2) NT	Mode (3) AC		
		Viet Nam	P	X			None (2),(3)	None (2),(3)		GATS	
		Thailand	P	X			No commitments on clearing services			GATS	
		Malaysia	P	X			No commitments on clearing services			GATS	
		Indonesia	P	X			No commitments on clearing services			GATS	
		Brunei	P	X			No commitments on clearing services			GATS	
		LAOS	P	X			No commitments on clearing services			GATS	
4	ASEAN – Korea, Republic of				Yes	14-Oct-10					
		Korea	P	X			No commitments on clearing services			GATS	
		Singapore	P	X			None (2)	None (2)		GATS	MA: (1) Unbound, except for the provision of settlement and clearing services for financial assets which are listed on overseas exchanges only. (3) These measures are also limitations on national treatment.

											Settlement and clearing services for exchange traded securities and financial futures can only be provided by Central Depository (Pte) Limited and SGX-DT respectively. Only one clearing house established under the Banking Act may provide clearing services for Singapore dollar cheques and inter-bank fund transfer.
		Cambodia	P	X			None (2)	None (1),(2),(3)		GATS	MA: (3) Unbound until the Government of Cambodia determines what types of entities can conduct these services, the related laws and regulation are established, and such business is authorised by the government or other relevant designated authority.
		Burma	P	X			No commitments on clearing services			GATS	
		Philippines	P	X			No commitments on clearing services			GATS	
		Viet Nam	P	X			None (2),(3)	None (2),(3)		GATS	
		Thailand	P	X			No commitments on clearing services			GATS	
		Malaysia	P	X			No commitments on clearing services			GATS	

(continued)

(Continued)

RTA No	RTA Name	Parties	Listing approach		FS Coverage	Entry into force	Commitments			Commitments' depth	Comments on MA, NT, AC
							Mode (1) MA	Mode (2) NT	Mode (3) AC		
		Indonesia	P	X			No commitments on clearing services			GATS	
		Brunei	P	X			No commitments on clearing services			GATS	
		LAOS	P	X			No commitments on clearing services			GATS	
5	Australia – Chile				Yes	6-Mar-09					
		Australia	N	X			None (2)	None (2),(3)		GATS plus	
		Chile	N	X			None (2)	None (2),(3)		GATS extra	Annex III: Section 2: MA: (3) Sector: Financial Services; Subsector: All Subsectors; Obligations Concerned: Market Access for Financial Institutions (Art 12.5); Description: Chile reserves the right to adopt or maintain any measure with respect to Art 12.5 (Market Access for Financial Institutions), except for the following sectors, subsectors and financial services defined in accordance with the relevant Chilean legislation, subject to the terms, limitations and conditions

											specified below: Clearing houses for futures contracts and options on securities must be established in Chile as corporations for that sole purpose and with an authorisation from the SVS. They may only be constituted by stock exchanges and their stockbrokers; Clearing houses of futures and options on cattle and agricultural commodities must be established as corporations for that sole purpose and with an authorisation from the SVS.
6	Australia – China				Yes	20-Dec-15					
		Australia	N	X			None (1),(2),(3)	None (1),(2),(3)		GATS plus	
		China	P	X			None (2)	None (1),(2),(3)		GATS	
7	Australia – New Zealand				Yes	1-Jan-89					
		Australia	N	X			None (1),(2),(3)	None (1),(2),(3)		GATS plus	
		New Zealand	N	X			None (1),(2),(3)	None (1),(2),(3)		GATS plus	
8	Brunei Darussalam – Japan				Yes	31-Jul-08					

(continued)

(Continued)

RTA No	RTA Name	Parties	Listing approach		FS Coverage	Entry into force	Commitments			Commitments' depth	Comments on MA, NT, AC
							Mode (1) MA	Mode (2) NT	Mode (3) AC		
		Brunei	P	X			No commitments on clearing services			GATS	
		Japan	P	U			None (2),(3)	None (1),(2),(3)		GATS plus	
9	Canada – Chile				No	5-Jul-97	Pursuant to Art G-01(2) and H-01(2)(a) the Agreement does not cover trade in financial services for either investment purposes or cross-border supply, respectively.				
10	Canada – Colombia				Yes	15-Aug-11					
		Canada	N	X			None (2),(3)	None (2),(3)		GATS	
		Colombia	N	X			None (2),(3)	None (2),(3)		GATS plus	
11	Canada – Honduras				Yes	1-Oct-14					
		Canada	N	X			None (2),(3)	None (2),(3)		GATS	
		Honduras	N	X			None (2)	None (2),(3)		GATS extra	

12	Canada – Panama				Yes	1-Apr-13					
		Canada	N	X			None (2),(3)	None (2),(3)		GATS	
		Panama	N	X			None (2),(3)	None (2),(3)		GATS extra	
13	Canada – Peru				Yes	1-Aug-09					
		Canada	N	X			None (2),(3)	None (2),(3)		GATS	
		Peru	N	X			None (2),(3)	None (2),(3)		GATS extra	
14	Canada – Rep. of Korea				Yes	1-Jan-15					
		Canada	N	X			None (2),(3)	None (2),(3)		GATS	
		Korea	N	X			None (2)	None (2),(3)		GATS extra	Annex III: Section A: MA: (3) Financial Services; Sub-Sector: Banking and other financial services (excluding insurance); Obligations Concerned: Market Access for Financial Institutions (Art 10.4); Level of Government: National; Measures: Financial Investment Services and Capital Markets Act (Law No 11758, 5 April 2013), Arts 298, 323-2, 323-3, 323-10 and 378 Description: Only the Korea Securities Depository and

(continued)

(Continued)

RTA No	RTA Name	Parties	Listing approach		FS Coverage	Entry into force	Commitments			Commitments' depth	Comments on MA, NT, AC
							Mode (1) MA	Mode (2) NT	Mode (3) AC		
											the Korea Exchange may perform clearing and settlement of securities and derivatives listed or traded on the Korea Exchange. Only central counterparties licensed under the Financial Investment Services and Capital Markets Act may perform clearing and settlement of financial investment services including securities and derivatives.
15	Chile – China				No	1-Aug-10	Pursuant to Art 2(a) of the Supplementary Aggreement on Trade in Services, financial services are not covered by the scope of the Free Trade Agreeement between Chile and China.				
16	Chile – Colombia				No	8-May-09	Pursuant to Art 9.1(4) and 10.1(4)(a) the Agreement does not cover financial services for either investment or cross-border supply, respectively.				

17	Chile – Costa Rica (Chile – Central America)				No	15-Feb-02	Pursuant to Art 11.02(3)(d) of the Agreement, financial services are not covered by the scope of the Free Trade Agreement.				
18	Chile – El Salvador (Chile – Central America)				No	1-Jun-02	Pursuant to Art 11.02(3)(d) of the Agreement, financial services are not covered by the scope of the Free Trade Agreement.				
19	Chile – Guatemala (Chile – Central America)				No	23-Mar-10	Pursuant to Art 11.02(3)(d) of the Agreement, financial services are not covered by the scope of the Free Trade Agreement.				
20	Chile – Honduras (Chile – Central America)				No	19-Jul-08	Pursuant to Art 11.02(3)(d) of the Agreement, financial services are not covered by the scope of the Free Trade Agreement.				
21	Chile – Japan				Yes	3-Sep-07					
		Chile	P	X				None (3)		GATS extra	MA: (3) Clearing houses for futures contracts and options on securities must be constituted in Chile as corporations for that sole purpose and with an authorisation from the SVS.They may only be constituted by stock exchanges and their stockbrokers.

(continued)

(Continued)

RTA No	RTA Name	Parties	Listing approach		FS Coverage	Entry into force	Commitments			Commitments' depth	Comments on MA, NT, AC
							Mode (1) MA	Mode (2) NT	Mode (3) AC		
		Japan	P	X			None (2),(3)	None (2),(3)		GATS	
22	Chile – Mexico				No	1-Aug-99	Pursuant to Art 9-02(3) and 10-02(3)(a) the Agreement does not cover financial services for either investment or cross-border supply, respectively.				
23	Chile – Nicaragua (Chile – Central America)				No	19-Oct-12	Pursuant to Art 11.02(3)(d) of the Agreement, financial services are not covered by the scope of the Free Trade Agreement.				
24	Chile – Thailand				Yes	5-Nov-15					
		Chile	P	X				None (3)		GATS extra	MA: (3) Clearing houses for futures contracts and options on securities must be constituted in Chile as corporations for that sole purpose and with an authorisation from the SVS. They may only be constituted by stock exchanges and their stockbrokers.
		Thailand	P	X			No commitments on clearing services			GATS	

25	China – Costa Rica				No	1-Aug-11	Pursuant to Art 91(3)(e) the Agreement does not cover financial services.				
26	China – Hong Kong, China				Yes	29-Jun-03	This Closer Economic Partnership although regulates financial services is not comprehensive and its trade disciplines are not fully-developed. When it comes to MA it is absent from the Agreement text and it is not implicitly existent in neither commercial presence (only NT & MFN) nor cross-border supply which is 3 lines about further liberalisation discussions. Therefore, I discarded it				
27	China – Korea, Republic of				Yes	20-Dec-15					
		China	P	X			None (2)	None (1),(2),(3)		GATS	
		Korea	P	X			No commitments on clearing services			GATS	
28	China – Macao, China				Yes	17-Oct-03	This Closer Economic Partnership although regulates financial services is not comprehensive and its trade disciplines are not				

(continued)

(Continued)

RTA No	RTA Name	Parties	Listing approach		FS Coverage	Entry into force	Commitments			Commitments' depth	Comments on MA, NT, AC
							Mode (1) MA	Mode (2) NT	Mode (3) AC		
							fully-developed. When it comes to MA it is absent from the Agreement text and it is not implicitly existent in neither commercial presence (only NT & MFN) nor cross-border supply which is 3 lines about further liberalisation discussions. Therefore, I discarded it				
29	China – New Zealand				Yes	1-Oct-08					
		China	P	X			None (2)	None (1),(2),(3)		GATS	
		New Zealand	P	U			None (2),(3)	None (2),(3)		GATS	
30	China – Singapore				Yes	1-Jan-09					
		China	P	X			None (2)	None (1),(2),(3)		GATS	
		Singapore	P	X			None (2)	None (2)		GATS	MA: (1) Unbound, except for the provision of settlement and clearing services for financial assets which are listed on overseas exchanges only. (3) These measures are also

											limitations on national treatment. Settlement and clearing services for exchange traded securities and financial futures can only be provided by Central Depository (Pte) Limited and SGX-DT respectively. Only one clearing house established under the Banking Act may provide clearing services for Singapore dollar cheques and inter-bank fund transfer.
31	Colombia – Mexico				Yes	1-Jan-95	According to Art 12-15 the parties shall submit their reservations to FS sectors. This has not yet happened, as of July 2023. Therefore, it is discarded				
32	Colombia – Northern Triangle (El Salvador, Guatemala, Honduras)				No	12-Nov-09	Pursuant to Art 12.2(5) and 13.2(4)(a) the Agreement does not cover financial services for either investment or cross-border supply, respectively.				
33	Costa Rica – Colombia				Yes	1-Aug-16					
		Costa Rica	N	X			None (2)	None (2),(3)		GATS extra	
		Colombia	N	X			None (2),(3)	None (2),(3)		GATS plus	

(continued)

(Continued)

RTA No	RTA Name	Parties	Listing approach		FS Coverage	Entry into force	Commitments: Mode (1) MA	Commitments: Mode (2) NT	Commitments: Mode (3) AC	Commitments' depth	Comments on MA, NT, AC
34	Costa Rica – Peru				No	1-Jun-13	Pursuant to Art 12.1(8) and 13.1(8) the Agreement does not cover financial services for either investment or cross-border supply, respectively.				
35	Costa Rica – Singapore				No	1-Jul-13	Pursuant to Art 11(3) and 10.2(7) the Agreement does not cover financial services for either investment or cross-border supply, respectively.				
36	Dominican Republic – Central America – United States Free Trade Agreement (CAFTA-DR)				Yes	1-Mar-06					
		Costa Rica	N	X			None (2)	None (2),(3)		GATS extra	
		Dominican Republic	N	X			None (2)	None (2),(3)		GATS extra	Annex III: Section A: MA: (3) Sector: Financial Services, Subsector: Securities; Obligations Concerned: Market Access (Art 12.4); Measures: Ley de

											Mercado de Valores, No 19-00, May 8, 2000, Arts. 46, 57, 62, 71, 76, 103, and 108; Description: The following entities must be incorporated under the laws of the Dominican Republic: (a) stock exchanges, (b) commodities exchanges, (c)brokers, (d) dealers, (e) clearing houses, (f) centralised depositories of securities, (g) investment fund managers, and (h) securities underwriters.
		El Salvador	N	X			None (2)	None (2),(3)		GATS extra	
		Guatemala	N	X			None (2)	None (2),(3)		GATS extra	
		Honduras	N	X			None (2)	None (2),(3)		GATS extra	Annex III: Section A: MA: (3) Sector: Financial Services Subsector: Centralised Depositories for the Custody, Compensation and Liquidation of Shares; Obligations Concerned: Market Access (Art 12.4); Level of Government: Central; Measures: Decree No 8-2001, Ley de Mercado de Valores, Art 139; Description: Depositories for the custody, compensation and liquidation of shares in Honduras must be constituted as public corporations.

(continued)

(Continued)

RTA No	RTA Name	Parties	Listing approach		FS Coverage	Entry into force	Commitments			Commitments' depth	Comments on MA, NT, AC
							Mode (1) MA	Mode (2) NT	Mode (3) AC		
		Nicaragua	N	X			None (2)	None (2),(3)		GATS extra	
		United States	N	X			None (2),(3)	None (2),(3)		GATS minus	
37	EFTA – Central America (Costa Rica and Panama)				Yes	19-Aug-14					
		Costa Rica	P	X			None (2)	None (2)		GATS extra	
		Panama	P	X			None (1),(2),(3)	None (1),(2),(3)		GATS extra	
		Iceland	P	U			None (2),(3)	None (2)		GATS	
		Lichtenstein	P	U			None (1),(2),(3)			GATS	
		Norway	P	U			None (2),(3)	None (1),(2),(3)		GATS plus	
		Switzerland	P	U			None (1),(2),(3)	None (2)		GATS	

38	EFTA – Chile				No	1-Dec-04	Pursuant to Art 45 of the Agreement, no commitments have been undertaken by the Parties in relation to trade in financial services.				
39	EFTA – Colombia				Yes	1-Jul-11					
		Colombia	P	X			None (2),(3)			GATS	
		Iceland	P	U			None (2),(3)	None (2)		GATS	
		Lichtenstein	P	U			None (1),(2),(3)			GATS	
		Norway	P	U			None (2),(3)	None (1),(2),(3)		GATS plus	
		Switzerland	P	U			None (1),(2),(3)	None (2)		GATS	
40	EFTA-Georgia				Yes	1-Sep-17					
		Georgia	P	X			None (1),(2),(3)	None (1),(2),(3)		GATS	
		Iceland	P	U			None (2),(3)	None (2)		GATS	
		Lichtenstein	P	U			None (1),(2),(3)			GATS	
		Norway	P	U			None (2),(3)	None (1),(2),(3)		GATS plus	

(continued)

(Continued)

RTA No	RTA Name	Parties	Listing approach		FS Coverage	Entry into force	Commitments			Commitments' depth	Comments on MA, NT, AC
							Mode (1) MA	Mode (2) NT	Mode (3) AC		
		Switzerland	P	U			None (1),(2),(3)	None (2)		GATS	
41	EFTA – Hong Kong, China				Yes	1-Oct-12					
		Hong Kong	N	X			No commitments on clearing services			GATS	
		Iceland	N	X			None (1),(2),(3)	None (1),(2),(3)		GATS plus	
		Lichtenstein	N	X			None (1),(2),(3)	None (1),(2),(3)		GATS plus	
		Norway	N	X			None (3)	None (3)		GATS minus	
		Switzerland	N	X			None (1),(2),(3)	None (1),(2),(3)		GATS plus	
42	EFTA – Korea, Republic of				Yes	1-Sep-05					
		Korea	P	X			No commitments on clearing services			GATS	
		Iceland	P	U			None (2),(3)	None (2)		GATS	
		Lichtenstein	P	U			None (1),(2),(3)			GATS	
		Norway	P	U			None (2),(3)	None (1),(2),(3)		GATS plus	

		Switzerland	P	U			None (1),(2),(3)	None (2)		GATS	
43	EFTA – Mexico				Yes	1-Jul-01					
		Mexico	N	X			None (1),(2),(3)	None (1),(2),(3)		GATS extra	
		Iceland	N	U			None (2),(3)	None (2)		GATS	
		Lichtenstein	N	U			None (1),(2),(3)			GATS	
		Norway	N	U			None (2),(3)	None (1),(2)		GATS	
		Switzerland	N	U			None (1),(2),(3)	None (2)		GATS	
44	EFTA – Singapore				Yes	1-Jan-03					
		Singapore	P	X			None (2)	None (2)		GATS	MA: (1) Unbound, except for the provision of settlement and clearing services for financial assets which are listed on overseas exchanges only. (3) Settlement and clearing services for exchange traded securities and financial futures can only be provided by Singapore Exchange Ltd (or its subsidiaries). Settlement and clearing services for Singapore dollar cheques and interbank funds transfer can only be provided by

(continued)

(Continued)

RTA No	RTA Name	Parties	Listing approach		FS Coverage	Entry into force	Commitments			Commitments' depth	Comments on MA, NT, AC
							Mode (1) MA	Mode (2) NT	Mode (3) AC		
											operators appointed by the Singapore Clearing House Association.
		Iceland	P	U			None (2),(3)	None (2)		GATS	
		Lichtenstein	P	U			None (1),(2),(3)			GATS	
		Norway	P	U			None (2),(3)	None (1),(2)		GATS	
		Switzerland	P	U			None (1),(2),(3)	None (2)		GATS	
45	EFTA-Ukraine				Yes	1-Jun-12					
		Ukraine	P	X			None (1),(2),(3)	None (1),(2),(3)		GATS	
		Iceland	P	U			None (2),(3)	None (2)		GATS	
		Lichtenstein	P	U			None (1),(2),(3)			GATS	
		Norway	P	U			None (1),(2)	None (1),(2),(3)		GATS plus	
		Switzerland	P	U			None (1),(2),(3)	None (2)		GATS	

46	El Salvador-Honduras – Chinese Taipei				No	1-Mar-08	Pursuant to Art 10.02(2)(a) and 11.02(3)(d) the Agreement does not cover financial services for either investment or cross-border supply, respectively.		
47	EU – Albania				Yes	1-Apr-09	Financial services are covered by the scope of the Stabilisation and Association Agreement to the extent that progressive liberalisation between the Parties shall occur in the coming years. MFN treatment is only explicitly extended for mode (3) of trade in services. There are no concrete MA and NT commitments, and that is reaffirmed by the absence of Schedules. Therefore, it is discarded		
48	EU – Bosnia Herzegovina				Yes	1-Jun-15	Financial services are covered by the scope of the Stabilisation and Association Agreement to the extent that progressive liberalisation between the Parties shall occur in the coming years. MFN treatment is only explicitly extended for mode (3) of trade in services. There are no concrete MA and NT		

(continued)

(Continued)

RTA No	RTA Name	Parties	Listing approach		FS Coverage	Entry into force	Commitments			Commitments' depth	Comments on MA, NT, AC
							Mode (1) MA	Mode (2) NT	Mode (3) AC		
							commitments, and that is reaffirmed by the absence of Schedules. Therefore, it is discarded				
49	EU – Canada				Yes	21-Sep-17					
		Canada	N	X			None (2),(3)	None (2),(3)		GATS	
		EU (–2)	N	X			None (2),(3)	None (2),(3)		GATS	
		EE & LT	N	X			None (1),(2),(3)	None (1),(2),(3)		GATS	
50	EU – CARIFORUM				Yes	1-Nov-08					
		EU (–2)	N	X			None (2),(3)	None (2),(3)		GATS	MA/NT: (1) RO: Unbound for financial leasing, for trading of money market instruments, foreign exchange, derivative products, exchange rate and interest rate instruments, transferable securities and other negotiable instruments and financial assets, for participation in issues of all kinds of securities, for asset management and for settlement and

											clearing services for financial assets. Payments and money transmission services are allowed only through a resident bank
		EE & LT	N	X			None (1,),(2),(3)	None (1),(2),(3)		GATS	
		CARIFORUM	P	X			No commitments on clearing services			GATS	
51	EU – Central America				Yes	1-Aug-13					
		Costa Rica	N	X			None (2),(3)	None (2),(3)		GATS extra	
		El Salvador	N	X			None (3)	None (3)		GATS extra	
		Honduras	N	X			None (2),(3)	None (2),(3)		GATS extra	
		Guatemala	N	X			None (3)	None (3)		GATS extra	
		Nicaragua	N	X			None (3)	None (3)		GATS extra	
		Panama	N	X			None (1),(2),(3)	None (1),(2),(3)		GATS extra	
		EU (–2)	N	X			None (2),(3)	None (2),(3)		GATS	MA/NT: (1) RO: Unbound for financial leasing, for trading of money market instruments, foreign exchange, derivative products, exchange rate and interest rate instruments, transferable securities and other negotiable instruments

(continued)

(Continued)

RTA No	RTA Name	Parties	Listing approach		FS Coverage	Entry into force	Commitments: Mode (1) MA	Commitments: Mode (2) NT	Commitments: Mode (3) AC	Commitments' depth	Comments on MA, NT, AC
											and financial assets, for participation in issues of all kinds of securities, for asset management and for settlement and clearing services for financial assets. Payments and money transmission services are allowed only through a resident bank
		EE & LT	N	X			None (1),(2),(3)	None (1),(2),(3)		GATS	
52	EU – Chile				Yes	28-Oct-05					
		Chile	P	X				None (3)		GATS extra	MA: (3) Clearing houses for futures contracts and options on securities must be constituted in Chile as corporations for that sole purpose and with an authorisation from the SVS. They may only be constituted by stock exchanges and their stockbrokers.
		EU	P	U			None (2),(3)	None (2),(3)		GATS	MA: (3) IT: Clearing services including the phase of final settlement may be conducted only by entities duly authorised and supervised by the Bank of Italy in agreement with Consob.

53	EU – Colombia and Peru				Yes	1-Mar-13					
		Colombia	N	X			None (2),(3)	None (2),(3)		GATS plus	
		Peru	N	X			None (3)	None (3)		GATS extra	
		EU (–2)	N	X			None (2),(3)	None (2),(3)		GATS	MA: (1) RO: Unbound for financial leasing, for trading of money market instruments, foreign exchange, derivative products, exchange rate and interest rate instruments, transferable securities and other negotiable instruments and financial assets, for partici-pation in issues of all kinds of securities, for asset management and for settlement and clear-ing services for financial assets. Payments and money transmission services are allowed only through a resident bank.
		EE & LT	N	X			None (1),(2),(3)	None (1),(2),(3)		GATS	
54	EU – Colombia, Peru – Accession of Equador				Yes	1-Jan-17					

(continued)

(*Continued*)

RTA No	RTA Name	Parties	Listing approach		FS Coverage	Entry into force	Commitments			Commitments' depth	Comments on MA, NT, AC
							Mode (1) MA	Mode (2) NT	Mode (3) AC		
		Equador	P	X			None (3)	None (3)		GATS extra	
		EU (–3)	N	X			None (2),(3)	None (2),(3)		GATS	MA: (1) RO: Unbound for financial leasing, for trading of money market instruments, foreign exchange, derivative products, exchange rate and interest rate instruments, transferable securities and other negotiable instruments and financial assets, for participation in issues of all kinds of securities, for asset management and for settlement and clearing services for financial assets. Payments and money transmission services are allowed only through a resident bank.
		EE & LT	N	X			None (1),(2),(3)	None (1),(2),(3)		GATS	
		HR	N	X			None (2)	None (2)		GATS	MA: (3) HR: None, except for settlement and clearing services where the Central Depositary Agency (CDA) is the sole supplier in Croatia. Access to the services of the CDA will be granted to non-residents on a non-discriminatory basis.

55	EU – Georgia				Yes	1-Sep-14					
		EU (–2)	H	X			None (2)	None (2),(3)		GATS minus	MA: (3) RO: Unbound for financial leasing, for trading of money market instruments, foreign exchange, derivative products, exchange rate and interest rate instruments, transferable securities and other negotiable instruments and financial assets, for participation in issues of all kinds of securities, for asset management and for settlement and clearing services for financial assets. Payments and money transmission services are allowed only through a resident bank
		EE & LT	H	X			None (1),(2)	None (1),(2),(3)		GATS minus	
		Georgia	H	X			None (1),(2)	None (1),(2),(3)		GATS minus	
56	EU – Korea, Republic of				Yes	1-Jul-11					
		EU (–2)	P	X			None (2),(3)	None (2),(3)		GATS	MA: (1) RO: Unbound for financial leasing, for trading of money market instruments, foreign exchange, derivative products, exchange rate and interest rate instruments, transferable securities and other negotiable instruments

(continued)

(Continued)

RTA No	RTA Name	Parties	Listing approach		FS Coverage	Entry into force	Commitments			Commitments' depth	Comments on MA, NT, AC
							Mode (1) MA	Mode (2) NT	Mode (3) AC		
											and financial assets, for participation in issues of all kinds of securities, for asset management and for settlement and clearing services for financial assets. Payments and money transmission services are allowed only through a resident bank
		EE & LT	P	X			None (1),(2),(3)	None (1),(2),(3)		GATS	
		Korea	P	X			No commitments on clearing services			GATS	
57	EU – Mexico				Yes	1-Oct-00					
		EU	N	U			None (2),(3)	None (2),(3)		GATS	MA: (3) Italy: Clearing and settlement of securities may be conducted only by the official clearing system. A company authorised by the Bank of Italy in agreement with Consob could be entrusted with the activity of clearing, up to the final settlement of securities.
		Mexico	N	X			None (1),(2),(3)	None (1),(2),(3)		GATS extra	

58	EU – Moldova, Republic of				Yes	1-Sep-14					
		EU (–2)	H	X			None (2)	None (2),(3)		GATS minus	MA: RO: Unbound for financial leasing, for trading of money market instruments, foreign exchange, derivative products, exchange rate and interest rate instruments, transferable securities and other negotiable instruments and financial assets, for participation in issues of all kinds of securities, for asset management and for settlement and clearing services for financial assets. Payments and money transmission services are allowed only through a resident bank.
		EE & LT	H	X			None (1),(2)	None (1),(2),(3)		GATS minus	
		Moldova	H	X			None (1),(2)	None (1),(2),(3)		GATS minus	
59	EU – Montenegro				Yes	1-May-10	Financial services are covered by the scope of the Stabilisation and Association Agreement to the extent that progressive liberalisation between the Parties shall occur in the coming years. MFN				

(continued)

(Continued)

RTA No	RTA Name	Parties	Listing approach		FS Coverage	Entry into force	Commitments			Commitments' depth	Comments on MA, NT, AC
							Mode (1) MA	Mode (2) NT	Mode (3) AC		
							treatment is only explicitly extended for mode (3) of trade in services. There are no concrete MA and NT commitments, and that is reaffirmed by the absence of Schedules. Therefore, it is discarded				
60	EU – Serbia				Yes	1-Sep-13	Financial services are covered by the scope of the Stabilisation and Association Agreement to the extent that progressive liberalisation between the Parties shall occur in the coming years. MFN treatment is only explicitly extended for mode (3) of trade in services. There are no concrete MA and NT commitments, and that is reaffirmed by the absence of Schedules. Therefore, it is discarded				
61	EU – FYROM				Yes	1-Apr-04	Financial services are covered by the scope of the Stabilisation and Association Agreement to the extent that progressive liberalisation				

							between the Parties shall occur in the coming years. MFN treatment is only explicitly extended for mode (3) of trade in services. There are no concrete MA and NT commitments, and that is reaffirmed by the absence of Schedules. Therefore, it is discarded				
62	EU – Ukraine				Yes	23-Apr-14					
		EU (–2)	H	X			None (2)	None (2),(3)		GATS minus	MA: RO: Unbound for financial leasing, for trading of money market instruments, foreign exchange, derivative products, exchange rate and interest rate instruments, transferable securities and other negotiable instruments and financial assets, for participation in issues of all kinds of securities, for asset management and for settlement and clearing services for financial assets. Payments and money transmission services are allowed only through a resident bank. HR: None, except for settlement and clearing services where the Central Depositary Agency (CDA) is the sole supplier in Croatia. Access to the services of the CDA will be granted to non-residents on a non-discriminatory basis.

(continued)

(Continued)

RTA No	RTA Name	Parties	Listing approach		FS Coverage	Entry into force	Commitments			Commitments' depth	Comments on MA, NT, AC
							Mode (1) MA	Mode (2) NT	Mode (3) AC		
		EE & LT	H	X			None (1),(2)	None (1),(2),(3)		GATS minus	
		Ukraine	H	X			None (1),(2)	None (1),(2),(3)		GATS minus	
63	Guatemala – Chinese Taipei				No	1-Jul-06	Pursuant to Art 10.02(2)(a) and 11.02(3)(d) the Agreement does not cover financial services for either investment or cross-border supply, respectively.				
64	Gulf Cooperation Council (GCC) – Singapore				Yes	1-Sep-13					
		United Arab Emirates	P	X			No commitments on clearing services			GATS	
		Kingdom of Bahrain	P	X			None (2)	None (2)		GATS plus	MA: (1) BH: Unbound, except for cross-listed equities that may be cleared on exchanges offering reciprocal privileges and that meet Bahrain information requirements. (3) BH: Unbound. Bahraini Dinar (BD) clearing must be through the Central Bank of Bahrain (CBB).

											BSE listed equities & securities must be cleared through the BSE.
		Kingdom of Saudi Arabia	P	X			No commitments on clearing services			GATS	MA: (2), (3) Unbound for all domestic settlement and clearing services provided exclusively by Saudi Arabian Monetary Agency (SAMA) under 'j.' This also limits national treatment.
		Sultanate of Oman	P	X			None (2),(3)	None (2),(3)		GATS	
		State of Kuwait	P	X			None (2)	None (2)		GATS	
		State of Quatar	P	X			None (1),(2),(3)	None (1),(2),(3)		GATS	
		Singapore	P	X			None (2)	None (2)		GATS	MA: (1) Unbound, except for the provision of settlement and clearing services for financial assets which are listed on overseas exchanges only. (3) Settlement and clearing services for exchange traded securities and financial futures can only be provided by Central Depository (Pte) Limited and SGX-DT respectively. Only one clearing house established under the Banking Act (Cap 19) may provide clearing services for Singapore dollar cheques and interbank fund transfer.

(continued)

(Continued)

RTA No	RTA Name	Parties	Listing approach		FS Coverage	Entry into force	Commitments			Commitments' depth	Comments on MA, NT, AC
							Mode (1) MA	Mode (2) NT	Mode (3) AC		
65	Hong Kong, China – Chile				Yes	9-Oct-14					
		Chile	P	X				None (3)		GATS extra	MA: (3) Clearing houses for futures contracts and options on securities must be constituted in Chile as corporations for that sole purpose and with an authorisation from the SVS. They may only be constituted by stock exchanges and their stockbrokers.
		Hong Kong	P	X			No commitments on clearing services			GATS	
66	Hong Kong, China – Macao, China				Yes	27-Oct-17					
		Hong Kong	P	X			No commitments on clearing services			GATS	
		Macao	P	X			None (2),(3)	None (1),(2),(3)		GATS	
67	Hong Kong, China – New Zealand				Yes	1-Jan-11					
		Hong Kong	N	X			No commitments on clearing services			GATS	

		New Zealand	N	X			None (2),(3)	None (2),(3)		GATS	
68	Iceland-China				Yes	1-Jul-14					
		Iceland	P	U			None (2),(3)	None (2)		GATS	
		China	P	X			None (2)	None (1),(2),(3)		GATS	
69	India – Japan				Yes	1-Aug-11					
		India	P	X			No commitments on clearing services			GATS	
		Japan	P	U			None (2),(3)	None (1),(2),(3)		GATS plus	
70	India – Malaysia				Yes	1-Jul-11					
		India	P	X			No commitments on clearing services			GATS	
		Malaysia	P	X			No commitments on clearing services			GATS	
71	India – Singapore				Yes	1-Aug-05					
		India	P	X			No commitments on clearing services			GATS	
		Singapore	P	X			None (2)	None (2)		GATS	MA: (1) Unbound, except for the provision of settlement and clearing services for financial assets which are listed on overseas exchanges

(continued)

(Continued)

RTA No	RTA Name	Parties	Listing approach		FS Coverage	Entry into force	Commitments Mode (1) MA	Commitments Mode (2) NT	Commitments Mode (3) AC	Commitments' depth	Comments on MA, NT, AC
											only.(3) Settlement and clearing services for exchange traded securities and financial futures and inter-bank transfers can only be provided by Central Depository (Pte) Limited, Singapore Exchange Derivatives Clearing Ltd, and Banking Computer Services Pte Ltd respectively. Only the clearing house established under the Banking Act may provide clearing services for Singapore dollar cheques and services for interbank fund transfers.
72	Japan – Australia				Yes	15-Jan-15					
		Japan	N	X			None (1),(2),(3)	None (1),(2),(3)		GATS plus	
		Australia	N	X			None (1),(2),(3)	None (1),(2),(3)		GATS plus	
73	Japan – Indonesia				Yes	1-Jul-08					
		Japan	P	U			None (2),(3)	None (1),(2),(3)		GATS plus	

		Indonesia	P	X						GATS	
74	Japan – Malaysia				Yes	13-Jul-06					
		Japan	P	U			None (2),(3)	None (1),(2),(3)		GATS plus	
		Malaysia	P	X			No commitments on clearing services			GATS	
75	Japan-Mexico				Yes	1-Apr-05	Pursuant to Art 108 of the EPA, the GATS commitments are applicable				
		Japan	N	X			None (2),(3)	None (1),(2)		GATS	
		Mexico	N	X			No commitments on clearing services			GATS	
76	Japan – Mongolia				Yes	7-Jun-16					
		Japan	P	U			None (2),(3)	None (1),(2),(3)		GATS	
		Mongolia	P	X			No commitments on clearing services			GATS	
77	Japan – Peru				Yes	1-Mar-12					
		Japan	N	X			None (1),(2),(3)	None (1),(2),(3)		GATS plus	
		Peru	N	X			None (2),(3)	None (2),(3)		GATS extra	

(continued)

(Continued)

RTA No	RTA Name	Parties	Listing approach		FS Coverage	Entry into force	Commitments			Commitments' depth	Comments on MA, NT, AC
							Mode (1) MA	Mode (2) NT	Mode (3) AC		
78	Japan – Philippines				Yes	11-Dec-08					
		Japan	P	U			None (2),(3)	None (1),(2),(3)		GATS plus	
		Philippines	P	X			No commitments on clearing services			GATS	
79	Japan – Singapore				Yes	30-Nov-02					
		Japan	P	U			None (2),(3)	None (1),(2)		GATS	
		Singapore	P	X			None (2)	None (2)		GATS	MA: (1) Unbound, except for the provision of settlement and clearing services for financial assets which are listed on overseas exchanges only. (3) Settlement and clearing services for exchange traded securities and financial futures can only be provided by the SGX or its subsidiaries. Settlement and clearing services for Singapore dollar cheques and interbank funds transfers can only be provided by operators appointed by the Singapore Clearing House Association.

80	Japan – Switzerland				Yes	1-Sep-09					
		Japan	N	X			None (1),(2),(3)	None (1),(2),(3)		GATS plus	
		Switzerland	N	X			None (1),(2),(3)	None (1),(2),(3)		GATS plus	
81	Japan – Thailand				Yes	1-Nov-07					
		Japan	P	U			None (2),(3)	None (1),(2),(3)		GATS plus	
		Thailand	P	X			No commitments on clearing services			GATS	
82	Japan – Viet Nam				Yes	1-Oct-09					
		Japan	P	U			None (2),(3)	None (1),(2),(3)		GATS plus	
		Viet Nam	P	X			None (2),(3)	None (2),(3)		GATS	
83	Jordan – Singapore				Yes	22-Aug-05					
		Jordan	P	X			None (2)	None (2)		GATS	MA: (3) Access restricted to the Depository Center at the Amman Bourse for securities, and to the Central Bank of Jordan for all other financial instruments.

(continued)

(Continued)

RTA No	RTA Name	Parties	Listing approach		FS Coverage	Entry into force	Commitments			Commitments' depth	Comments on MA, NT, AC
			P	X			Mode (1) MA	Mode (2) NT	Mode (3) AC		
		Singapore	P	X			None (2)	None (2)		GATS	MA: (1) Unbound, except for the provision of settlement and clearing services for financial assets which are listed on overseas exchanges only. (3) Settlement and clearing services for exchange traded securities and financial futures can only be provided by Central Depository (Pte) Limited and Singapore Exchange Derivatives Clearing Ltd respectively. Only one clearing house established under the Banking Act may provide clearing services for Singapore dollar cheques and interbank fund transfer.
84	Korea, Republic of – Colombia				No	15-Jul-16	Pursuant to Art 8.1(4) and 9.1(4)(a) the Agreement does not cover trade in financial services for either investment purposes or cross-border supply, respectively.				
85	Korea, Republic of – Australia				Yes	12-Dec-14					

		Korea	N	X			None (2)	None (2),(3)		GATS extra	Annex III: Sector: Financial Services; Sub-Sector: Banking and other financial services (excluding insurance) Obligations Concerned: Market Access for Financial Institutions (Art 8.4); Level of Government: Central Measures: Financial Investment Services and Capital Markets Act (Law No 9407, February 3, 2009), Arts 298, 378 and 166 Enforcement Decree of the Financial Investment Services and Capital Markets Act (Presidential Decree No 21291, February 3, 2009), Art 178; Description: Only the Korea Securities Depository and the Korea Exchange may perform liquidation and settlement of securities and derivatives listed or traded on the Korea Exchange.
		Australia	N	X			None (2),(3)	None (2),(3)		GATS plus	
86	Korea, Republic of – Chile				No	1-Apr-04	Pursuant to Art 10.2(3)(a) and 11.2(3)(a) the Agreement does not cover trade in financial services for either investment purposes or cross-border supply, respectively.				

(continued)

(Continued)

RTA No	RTA Name	Parties	Listing approach		FS Coverage	Entry into force	Commitments: Mode (1) MA	Commitments: Mode (2) NT	Commitments: Mode (3) AC	Commitments' depth	Comments on MA, NT, AC
87	Korea, Republic of – India				Yes	1-Jan-10					
		Korea	P	X			No commitments on clearing services			GATS	
		India	P	X			No commitments on clearing services			GATS	
88	Korea, Republic of – New Zealand				No	20-Dec-15	Pursuant to Art 10.3(4) and 8.3(3)(a) the Agreement does not cover trade in financial services for either investment purposes or cross-border supply, respectively.				
89	Korea, Republic of – Singapore				Yes	2-Mar-06					
		Korea	P	X			No commitments on clearing services			GATS	
		Singapore	P	X			None (2)	None (2)		GATS	MA: (1) Unbound, except for the provision of settlement and clearing services for financial assets which are listed on overseas exchanges only. (3) Settlement and clearing services for exchange traded

											securities and financial futures can only be provided by Central Depository (Pte) Limited and Singapore Exchange Derivatives Clearing Ltd respectively. Only one clearing house established under the Banking Act may provide clearing services for Singapore dollar cheques and interbank fund transfer.
90	Korea, Republic of – US				Yes	15-Mar-12					
		Korea	N	X			None (2)	None (2),(3)		GATS extra	Annex III: Sector: Financial Services Sub-Sector: Banking and other financial services (excluding insurance) Obligations Concerned: Market Access for Financial Institutions (Ar 13.4); Level of Government: Central Measures: Arts 173-3 and 194 of the Securities and Exchange Act (Law No 7762, December 29, 2005) Art 84-27 of the Enforcement Decree of the Securities and Exchange Act (Presidential Decree No 19806, December 29, 2006); Description: Only the Korea Securities Depository and the Korea Exchange may perform liquidation and

(continued)

(Continued)

RTA No	RTA Name	Parties	Listing approach		FS Coverage	Entry into force	Commitments			Commitments' depth	Comments on MA, NT, AC
							Mode (1) MA	Mode (2) NT	Mode (3) AC		
											settlement of securities and derivatives listed or traded on the Korea Exchange.
		US	N	X			None (2),(3)	None (2),(3)		GATS minus	
91	Korea, Republic of – Viet Nam				Yes	20-Dec-15					
		Korea	P	X			No commitments on clearing services			GATS	
		Viet Nam	P	X			None (2),(3)	None (2),(3)		GATS	
92	Malaysia – Australia				Yes	1-Jan-13					
		Malaysia	P	X			No commitments on clearing services			GATS	
		Australia	P	U			None (2),(3)			GATS	
93	Mexico – Central America				No	1-Sep-12	Pursuant to Art 11.2(3)(a) and 12.2(2)(b) the Agreement does not cover trade in financial services for either investment purposes or cross-border supply, respectively.				

94	Mexico – Panama				Yes	1-Jul-15					
		Mexico	N	X			None (2),(3)	None (2),(3)		GATS extra	
		Panama	N	X			None (2),(3)	None (2),(3)		GATS extra	
95	Mexico – Uruguay				No	15-Jul-04	Pursuant to Art 13-02(4) and 10-02(2)(a) the Agreement does not cover trade in financial services for either investment purposes or cross-border supply, respectively.				
96	New Zealand – Chinese Taipei				Yes	1-Dec-13					
		New Zealand	N	X			None (2),(3)	None (2),(3)		GATS	
		Chinese Taipei	N	X			None (1),(2),(3)	None (1),(2),(3)		GATS plus	Section I: Sector: Financial Services, Sub-Sector: Industry Classification: Securities & Futures; Obligations Concerned: Local Presence (Chapter 13 (Cross-Border Trade in Services) Art 7). Measures: Securities and Exchange Act, January 4 2012 Futures Trading Act, June 9 2010 Securities Investment Trust and Consulting Act, June 9 2010 Standards Governing the Establishment

(continued)

(Continued)

RTA No	RTA Name	Parties	Listing approach		FS Coverage	Entry into force	Commitments			Commitments' depth	Comments on MA, NT, AC
							Mode (1) MA	Mode (2) NT	Mode (3) AC		
											of Securities Firms, June 16 2009 Standards Governing the Establishment of Futures Commission Merchants, October 2 2007 Description: Cross-Border Trade in Services Cross-border financial services suppliers shall not supply any financial services related to securities and futures, including solicitation or marketing thereof, to any entities or persons located in the Separate Customs Territory of Taiwan, Penghu, Kinmen and Matsu without prior approval and obtaining related business licenses from the competent authorities.
97	New Zealand – Malaysia					1-Aug-10					
		New Zealand	P	U			None (2),(3)	None (2),(3)		GATS	
		Malaysia	P	X			No commitments on clearing services			GATS	
98	New Zealand – Singapore				Yes	1-Jan-01					

		New Zealand	P	X			None (2),(3)	None (2),(3)		GATS	
		Singapore	P	X			None (2)	None (2)		GATS	MA: (1) Unbound, except for the provision of settlement and clearing services for financial assets which are listed on overseas exchanges only. (3) Settlement and clearing services for exchange traded securities and financial futures, and Singapore dollar cheques and inter-bank funds transfer can only be provided by SGX or its subsidiaries and Banking Computer Services Pte Ltd.
99	Nicaragua – Chinese Taipei				Yes	1-Jan-08					
		Nicaragua	N	X			None (2)	None (2),(3)		GATS extra	
		Chinese Taipei	N	X			None (2),(3)	None (2),(3)		GATS	
100	North American Free Trade Agreement (NAFTA)				Yes	1-Jan-94					
		Canada	N	X			None (2),(3)	None (2),(3)		GATS	

(continued)

(Continued)

RTA No	RTA Name	Parties	Listing approach		FS Coverage	Entry into force	Commitments			Commitments' depth	Comments on MA, NT, AC
							Mode (1) MA	Mode (2) NT	Mode (3) AC		
		Mexico	N	X			None (1),(2),(3)	None (1),(2),(3)		GATS extra	
		US 2 Canada	N	X			None (2),(3)	None (2),(3)		GATS minus	
		US 2 Mexico	N	X			None (1),(2),(3)	None (1),(2),(3)		GATS plus	
101	Pacific – Alliance				Yes	1-May-16					
		Chile	N	X			None (2),(3)	None (2),(3)		GATS extra	7. Sector: Servicios Financieros; Subsector: Servicios bancarios y demás servicios financieros; Obligaciones Afectadas: Derecho de Establecimiento (Artículo 11.5); Nivel de Gobierno: Central Medidas: Ley N° 20345, Diario Oficial de 6 de junio de 2009, Ley sobre Sistemas de Compensación y Liquidación de Instrumentos Financieros, artículo 21 Ley N° 18.046, Diario Oficial de 22 de octubre de 1981, Ley de Sociedades Anónimas, Título XIII, artículos 126 a 132. Descripción: Sólo los agentes de valores,

											corredores de bolsas de valores, corredores de bolsas de productos, bancos y demás personas que autorice la Superintendencia de Valores y Seguros a través de normas de carácter general podrán ser miembros de sistemas de compensación y liquidación de instrumentos financieros.
		Colombia	N	X			None (2),(3)	None (2),(3)		GATS plus	
		Mexico	N	X			None (2),(3)	None (2),(3)		GATS extra	
		Peru	N	X			None (2),(3)	None (2),(3)		GATS extra	
102	Pakistan – China				Yes	10-Oct-09					
		Pakistan	P	X			No commitments on clearing services			GATS	
		China	P	X			None (2)	None (1),(2),(3)		GATS	
103	Pakistan – Malaysia				Yes	1-Jan-08					
		Pakistan	P	X			No commitments on clearing services			GATS	
		Malaysia	P	X			No commitments on clearing services			GATS	

(continued)

(Continued)

RTA No	RTA Name	Parties	Listing approach		FS Coverage	Entry into force	Commitments			Commitments' depth	Comments on MA, NT, AC
							Mode (1) MA	Mode (2) NT	Mode (3) AC		
104	Panama – Chile				No	7-Mar-08	Pursuant to Art 10.1(3)(a) the Agreement does not cover financial services.				
105	Panama – Chinese Taipei				Yes	1-Jan-04					
		Panama	N	X			None (1),(2),(3)	None (1),(2),(3)		GATS extra	
		Chinese Taipei	N	X			None (2),(3)	None (2),(3)		GATS	
106	Panama – Costa Rica (Panama – Central America)				Yes	23-Oct-08					
		Panama	N	X			None (2),(3)	None (2),(3)		GATS extra	
		Costa Rica	N	X			None (2),(3)	None (2),(3)		GATS extra	
107	Panama – El Salvador (Panama – Central America)				Yes	11-Apr-03					

		Panama	N	X			None (1),(2),(3)	None (1),(2),(3)		GATS extra	
		El Salvador	N	X			None (1),(2),(3)	None (1),(2),(3)		GATS extra	
108	Panama – Guatemala (Panama – Central America)				Yes	20-Jun-09					
		Panama	N	X			None (1),(2),(3)	None (1),(2),(3)		GATS extra	
		Guatemala	N	X			None (2)	None (2)		GATS extra	
109	Panama – Honduras (Panama – Central America)				Yes	9-Jan-09					
		Panama	N	X			None (1),(2),(3)	None (1),(2),(3)		GATS extra	
		Honduras	N	X			None (1),(2),(3)	None (1),(2),(3)		GATS extra	
110	Panama – Nicaragua (Panama – Central America)				Yes	21-Nov-09					

(continued)

(Continued)

RTA No	RTA Name	Parties	Listing approach		FS Coverage	Entry into force	Commitments			Commitments' depth	Comments on MA, NT, AC
							Mode (1) MA	Mode (2) NT	Mode (3) AC		
		Panama	N	X			None (1),(2),(3)	None (1),(2),(3)		GATS extra	
		Nicaragua	N	X			None (1),(2),(3)	None (1),(2),(3)		GATS extra	
111	Panama-Peru				Yes	1-May-12					
		Panama	N	X			None (2),(3)	None (2),(3)		GATS extra	
		Peru	N	X			None (2),(3)	None (2),(3)		GATS plus	
112	Panama – Singapore					24-Jul-C6					
		Panama	N	X			None (2),(3)	None (2),(3)		GATS extra	
		Singapore	N	X			None (2)	None (2)		GATS	Annex III: Section A (Non-Conforming Measures): Sector: Financial Services, Sub-Sector All sectors; Industry Classification; Type of Reservation: Market Access for Financial Institutions, National Treatment; Measure Companies Act, Cap 50, Part IV Division 7A,Securities and Futures Act, Cap 289, Part III,Banking Act, Cap 19, section 59;

											Description of Reservation: Clearing and settlement services for exchange-traded securities and financial futures and inter-bank transfers can only be provided by Central Depository (Pte) Limited, Singapore Exchange Derivatives Clearing Ltd and Banking Computer Services Pte Ltd respectively | Section B (Future Measures): Sector Financial Services; Sub-Sector Settlement and clearing services for financial assets, including securities, derivative products and other negotiable instruments; Industry Classification, CPC 81329 Other services related to securities market; Type of Reservation: Market Access for Financial Institutions, National Treatment; Description of Reservation: Singapore reserves the right to adopt or maintain any measure affecting the supply of clearing and settlement services for exchange traded securities and financial futures and Singapore dollar cheques and interbank transfers. Existing Measures: Companies Act, Cap 50, Securities and Futures Act 2001, Cap 289

(continued)

(Continued)

RTA No	RTA Name	Parties	Listing approach		FS Coverage	Entry into force	Commitments			Commitments' depth	Comments on MA, NT, AC
							Mode (1) MA	Mode (2) NT	Mode (3) AC		
113	Peru – Chile				No	1-Mar-09	Pursuant to Art 11.1 (4) (a) and 12.1 (3) (a) the Agreement does not cover trade in financial services for either investment purposes or cross-border supply, respectively.				
114	Peru – China				Yes	1-Mar-10					
		Peru	P	X			None (2),(3)	None (2),(3)		GATS plus	
		China	P	X			None (2)	None (1),(2),(3)		GATS	
115	Peru – Korea, Republic of				Yes	1-Aug-11					
		Peru	N	X			None (2),(3)	None (2),(3)		GATS plus	
		Korea	N	X			None (2),(3)	None (2),(3)		GATS extra	
116	Peru – Mexico				Yes	1-Feb-12					
		Peru	N	X			None (2),(3)	None (2),(3)		GATS extra	
		Mexico	N	X			None (2),(3)	None (2),(3)		GATS extra	

117	Peru – Singapore				No	1-Aug-09	Pursuant to Art 10.2(4) and 11.2(7) the Agreement does not cover trade in financial services for either investment purposes or cross-border				
							supply, respectively. However, the GATS obligations are incorporated to FTA				
		Peru	P	X			None (3)	None (3)		GATS	
		Singapore	P	X			None (2)	None (2)		GATS	
118	Singapore – Australia				Yes	28-Jul-03					
		Singapore	N	X			None (2)	None (2),(3)		GATS plus	Annex Vi: Section B: Sector: Financial Services, Sub-Sector: Settlement and clearing services for financial assets, including securities, derivative products and other negotiable instruments; Obligations Concerned: Market Access for Financial Institutions; Level of Government: National; Measure: Companies Act, Cap 50. Securities and Futures Act, Cap 289; Reservation: Singapore reserves the right to adopt or maintain any measure affecting the supply of clearing and settlement services for exchange traded securities,

(continued)

(Continued)

RTA No	RTA Name	Parties	Listing approach		FS Coverage	Entry into force	Commitments			Commitments' depth	Comments on MA, NT, AC
							Mode (1) MA	Mode (2) NT	Mode (3) AC		
											financial futures and interbank transfers. | Sector: Financial Services; Obligations Concerned: National Treatment, Market Access for Financial Institutions; Level of Government: National; Reservation: Singapore reserves the right to adopt or maintain any measure in the form of subsidies or grants provided by Singapore in connection with the supply of any financial service involving what Singapore deems as systemically important financial markets infra-structure, including: (a) Exchanges; (b) Central Depositories; (c) Repositories; (d) Clearing and Settlement facilities; and (e) Market operators.
		Australia	N	X			None (2),(3)	None (2),(3)		GATS plus	
119	Singapore – Chinese Taipei				No	22-Apr-14	Pursuant to Art 9.3(1) and 8.2(3)(a) the Agreement does not cover trade in financial services for either investment purposes or cross-border				

							supply, respectively. However, the GATS commitments are incormporated.				
		Singapore	P	X			None (2)	None (2)		GATS	
		Chinese Taipei	P	X			None (2),(3)	None (2),(3)		GATS	
120	Switzerland – China				Yes	1-Jul-14					
		Switzerland	P	U			None (1),(2),(3)	None (2)		GATS	
		China	P	X			None (2)	None (1),(2),(3)		GATS	
121	Thailand – Australia				Yes	1-Jan-05					
		Thailand	H	X			No commitments on clearing services			GATS	
		Australia	H	X			None (2),(3)	None (2),(3)		GATS plus	
122	Thailand – New Zealand				No	1-Jul-05	Pursuant to Art 8.1 trade in services is not captured by the scope of the current Agreement. Services trade is regulated by ASEAN – Australia – NZ.				

(continued)

(Continued)

RTA No	RTA Name	Parties	Listing approach		FS Coverage	Entry into force	Commitments Mode (1) MA	Mode (2) NT	Mode (3) AC	Commitments' depth	Comments on MA, NT, AC
123	Trans-Pacific Strategic Economic Partnership				No	28-May-06	Pursuant to Art 12.3(2)(a) the Agreement does not cover trade in financial services.				
124	Ukraine – Montenegro				Yes	1-Jan-13					
		Ukraine	P	X			None (1),(2),(3)	None (1),(2),(3)		GATS	
		Montenegro	P	X			None (2)	None (1),(2),(3)		GATS	MA: (3) This type of services may be provided by Central Depository of Securities only
125	US – Australia				Yes	1-Jan-05					
		US	N	X			None (2),(3)	None (2),(3)		GATS minus	
		Australia	N	X			None (2),(3)	None (2),(3)		GATS plus	
126	US – Bahrain				Yes	1-Aug-06					
		US	N	X			None (2),(3)	None (2),(3)		GATS minus	

		Bahrain	N	X			None (2),(3)	None (2),(3)		GATS plus	
127	US – Chile				Yes	1-Jan-04					
		US	N	X			None (2),(3)	None (2),(3)		GATS minus	
		Chile	N	X			None (2)	None (2),(3)		GATS extra	Annex III: Section A: MA: (3) Sector: Financial Services; Subsector: Banking and Other Financial Services; Obligations Concerned: Right of Establishment Measures: Ley N° 18.045, Official Gazette of October 22, 1981, Ley de Mercado de Valores, Title XIX, Art 155. Ley N° 18.046, Official Gazette of October 22, 1981, Ley de Sociedades Anónimas, Title XIII, Arts 126 to 132; Description: Clearing houses of futures, options and other contracts of similar nature that the Superintendencia de Valores y Seguros may authorise, must be established as special purpose corporations (sociedades anónimas especiales) under Chilean law. Only stock exchanges established in Chile and stock brokers who are members of those exchanges can be shareholders of clearing houses. | Sector: Financial

(continued)

(Continued)

RTA No	RTA Name	Parties	Listing approach		FS Coverage	Entry into force	Commitments Mode (1) MA	Mode (2) NT	Mode (3) AC	Commitments' depth	Comments on MA, NT, AC
											Services; Subsector: Banking and Other Financial Services Obligations Concerned: Right of Establishment Measures: Ley N° 19.220, Official Gazette of May 31, 1993, Ley de Bolsa de Productos Agropecuarios, Title IV, Arts 24, 25 and 26. Ley N° 18.046, Official Gazette of October 22, 1981, Ley de Sociedades Anónimas, Title XIII, Arts 126 to 132. Description: Clearing houses of futures and options on cattle and agricultural commodities must be established as special purpose corporations (sociedades anónimas especiales) under Chilean law.
128	US – Colombia				Yes	15-May-12					
		US	N	X			None (2),(3)	None (2),(3)		GATS minus	
		Colombia	N	X			None (2),(3)	None (2),(3)		GATS plus	
129	US – Jordan				Yes	17-Dec-01					

		US	P	U			None (2),(3)	None (2),(3)		GATS minus	
		Jordan	P	X			None (2)	None (2)		GATS	MA: (3) Access restricted to the Depository Center at the Amman Bourse for securities, and to the Central Bank of Jordan for all other financial instruments.
130	US – Morocco				Yes	1-Jan-06					
		US	N	X			None (2),(3)	None (2),(3)		GATS minus	
		Morocco	N	X			None (2),(3)	None (2),(3)		GATS extra	
131	US – Oman				Yes	1-Jan-09					
		US	N	X			None (2),(3)	None (2),(3)		GATS minus	
		Oman	N	X			None (2),(3)	None (2),(3)		GATS	
132	US – Panama				Yes	31-Oct-12					
		US	N	X			None (2),(3)	None (2),(3)		GATS minus	
		Panama	N	X			None (2),(3)	None (2),(3)		GATS extra	
133	US – Peru				Yes	1-Feb-09					
		US	N	X			None (2),(3)	None (2),(3)		GATS minus	

(continued)

(Continued)

RTA No	RTA Name	Parties	Listing approach		FS Coverage	Entry into force	Commitments			Commitments' depth	Comments on MA, NT, AC
							Mode (1) MA	Mode (2) NT	Mode (3) AC		
		Peru	N	X			None (2),(3)	None (2),(3)		GATS plus	
134	US-Singapore				Yes	1-Jan-04					
		US	N	X			None (2),(3)	None (2),(3)		GATS minus	
		Singapore	N	X			None (2)	None (2)		GATS	Annex 10B: Section B: Type of Reservation: Market Access for Financial Institutions and National Treatment; Level of Government: National; Measures: Companies Act, Cap 50, Part IV Division 7A Securities and Futures Act, Cap 289, Part III Banking Act, Cap 19, Section 59; Description: Clearing and settlement services for exchange-traded securities and financial futures and inter-bank transfers can only be provided by Central Depository (Pte) Limited, Singapore Exchange Derivatives Clearing Ltd, and Banking Computer Services Pte Ltd respectively
135	China – Georgia					1-Jan-18					

		China	P	X			None (2)	None (1),(2),(3)		GATS	
		Georgia	P	X			None (1),(2),(3)	None (1),(2),(3)		GATS	
136	EAEU – Viet Nam					5-Oct-16					
		Viet Nam	H	X			None (2),(3)	None (2),(3)		GATS	
		Russian Federation	H	X			None (2)	None (2)		GATS	

Bibliography

Adlung, R, 'Negotiations on Safeguards and Subsidies in Services: A Never-Ending Story?' (2007) 10 *Journal of International Economic Law* 235

Adlung, R and Mattoo, A, 'The GATS' in A Mattoo, RM Stern and G Zanini (eds), *A Handbook of International Trade in Services* (Oxford, Oxford University Press, 2007)

Alexander, K, 'Global Financial Standard Setting, the G10 Committees, and International Economic Law' (2008) 34 *Brooklyn Journal of International Law* 861

Allen, J, 'Derivatives Clearinghouses and Systemic Risk: A Bankruptcy and Dodd-Frank Analysis' (2012) 64 *Stanford Law Review* 1079

Bagwell, K and Staiger, R, 'An Economic Theory of GATT' (1999) 89 *American Economic Review* 215

—— 'Reciprocity, Non-Discrimination and Preferential Agreements in the Multilateral Trading System' (2001) 17 *European Journal of Political Economy* 281

—— *The Economics of the World Trading System* (Cambridge, MIT Press, 2002)

Baldwin, R, *The Political Economy of US Import Policy* (Cambridge, MIT Press, 1985)

Baldwin, R, McLaren, J and Panagariya, A, 'Regulatory Protectionism, Developing Nations, and a Two-Tier World Trade System [with Comments and Discussion]' (Brookings Institution Press, 2000)

Barth, J et al, 'World Trade Organization Commitments vs Reported Practices on Foreign Bank Entry and Regulation: A Cross-Country Analysis' in AN Berger, P Molyneux and JOS Wilson (eds), *The Oxford Handbook of Banking* (Oxford, Oxford University Press, 2012)

Baumol, W, Panzar, J and Willig, R, *Contestable Markets and the Theory of Industry Structure* (New York, Harcourt Brace Jovanovich, 1982)

Berkey, J, *A Framework Agreement for Electronic Commerce Regulation under the GATS 1-2* (Institution of International Finance, 2001)

Bhagwati, J, 'The Pure Theory of International Trade: A Survey' (1964) 74 *The Economic Journal* 1

Bhuiyan, S, 'Mandatory and Discretionary Legislation: The Continued Relevance of the Distinction under the WTO' (2002) 5 *Journal of International Economic Law* 571

Bismuth, R, 'Financial Sector Regulation and Financial Services Liberalization at the Crossroads: The Relevance of International Financial Standards in WTO Law' (2010) 44 *Journal of World Trade* 489

Booth, P, 'Is 'Market Failure' a Good Justification for Financial Regulation?' [2021] Institute for International Monetary Research Discussion Paper

Bradford, A, 'The Brussels Effect' (2012) 107 *Northwestern University Law Review* 1

—— *The Brussels Effect: How the European Union Rules the World* (Oxford, Oxford University Press, 2020)

Brummer, C, 'How International Financial Law Works (and How It Doesn't)' (2010) 99 *Georgetown Law Journal* 257

—— 'Why Soft Law Dominates International Finance – and Not Trade' (2010) 13 *Journal of International Economic Law* 623

Brunnermeier, M et al, *The Fundamental Principles of Financial Regulation*, vol 11 (Geneva, International Center for Monetary and Banking Studies, 2009)

Bullard, J, Neely, C and Wheelock, D, 'Systemic Risk and the Financial Crisis: A Primer' (2009) 91 *Federal Reserve Bank of St. Louis Review*

Cantore, C, *The Prudential Carve-out for Financial Services: Rationale and Practice in the GATS and Preferential Trade Agreements* (Cambridge, Cambridge University Press, 2018)

Cerezetti, F et al, 'Market Liquidity, Closeout Procedures and Initial Margin for CCPs' (2019) 25 *The European Journal of Finance* 599

Chang, F, 'The Systemic Risk Paradox: Banks and Clearninghouses under Regulation' (2014) 14 *Columbia Business Law Review* 747

Claessens, S et al, 'Lessons and Policy Implications from the Global Financial Crisis' [2010] IMF Working Paper No 2010/044

—— *Financial Crises: Causes, Consequences, and Policy Responses* (Washington DC, International Monetary Fund, 2014)

Claessens S and Jansen M, *The Internationalization of Financial Services: Issues and Lessons for Developing Countries* (Heidelberg, Springer Netherlands, 2000)

Commission Staff Working Document, 'EU Equivalence Decisions in Financial Services Policy: An Assessment' SWD (2017) 102 final

—— 'Impact Assessment Accompanying the Proposal for a Regulation of the European Parliament and of the Council Amending Regulation (EU) No 1095/2010 Establishing a European Supervisory Authority (European Securities and Markets Authority)' COM (2017) 331 final

'Communication from the Commission – The Recapitalisation of Financial Institutions in the Current Financial Crisis: Limitation of Aid to the Minimum Necessary and Safeguards against Undue Distortions of Competition', OJ C 10, 15 January 2009'

'Communication from the Commission on the Application, from 1 August 2013, of State Aid Rules to Support Measures in Favour of Banks in the Context of the Financial Crisis' (Banking Communication), OJ C 216, 30 July 2013

'Communication from the Commission on the Return to Viability and the Assessment of Restructuring Measures in the Financial Sector in the Current Crisis under the State Aid Rules', OJ C 195/9, 19 August 2009

'Communication from the Commission on the Treatment of Impaired Assets in the Community Banking Sector', OJ C 72, 26 March 2009

Cottier, T and Krajewski, M, 'What Role for Non-Discrimination and Prudential Standards in International Financial Law?' (2010) 13 *Journal of International Economic Law* 817

Crochet, V and Gustafsson, M, 'Lawful Remedy or Illegal Response? Resolving the Issue of Foreign Subsidization under WTO Law' (2021) 20 *World Trade Review* 343

Crotty, J, 'Structural Causes of the Global Financial Crisis: A Critical Assessment of the "New Financial Architecture"' (2009) 33 *Cambridge Journal of Economics* 563

Crotty, J and Epstein, G, 'Proposals for Effectively Regulating the US Financial System to Avoid yet Another Meltdown' (2008) No 2008-15 Working Paper, University of Massachusetts

De Meester, B, 'Testing European Prudential Conditions for Banking Mergers in the Light of Most Favoured Nation in the GATS' (2008) 11 *Journal of International Economic Law* 609

—— 'The Global Financial Crisis and Government Support for Banks: What Role for the GATS?' (2010) 13 *Journal of International Economic Law* 27

—— *Liberalization of Trade in Banking Services: An International and European Perspective* (Cambridge, Cambridge University Press, 2014)

Delimatsis, P, 'Don't Gamble with GATS – The Interaction between Articles VI, XVI, XVII and XVIII GATS in the Light of the US – Gambling Case' (2006) 40 *Journal of World Trade* 1059

—— 'Due Process and "Good" Regulation Embedded in the Gats – Disciplining Regulatory Behaviour in Services through Article vi of the Gats' (2007) 10 *Journal of International Economic Law* 13

—— *International Trade in Services and Domestic Regulations: Necessity, Transparency, and Regulatory Diversity* (Oxford, Oxford University Press, 2007)

—— 'Concluding the WTO Services Negotiations on Domestic Regulation – Hopes and Fears' (2010) 9 *World Trade Review* 643

—— 'Financial Innovation and Prudential Regulation: The New Basel III Rules' (2012) 46 *Journal of World Trade* 1309

—— 'Transparent Financial Innovation in a Post-Crisis Environment' (2013) 16 *Journal of International Economic Law* 159

Delimatsis, P and Herger, N, *Financial Regulation at the Crossroads: Implications for Supervision, Institutional Design and Trade* (Alphen aan den Rijn, Kluwer Law International BV, 2011)

Delimatsis, P and Hoekman, B, 'National Tax Regulation, Voluntary International Standards, and the GATS: Argentina – Financial Services' (2018) 17 *World Trade Review* 265

Delimatsis, P and Sauvé, P, 'Financial Services Trade after the Crisis: Policy and Legal Conjectures' (2010) 13 *Journal of International Economic Law* 837

Dobson, W and Jacquet, P, *Financial Services Liberalization in the WTO* (Washington DC, Peterson Institute for International Economics, 1998)

Ehlermann, C-D and Ehring, L, 'WTO Dispute Settlement and Competition Law: Views from the Perspective of the Appellate Body's Experience' (2002) 26 *Fordham International Law Journal* 1505

Erixon, F and Sally, R, 'Trade, Globalisation and Emerging Protectionism since the Crisis' (2010) No 02/2010 ECIPE Working Paper

European Commission, 'Draft Technical Standards for the Regulation on OTC Derivatives, CCPs and Trade Repositories' ESMA/2012/379

Feketekuty, G, 'Regulatory Reform and Trade Liberalisation in Services' in P Sauvé and RM Stern (eds), *GATS 2000: New Directions in Services Trade Liberalization* (Washington DC, Brookings Institution Press, 2000)

Financial Stability Board, 'Improving Financial Regulation – Report of the Financial Stability Board to G20 Leaders' (2009)

Fiorentino, R and Crawford, J-A, 'The Changing Landscape of Regional Trade Agreements' [2005] WTO Discussion Paper No 8

Footer, M and George, C, 'The General Agreement on Trade in Services' in PFJ Macrory, AE Appleton and MG Plummer (eds), *The World Trade Organization: Legal, Economic and Political Analysis* (New York, Springer Publishing, 2005)

Goncalves, M and Stephanou, C, 'Financial Services and Trade Agreements in Latin America and the Caribbean: An Overview' (2007) 4181 World Bank Policy Research Working Paper

Goodhart, C et al, *Financial Regulation: Why, How and Where Now?* (Abingdon, Routledge, 1998)

Griffin, P, 'The Delaware Effect: Keeping the Tiger in Its Cage – The European Experience on Mutual Recognition in Financial Services' (2001) 7 *Columbia Journal of European Law* 337

Grima, S, 'The Current Financial Crisis and Derivative Misuse' (2012) 1 *Online Journal of Social Sciences Research* 265

Hasen, R, 'Lobbying, Rent-Seeking, and the Constitution' (2012) 64 *Stanford Law Review* 191

Hoekman, B and Mattoo, A, 'Services Trade and Growth' (2008) 4461 Policy Research Working Paper

—— 'Services Trade Liberalisation and Regulatory Reform: Re-Invigorating International Cooperation' [2011] World Bank Policy Research Working Paper

Hoekman, B, Mattoo, A and Sapir, A, 'The Political Economy of Services Trade Liberalization: A Case for International Regulatory Cooperation?' (2007) 23 *Oxford Review of Economic Policy* 367

Hoekman, B and Mavroidis, P, 'Embracing Diversity: Plurilateral Agreements and the Trading System' (2015) 14 *World Trade Review* 101

—— 'WTO "à La Carte" or "Menu Du Jour"? Assessing the Case for More Plurilateral Agreements' (2015) 26 *European Journal of International Law* 319

Hoekman, B and Messerlin, P, 'Liberalizing Trade in Services: Reciprocal Negotiations and Regulatory Reform' in P Sauvé and RM Stern (eds), *GATS 2000: New Directions in Services Trade Liberalization* (Washington DC, Brookings Institution Press, 2000)

Hoekman, B and Primo Braga, C, 'Protection and Trade in Services: A Survey' (1997) 8 *Open Economies Review* 285

Hoekman, B and Sauvé, P, 'Liberalizing Trade in Services' [1994] WTO Discussion Paper No 243

ISDA, 'Whitepaper: Cross-Border Harmonization of Derivatives Regulatory Regimes: A Risk-Based Framework for Substituted Compliance via Cross-Border Principles' (ISDA, 2017)

Jackson, O, 'Could EU Go down the Equivalence Route for London CCPs?' (14 February 2018) International Financial Law Review

Johnson, K, Pasquale, F and Chapman, J, 'Artificial Intelligence, Machine Learning, and Bias in Finance: Toward Responsible Innovation' (2019) 88 *Fordham Law Review* 499

Johnston, B, 'Sequencing Capital Account Liberalizations and Financial Sector Reform' (1998) 98 IMF Paper on Policy Analysis and Assessment

Kaminsky, G and Schmukler, S, 'Short-Run Pain, Long-Run Gain: The Effects of Financial Liberalization' [2003] IMF Working Paper No 2003/034

—— 'Short-Run Pain, Long-Run Gain: The Effects of Financial Liberalization' [2003] NBER Working Paper 9787

Key, S, 'Financial Services in the Uruguay Round and the WTO' [1997] Group of Thirty Occasional Papers 54

—— *The Doha Round and Financial Services Negotiations* (Washington DC, American Enterprise Institute, 2003)

Khwaja, A and Mian, A, 'Rent Seeking and Corruption in Financial Markets' (2011) 3 *Annual Review of Economics* 579

Kidd, J, 'FinTech: Antidote to Rent-Seeking' (2018) 93 *Chicago-Kent Law Review* 165

Kono, M et al, 'Opening Markets in Financial Services and the Role of the GATS' (WTO 1997) WTO Speical Studies No 1

Lamandini, M, 'Recovery and Resolution of CCPs: Obsessing over Regulatory Symmetry?' (Centre for European Policy Studies, 2018)

Lewis, M, *The Big Short: Inside the Doomsday Machine* (London, Penguin, 2011)

Lianos, I et al, *Regulating Blockchain: Techno-Social and Legal Challenges* (Oxford, Oxford University Press, 2019)

Llewellyn, D, *The Economic Rationale for Financial Regulation*, vol 21 (London, Financial Services Authority, 1999)

Lubben, S, 'Failure of the Clearinghouse: Dodd-Frank's Fatal Flaw' (2015) 10 *The Virginia Law & Business Review* 127

Marchetti, J, 'Financial Services Liberalization in the WTO and PTAs' in JA Marchetti and M Roy (eds), *Opening Markets for Trade in Services, Countries and Sectors in Bilateral and WTO Negotiations* (Cambridge, Cambridge University Press, 2009)

—— 'Do PTAs Actually Increase Parties' Services Trade?' in KW Bagwell and PC Mavroidis (eds), *Preferential Trade Agreements: A Law and Economics Analysis* (Cambridge, Cambridge University Press, 2011)

—— 'Technical Standard-Setting in the Financial Sector' in P Delimatsis (ed), *The Law, Economics and Politics of International Standardisation* (Cambridge, Cambridge University Press, 2015)

Marchetti, J and Mavroidis, P, 'The Genesis of the GATS (General Agreement on Trade in Services)' (2011) 22 *European Journal of International Law* 689

—— 'I Now Recognise You (and Only You) as Equal: An Anatomy of (Mutual) Recognition Agreements in the GATS' in I Lianos and O Odudu (eds), *Regulating Trade in Services in the EU and the WTO: Trust, Distrust and Economic Integration* (Cambridge, Cambridge University Press, 2012)

Marconini, M, 'Services in Regional Agreements between Latin American and Developed Countries' (2006) serie 71 *Comercio Internacional*

Mattoo, A, 'National Treatment in the GATS: Corner-Stone or Pandora's Box?' (1997) 31 *Journal of World Trade* 107

—— 'MFN and the GATS' in T Cottier and PC Mavroidis (eds), *Regulatory Barriers and the Principle of Non-Discrimination in World Trade Law*, vol 2 (Ann Arbor, University of Michigan Press, 2000)

Mavroidis, P, 'Highway XVI Re-Visited: The Road from Non-Discrimination to Market Access in GATS' (2007) 6 *World Trade Review* 1

Mavroidis, P and Davey, W, 'Is the WTO Dispute Settlement Mechanism Responsive to the Needs of the Traders? Would a System of Direct Action by Private Parties Yield Better Results?' (1998) 32(2) *Journal of World Trade* 147

Moloney, N, 'I. Reform or Revolution? The Financial Crisis, EU Financial Markets Law, and the European Securities and Markets Authority' (2011) 60 *International & Comparative Law Quarterly* 521

—— 'The European Securities and Markets Authority and Institutional Design for the EU Financial Market – a Tale of Two Competences: Part (1) Rule-Making' (2011) 12 *European Business Organization Law Review* 41

—— 'The European Securities and Markets Authority and Institutional Design for the EU Financial Market–a Tale of Two Competences: Part (2) Rules in Action' (2011) 12 *European Business Organization Law Review* 177

Monnet, C, 'Let's Make It Clear: How Central Counterparties Save(d) the Day' (2010) Issue Q1 *Business Review, Federal Reserve Bank of Philadelphia* 1

Moreno-Villalaz, J, 'Financial Integration and Dollarization: The Case of Panama' (2005) 25 *Cato Journal* 127

Nakatomi, M, 'Plurilateral Agreements: A Viable Alternative to the World Trade Organization?' [2013] Asian Development Bank Institute Working Papers No 439

Nicolaidis, K, 'Non-Discriminatory Mutual Recognition: An Oxymoron in the New WTO Lexicon?' in PC Mavroidis and P Blatter (eds), *Non Discrimination in the WTO: Past and Present, Journal of World Trade* (Ann Arbor, University of Michigan Press, 2000)

Nicolaidis, K and Shaffer, G, 'Transnational Mutual Recognition Regimes: Governance without Global Government' (2004) 68 *Law and Contemporary Problems* 263

Nicolaïdis, K and Trachtman, J, 'From Policed Regulation to Managed Recognition: Mapping the Boundary of GATS' in P Sauvé and RM Stern (eds), *GATS 2000: New Directions in Services Trade Liberalization* (Washington DC, Brookings Institution Press, 2000)

Ortino, F, 'Treaty Interpretation and the WTO Appellate Body Report in US – Gambling: A Critique' (2006) 9 *Journal of International Economic Law* 117

Papaconstantinou, G, 'The GATS and Financial Regulation: Time to Clear-House?' (2020) 19 *World Trade Review* 379

—— 'Investment Bankers in Conflict: The Regime of Inducements in MiFID II and the Member States' Struggle for Fairness' (2016) 12 *European Review of Contract Law* 356

—— 'Financial Services Liberalization under EU FTAs: The Case of Clearing and Settlement Services' in *Yearbook of International Economic Law* (Springer International Publishing, 2020) 65.

—— 'Clearing & Settlement' by D Turing, Book Review' (2018) 42 *European Law Review* 131

Papaconstantinou, G and Pedreschi, L, 'Alternative Dispute Settlement and the Jurisprudential Legacy of the World Trade Organization's Appellate Body' (2022) 56(2) *Journal of World Trade* 261

Peirce, H, 'Derivatives Clearinghouses: Clearing the Way to Failure' (2015) 64 *The Cleveland State Law Review* 589

Petit, N, 'EU Competition Law Analysis of FRAND Disputes' in J Contreras (ed), *The Cambridge Handbook of Technical Standardization Law: Competition, Antitrust, and Patents* (Cambridge: Cambridge University Press, 2017) 290

Pinotti, P, 'Trust, Regulation and Market Failures' (2012) 94 *Review of Economics and Statistics* 650

Pirrong, C, 'The Economics of Central Clearing: Theory and Practice' (2011) 1 ISDA Discusson Papers Series

Poretti, P, 'Waiting for Godot: Subsidy Disciplines in Services Trade' in M Panizzon, N Pohl and P Sauvé (eds), *GATS and the Regulation of International Trade in Services* (Cambridge, Cambridge University Press, 2008)

Quaglia, L, 'The Politics of 'Third-country Equivalence'in Post-Crisis Financial Services Regulation in the European Union' (2015) 38 *West European Politics* 167

Rehlon, A and Nixon, D, 'Central Counterparties: What Are They, Why Do They Matter, and How Does the Bank Supervise Them?' [2013] Bank of England Quarterly Bulletin Q2
Rennison, J and Stafford, P, 'Reforming the Derivatives Market: An Explainer' (*Financial Times*, 22 September 2016) http://www.ft.com/content/6b5e97e0-7029-11e6-9ac1-1055824ca907 accessed 1 June 2023
Ricardo, D, *Principles of Political Economy and Taxation* (London, G Bell and Sons, 1891)
Roe, M, 'Clearinghouse Overconfidence' (2013) 101 *California Law Review* 1641
Roy, M, Marchetti, J and Lim, A, 'The Race towards Preferential Trade Agreements in Services: How Much Market Access Is Really Achieved?' in M Panizzon, N Pohl and P Sauvé (eds), *GATS and the Regulation of International Trade in Services: World Trade Forum* (Cambridge, Cambridge University Press, 2008)
Roy, M, Marchetti, J and Lim, H, 'Services Liberalization in the New Generation of Preferential Trade Agreements (PTAs): How Much Further than the GATS?' (2007) 6 *World Trade Review* 155
Schammo, P, 'The European Securities and Markets Authority: Lifting the Veil on the Allocation of Powers' (2011) 48 *Common Market Law Review* 1879
—— 'Caught in a Cross-Fire? The US CFTC and the European Commission's Proposals on Third-Country CCPs' (2018) 39 *Company Lawyer* 277
Schleyer, G, 'Power to the People: Allowing Private Parties to Raise Claims Before the WTO Dispute Resolution System' (1996) 65 *Fordham Law Review* 2275
Scholes, M, 'Foreword' in TF Cooley et al (eds), *Regulating Wall Street: The Dodd-Frank Act and the New Architecture of Global Finance* (Hoboken, John Wiley & Sons, 2010)
Schwartz, A, 'Regulating for Rationality' (2015) 67 *Stanford Law Review* 1373
Shiller, R, *The Subprime Solution: How Today's Global Financial Crisis Happened, and What to Do about It* (Princeton, Princeton University Press, 2012)
Shy, O, *The Economics of Network Industries* (Cambridge, Cambridge University Press, 2001)
Song, W, 'Bullish on Blockchain: Examining Delaware's Approach to Distributed Ledger Technology in Corporate Governance Law and Beyond' (2017) 8 *Harvard Business Law Review Online* 9
Stern, R, 'Quantifying Barriers to Trade in Services', *Development, Trade, and the WTO: A Handbook. Washington, DC: The World Bank* (Washington DC, World Bank Publications, 2002)
Sykes, A, 'Regulatory Protectionism and the Law of International Trade' (1999) 66 *The University of Chicago Law Review* 15
Trachtman, J, 'Embedding Mutual Recognition at the WTO' (2007) 14 *Journal of European Public Policy* 780
Turing, D, *Clearing and Settlement* (Oxford, Bloomsbury Publishing, 2016)
Verdier, P-H, 'Mutual Recognition in International Finance' (2011) 52 *Harvard International Law Journal* 55
Vives, X, *Competition and Stability in Banking* (Princeton, Princeton University Press, 2016)
Wagner, C, 'The New WTO Agreement on Financial Services and Chapter 14 of NAFTA: Has Free Trade in Banking Finally Arrived' (1999) 5 *NAFTA: Law and Business Review of the Americas* 5
Weiler, JHH, 'Mutual Recognition, Functional Equivalence and Harmonization in the Evolution of the European Common Market and the WTO' in FK Padoa Schioppa (ed), *The Principle of Mutual Recognition in the European Integration Process* (London, Palgrave Macmillan UK, 2005)
Wendt, F, 'Central Counterparties: Addressing Their Too Important to Fail Nature' [2015] IMF Working Paper No 2015/021
Werbach, K, 'Trust, but Verify: Why the Blockchain Needs the Law' (2018) 33 *Berkeley Technology Law Journal* 487
Wolfrum, R, Stoll, P-T and Feinäugle, C, 'Understanding on Commitments in Financial Services' in R Wolfrum, PT Stoll and C Feinäugle (eds), *WTO – Trade in Services* (Leiden, Brill Nijhoff, 2008)
Wolkoff, N and Werner, J, 'The History of Regulation of Clearing in the Securities and Futures Markets, and Its Impact on Competition' (2010) 30 *Review of Banking and Financial Law* 313
WTO, *The Legal Texts: The Results of the Uruguay Round of Multilateral Trade Negotiations* (Cambridge, Cambridge University Press, 2000)

WTO Secretariat, 'Report on the Meeting Held on 11 May 2001' S/WPDR/M/11, 7 June 2001
Yadav, Y, 'The Problematic Case of Clearinghouses in Complex Markets' (2012) 101 *Georgetown Law Journal* 387
—— 'Clearinghouses and Regulation by Proxy' (2014) 43 *The Georgia Journal of International and Comparative* Law 161
Yadav, Y and Turing, D, 'The Extraterritorial Regulation of Clearinghouses' (2016) 2 *Journal of Financial Regulation* 21
Yanovich, A and Voon, T, 'What Is the Measure at Issue?' in A Mitchell (ed), *Challenges and Prospects for the* WTO (Cameron May Ltd, 2005)
Yeoh, P, 'Regulatory Issues in Blockchain Technology' (2017) 25(2) *Journal of Financial Regulation and Compliance* 196
Zampetti, A, 'Mutual Access through Mutual Recognition: The Promise and Limits of GATS Article VII' in P Sauvé and RM Stern (eds), *GATS 2000: New Directions in Services Trade Liberalization* (Washington DC, Brookings Institution Press, 2000)

Index

www.ingramcontent.com/pod-product-compliance
Ingram Content Group UK Ltd.
Pitfield, Milton Keynes, MK11 3LW, UK
UKHW020241290926
15470UKWH00002B/678